# Jeremiah's God

## A Daily Devotional

~

By

### David C. Coldwell

Interact International Publications
Post Office Box 329
Buda, Texas 78610

ISBN 978-0-6152-1960-8

This book may be purchased online at
http://stores.lulu.com/InteractPublications

## Author's Note

Ever since I was a young university student seriously pursuing the Lord, I have used daily devotional books. I realized early that my relationship with God must be based on a daily time with Him. Only God's grace is responsible for any spiritual growth that I may have experienced through the years. Through His grace, I believe I have grown closer to God from regular times of Bible meditation and prayer with the aid of devotional books.

For many years, one of my Biblical mentors has been Jeremiah the prophet. His deep relationship with the Lord has inspired me to seek the same degree of spiritual intimacy that he had. Jeremiah was a mere man. Yet his commitment to the Lord and to his calling has stirred human hearts for more than 2500 years.

The relevance of the prophet's life to today's world became increasingly obvious to me. Jeremiah knew the same God that true believers follow today. Jeremiah's Lord actively and consistently intervenes in people's lives today. The God whom Jeremiah knew now holds the present-day world in His hand.

As Jeremiah served the Lord, he encountered a broad array of human beings. He knew powerful kings, deceptive prophets, simple farmers and diligent potters. I have counted dozens of individual names of people in Jeremiah's book who lived during Jeremiah's time. He knew that every human encounter was a divine arrangement. Jeremiah was acquainted with many, but he had close friendships with just a few.

Jeremiah was a fascinating and complex man. As you learn more about him, I hope you will draw closer to his God. Jeremiah knew and understood the Lord. He was aware that the Lord implements

kindness, justice and righteousness on the earth (Jeremiah 9:24).
May you have the same understanding.

Do not worry if the busyness of some days causes you to neglect your
devotional reading. My intention was not to create a legalistic burden.
Read about and meditate on Jeremiah's God as many days as you can.
To aid your personal use of these studies, a question or application
ends each reading. My prayer is that these daily thoughts can help you
know the Lord better.

## Day 1
### THE GOD OF HISTORY

*Jeremiah 1:1–2. The words of Jeremiah son of Hilkiah, one of the priests at Anathoth in the territory of Benjamin. The word of the LORD came to him in the thirteenth year of the reign of Josiah son of Amon king of Judah....*

Jeremiah's opening words assure us of his core beliefs: God exists, and God communicates to people. Jeremiah wrote these words because the Lord had first sent His words to him. Unlike the many mute idols in that period of history, the Lord spoke to select people like Jeremiah.

Jeremiah grew up in a religious home. His hometown was Anathoth, which was one of the towns originally assigned to the priests. As Jeremiah grew up, he could observe the lifestyles of many priests and their families. His upbringing gave him experiences similar to those of many young people today. He may have seen injustices and hypocrisy in the religious system of his father. However, problems in the priesthood did not deter him from following the Lord.

The Lord first spoke to Jeremiah when Josiah governed Judah. Josiah was a good king who tried to improve the spiritual and moral lives of his people. When Jeremiah began his ministry, the king had already begun some national reforms. Several years later King Josiah would lead his nation into a spiritual reformation. Who knows how much influence Jeremiah had on the king's policies?

Historians pinpoint Josiah's thirteenth year as 627 BC. Unfortunately, many people are not interested in Biblical history. They think that any information about God from a time period that old would have changed by now. However, people need to learn that postmodern times have not changed Jeremiah's God. Jeremiah's God continues to direct the course of history.

The God whom Jeremiah knew is the Lord of history. The thirteenth year of Josiah's reign was the opportune time for Jeremiah to begin his ministry. The Lord matches His people with the era in which they live. He matches them perfectly.

Are you aware of your timely moment in history? God has arranged for you to live in the absolutely best time for you personally. You should therefore seek to know God better. Jeremiah's God can show you how to live fully in the years He has allotted for you.

**In what way does God's timeliness affect you?**

## Day 2
### THE GOD WHO EXILES

**Jeremiah 1:3.** *... and through the reign of Jehoiakim son of Josiah king of Judah, down to the fifth month of the eleventh year of Zedekiah son of Josiah king of Judah, when the people of Jerusalem went into exile.*

Several of Josiah's descendants became kings after him. Two of them each reigned for more than a decade. Sadly, neither Jehoiakim nor Zedekiah kept the faith of their father Josiah.

The best I can write about Jehoiakim is that he was consistent. However, he was consistently godless! Jeremiah continually knew what to expect from King Jehoiakim. The king was always hostile toward spiritual truth and was Jeremiah's constant enemy.

In contrast to Jehoiakim's antagonism, Zedekiah had indifference toward God. He was a weak man who never quite knew how to deal with Jeremiah. He was a vacillating politician who finally broke a treaty with the Babylonians. That led to his downfall.

These kings' policies contributed to the death of their nation. Jeremiah would live to see Judah's kings come and go. When it was time for Zedekiah to go, the whole city went with him! Jerusalem's exile was one of the defining events in Judah's history. The exile was such an important and traumatic episode that Jeremiah recorded the exact month it happened. In the fifth month of Zedekiah's eleventh year, the nation of Judah came to an end.

For everyone who ignores God, there is coming a fifth month! A doubter of God may have a prosperous third and even fourth month. But the fifth month always comes. Jeremiah's God did not tolerate the long-term crimes of individuals and nations. Jeremiah's God used the Babylonians to judge spiritual rebels.

Many people today wish to believe in a god who tolerates just about everything. They reject Jeremiah's God of judgment. Their god has evolved beyond tendencies to cast judgments. They need to understand more about Jeremiah's God.

Jeremiah's God is the supreme judge. If He were not, He would be morally apathetic. If He were not the judge, He would do nothing about the evil in the universe. If He were not the judge, the war between good and evil would continue indefinitely. Are you ready for the conflict to end? Be glad that Jeremiah's Lord is the judge!

**Will God judge you like He judged Jeremiah, or like He judged Zedekiah? How can Romans 5:1 give you confidence when you stand before the Supreme Judge?**

## Day 3
### GOD'S CALL

**Jeremiah 1:4-5.** *The word of the LORD came to me, saying, "Before I formed you in the womb I knew you, before you were born I set you apart; I appointed you as a prophet to the nations."*

God always takes the initiative with people. The Lord invaded Jeremiah's life with a plan. God planned for Jeremiah to be a prophet. Jeremiah had no doubt grown up with a different plan. He was probably expecting to be a priest, just like his father.

Being a prophet would be radically different from being a priest. Priests were members of a closely-knit community who provided religious services for the nation. They offered sacrifices to God on behalf of the people. In contrast, a prophet spoke to people on behalf of God. Jeremiah would often be the only voice that spoke the truth. He would not have the support of the religious community.

As a prophet, Jeremiah would need to depend on God constantly. Jeremiah did not have the entire written Bible like we do. He often heard God speaking to him directly. Jeremiah could choose to listen or ignore, just as we can choose how we respond to the written Word of God. The wise choice is to always listen to God.

The Lord mentioned the parameters of Jeremiah's calling. He would be a prophet to the nations. He would not just preach about his own country. He would have an international ministry by speaking about Babylon, Egypt and many other nations.

Jeremiah's God continues to call people today. He first calls them to be saved from their sins by believing in the person that Jeremiah would later describe as David's righteous Branch (23:5). Next, the Lord calls believers to live in a relationship with Him. The specifics of each unique calling usually do not come all at once like they did for Jeremiah. The Lord called me out of my forestry profession while I was working in a National Forest in Colorado, but then He gradually unfolded His particular plans for me through the years.

God calls you. You do not submit your own resume to God! Once God has called you, you do not have a choice. Answering God's call is not optional. You will always have other ministry opportunities, but you must stay focused on your own calling. By listening to God's call, you avoid many other demands on your life. Jeremiah's God is the God who calls and He is calling you.

**How has the Lord taken the initiative in your life?**

## Day 4
### INTIMATE KNOWLEDGE

**Jeremiah 1:5.** *"Before I formed you in the womb I knew you, before you were born I set you apart; I appointed you as a prophet to the nations."*

God was already working in his life before Jeremiah was born. While Jeremiah was yet unborn, God knew him. The Hebrew word that is translated as *knew* is a strong word. The word includes the idea of choosing and knowing intimately.

God knew Jeremiah. He knew him more closely than a husband and wife know each other. God never even briefly forgot about Jeremiah. The Lord constantly thought about him, valued him, loved him. What a relationship!

Not only had He known him, Jeremiah's God had formed him in his mother's womb. The Lord had painstakingly produced a unique human being, as He does with everyone. Jeremiah's conception was not an accident. His birth did not happen by chance. God personally fashions each human baby.

There was a third action that God took toward Jeremiah before he was even born. The Lord set him apart for a special life. God had consecrated him to be in an exceptional class of people who serve Him wholeheartedly. Jeremiah would not live for the worldly ambitions that the masses pursue.

The fourth action that God took before Jeremiah was born was that He appointed him to a specific job. Jeremiah would be a prophet to the nations. He would not be able to travel to every nation, but he would become knowledgeable in international events. God would give him unique insight into the future of the nations in Jeremiah's world.

As a prophet, Jeremiah would need to know God. As a prophet to the nations, he would need to know the world. You also should be serious about God and the world. Keep a Bible on your desk and a world map on your wall!

I remember very clearly when each of my three children was born. Of course, I thought that all three of them were very cute babies! As I think back on their births, I realize that the Lord had a plan for each one of them. When Jeremiah was a tiny baby in the arms of his mother, the Lord had already mapped out the days of his life. When my children were infants, the Lord had already planned a unique destiny for each of them.

Jeremiah could know God only because God had first known him. As a prophet, Jeremiah would need to know the Lord deeply. Jeremiah's life can help you know how to know his God intimately.

**In what ways do you recognize God's intimacy in your daily life?**

## Day 5
### A PRAYER OF EXCUSES

**Jeremiah 1:6.** *"Ah, Sovereign LORD," I said, "I do not know how to speak; I am only a child."*

When he first heard about God's plan for his life, Jeremiah did not like it. If you knew God's plan for your entire life, you might not like it either. That is one of the reasons that God does not reveal your entire personal future to you!

Jeremiah had two excuses ready for God to ponder. Jeremiah considered himself to be (1) too inexperienced and (2) too young. What excuses do you have for not doing the part of God's will that you do clearly understand?

Being a prophet to all the nations is an awesome responsibility. Jeremiah knew that he lacked the right words to say to all those nations.

I can identify with Jeremiah's objection. When I was a pastor, I had to prepare two sermons a week. I occasionally would have a certain fear as I stood behind the pulpit. I was afraid that I might stand up and have nothing to say!

Jeremiah told God that he did not know what to say to the nations. In doing so, he started a pattern of openly frank conversations with God. He would continue to pray candidly for the rest of his life.

Perhaps Jeremiah called himself a child because he was only a teenager. We do not know his exact age when God called him. He was probably not yet old enough to be a priest, the profession of his father. How could he now be mature enough to become a famous prophet?

There is a positive side to Jeremiah's excuses. In the future, Jeremiah could never accuse himself of desiring to become a celebrity who was famous throughout the nations! Also, he could never accuse himself of responding to God's call because he took pleasure in preaching doom!

Jeremiah could question his call, because he was on speaking terms with God. He knew how to pray, and he knew that God welcomed his prayers. God eagerly receives the prayers of His people today, even when they are as self-questioning as Jeremiah.

**How can sincerely expressing your weaknesses, doubts or fears to God actually help you grow closer to Him?**

## Day 6
### THE GOD WHO SENDS

*Jeremiah 1:7. But the LORD said to me, "Do not say, 'I am only a child.' You must go to everyone I send you to and say whatever I command you…."*

The Lord had His plan for Jeremiah. Jeremiah's objections would not change the plan. The Lord responded to Jeremiah's reasons for wanting to avoid the call. The Lord gave encouraging words to Jeremiah.

When he heard these words, Jeremiah perhaps realized that his excuses had been just like those of Moses. When God first called Moses to lead the people out of Egypt, Moses gave many excuses. The Lord gave Moses His promise that He would help him speak and would teach him what to say (Exodus 4:12).

God was not requiring Jeremiah to be an eloquent speaker. God wanted him to be merely a man who delivered God's words. Nor would Jeremiah need to carefully plan his journeys. The Lord would tell Jeremiah what to say and where to say it.

Jeremiah would not need to wait twenty years before he had a more mature outlook on life. He would not tell people his own ideas about God. He would speak the words that God would give him.

Only words from God compose the Bible. The Bible is not a collection of people's ideas about God. The Bible *is* God's Word. Belief in the truth of the Bible can give you just as much confidence as Jeremiah had when he heard the words directly from the Lord.

Jeremiah's God always sends people. The Lord sends whomever He wishes to the places He chooses at the time He pleases. He may send you across the ocean, or across the street to talk to a neighbor. God uses your job to send you among people to whom you can be a light.

Do you have excuses for not going where God is sending you? Do you think you are too young? Do you think you are too old? Forget your excuses! You must go where God sends you.

God would send Jeremiah to many locations. He did what the Lord told him to do. Are you willing to go to wherever the Lord may send you? You should be more than willing. You should also be ready, because Jeremiah's God is the God who sends. God has special plans for each of His children.

**What is your current thinking about God's call to you?**

### Day 7
### THE GOD WHO DELIVERS

**Jeremiah 1:8.** *"Do not be afraid of them, for I am with you and will rescue you,"* *declares the LORD.*

Jeremiah had objected to the Lord's call because he considered himself too young. The Lord knew the real reason why Jeremiah hesitated. The young man was fearful.

Jeremiah was aware of the level of ungodliness in his country. He knew that his countrymen did not often accept words from the Lord. He was afraid for his personal safety.

I remember feeling fearful before my first missionary trip during the days when Eastern Europe was Communist. I was going to take a train from Austria to a country to the north. I could not travel into that country openly as a missionary. I thought about what the government might do to me if I was caught teaching the Bible to pastors. It was February. My children were afraid that I would freeze to death!

Fear is a normal emotion. If you sense danger, you will probably be afraid. Jeremiah's life would be perilous. The Lord did not promise to remove all hazards. However, the Lord did promise that He would rescue him out of every difficulty.

Throughout his life Jeremiah faced many life-threatening dangers. The Lord did not keep him isolated from problems. Jeremiah had many enemies who persecuted him without mercy, but the Lord kept His promise. The Lord always delivered him.

Jeremiah knew that there were many examples of God's people being delivered in the past. The Lord rescued His people from Egypt under the leadership of Moses. On an individual level, the Lord rescued David from lions and bears. There is a lengthy history of God rescuing His people from many dangers. Jeremiah knew the stories. He had no reason to doubt that the Lord would rescue him also.

The Lord promised Jeremiah that He would be with him. You can find these simple words repeated throughout the Bible. "I am with you." God's presence with His people is one of the great spiritual encouragements.

**What are three ways in which you can grow more aware of God's presence in your life?**

## Day 8
### GOD'S SPEAKER

**Jeremiah 1:9. *Then the LORD reached out his hand and touched my mouth and said to me, "Now, I have put my words in your mouth."***

When the Lord called him to be a prophet to the nations, Jeremiah was concerned about what he would say. Now he would have confidence that God would give him the right words every time he needed to speak. He would never again wonder about what to say. Now he had the Lord's words. Jeremiah received from the Lord a multi-sensory experience. He saw, he felt and he heard.

Jeremiah *saw* the Lord's hand. He knew from his upbringing that God does not have a body. God is the ultimate free spirit. So what did Jeremiah really see? The Lord extended a mental image of Himself to make Himself vividly real to Jeremiah.

Isaiah was another great prophet who had a similar experience when the Lord called him. In Isaiah's vision, an angel touched his mouth with a burning coal. Also, Ezekiel had a vision in which he ate a scroll. From that point on, God's Word became an inseparable part of who those prophets were. It was the same way with Jeremiah.

Jeremiah *felt* the Lord's touch. The young man's mouth would be God's sound system. Jeremiah's preaching career began with this exceptional touch from the Lord.

Jeremiah *heard* the Lord's words. He heard the Lord say that he now had the Lord's words in his mouth. The Lord had first given this statement to Moses. Jeremiah could be encouraged that he would stand in a long tradition of prophets that included Moses.

Jeremiah could never forget such an experience as this. He was now the Lord's mouthpiece. He still had his unique individuality through which he would express the Lord's messages. Nevertheless, he would not distort any word that the Lord would give to him. The primary force behind Jeremiah's preaching would not be his compelling personality, but the Lord's authority. Jeremiah would speak with clout because he had the Lord's power.

Jeremiah did not have all the Scriptures like you do, so he needed this vision of God's hand touching his mouth. Today, your Bibles are God's hands reaching down toward you. You can find your needed strength and comfort from God in the Bible, and as you pray to Him.

**What is one reason why you need to hear God's words today?**

## Day 9
### UPROOTING AND PLANTING

**Jeremiah 1:10.** *"See, today I appoint you over nations and kingdoms to uproot and tear down, to destroy and overthrow, to build and to plant."*

Jeremiah would be like a builder and a farmer. When contractors build buildings, they often need to tear down the old ones on the site. Before farmers plant a crop, they have to uproot the weeds.

God planned to replace certain nations. Jeremiah's job was to tell them this bad news. God replaces people in the same way that my wife and I replace useless plants in our garden. We uproot them and throw them in our compost bin! Then we prepare the soil so that we can plant something more promising.

Why does God replace people? He has many reasons. In the case of Jeremiah's contemporaries, they had turned away from the Lord. Totally. The Lord always desires to have people on earth who follow and worship Him. God does not hesitate to replace those who merely give Him lip service. After the demolition, He can then build up others who have willing hearts to know Him.

If only those people had torn down the idols themselves. If only they themselves had repented of their false beliefs and practices. If they had done this and turned back to the Lord, then the Lord would not have destroyed Jerusalem. They chose to keep their idols, so the Lord had to destroy them Himself.

Jeremiah's message from God was not entirely bad news. He also had good news. God does not destroy just to wreck things. God destroys in order to build up again. Ecclesiastes 3:3 says that there is a time to tear down, and a time to build up. Jeremiah's ultimate message was one of hope. The Lord would replant with a new people for Himself. The Lord would build them up.

This same process is happening to you, if you are seeking to know the Lord better. God must first uproot and break down those things in your life that are offensive to Him. Do not whine! The Lord will then build you up and you can know Him more deeply.

**What are two recent events in your life where God used the process of tearing down and building up?**

## Day 10
### VISION ABOUT GOD

**Jeremiah 1:11-12.** *The word of the LORD came to me: "What do you see, Jeremiah?" "I see the branch of an almond tree," I replied. The LORD said to me, "You have seen correctly, for I am watching to see that my word is fulfilled."*

The Lord gave Jeremiah a special word to encourage him as he began his ministry. The Lord showed him an almond branch to exhibit a notable truth about Himself.

Almond trees were plentiful where Jeremiah lived. He knew that they were the first trees to bud in the spring. They "awoke" while the other trees were still dormant. The word for *almond* in Hebrew is similar to the word for *watching*. Almond trees watched for warmer weather. They then budded to let everyone know that springtime was coming.

Like the almond tree, the Lord also watches. God does not sleep. He is always aware. He has been watching His people from the beginning. He watches other nations too. God knows when He needs to deal with each nation. He will do as He has promised, as certainly as spring comes after the almond has budded.

The almond branch would give Jeremiah confidence as he warned people with God's words. The Lord continues today to watch over His word. You can be sure that God watches over every word in the Bible.

If the Lord were to give me a similar vision, He might show me the branch of a Texas mesquite tree! Unlike the mesquite, many plants in Texas are deceived by warmer weather in the late winter. Other plants can start budding and even flowering. They are not reliable indicators that spring is coming, because the irregular Texas weather may bring yet another freeze. The mesquite tree is seldom fooled. The mesquite buds only when the freezing weather has ended.

Like the almond tree in Israel and the mesquite in Texas, God is never fooled. God carries out His word. He controls every outcome. People in Jeremiah's day did not believe this way. They believed that God was doing nothing. This is the sentiment of many people today. Do not live their way. Do not live according to the popular idea that God does not actively watch everything. Remember the almond tree and live according to the truth.

**Write three reasons why the Lord's constant watchfulness encourages you?**

## Day 11
### VISION ABOUT THE NATIONS

**Jeremiah 1:13-14.** *The word of the LORD came to me again: "What do you see?" "I see a boiling pot, tilting away from the north," I answered. The LORD said to me, "From the north disaster will be poured out on all who live in the land."*

The Lord gave Jeremiah another vision. He showed the young prophet a boiling kettle. A pot used for cooking or washing was a common sight in Jeremiah's day. The people put their cauldrons on open flames that were fanned by the wind. If the coals beneath the pot became uneven, the kettle would tilt. The steaming contents would start to spill.

If I had a vision like this, perhaps I would see a boiling pot tilting toward a mound of fire ants. I have actually poured scalding water on fire ant beds near my house. Hot water does not harm the environment and many of the ants die. The rest are agitated and move away with their queen ant. Goodbye, fire ants!

The Lord explained the meaning of the vision. Like hot spillage sizzling everything in its path, armies from the north would conquer the land. The conquest would be total.

No one likes to hear about future disaster. People would dismiss Jeremiah's warnings. They would also mock him, because they thought he had it all wrong. Military threats from the north no longer existed. The superpower was now Egypt, to the south. The people would think that Jeremiah was not in touch with current politics.

A nation does not remain a superpower forever! Egypt's power would soon diminish. Babylon would begin conquering the world.

God is the one who brings disaster. People hate this description of God, because they want God to bring them nothing but goodness. Unfortunately, history demonstrates that catastrophes do happen. If you think that the Lord has no control over tragedies, then your god is less than God! You need Jeremiah's God!

Just like the Lord keeps fire ants from taking over the earth, He subdues the wicked. This is just one of the reasons why calamities happen. Usually we do not understand why the disasters happen, because good people suffer along with the bad. If you get caught in a disaster, do you look to the One who is always in control? The Lord may not give you complete understanding why misfortunes happen, but He can give you the strength to endure.

**What is one reason why it is difficult to believe that God causes disasters?**

## Day 12
### SUMMONS FROM GOD

**Jeremiah 1:15.** *"I am about to summon all the peoples of the northern kingdoms,"
declares the LORD. "Their kings will come and set up their thrones in the entrance of
the gates of Jerusalem; they will come against all her surrounding walls and against
all the towns of Judah...."*

Jeremiah's God is the Lord who summons. He assembles all peoples to do
what He wants done. They do what He wants even when they are not aware of His
presence and His plans.

My earliest memory of a summons was when I was a child in school. If a child
got in trouble, he was ordered to the principal's office. None of us wanted to go to
the principal's office, but we had to go if we were commanded. We had no choice.
The summons from the school principal was binding!

Jeremiah's message would be about a particular summons forty years into the
future. The Lord would assemble all the leaders of the vast Babylonian Empire.
They would march toward Jerusalem with the intention of conquering the city.
They would sit on thrones in the city gates, showing that they had terminated the
nation of Judah.

Even though Babylon was east of Judah, the conquering armies would come
from the north. The military itinerary was not on a straight east-west line. The
soldiers would have to go around the sprawling Arabian Desert. The Babylonians
from the east would conquer Judah from the north. They would set up thrones to
symbolize their conquest.

Thrones were symbols of both triumph and judgment. The defeated people of
Jerusalem would have to stand before these thrones and receive their punishment
for resisting Babylon. In reality, they would receive punishment from the Lord. The
Babylonians were just the instruments that the Lord would use. The Babylonian
thrones would symbolize the Lord's throne of judgment.

The Lord summons both the willing and the unwilling. You do not understand
His entire plan, but you can certainly answer His summons. The Lord called
Jeremiah, who considered himself willing but weak. The Lord summoned the
northern peoples, who thought themselves strong and independent. Follow the
example of Jeremiah!

**What picture comes to your mind when you think about God's universal
summons?**

### Day 13
#### REPLACING GOD WITH GODS

**Jeremiah 1:16.** *"I will pronounce my judgments on my people because of their wickedness in forsaking me, in burning incense to other gods and in worshiping what their hands have made."*

The Babylonians were the ones who would conquer the city. What they thought was their own conquest was really God's way of bringing judgment.

When disaster falls on us, we do not usually know why. However, the reason for the coming Jerusalem catastrophe was clear. Jeremiah would repeat the reason many times. The people had left God for other gods.

Why did they forsake the Lord? Every generation faces the same choice. People can trust in the real God for their well-being, or they can depend on little gods. Small gods tempt them when they imagine themselves to be self-sufficient. They may think they can control the gods as they pursue their own agenda, but they cannot control God.

They had replaced their Lord with other gods. Wood carvers and stonemasons used their skills to make human images. These were intriguing images. Worshipping them probably helped relieve the boredom and stresses of life. Everyone needs a little diversion, but Jeremiah's God was and is totally against idolatry.

Later in his preaching, Jeremiah would refer to an example of an idol. He would describe the widespread worship of the Queen of Heaven (44:17). The Queen of Heaven was one of many gods and goddesses that many of the people worshipped. Entire families were involved in offering sacrifices to this wooden statue named the Queen of Heaven. The children gathered the wood, and then the fathers built fires with it (7:18). The women mixed dough to bake cakes to offer to the Queen of Heaven. They even made the cakes to resemble the goddess.

Instead of caring about obedience to the Lord, many people lived for their idols. Their idols brought them short-term pleasure. Jeremiah would warn that idol worship brings long-term results of grief and shame.

As well as being personally harmful, idolatry is a flagrant disregard for God's clear commands. God desires to keep you from idols because He has your best interests in mind. God loves you! What has a human-made idol done for you lately!?

**What idols are temptations to you?**

## Day 14
### A TIME TO START

**Jeremiah 1:17.** *"Get yourself ready! Stand up and say to them whatever I command you. Do not be terrified by them, or I will terrify you before them."*

It was time for Jeremiah to begin his ministry. The Lord told him to get up and get dressed! The Lord wanted Jeremiah to roll up his sleeves and get ready to work! The Lord told him that it was time to start preaching. Jeremiah could not remain a holy hermit for the rest of his life.

As always, the Lord knew Jeremiah's feelings. He knew that the young man was petrified with fright. He told Jeremiah not to be scared. Then the Lord gave him a stern warning.

The Lord gave Jeremiah such a harsh warning so that the prophet would realize that he now had everything he needed for his ministry. The Lord had given him a purposeful life, supernatural strength and His presence with him at all times. There was no reason for Jeremiah to be terrified.

During my last year of seminary studies, one of my professors told the class, "You are equipped!" He meant that we were ready to begin ministering in other places. We did not need to stay in the safe confines of the seminary any longer.

The Lord wanted his prophet to boldly represent Him in front of the people. Jeremiah must not panic. If he quaked with fear, they would laugh at him. They would terrorize him and treat him like a fool. If they rejected his message, the Lord did not want the reason to be because the messenger was a wimp!

Fear is a common emotion. If the Lord had told me to do what He told Jeremiah to do, I know that I would be extremely fearful also!

The Lord told Jeremiah to tell them whatever He commanded him to say. Jeremiah would speak the words of the Lord. If you had lived in those days, would you have listened? Are you listening to the Lord's commands today?

Jeremiah had listened to the Lord. As much as he might have liked to do nothing else but continue to listen, it was time for him to start. He knew what to do. The hour had come for him to start doing it. What about you? Is it now time for you to start doing what you know you should do?

**What is keeping you from doing something that God has asked you to do?**

## Day 15
### ONE TOUGH PROPHET

**Jeremiah 1:18.** *"Today I have made you a fortified city, an iron pillar and a bronze wall to stand against the whole land—against the kings of Judah, its officials, its priests and the people of the land."*

Jeremiah would face much resistance as he lived for his God. The Lord gave him three graphic images of how strong He would make him.

The Lord made him like a fortified city. Cities in Jeremiah's day were fortresses. People thought the city was the safest place to live. Enemy troops could not easily capture a well-protected city. Enemies would surround Jeremiah, but he would remain unbeatable.

Also, the Lord made him like an iron pillar. The pillars that Samson pulled down were made of either wood or stone. I have not heard of any archaeologist unearthing a column made of iron! As an iron pillar, Jeremiah would not be pushed around. Men would inflict pain, but none would topple him. Jeremiah would be a pillar of strength.

In addition, the Lord made the young prophet like a bronze wall. The Lord would repeat this promise to him later when Jeremiah was in a crisis (15:20). Unlike walls of stone, a bronze wall was invincible. Ironically, the walls of the impregnable Jerusalem would fall. Jeremiah would not.

The people of the land were under the political power of kings and religious power of priests. Jeremiah would stand firm against all of them and against their ungodly beliefs. Corrupt kings do not want to hear about God. What about the priests? Jeremiah would later write that all the priests are godless. Religion in Judah had utterly deteriorated.

Jeremiah would stand against the whole land. Without considering what others might think, he would be all that God wanted him to be. He would not allow negative peer pressure to influence him.

As Jeremiah depended on the Lord, God made him tough. No king or priest would be able to deter him from his God-given work. What about you? The Lord has a plan for you. Are you trusting Him to make you spiritually tough?

**In what ways does your dependence on the Lord make you strong like Jeremiah?**

## Day 16
### THE LORD'S PRESENCE

**Jeremiah 1:19.** *"They will fight against you but will not overcome you, for I am with you and will rescue you," declares the LORD.*

Jeremiah would not have a trouble-free life and ministry. He would have enemies who would oppose him. You will too, if you strive to live for the Lord. Remember that Jesus told His disciples that they would have trouble in this world. Then Jesus encouraged them with His words that He had overcome the world (John 16:33).

Jeremiah would not be able to avoid fights. His mightiest weapon would be the Lord's presence. This is the second time that the Lord promised to be with him. Earlier, the Lord had told him not to be afraid, because He would be with him (1:8).

God did not give Jeremiah a book of sermons and then thrust him out into a hostile environment. Nor did He tell Jeremiah to organize an army of bodyguards to protect himself! The Lord assured him of His presence, which was a promise given to many of Jeremiah's predecessors.

Many centuries earlier, God had promised to take care of Jacob. In a dream, God promised Jacob that He was with him and would not leave him (Genesis 28:15). Joshua was another recipient of this promise. After Moses died, Joshua was the leader of God's people. The Lord promised Joshua that just as He had been with Moses, so also would He be with Joshua (Joshua 1:5).

All believers in Jesus Christ can have assurance of God's presence. Knowing that God is with you will enable you to be content. You can claim His promise that He will never leave you or abandon you (Hebrews 13:5).

The Lord had privately given Jeremiah visions and promises. Now Jeremiah was ready to go public. What about your own relationship with the Lord? Are you ready to go public with words about God? Or do you need to spend more personal time with Him?

If I did not have confidence that the Lord was with me, I would not be writing these meditations about Jeremiah's God! If you know Jeremiah's God, then you know that He is with you wherever you go today. God will never leave you nor forsake you. Nothing in the financial markets has ever made this promise!

**How does God's call to Jeremiah help you trust God for your life's circumstances?**

## Day 17
### LOST DEVOTION

**Jeremiah 2:1-2.** *The word of the LORD came to me: "Go and proclaim in the hearing of Jerusalem: 'I remember the devotion of your youth, how as a bride you loved me and followed me through the desert, through a land not sown.'"*

God had called Jeremiah to be His spokesman, and now Jeremiah spoke with compelling passion. He left no doubts with his audience that he was sharing God's words with them. These words were not Jeremiah's fabrication. The Lord spoke to Jeremiah, and Jeremiah knew that he had to convey those words to the people.

Jeremiah did not deliver his message in obscure and safe farmlands. The Lord told him to preach to the city people. I grew up in a city and wanted to escape from it! But like Jeremiah, the Lord called me to a city ministry. Jeremiah would face hostile opposition in the city, especially from false prophets, unprincipled politicians and godless priests.

Jeremiah's sermon began with a reminder of how God's people used to be staunchly loyal to Him. They were as devoted to Him as a bride is to her husband on their wedding night. God's marriage with His people began centuries earlier on Mount Sinai. The people followed Him faithfully in those youthful years.

Yes, there were problems with Moses' people. They rebelled, and the Lord raised up a new generation in the wilderness. Even the best marriages have their weak moments. But overall, those years in the wilderness were nostalgic to godly men like Jeremiah.

After they entered the promised land, the Lord gave His people many occasions to demonstrate their ongoing loyalty to Him. They failed. But the Lord remained faithfully committed to them through the centuries. Jeremiah lived 800 years after the wilderness generation. Through Jeremiah's preaching, the Lord gave His people one more chance.

What about you? Were you, like the people who followed Moses, formerly devoted to the Lord? What happened to your former devotion? The Lord still wants you to follow Him. Follow Him today.

**If you have lost your former devotion to the Lord, how can you return to Him?**

## Day 18
### LIKE FIRST FRUITS

**Jeremiah 2:3.** *"Israel was holy to the LORD, the firstfruits of his harvest; all who devoured her were held guilty, and disaster overtook them,'" declares the LORD.*

Early in his sermon, Jeremiah told the people the truth that the Lord had set them apart for Himself. The Lord considered them to be His holy people. The Lord faithfully protected them from extinction from their enemies. Jeremiah was merely reminding them of this truth. Throughout the history of their nation, they had heard this wonderful promise. Therefore, their current rebellion against the Lord was enormously unwise.

The Lord had given specific instructions to Moses about firstfruits. Every year when the people gathered their harvest from the land, they were to bring the sheaf of the first fruit of their harvest to the priest. The priest would wave the sheaf before the Lord to be accepted for their benefit. The people were commanded to bring a burnt offering, grain offering and drink offering to the Lord along with the firstfruits (Leviticus 23:9-14).

When they offered their firstfruits to the Lord, they were admitting that that their entire harvest belonged to Him. Their first fruits were a sacrifice to the Lord. They could not eat the first fruits themselves.

Some churches today have a firstfruits celebration every year. I once visited a large church in the Ukraine on Harvest Sunday. The believers who owned gardens brought the first crops they had harvested to church. They had stacked all varieties of fruit and vegetables on wooden tiers in front of the choir loft. This massive display towered eight feet above the congregation. The church distributed the food to the poor the following day.

Jeremiah made a spiritual application of these literal firstfruits. The people of Israel were the Lord's firstfruits. No political enemies could successfully devour the Lord's firstfruits. As firstfruits, Moses' people were the first nation to worship the true God. As firstfruits, they were signs that masses of people would later become the Lord's worshippers as well.

If you are a true believer, then you are the result of the firstfruits of a harvest to Him. You are the firstfruits of all He created (James 1:18). You will join those who were redeemed from humanity as firstfruits to God and to the Lamb (Revelation 14:4). Do not trivialize your identity as the Lord's first fruit!

**How is your relationship with the Lord like His first fruit?**

## Day 19
### INGRATITUDE

**Jeremiah 2:4-5.** *Hear the word of the LORD, O house of Jacob, all you clans of the house of Israel. This is what the LORD says: "What fault did your fathers find in me, that they strayed so far from me? They followed worthless idols and became worthless themselves...."*

As Jeremiah preached, he emphasized that his words were not his own. He gave the people the Lord's words. He gave the Lord's assessment that the Lord's people had wandered far from Him.

Instead of following the Lord, they now paid allegiance to worthless idols. An idol is anything other than the true God on which people place their confidence. Idols caused major problems. Worshippers of idols eventually became just like the idols (Psalm 115:8). Being idol-like means that they lost their humanity.

Because their commitment was to worthless idols, they became worthless to the Lord. The Hebrew word for *worthless* can also mean *empty*. Idols are as empty as my bank account was during my last year of graduate school! Idols have nothing of substance to offer to anyone.

Idols illustrate the emptiness of many people's lives. People who do not give appreciation to God have no one else to thank. Since an idol is always empty, only the superstitious and the foolish would try to give thankfulness to it.

What possible fault could the people have found in the Lord that they strayed so far from Him? People who are not thankful to God think that He is somehow to blame for something. How sad! They do not know that God cannot be blamed for evil. They do not know that God is perfect goodness. They do not know that God is unlimited love.

Jeremiah would preach against idolatry all his life. He knew the disastrous effects of false gods. Idol worshippers became hardened against the true God and lost any gratitude that they may have shown Him in the past.

A person who has known about the Lord and turns to idols anyway shows deep ingratitude to God. That person's life is empty. Stay away from idols and give thanks only to Him.

**What is your level of gratefulness to the Lord?**

## Day 20
### FRUIT AND BOUNTY

**Jeremiah 2:6-7.** *"They did not ask, 'Where is the LORD, who brought us up out of Egypt and led us through the barren wilderness, through a land of deserts and rifts, a land of drought and darkness, a land where no one travels and no one lives?' I brought you into a fertile land to eat its fruit and rich produce. But you came and defiled my land and made my inheritance detestable."*

Like a compelling preacher, Jeremiah drew a vivid contrast between the wilderness and the promised land. The wilderness was a land of desert sand where windstorms darkened the skies. It was known for its drought and its life-threatening valleys. Most people tried to avoid traveling and living in the wilderness.

In contrast, the Lord's promised land was lush. The Lord brought His people into a land that was known for its fruitfulness. God intended for them to enjoy the land's fruit and rich bounty. The Lord had delivered His people out of a nation that was loathsome to Him. Sadly, they turned the promised land into the same high level of loathsomeness. They rejected the Lord's goodness.

Do not forget the full extent that the Lord showered the land with His goodness. Even before they entered the land, they knew about the land's vast richness. It was a land flowing with milk and honey (Exodus 3:8).

The Lord planned to bring them to a land that flowed with brooks, springs and fountains. It was a land of wheat, barley, vines, fig trees, pomegranates and olive trees. It was a land where the people would always have plenty of food. They would be able to mine iron and copper from the hills. The promised land lacked nothing. The people would eat, drink and praise the Lord because of the superior land He gave them (Deuteronomy 8:7-10).

The Lord's pleasurable gifts to His people are evidence of His goodness. The Lord is eternally good. His goodness is a reality even during those times when you do not see His gifts or feel aware of His kindness.

Are you sensitive to all the fruit and bounty that the Lord has showered on you? You are alive as you read this, so you must have had adequate food all your years. You may not have had the variety that you desired, but you did have food. The Lord has deluged you with gifts so that you may grow close to the Giver.

**What are you doing with the "fruit" that God has given you?**

Day 21

IDOL LEADERS

**Jeremiah 2:8.** *"The priests did not ask, 'Where is the LORD?' Those who deal with the law did not know me; the leaders rebelled against me. The prophets prophesied by Baal, following worthless idols".*

Jeremiah boldly preached the reason why there was a problem. He had said that the people had wandered away from the Lord and worshipped idols. They had stopped seeking the Lord and they had made the land repugnant to Him (2:5-7). The people had strayed, because their leaders were idolatrous.

The spiritual leaders of Jeremiah's day did not teach people about the Lord. They were in rebellion against Him. The priests, prophets, rulers and those responsible for teaching God's law had no relationship with the Lord. Instead, they tried to have relationships with idols. Jeremiah named one of the main gods that they worshipped. He said that their prophets foretold the future in the name of Baal.

Baal was the pagan storm god. People thought that Baal was responsible for the rainstorms, and they also worshipped him as the god of fertility. Jeremiah preached against Baal throughout his long career. He did not fear offending the Baalites!

Jeremiah later used their worship of Baal as an illustration of their breaking the Ten Commandments (7:9). He preached that the citizens of Jerusalem had set up as many altars to sacrifice to the repulsive god Baal as they have streets in the city (11:13). He predicted that disaster would come on them because they had angered the Lord by offering sacrifices to Baal (11:17).

Jeremiah exposed the truth that the people had built places of idolatrous worship so that they could sacrifice their children as burnt offerings to Baal in the fire (19:5). They had built places of worship for Baal in the Valley of Ben Hinnom so that they could sacrifice their sons and daughters. God never intended for them to have such a deplorable practice. Judah was now liable for punishment (32:35). Jeremiah prophesied that the Babylonians would set Jerusalem on fire. They would burn the city down along with all the houses where people offered sacrifices to Baal (32:29).

Unfortunately, every generation sees religious leaders who lead people away from the Lord. Do not be persuaded by their lies and by their deceptively attractive lives. Follow the truth, and live in an ever-tightening bond with the Lord.

**How can you identify religious leaders who are not teaching what God approves?**

## Day 22
### WHY DID THEY FORSAKE THE GOOD LORD?

**Jeremiah 2:11. *Has a nation ever changed its gods? (Yet they are not gods at all.) But my people have exchanged their glory for worthless idols.***

The Lord asked a rhetorical question through Jeremiah. The question was, "Has a nation changed gods?" The expected answer was, "No!" The nations had kept their same idols for centuries.

In order to highlight the question, Jeremiah called for an international audience. God summoned messengers to travel as far west as Kittim and as far east as Kedar (2:10). None of these nations had given up their gods. How much more should the Judeans have kept their worship of the true God!

The Lord had been so good to them. He had made them His holy people (2:3) and He had given them a fruitful land (2:7). Why did they want to abandon Him?

The history of Jeremiah's people reveals the answer. Their ancestors soon forgot that God delivered them from Egypt (Psalm 106:13). They made an idol of a golden calf, and thus exchanged their glory for an image that eats grass. They forgot the God who had delivered them (Psalm 106:19-21).

They failed to remember because they focused on themselves. When they forgot the Lord, it was easy for them to take the next step to forsake Him. Jeremiah's unmistakable message was that God's people had forsaken Him (2:13). They had given up their glory by turning away from His glory.

Jeremiah preached that they had exchanged their glory for that which was worthless. The majesty of God had been their glory. By their own foolish choices, they had forgotten the glory. So they replaced it.

Many centuries later, people were no wiser. They thought they were prudent, but they were really fools. They exchanged what they knew about God's glory for images of creation. (Romans 1:23).

They forgot, they forsook and they exchanged. You must never follow their bent! Never ever forget the Lord!

**How does your daily schedule guard against the possibility that you will forget God?**

## Day 23
### BROKEN CISTERNS

**Jeremiah 2:13.** *"My people have committed two sins: They have forsaken me, the spring of living water, and have dug their own cisterns, broken cisterns that cannot hold water."*

Jeremiah used the illustration of broken cisterns to warn against idolatry. The people had abandoned the Lord and turned to idols. Turning to idols was just as foolish as digging an inferior cistern on your farmland when your land already has a gushing stream of sparkling water.

According to Proverbs 18:4, the words of a person's mouth are deep waters, and the fountain of wisdom is a flowing brook. If the author of this proverb intended for the two lines to be in contrast, then the proverb means that people's own thoughts are like deep water in a cistern. That deep water is stagnant, unlike bubbling water of wisdom.

If people turn their backs on the Lord's living water and try to draw water from the cisterns of their own minds, they will get murky water. Jeremiah went a step further than the proverb. Jeremiah preached that if people dig their own cisterns, those receptacles would not endure. They will crack and hold no water at all.

Jeremiah later used other examples to describe the Lord's spring of living water. He asked if the snow ever completely disappeared from the rocky slopes of Lebanon. He also asked if the cool waters from the distant foreign mountains ever stopped flowing. The implied answer was, "No". Yet God's people had forgotten Him and were offering sacrifices to worthless idols (18:14-15).

It would seem that the choice between fresh water and no water at all would be easy. Why wouldn't people always choose the pure water? With the living water always available, why would they want to dig their own useless cisterns?

A possible answer to these questions today is that people do not know or understand about living water. Many people, like the woman with whom Jesus spoke at the well, are asking where one can get this living water. Jesus explained to the woman that the water He gives is eternal life (John 4:13-14).

Do you know people like this woman who do not understand about the living water? How can you talk to them about it? Are you drinking this living water every day? Is your relationship with the Lord fresh today? What would you like to say to Him?

**Describe the level of freshness of your relationship with the Lord.**

## Day 24
### WEAK SOAP

**Jeremiah 2:22.** *"Although you wash yourself with soda and use an abundance of soap, the stain of your guilt is still before me," declares the Sovereign LORD.*

Jeremiah preached that no quantity of soap was enough to spiritually cleanse the people. Guilt had permanently stained them. And the Lord constantly observed their sin.

Jeremiah's sermon had led to this seemingly hopeless conclusion. He had challenged his listeners to look around to see if they could find any other country that had bartered its national gods for new ones. Yet the Lord's people had abandoned their true God for empty idols (2:10-11).

Jeremiah then preached that the Lord's people committed a shocking pair of wrongs. Their first sin was leaving the Lord, who was their fountain of life-giving water. Their second sin was digging idolatrous cisterns for themselves. Ironically, these were cracked cisterns that could not even hold water (2:12-13).

Therefore, slavery would be their punishment. Other nations would enchain them like in the past. The Egyptians and Assyrians had burned their cities and taken prisoners. Yet the Lord's people insisted on looking for help from these and other nations instead of depending on the Lord (2:14-18).

Their own wickedness would bring about their punishment. They were guilty of many unfaithful acts. They walked out on God and showed Him no respect. Their abandonment of Him brought on themselves nothing but harm (2:19).

The people had a history of throwing off God's authority and refusing to be subject to Him. The people blatantly told the Lord that they would not serve Him. Instead, they made for themselves idols on every hill and under every tree. The Lord had graciously planted them in the land like a special vine of the very best stock. Yet the people rejected His grace. Consequently, they turned into wild vines that produce foul smelling grapes (2:20-21).

There was no detergent available at the market that could wash away their guilt. Their only hope was divine forgiveness. Jeremiah would later reveal the Lord's offer of forgiveness under the new covenant (31:34). Total forgiveness through Jesus Christ can clean the deepest stains. Live in a guilt-free relationship with the Lord today.

**Describe how your relationship with the Lord can be "guilt-free."**

Day 25

DELUSIONAL PURITY

**Jeremiah 2:23.** *"How can you say, 'I am not defiled; I have not run after the Baals'? See how you behaved in the valley; consider what you have done. You are a swift she-camel running here and there...."*

Jeremiah asked the people a rhetorical question. How could they deny that their lives were focused on their images of the fertility god named Baal? How could they claim to be morally pure?

He wanted them to notice how far their thinking had strayed from the truth. He wanted them to consider what they had done. He had already exposed the prophets who prophesied by Baal (2:8). He would later rebuke the people for offering sacrifices to Baal (7:9).

Jeremiah accused them of going after the Baals in the valley. He probably had in mind the valley just outside the gates of Jerusalem. The people had built altars to Baal in the valley of Ben Hinnom. They sacrificed their sons and daughters in that valley (32:35).

They had completely deceived themselves! Just like the people about whom the Apostle Paul wrote had exchanged the truth of God for a lie (Romans 1:25), Jeremiah's people believed the same falsehood. They thought that they could live autonomously apart from God. They thought that they did not need God to supply their needs.

Perhaps they thought they were still spiritually clean because they remembered a moment in their past when they did a good deed. I had a similar thought pattern when I still considered myself a runner even though I had not jogged for years! What an illusory way to think!

Once they turned their backs on God's truth, they did not think sensibly. Jeremiah said that they were like a fast young camel running back and forth. The camel would go a few steps in one direction, then suddenly turn and run a different way. She would leave a crisscross of tracks in the sand and would end up going nowhere.

Beware of thinking that you are pure when you are really not. Keep yourself in touch with reality. Examine yourself before the Lord.

**What are some specific ways that you can ask the Lord to keep you from being deceived about how pure you really are?**

## Day 26
### ADDICTION

**Jeremiah 2:25.** *Do not run until your feet are bare and your throat is dry. But you said, 'It's no use! I love foreign gods, and I must go after them.'*

Jeremiah lived among people who were obsessed with their idols. They pursued foreign gods like fanatics who run until their shoes wear out. They were so consumed with their idols that they gave no thought to simple needs like thirst.

It was not the Lord's plan for His people to worship anything other than Himself. The Lord considered any other object of worship to be foreign. Many people think that the idol worship against which Jeremiah preached is irrelevant today. They are wrong. Jeremiah described idol worship as an addiction.

People told Jeremiah that they loved their strange gods. But they used the wrong word. They used the word *love*. They did not realize that a person could not truly love an idol. All a person can do is lust for it! Idols can never satisfy one's quest for 'human-ness'. Sooner or later, the person cries out, "It is hopeless!" The addict is desperate. People who are addicted to idols are prisoners of their own idols.

One of the great messages of the Bible is that the Lord desires to set prisoners free and give them significant lives. A believer's maturing relationship with the Lord is the most effective way to break free of idolatrous addictions.

Jeremiah had preached that the Lord's people committed a terrible twosome of offenses. Their first sin was abandoning the Lord, who was their spring of life-giving water. Their second sin was hollowing out idolatrous cisterns for themselves. Ironically, these were fractured cisterns that could not even hold water (2:12-13).

Without the life-giving water that only God can give, people are addicts to their own gods. They futilely attempt to dig their own cisterns. Even the counterfeit spiritual water that they try to collect oozes away through the cracks in their cisterns.

At the end of his first letter in the New Testament, John wrote that believers should keep themselves from idols (1 John 5:21). Paul wrote that greed is idolatry (Colossians 3:5). Idols are a grave temptation for believers today. You must avoid greedily seeking other things instead of God. Draw nearer to Jeremiah's God. Keep yourself from idols.

**Name three reasons why idols are so addictive. How can you overcome this addiction?**

Day 27
CONFUSION

**Jeremiah 2:26-27.** *As a thief is disgraced when he is caught, so the house of Israel is disgraced—they, their kings and their officials, their priests and their prophets. They say to wood, 'You are my father,' and to stone, 'You gave me birth.' They have turned their backs to me and not their faces; yet when they are in trouble, they say, 'Come and save us!'*

Jeremiah preached powerfully and boldly. He knew he was attacking those wooden and stone idols that most people accepted as part of their culture. And Jeremiah knew he would offend the political and religious leaders of Judah by comparing the leaders of Israel to a humiliated captured thief.

Jeremiah did not fear offending the leaders, because he remembered his calling. The Lord had promised to make Jeremiah a fortified city, iron pillar and bronze wall against all the leaders and people of the land (1:18).

The entire population, including the political and religious leaders, had turned their backs to the Lord. They did not acknowledge their own Creator. Instead, they claimed their wooden idols were their father and their stone idols gave them birth. Jeremiah later named the specific wooden idol of Asherah (17:2) and he had already named the stone idol of Baal (2:8).

Perhaps the people argued with Jeremiah that the wooden and stone images actually helped them worship the true Lord. The Lord created trees and stones, and seeing His creation helped them think about Him. Jeremiah's response was to fully ridicule them.

Asherah was the female idol of fertility, and Baal was the male god of fertility. Jeremiah declared that the people looked to their wooden female goddess as their father and their stone male god as giving them birth! Jeremiah derided their idolatry by reversing the sexes. Jeremiah did this to emphasize how spiritually confused the people were!

Among other dangers, idolatry leads to sexual confusion. Idolaters are dismally confused people. You must rise above the disorder of the world and pursue the truth. Do not exchange your relationship with the Creator for a lie.

**List three reasons why people do not pursue the truth.**

## Day 28
### WHERE ARE THE 'GODS'?

**Jeremiah 2:28.** *Where then are the gods you made for yourselves? Let them come if they can save you when you are in trouble! For you have as many gods as you have towns, O Judah.*

As Jeremiah continued preaching, he asked the people where their gods were. He challenged their idols to come and save the people during times of difficulty. Jeremiah expressed doubt that the wooden and stone idols could help them.

Jeremiah told them the sad fact that the nation of Judah had as many gods as it had towns. In many cases, each ancient town had its own patron god. In fact, towns were often named after idols. Even Jeremiah's hometown was named after the Canaanite goddess Anath.

The people had spiritually regressed to the idols of the land that their ancestors had conquered. Ironically, they were trusting in the idols that Moses had mocked. Moses had asked the same question that Jeremiah now posed. "Where are their gods?" (Deuteronomy 32:37).

I have seen ancient idols in museums. Some of them looked sinister, others looked comical. None of them looked like they would lift a stony finger to help anyone!

Moses sarcastically challenged the gods to rise up and help the people who worshipped them (Deuteronomy 32:38). Jeremiah now issued the same demand. Let the idols come and help, if they can!

Jeremiah's people also imported gods and goddesses from other nations. Perhaps they thought that having so many gods would assure that at least one would come to their aid. However, none of the idols helped them in any way! The gods never came!

In contrast, the Lord always comes. The entire Bible narrates how the Lord came to men and women. The Bible ends with the promise, "I am coming soon" (Revelation 22:20).

God is your helper. He is your shield and your sword (Deuteronomy 33:29). You can call on Him whenever you are in trouble, and He will hear you and help you (Psalm 18:6). God is your helper and you never need to be afraid (Hebrews 13:6).

**How has the Lord helped you during the past month?**

## Day 29
### SILENCING THE PROPHETS

Jeremiah 2:29-30. *"Why do you bring charges against me? You have all rebelled against me," declares the LORD. "In vain I punished your people; they did not respond to correction. Your sword has devoured your prophets like a ravening lion...."*

Jeremiah asked the people why they were trying to refute the Lord. The question was rhetorical. Jeremiah did not expect an answer from his listeners. He may have wondered if they were even listening.

Their case against God was the same one that many people bring against Him today. Their charge is simply that they cannot get God to do their will. They cannot control God.

Jeremiah answered the question by reversing the charges. The people had no reasons for refuting the Lord. Instead, the Lord had every reason for bringing a lawsuit against them. Jeremiah expressed the Lord's verdict that all the people had rebelled against Him. In fact, nothing positive resulted even when the Lord punished His people. They did not respond to such correction. They merely slaughtered the Lord's prophets just like a voracious lion would devour its prey.

I have watched documentary movies about lions. I have seen how they satisfy their huge appetites. They pounce on weaker animals and tear them apart. The people of Judah had done the same with their prophets!

In contrast to the good King Josiah, his father was an extremely evil king who shed much innocent blood in Jerusalem (2 Kings 21:16). Among those he murdered were countless numbers of prophets. Jesus condemned His own people for having a history of killing the prophets (Matthew 23:37). Stephen accused his people of persecuting every one of the prophets (Acts 8:52).

The prophets were those through whom God spoke. The prophets wrote the Old Testament. After many centuries of speaking through the prophets, God gave His final message through His Son (Hebrews 1:1-3).

If only they had listened to the prophets instead of killing them! If only we would listen! Listen to the Lord speak through His prophets and apostles. Do not silence the prophets by ignoring them. Listen to Jeremiah's words. Do not bring charges against God. When the Lord corrects you, respond and learn.

**In what ways has the Lord corrected you during the past month? How have you responded?**

Day 30

DELUSIONAL FREEDOM

**Jeremiah 2:31.** *"You of this generation, consider the word of the LORD: Have I been a desert to Israel or a land of great darkness? Why do my people say, 'We are free to roam; we will come to you no more'?"*

Jeremiah spoke on behalf of the Lord when he asked what the people thought about Him. The people were thinking untrue word pictures about God. They thought that God was like a desert and like a dark land.

Each time I travel back to the city of my birth (El Paso, Texas) and see the vast hot desert, I am reminded that a desert does not have provisions for basic human needs. And the Texas desert at night conceals dangers. When Jeremiah's people compared God with desert and darkness, they claimed that the Lord neither provided nor protected.

The truth was that the Lord had led Moses' people through the desert and had sustained them every step of the way (Deuteronomy 8:15). The Lord had not left them in threatening darkness. His pillar of fire had been with them every night (Exodus 13:21-22).

You can have the same provision and protection. The Lord is your light and your salvation (Psalm 27:1). You can always see light because of His light (Psalm 36:9). God's word is a lamp and a light (Psalm 119:105).

I keep a small flashlight next to my bed. I take it with me when I travel to other countries. I always wake up before dawn and sometimes I do not remember if I am at home or abroad! I reach for my tiny flashlight as I get out of bed, and the light gives me my bearings.

God provides bearings in life along with everything else that you need. He gives grace and glory (Psalm 84:11). As you seek Him, He will provide absolutely everything that you need (Psalm 34:10).

With such a Provider and Protector, why would anyone want to stray from God? The people thought that they could be truly free if they freed themselves from God. They were wrong. They believed in delusional freedom, and they became slaves of sin.

Do not fantasize about freedom that is sin-drenched. Remember Jesus' words about being free (John 8:31-32). Continue being His disciple by following His word.

**Give a specific example of how your relationship with the Lord has given you genuine freedom.**

## Day 31
### FAITHLESS FORGETFULNESS

*Jeremiah 2:32. Does a maiden forget her jewelry, a bride her wedding ornaments? Yet my people have forgotten me, days without number.*

On her wedding day, a young Judean woman did not come dressed for farm work! No, she wore her bridal dress and her marriage jewels. Then she kept her wedding apparel for the rest of her life.

A young Judean bride wore an embroidered dress of fine linen and silk. On her feet were beautiful leather sandals. She was adorned with jewelry, including bracelets, rings, earrings and a necklace. On her head was a lovely bridal crown. The bride was gorgeous (Ezekiel 16:10-14).

For a young woman to forget what she was supposed to wear on her wedding day was unimaginable. Sadly, the unimaginable had happened to the people spiritually. They had forgotten their Lord. It was not an occasional memory loss. They had stopped thinking about the Lord for more days than could be counted.

The people had forgotten God, and they acted like an adulterous woman who had forgotten her wedding. They were like the most promiscuous women who chased after their lovers! Even the worst of women could learn from them. Forgetting about the Lord also led to social injustice. Jeremiah accused the people of having clothes stained with the lifeblood of the poor who were not guilty of doing anything wrong. They had not caught the poor people breaking into their homes, yet they still put them to death. The people were guilty of oppressing the poor, yet they claimed they were innocent (2:33-35).

They had also demonstrated their unfaithfulness to the Lord by changing their political allegiances. They had tried a treaty with Assyria, but Assyria had given them no help. Now they were trying to get help from Egypt. But Jeremiah prophesied that they would come away from Egypt with their hands covering their faces in sorrow and shame. They were trusting in international politics instead of the Lord. The Lord would not allow their reliance on foreign nations to be successful (2:36-37).

Do not be like these forgetful, faithless people. Remember the great wedding of the future, the wedding of the Lamb. The Lamb's bride will wear bright, clean linen that will result from believers' righteous deeds (Revelation 19:7-8). Never, never forget!

**What might cause you to forget your spiritual "wedding clothes"?**

## Day 32
### To and Fro

**Jeremiah 2:36.** *Why do you go about so much, changing your ways? You will be disappointed by Egypt as you were by Assyria.*

Jeremiah had described his people as being like a swift young camel running here and there (2:23). They had shown themselves morally unstable. This spiritual wavering was the basis for their erratic political opinions.

Jeremiah had told them not to drink the waters from either the Nile River or the Euphrates. These rivers symbolized the powerful nations of Egypt and Assyria. Instead of following the Lord's way, they were traveling on the roads to these two nations (2:18-19).

In the past, they had followed their kings into disastrous foreign policies with both Egypt and Assyria. At one time, their nation of Judah was aligned with powerful Assyria. Ahaz was king of Judah, and he asked the Assyrians for help against other nations that were attacking Judah. The Assyrians came, but their assistance resulted only in Judah's bondage to Assyria. Ahaz gave a substantial amount of wealth to the Assyrians from both his palace and the temple, but the Assyrian oppression continued (2 Chronicles 28:16-21).

Later during Jeremiah's lifetime, King Josiah led the Judean army to fight against the Egyptians. Josiah died in battle. The Egyptians took the next king of Judah back to Egypt as a prisoner and forced Judah to pay taxes to Egypt (2 Kings 23:29-35).

They would again be disappointed by Egypt when the Babylonians later began their siege of Jerusalem. The Judeans would trust in Egypt to defend them against Babylon. Egypt would let them down (Jeremiah 37:5-8).

Trusting other nations instead of the Lord was a fatal mistake. This misplaced trust led to their embracing the idols of other nations. Idolatry then resulted in religious irregularity.

People face the same choice even today. The Apostle Paul warned believers not to be frequently changing their doctrines. Believers in Jesus should not be like a ship being tossed to and fro by waves and by every wind of doctrine. They should concentrate on their own spiritual growth and unity with other believers (Ephesians 4:13-15).

**What are some definite actions you can take to become more stable in your beliefs about God?**

## Day 33
### SPIRITUAL DIVORCE

**Jeremiah 3:1.** *"If a man divorces his wife and she leaves him and marries another man, should he return to her again? Would not the land be completely defiled? But you have lived as a prostitute with many lovers—would you now return to me?" declares the LORD.*

Jeremiah's text for his sermon was a reference from Moses' law about divorce. The law allowed divorce under certain circumstances. If a husband was not pleased with his new wife, he could draw up a divorce document and expel her from his house. She could then become someone else's wife. If her second husband divorced her, she could not return to her first husband. She had become impure before the Lord. If she returned to her first husband, the land would be defiled (Deuteronomy 24:1-4).

Jesus explained that the Lord gave this divorce law because of humanity's hardness of heart. Jesus emphasized that the Lord established marriage as a permanent bond between a man and a woman at the beginning of creation. Jesus taught clearly against divorce (Mark 10:5-9).

Instead of highlighting laws about divorce, Christian marriage emphasizes God's grace in keeping the marriage together. Jeremiah's sermon also stressed grace. Moses' law did not permit a man to take back his twice-divorced wife, but the Lord was willing to be a husband again to His immoral people.

However, the question of returning to the Lord was an incredulous one. The people could not return in their present condition. The outward religious reforms of King Josiah had not caused them to change their hearts.

Their immorality was blatant. They waited for lovers like a prostitute sitting beside the road. They refused to be ashamed of what they had done. Outwardly they kept referring to the Lord as their Father and faithful companion, but the Lord accused them of doing all the evil that they could (3:2-5).

Even as they spoke words about the Lord, in their hearts they were pursuing three classes of lovers. First, they chased literal lovers and were unfaithful to their marriage vows. Secondly, they ran after religious lovers and worshiped idols. Thirdly, they pursued political lovers and trusted alliances with foreign nations instead of the Lord. They had divorced themselves from Him. Do not even think of being like them!

**Describe how your relationship with the Lord can protect you from these three classes of sinful "lovers".**

## Day 34
### FATHER AND FRIEND

**Jeremiah 3:4-5.** *"Have you not just called to me: 'My Father, my friend from my youth, will you always be angry? Will your wrath continue forever?' This is how you talk, but you do all the evil you can."*

During the days of Jesus' earthly life, He taught His followers to pray to God as their Father. However, "Father" as a name for God is not solely a New Testament idea. Jeremiah preached that even backsliders in his day called God "Father".

They were backsliders because they had slipped away from the Lord and turned to idols. In fact, they even called certain of their idols "father" (2:27). In the preceding sentences of his sermon, Jeremiah gave the Lord's scathing exposure of their lifestyle.

Anyone could look up at the hilltops and see that they were doing all the evil that they could. On every one of the hills, the backsliders were intimately involved with idols. They waited on those gods like a prostitute sitting beside the road. They were like a thief lying in wait in the desert, looking for someone to rob. They had defiled the land by wickedly prostituting themselves to other gods (3:2).

Because of their evil lives, the Lord had withheld the rains. The critical spring rains had not come, but the people had not learned from the drought. Jeremiah said that they were as stubborn as prostitutes. They refused to be ashamed of what they had done (3:3).

The people still wanted rain. They thought that the Lord might be holding a grudge against them along with holding back the rain. They thought that any divine resentment against them would be temporary.

They wanted it both ways. They wanted to keep asking their idols to send rain at the same time that they wanted the Lord to be their Father and Friend. They thought that they could say niceties to God and that He would then be nice to them. They were wrong. They offered polite prayers, but they had horrible hearts. Their disgusting deeds came from their malicious minds. They made no attempt to genuinely repent.

In contrast, true believers speak from their hearts when they call God their Father and their Friend. Do not wait until the next drought. Get near to Him now.

**What recent incident strengthened your belief that God is both your Father and your Friend.**

## Day 35
### LEARNING FROM EVENTS

*Jeremiah 3:6-7. During the reign of King Josiah, the LORD said to me, "Have you seen what faithless Israel has done? She has gone up on every high hill and under every spreading tree and has committed adultery there...."*

King Josiah reformed the whole country's religious structures. He tried to bring the nation back to God. Because he was king, no one tried to oppose him. The people supported his reforms outwardly, but most of their hearts still followed the idols that Josiah's evil father and grandfather had worshipped.

The nation of Judah had seen what happened to the nation of Israel (3:7). The Lord had judged Israel. The Lord had used the nation of Assyria to conquer and scatter the Israelites because they had been unfaithful to the Lord.

They were unfaithful because they chose to worship idols. They had allowed idolatry to invade the land of Israel. Idols were on top of every peak and under every tree.

The people of Judah had seen both the sin and the judgment for that sin. They saw how the Lord sent the Israelites away because of their worship of other gods. However, the people of Judah did not seem to be fazed. They did not think that the same thing would happen to them even as they gave themselves to other gods. Jeremiah warned them by calling their idolatry "prostitution" and "adultery" (3: 8-9).

King Josiah wanted his nation of Judah to return to the Lord. He began seeking God when he was sixteen years old. As the Lord worked in his heart, Josiah increasingly realized the hideousness of idolatry. When Josiah was twenty, he began to destroy the idols throughout Judah (2 Chronicles 34:1-4). The next year, the Lord called Jeremiah (1:1).

The Lord was using two immense historical events to urge the people of Judah to return to Him. God was teaching the people through (1) Josiah's reforms and (2) Israel's example of being judged. The people should have learned from observing these two events.

**What specific events in your life is the Lord using to teach you or to warn you?**

## Day 36
### DECEPTIVE HEARTS

**Jeremiah 3:10.** *"In spite of all this, her unfaithful sister Judah did not return to me with all her heart, but only in pretense," declares the LORD.*

Judah and Israel were sister nations. Israel had already been conquered and scattered. The Lord referred to Judah as Israel's unfaithful sister. If Israel deserved judgment, Judah deserved it even more.

Jeremiah preached that wayward Israel was less guilty than unfaithful Judah (3:11). Judah had refused to learn from Israel's wrongdoing. Judah was committing a worse offense against God by faking godliness.

Israel had done nothing to conceal her sin. Israel had sinned unreservedly and explicitly. In contrast, Judah was sinning secretly. Judah only pretended to return to the Lord. There was no sincerity behind Judah's repentance. Judah was committing the greater sin, the sin of hypocrisy.

King Josiah did everything that he could to bring his people back to the Lord. He destroyed idols, repaired the temple, publicly read the Scriptures, and celebrated the Passover. Since he was the king, the people obeyed him.

Throughout the rest of Josiah's reign, the people followed the Lord (2 Chronicles 34:33). Josiah made them do it, but they did not serve the Lord willingly.

In spite of Josiah's efforts of dismantling the idols, Jeremiah still saw statues to pagan gods everywhere. The king could be in only one place at a time. The people could hide their idols from him.

Josiah exemplified how a godly king should live. His obedience to the Lord was sincere. He followed the Lord with all his heart, soul and strength (2 Kings 23:25).

To have intimacy with God, you must let Him have your heart. If you do not release the deception in your heart, your relationship with Him will remain aloof. If you pretend that your relationship with the Lord is closer than it really is, you are imitating the unfaithful Judeans!

**Write a prayer in your own words, asking the Lord to search your heart and remove deceit from it.**

## Day 37
### THE MERCIFUL LORD

**Jeremiah 3:12.** *Go, proclaim this message toward the north: "Return, faithless Israel," declares the LORD, "I will frown on you no longer, for I am merciful," declares the LORD, "I will not be angry forever."*

Jeremiah preached that the people must repent. Many of them may have rejected his message because they believed they had already repented. Jeremiah was preaching during King Josiah's reign (3:6), and Josiah had led the people to return to God.

However, the people's repentance had been superficial and false. Unfaithful Judah had not turned back to the Lord with sincerity (3:10). The nation had only pretended to repent.

The nation of Judah had given herself like a prostitute to idols (3:8). Judah had defiled the land through her adulterous worship of the gods of wood and stone (3:9). Judah was more guilty than the nation of Israel (3:11), and the Lord had already punished Israel.

More than one hundred years earlier, the Assyrians had taken Israel into captivity (2 Kings 17:6). Only the nation of Judah was left (2 Kings 17:18). In the presence of the Judeans, Jeremiah was calling on the captive Israelites in the north to repent.

The Judeans should have learned a wonderful lesson about God's mercy from Jeremiah's sermon. If the Lord could be merciful to the scattered Israelites, who were obviously under His judgment, then He could also show mercy to the Judeans.

When certain people are under the Lord's mercy, it means that they no longer offend Him. He has withdrawn His anger toward them. Living under His mercy is the only safe existence for you and me.

God has absolute freedom to show His mercy to whomever He wishes. If the Lord did not have this freedom, no one would receive His mercy. You do not deserve His mercy, and you can do nothing to earn it.

Are you growing in your awareness of the depths of God's mercy? Are you aware that the Lord has enabled you to be born again according to His great mercy (1 Peter 1:3)? Go before His throne and receive His mercy (Hebrews 4:16).

**What does the Lord's mercy mean to you?**

## Day 38
### WISE SHEPHERDS

**Jeremiah 3:15.** *"Then I will give you shepherds after my own heart, who will lead you with knowledge and understanding."*

The people in Jeremiah's day needed shepherds. They needed leaders who followed the Lord's heart. Jeremiah preached compellingly about the desperate need that they had for shepherds.

Jeremiah had summed up the reasons for their need of shepherds. First, they had given themselves repeatedly to foreign idols under every tree. Secondly, they had disobeyed the Lord's commands (3:13).

Jeremiah had given them the good news that the Lord was inviting them to return to Him. They were wayward people and needed to repent, but then the Lord would bring them back to Him. They could return to their true Master (3:14).

Jeremiah now gave them more good news. The Lord promised to give them shepherds. These would be shepherds who would have the same heart that God had. They would lead the people wisely and "feed" them knowledge and understanding. In his early years, Solomon had been such a shepherd.

The Hebrew word for "shepherds", which is sometimes translated as "pastors", means "leaders". Jeremiah was primarily referring to political leaders, to kings. God's purpose for the kings of Israel was to shepherd the people (2 Samuel 7:7). Jeremiah later preached about political rulers being shepherds (23:1-5).

I once drank coffee with a real shepherd on a hillside in Colorado. He was always listening for any problems that his nearby sheep might have. His constant concern for his sheep's welfare illustrated for me God's model for leaders.

Jeremiah could reflect on his nation's history and see that many of the kings had failed to be good shepherds. He knew that the Lord was sending imminent judgment, but the prophet was extremely hopeful about the distant future. God would someday send a righteous Branch who would be a wise king reigning with justice (23:5).

During the days that Jesus was on earth, He saw people as sheep without a shepherd (Matthew 9:36). Jesus claimed that He was the Good Shepherd (John 10:11). You have a shepherd now. Follow Him.

**What specific needs do you have that the Good Shepherd can help you with today?**

## Day 39
### THE ARK OF THE COVENANT

**Jeremiah 3:16a.** *"In those days, when your numbers have increased greatly in the land," declares the LORD, "men will no longer say, 'The ark of the covenant of the LORD.' It will never enter their minds or be remembered; it will not be missed, nor will another one be made."*

The ark of the covenant was the most holy furnishing of the temple. It was situated behind the curtain of the most holy place. The ark was a little more than a meter long, and it was about seven tenths of a meter high. It was made of acacia wood and was overlaid with pure gold, and it had a gold molding around it. The ark had a golden ring at each corner, so that men could carry the ark on poles (Exodus 25:10-16).

An ungodly king had removed the ark so that he could endow the temple with his idols. During the religious reformation, King Josiah commanded the Levites to move the ark back into the temple (2 Chronicles 35:3). This must have been an emotional event for those people who had prayed that godliness would return to Judah.

Possibly, Jeremiah was not impressed with the ark's return to the temple. Perhaps he suspected that the ark would have little effect on people's inward spiritual hearts. He suspected that people were chanting, "The ark of the covenant of the Lord" as a meaningless ritual. Jeremiah knew that spiritual reformation needed to be inward.

Three extraordinary items were initially inside the ark of the covenant. In the early years, the ark contained a jar filled with manna, Aaron's staff, and stone tablets of God's commandments (Hebrews 9:4). These contents of the ark represented the old covenant. The manna signified God's temporary provision. The staff symbolized the priesthood that began with Aaron. The stone tablets stood for the law that the Lord gave to Moses.

By the time of King Solomon, only the tablets of stone were inside the ark (1 Kings 8:9). By the time of Jeremiah, the people disobeyed every law that was on those tablets (7:9). The Lord revealed to Jeremiah that He would replace the old covenant (31:31-32). The old covenant would become obsolete (Hebrews 8:13). Consequently, the ark of the covenant would become irrelevant.

As you grow closer to God, do not cling to visible aids. The ark of the covenant is gone. Jesus said that people would worship God in spirit and truth (John 4:23).

**What visible image may be restraining you from a deeper relationship with God?**

## Day 40
### FORGETTERS OF THE LOST ARK

**Jeremiah 3:16b.** *"In those days, when your numbers have increased greatly in the land," declares the LORD, "men will no longer say, 'The ark of the covenant of the LORD.' It will never enter their minds or be remembered; it will not be missed, nor will another one be made."*

During the days of Jeremiah, the ark of the covenant vanished. Jeremiah never mentioned the ark again. When the Babylonians destroyed Jerusalem, the ark was not on the list of temple contents that they took back to Babylon (52:17-23).

What happened to the ark? A legend arose that Jeremiah hid it! He ordered men to carry the ark to Mount Nebo, where Jeremiah hid it in a cave (2 Maccabees 2:1-7).

No one has ever found the ark on Mount Nebo, but legends and fictional ideas continue. Forget about the lost ark! True believers do not long for its return.

The ark had a temporary place in God's plan, but it was still important. Along with the rest of the tabernacle that Moses constructed, the ark was a symbol of heavenly realities (Hebrews 8:5). In contrast to the wooden and gold ark that Moses made, the eternal ark of the covenant is in heaven (Revelation 11:19).

The top of the earthly ark had a golden mercy seat between two cherubim of gold (Exodus 25:17-22), and it was considered to be the Lord's throne on earth (1 Samuel 4:4). Only the high priest could approach that throne, but he had to bring the blood of animals. He sprinkled the blood on the mercy seat as atonement for the sins of the people (Leviticus 16:14-16).

When Jesus Christ died, His blood atoned for your sins. He now sits on a throne in heaven. He sits on the throne of grace and you have unrestricted access to Him (Hebrews 4:16).

You can approach the throne of grace at anytime. You can draw near to His throne with complete boldness. The One on the throne of grace has absolute sympathy with your situation and He always understands your needs.

When you pray, you obtain the mercy of Jesus and find the grace of Jesus. In His mercy He forgives, and in His grace He gives. He gives grace and mercy as frequently as you choose to come to His throne!

**What personal needs will you bring now before the throne of grace?**

Day 41
THE LORD'S THRONE

**Jeremiah 3:17.** *At that time they will call Jerusalem The Throne of the LORD, and all nations will gather in Jerusalem to honor the name of the LORD. No longer will they follow the stubbornness of their evil hearts.*

As Jeremiah grew closer to the Lord, he understood more clearly that God is on a throne. His throne makes Him worthy of every honor. In the future, God's throne will become obvious to all the nations and they will honor Him.

Throughout the history of Jeremiah's nation, the Lord's throne was the ark of the covenant. The priests had placed the ark in the temple that King Solomon built (1 Kings 8:6). Jeremiah preached that people would no longer remember this ark (3:16). He predicted that the temple would be destroyed (7:14).

When I visited Jerusalem, I saw the only remains of the temple that King Herod rebuilt. One wall. The descendants of Jeremiah's people continue to pray at that wall. They live on memories of God's throne being in the temple long ago.

God's throne in the future will be greater and more inclusive. The Lord's earthly throne will be an entire city. Today, He continues to occupy His heavenly throne.

God's throne always has been and always will be in heaven. He chose to have an earthly expression of His throne so that people would have opportunities to know Him. The time is coming when His throne will be obvious to the entire world.

The nations need to see God's throne. They are following the stubbornness of their evil hearts and they ought to know that God holds them accountable for their deeds. They should follow God instead of their hearts.

Jeremiah's people had a problem with stubborn hearts. Their hearts caused them to follow Baal (9:14) and every other available idol (13:10). When they followed their own stubborn hearts, they did not listen to the Lord (16:12).

Does your heart have stubborn tendencies? Is your obstinacy keeping you from growing closer to the Lord? Do you consider your heart to be your own throne? If so, your heart's throne is microscopic! Remember that the Lord is on His unrivaled throne.

**What definite results does God's throne have on your relationship with Him?**

Day 42

RAUCOUS REPENTANCE

**Jeremiah 3:21.** *A cry is heard on the barren heights, the weeping and pleading of the people of Israel, because they have perverted their ways and have forgotten the LORD their God.*

Jeremiah had preached clearly about his nation's problem. The people lived as if the Lord were not there, for they were unfaithful to God. They were like an unfaithful marriage partner (3:20).

This unfaithfulness made no sense. The Lord had blessed His people in every way. His desire was to treat them like His own sons and daughters. He planned to give them a beautiful inheritance. He wanted them to call Him "Father" (3:19).

Now Jeremiah paused in his sermon and listened. He could hear noise coming from the nearby hilltop. He said that he heard human voices weeping and crying out for help.

Those who heard Jeremiah might think that the loud hilltop weeping was a positive event. They might think that certainly Jeremiah would commend the summit shouters for their emotional worship and repentance. No, he did not extol them, since they were probably begging their idols to hear their prayers. The barren heights were known as places of idolatry (3:2).

They were not praying to the Lord. Jeremiah claimed that they had forgotten Him. Consequently, their lives were perverted.

Jeremiah often preached that the people had forgotten the Lord. Their ancestor Moses also had warned against forgetting the Lord (Deuteronomy 8:11). They had apparently forgotten Moses' words!

Jeremiah then issued an intense invitation from the Lord (3:22). In an extraordinary act of grace, the Lord asked His faithless people to return to Him. If they would return, the Lord would heal them from their faithlessness.

Jeremiah voiced the answer that he wished they would say. He wanted them to truly repent. He yearned for them to say, "Yes, we will come to you, for you are the Lord our God (3:22)."

**How can you avoid saying insincere prayers to the Lord?**

Day 43
FINANCIAL PROBLEMS

**Jeremiah 3:24.** *From our youth shameful gods have consumed the fruits of our fathers' labor—their flocks and herds, their sons and daughters.*

Jeremiah had preached mightily about the spiritual ruin caused by idols. Then he introduced another terrible result. He said that idols could also cause economic ruin.

Jeremiah used the words that he hoped the people would say. He wanted them to admit that idolatry had brought them to poverty. He wanted them to acknowledge that they had sinned against the Lord.

They had wasted their assets. In a rural economy, wealth was measured in flocks and herds. The people had foolishly sacrificed their animals to useless idols.

Substantially worse, they had sacrificed their own children. Jeremiah later preached that they built altars on which they burned their sons and daughters (7:31). They murdered the very future of their families.

Jeremiah referred to idols as "shameful gods". The Hebrew word for "shame" was sometimes used as a name for Baal, one of the popular idols. These Baal idols of shame devoured the time, assets and souls of many.

Jeremiah wanted the people to express their repentance by lying down in shame and dishonor on the bare ground (3:25). He wanted them to confess that they and their ancestors had disobeyed God by worshipping idols. Giving their hearts to idols caused their fiscal problems. Their money followed the direction of their hearts.

The definitive waste of children and resources happened when the Babylonians came. The people did not repent, so the Lord sent the Babylonians. The Babylonians killed or exiled everyone in Judah except the poorest. Judah was left with no economy at all.

Are your finances in disarray? Have postmodern idols consumed your resources? Do you have the spiritual potency to reject the idols of obsessive gambling, excessive pleasure, unchecked consumerism and abhorrent abortion? Do you remember that Jesus said that you could not serve both God and money (Matthew 6:24)? Serve the Lord today.

**In what specific way can you use your money to serve the Lord?**

## Day 44
### GLOBAL OUTCOMES

**Jeremiah 4:1-2.** *"If you will return, O Israel, return to me," declares the LORD. "If you put your detestable idols out of my sight and no longer go astray, and if in a truthful, just and righteous way you swear, 'As surely as the LORD lives,' then the nations will be blessed by him and in him they will glory."*

Jeremiah kept preaching, pleading with his people to return to the Lord. He gave the people a direct divine invitation. If the people would come back to Him, their repentance would have international effects. God would then bless all the nations because of them.

First, a major problem needed to be corrected. The people could not return to the Lord without first getting rid of their idols. God considered their idols to be repugnant. The idols led them to wander and caused them to speak hypocritically about God. The people were saying, "As surely as the Lord lives," without believing a word of it!

God wanted them to say truthfully, "As surely as the Lord lives." Instead of their going astray, He desired for them lives of truth, justice and righteousness. The true prophets stressed these three attributes repeatedly. God's people must speak the truth to each other (Zechariah 8:16). God requires His people to do justice (Micah 6:8). You should plant seeds of righteousness (Hosea 10:12).

Truthful, just and righteous people who follow the Lord will influence the earth. From the very beginning of the history of God's people, the Lord had a plan for Abraham's descendants to cause all the nations to be blessed (Genesis 12:3). As prophet to the nations, Jeremiah contributed to God's global strategy.

Your relationship with the Lord is much more expansive than your own personal concerns. God has a worldwide plan that will result from those who know Him. Sin is universal, but God's grace on the nations saturates the planet even more than sin.

As you interact with the Lord, seek to live truthfully, justly and righteously. Your relationship with God has global implications. Grow closer to Him and influence the planet!

**In what particular ways would you like for the Lord to use you to influence others?**

## Day 45
### HEARTS OF THORNS

**Jeremiah 4:3.** *This is what the LORD says to the men of Judah and to Jerusalem: "Break up your unplowed ground and do not sow among thorns."*

As he preached on the need to return to the Lord, Jeremiah called on his people to do a specific act. He said that the Lord wanted them to hoe their hearts, like a farmer would plow long-neglected land.

Before Jeremiah's time, another prophet had preached the same message. Hosea spoke about how the Lord wanted His people to cultivate the hard ground of their hearts, so that He could plant seeds of righteousness. The Lord desired that they harvest the fruit of His love (Hosea 10:12).

The situation had worsened in Jeremiah's day. The people's devotion to idols had allowed weeds and thorns to grow in their spiritual hearts. The thorns in their hearts were sin.

Thorns began growing on the earth as a result of sin (Genesis 3:17-18). I think of these results often as I walk through the grass outside my house. Thorns frequently cling to my pants and shoes!

Unless a farmer works his land diligently, thorns will cover it (Proverbs 24:30-31). Thorns and thistles grow up among the ruins of defeated cities (Isaiah 34:23). Thorns and snares lie in the paths of the wicked (Proverbs 22:5).

Jeremiah preached that his people had sown wheat but had reaped thorns (12:13). Who can deliver us from all these thorns? Jesus Christ wore a crown of thorns (John 19:5), and He came to save us from sin. Because of His death for sin, in the coming kingdom there will be no more thorns (Isaiah 55:13).

Are there too many thorns in your life? Do you feel like you are missing out on the Lord's best for your life? Do you need some major tilling in your heart?

Perhaps the soil of your heart has lain fallow for a while. It is time to let the Lord begin to cultivate you. Even though you will feel the pain of the digging, you should allow God's Word to plow your heart. Let Him hoe you.

**Name three definite "thorns" that have a tendency to grow in your heart. Ask the Lord to plow them up.**

## Day 46
### CIRCUMCISED HEARTS

**Jeremiah 4:4.** *Circumcise yourselves to the LORD, circumcise your hearts, you men of Judah and people of Jerusalem, or my wrath will break out and burn like fire because of the evil you have done—burn with no one to quench it.*

Jeremiah was the heart prophet. His wrote about the heart more times than any other Old Testament prophet. He knew that the heart was deceitful and desperately sick (17:9). He preached that radical surgery must be done on the spiritual heart. He proclaimed, "Circumcise your hearts!"

Circumcision of the heart was not a new metaphor for God's people. Moses had used the same illustration. Moses had urged his people to circumcise the foreskins of their hearts (Deuteronomy 10:16). He told them that the Lord would circumcise their hearts and the hearts of their descendants (Deuteronomy 30:6).

Both Moses and Jeremiah knew that outward circumcision was not enough. Many of the gentile nations in Jeremiah's day practiced physical circumcision, but their hearts were still uncircumcised (9:25-26). Even though Israel devotedly performed the rite circumcision on all male babies, Israel was no closer to the Lord than the neighboring pagan nations.

Centuries later, the apostle Paul used the same spiritual circumcision metaphor. He wrote that the Holy Spirit performs the circumcision of the human heart (Romans 2:29). In spiritual circumcision, Jesus Christ cut away at the entire body of flesh (Colossians 2:11). He gave His people new hearts (Ezekiel 36:26), hearts that would know Him (Jeremiah 24:7).

Only Christ can successfully perform the spiritual surgery of circumcision. Spiritual circumcision is urgent. A person who postpones circumcising his or her heart, who delays coming to Christ through faith, is in imminent danger. God's wrath comes on those whose hearts still have the foreskins of evil.

Literal circumcision was a sign of God's covenant with Abraham (Genesis 17:10). Literal circumcision removes a tiny part of a man's body. Circumcision of the heart removes much more. A circumcised heart allows you to have an unending covenant with God.

**In your own words, describe how the Lord has circumcised your heart.**

## Day 47
### LOOSE LION

Jeremiah 4:7. *A lion has come out of his lair; a destroyer of nations has set out. He has left his place to lay waste your land. Your towns will lie in ruins without inhabitant.*

Jeremiah tried to warn his people that an awful danger was coming. Their small nation of Judah was in the path of a destroyer of nations. A lion was on the loose.

Even though the people desperately wanted peace, Jeremiah tried to caution them that war was coming. He wanted them to blow a trumpet to alert everyone in the countryside to go into the fortified cities (4:5). They would be attacked from the north (4:6), just like the Lord had told Jeremiah when He first called him to be a prophet (1:14-15).

What was this danger from the north? Who was this lion? Those who paid attention to Jeremiah's subsequent sermons would know the answers.

Like a killer lion coming out of a forest (5:6), a hostile nation would eventually destroy Judah (5:17). Jeremiah later identified that nation as Babylon (20:4). The king of Babylon was the lion that crushed and scattered Israel (50:17).

However, Babylon would not be the world's super power forever. Finally Babylon would become ruins. The ravenous Babylonian lions would eat their last feast and perish (51:37-39). Sooner or later, all lions die!

For now, Jeremiah wanted to defend his people from the Babylonians. If only they would wash their hearts from evil and be saved (4:14)! The Babylonians were coming because Jeremiah's people had rebelled against the Lord (4:17).

Lions symbolize dangerous power. Their power can devastate you. Yet the Lord will save His faithful ones from harm. He would protect His faithful prophet Jeremiah from the Babylonians.

There is a loose lion in a neighborhood near you! Your spiritual enemy is like a roaring lion on the prowl. This adversarial lion is the devil. He is looking for people to devour, so you must resist him through faith (1 Peter 5:8-9).

**What is an explicit way that your relationship with the Lord can help you resist the devil?**

## Day 48
### DECEPTION

*Jeremiah 4:10. Then I said, "Ah, Sovereign LORD, how completely you have deceived this people and Jerusalem by saying, 'You will have peace,' when the sword is at our throats."*

Since the Lord is the supreme ruler, Jeremiah gave Him credit for deceiving the people! The people of Judah thought they would see peace in their land. The Lord sovereignly allowed them to believe a lie.

Was the Lord the source of their deception? No. God is good (Psalm 31:19). God was not the one who told the people, "You will have peace." These were the words of the false prophets (14:13-14).

Why did Jeremiah accuse the Lord of deceiving the people? Jeremiah felt a deep love for his people and wanted them to repent and avert terrible judgment. He was pouring out his heart to God and wondering why He authorized the false teachers to delude the people. He perhaps included this prayer in his sermon as another effort to bring the people to their spiritual senses.

Why did the Lord allow false words about peace to be spoken? The Lord obviously allows all sorts of evil to permeate the planet. In ways beyond our perception, He uses evil to bring about good.

The false prophets were still responsible before God for their deceitful words. Even though they may have sincerely believed that peace was coming, their sermons were deceptive. They misled the people and caused them to believe a lie.

The truth was that there was a lion on the loose (4:7). God's fierce anger was coming toward them, so they should put on sackcloth and repent (4:8). When the destruction of war came, all the leaders would be disheartened (4:9).

The people chose to listen to the false prophets instead of Jeremiah. Their spiritual hearts were as hardened as unplowed land (4:3), and their distance from the Lord prevented them from being discerning. What about you? Are you asking the Lord for wisdom so that you can discern what is deceptive? Are you snubbing false teachers and listening to the truth?

**Describe an incident in which you were deceived. How can your relationship with the Lord prevent an incident like this from occurring again?**

Day 49
### MORE THAN A LIGHT BREEZE

*Jeremiah 4:11-12. At that time this people and Jerusalem will be told, "A scorching wind from the barren heights in the desert blows toward my people, but not to winnow or cleanse; a wind too strong for that comes from me. Now I pronounce my judgments against them."*

During days of gentle winds, the farmers could harvest and winnow their grain. They would toss the crop into the air. The breeze would blow away the chaff, while the desirable wheat would remain.

Jeremiah announced that there would be no light breeze in the future. There would be only hot unbearable winds. The people knew about these windstorms. The farmers could not separate the grain from the chaff during these winds, which could last for many days. The wheat as well as the chaff would blow away.

Jeremiah preached that God's judgment would be like a blistering wind. Not only would the gust of judgment drive away the chaff of humanity. God's blast of air would blow away everyone.

Jeremiah had their attention. He kept using vivid illustrations as he preached. He warned that the approach of the Babylonians would be like clouds, a whirlwind and eagles (4:13).

The Babylonians were coming like clouds. They would cover the entire nation like clouds cover the sky. The Babylonian chariots were coming like a whirlwind. They would arrive before the Judeans were ready for them. And the Babylonian horses were swifter than eagles. They would swoop down on Jeremiah's people.

Was there any hope? Could the people avoid this disaster? Yes. Jeremiah believed that there was still time for them to repent.

They had evil in their hearts. They had hidden wicked thoughts deep within themselves. To be saved from the Babylonians, they had to wash their hearts (4:14).

Jeremiah used an abrasive Hebrew word for "wash". He did not refer to a light rinsing. The people had washed themselves gently by outwardly following King Josiah's spiritual reforms. However, their hearts were still foul. They needed to allow the Lord to totally scrub their hearts.

**Precisely how has the Lord cleansed your heart to enable you to escape His severe judgment?**

Day 50
### JEREMIAH'S ANGUISH

**Jeremiah 4:19.** *"Oh, my anguish, my anguish! I writhe in pain. Oh, the agony of my heart! My heart pounds within me, I cannot keep silent. For I have heard the sound of the trumpet; I have heard the battle cry."*

Jeremiah preached with incredible empathy. His deep feelings finally exploded into his sermon. He expressed his emotional torment over the coming cruelty of the Babylonians.

The Lord had apparently revealed His judgment to Jeremiah with frightening sensory visions. God had communicated through Jeremiah's sense of hearing. Jeremiah actually heard a Babylonian trumpet sounding the beginning of battle. He heard the warriors' shouts.

He heard a voice from the northern region of Dan. The warning was about the disaster that was coming. Then he heard a voice from Mount Ephraim shouting the same alarm (4:15). Words about the calamity were nearing Jerusalem.

Jeremiah heard a voice directing him to tell all the nations about the future fate of Jerusalem. A destructive army from a distant country was coming. All the cities of Judah were at risk (4:16). The Babylonian soldiers were like watchmen guarding a field (4:17). Escape attempts would be futile.

The Babylonian catastrophe would happen as God's way of punishing the people for their evil ways. The people would feel bitter about this looming divine judgment. Their guilt would pierce their hearts (4:18).

The Lord also communicated through Jeremiah's sense of seeing. Jeremiah saw the future destruction of his nation. The whole land lay desolate. All family homes were demolished. He saw his own tent being ripped to shreds (4:20).

Jeremiah asked how long he must keep seeing and hearing these visions of warfare (4:21). He felt the pain of the miserable future that lay ahead for his ungodly countrymen. Sadly, Jeremiah's people would also hear and see the enemy for a long time. The consequences of their spiritual rebellion would be permanent.

**How can you follow Jeremiah's example and sympathize with the lost condition of unbelievers?**

## Day 51
### CREATION REVERSAL

**Jeremiah 4:23.** *I looked at the earth, and it was formless and empty; and at the heavens, and their light was gone.*

The Lord gave Jeremiah a breathtaking vision of both the distant past and the far-away future. Jeremiah saw the earth just as it was before the Lord began His creative work. The earth was formless, empty and dark (Genesis 1:2).

Jeremiah realized that God's future judgment would reverse His creation. The earth would once again become like it was before God created light, formed the earth and filled it. When people sin, they reverse what God has done. Sin always results in chaos and darkness.

Perhaps Jeremiah understood that the Lord would bring about an even more complete judgment afterward. The Lord later revealed to him that a day of distress would come that would be worse than any other (30:7). Jesus prophesied about the coming great tribulation (Matthew 24:21).

Jeremiah saw mega earthquakes moving all the mountains and hills (4:24). He could see no people and not even any birds (4:25). He saw the earth as a giant desert, and all the cities were piles of rubble (4:26).

After seeing the vision, Jeremiah heard the Lord explain it. God reassured Jeremiah that He would not destroy the nation entirely (4:27). He definitely would send His judgment. Many people would mourn and it would be a dark time (4:28). The enemy soldiers on horses and the archers would empty all the towns. The people of Judah would hide in the rocks and thickets (4:29). Some would not hide, but they would try to entice Babylon to form a relationship with Jerusalem (4:30). It would not work. Jeremiah heard the helpless cries as Jerusalem gasped for breath (4:31).

Before sharing his vision about the formless and empty earth, Jeremiah had preached about skillful fools. His people did not know the Lord, so they were fools. They were skilled at doing evil (4:22). Jeremiah used language from the Proverbs about wisdom and fools to illustrate their problem. Their problem was "wisdom reversal".

The reason for the Lord's creation reversal was because of the people's wisdom reversal. Wisdom reversal is rampant today. Even though you can do nothing about the coming cataclysmic creation reversal, you can help curb wisdom reversal. Ask God for wisdom (James 1:5) and live wisely.

**Write a detailed prayer request asking the Lord to give you wisdom.**

## Day 52
### LOOKING FOR HONESTY

**Jeremiah 5:1.** *"Go up and down the streets of Jerusalem, look around and consider, search through her squares. If you can find but one person who deals honestly and seeks the truth, I will forgive this city."*

The Lord told Jeremiah to survey the people in the city. Jerusalem was put under spiritual investigation! God wanted Jeremiah to learn about the standard of honesty that the majority accepted. That standard had slipped to an all time low. The Lord implied that Jeremiah would not find even one honest person.

The Lord wanted Jeremiah to search thoroughly. The prophet was to walk every street and visit every square. The people would hear him preach for the next forty years. The Lord wanted the young prophet to know his audience.

Centuries earlier, the Lord told Abraham that He would spare Sodom if ten righteous men were found in the city (Genesis 18:32). Jerusalem had now sunk to a lower level than Sodom. Instead of ten, the Lord told Jeremiah to find just one! The Lord's invitation to tour the city was given to others besides Jeremiah. The Hebrew verbs are plural. Apparently, Jeremiah was the only one who accepted the invitation.

Jeremiah found that the entire population was corrupt. He tried to understand why there was wholesale rejection of the Lord's truth. He thought that lack of education had made people too ignorant to understand the Lord's requirements for truth (5:4). Jeremiah decided to go and investigate what the rich and the privileged believed (5:5).

It must have been a discouraging day for Jeremiah when he talked to the leaders of the city. He thought that certainly they would know about the ways of the Lord. Jeremiah discovered that even if they did know, they did not seem to care. They had rejected the Lord's authority over their lives.

King Josiah and the prophet Zephaniah were among the few exceptions. A few other godly men would surface later, like Baruch, Daniel, Ezekiel and Ebed-Melech. Looking for men like these would be like looking for a needle in a haystack. Disregard for truth was so widespread that these exceptions were relatively insignificant.

Honesty is sadly lacking in much of the world. Intimacy with the Lord will strengthen your own honesty. Live for truth, and influence a city!

**Specifically how do you keep your life honest?**

## Day 53
### REJECTING LUST

**Jeremiah 5:8.** *They are well-fed, lusty stallions, each neighing for another man's wife.*

Even though Jeremiah was single and celibate, he still knew how to talk about sex! He used an illustration of sexually-active horses to get the attention of his audience. Jeremiah vividly described the people of his nation as always being ready for sexual sin.

Jeremiah had earlier compared the sexual practices of his people to camels (2:23) and wild donkeys (2:24). The people had sunk to sub-human morals. The Lord did not intend for the sex habits of animals to be the benchmark for human behavior. God created men and women in His own image (Genesis 1:27). The Lord has a standard of holiness for His people (1 Peter 1:15-16).

The people in Jeremiah's day were habitually committing adultery and frequenting houses of prostitution (5:7). The entire nation was full of adulterers (23:10). The Lord had sufficient cause to judge the people instantly.

What went wrong with Jeremiah's people? Why had they lowered themselves to animalistic behavior? The answer was in the idols. The people had left the Lord and had sworn oaths by gods that are not gods at all (5:7).

An earlier prophet had described the connection between idolatry and immorality. When the people consulted their wooden idols, they committed spiritual adultery against their God. Sacrifices to idols directly led to young women becoming cult prostitutes. Men went to these temple prostitutes as they offered sacrifices to their idols. Because of idolatry, men and women committed adultery (Hosea 4:12-14).

When King Josiah led a religious reformation, he tore down the homes of the male cultic prostitutes in the temple, where women were weaving tents for the goddess Asherah (2 Kings 23:7). Temple prostitutes had become culturally acceptable, even though the Lord had specifically forbidden this sexual activity (Deuteronomy 23:17-18).

Those who claim to know God must live according to His standards. Both singles and married people must stay pure. Sex between husband and wife (the marriage bed) is pure (Hebrews 13:4). Married people must stay faithful to their husband or wife. Reject your culture's chasing after lust and pursue the Lord.

**How does idolatry lead to impurity?**

## Day 54
### INSULTS

**Jeremiah 5:13.** *"The prophets are but wind and the word is not in them; so let what they say be done to them."*

The people did not believe Jeremiah's words. They insulted him and the other true prophets by calling them "windbags"! They used the Hebrew word for "wind", which can also be translated as "Spirit". Instead of letting God's Spirit guide them, the prophets were blowing hot air!

The people claimed that the prophets did not have God's Word in them. They wanted the words about divine punishment to fall back on the prophets who said them. They wanted the prophets themselves to be attacked and ravaged.

Jeremiah was not the only true prophet of the Lord during his day. Zephaniah also lived during the days of King Josiah (Zephaniah 1:1). Perhaps Habakkuk did too, since he prophesied the imminent invasion of the Babylonians (Habakkuk 1:6). Uriah lived during that time as well (Jeremiah 26:20-23).

The people insulted them all. It was their way of retaliating against the prophets' condemnation of their idolatry. Jeremiah had exposed their sins (5:7-8), and he warned that the Lord would punish them (5:9). He said that God was telling Judah's enemies to ravage the Judean countryside (5:10), because the Judeans had been unfaithful to Him (5:11).

In response to the words of the true prophets, the people lied about the Lord. They said that God would not really bring judgment on them. They claimed that the Lord would do nothing (5:12).

The Lord did not tolerate their insults of His prophets. He told Jeremiah that He would make the words of his sermons like a fire. The words would consume the people like a fire burns wood (5:14).

Jesus taught that those people who reject the true prophets also reject Him and they reject the One who sent Him (Luke 10:16). He told His disciples that the world would hate them after first hating Him (John 15:18). Do not melt when others insult you because of your faith. Insults against godly people are not innovative.

**Have others insulted you lately because of your relationship with the Lord? How can you ignore the insults and grow even closer to Him?**

## Day 55
### LANGUAGE BARRIER

**Jeremiah 5:15.** *"O house of Israel," declares the LORD, "I am bringing a distant nation against you—an ancient and enduring nation, a people whose language you do not know, whose speech you do not understand."*

Just like the Babylonian invasion would result in a creation reversal (4:23), it would also result in a reversal of communication. It would be like the confusion of speech after the tower of Babel (Genesis 11:9). The people of Judah would not be able to understand the Babylonian language.

Centuries earlier, Moses warned that this would happen. He said that the Lord would raise up a distant nation against the people. The Judeans would not understand the language of this nation (Deuteronomy 28:49).

Moses explained that this fierce nation would have no regard for the lives of either young or old. This nation would devour their flocks and herds, grain and fruit trees. This enemy would cause their sons and daughters to be devoured (Deuteronomy 28:50-53). Jeremiah described the same dreadful scene (5:16-18).

Why would the Lord allow this horrible Babylonian invasion? Jeremiah gave the Lord's reason. Because they had turned from the Lord and served foreign idols, some of them would survive and go to Babylon to serve foreign people (5:19). The Lord would punish them by giving them the full measure of what they were seeking.

The idols that they worshipped could not speak to them (10:5). There was no real communication between the people and their idols. Because of the language barrier in Babylon, they would suffer the same lack of communication.

Being among people whose language you do not understand affects every area of life. When my family and I moved overseas, we knew we would need to learn the language of our new host country. When we had been there only a week, our six-year-old son ran ahead of us into a pastry shop. The woman behind the counter spoke to him in a language that he did not understand. He burst into tears!

With the Lord, there is no language barrier! He always understands you. And you can understand what He says to you. He has spoken clearly through His Word. He communicates to His people through His Spirit.

**Explain how the lack of a language barrier between you and the Lord affects your relationship with Him.**

## Day 56
### OCEAN BARRIER

Jeremiah 5:22. *"Should you not fear me?" declares the LORD. "Should you not tremble in my presence? I made the sand a boundary for the sea, an everlasting barrier it cannot cross. The waves may roll, but they cannot prevail; they may roar, but they cannot cross it."*

When God created the oceans, He made boundaries to keep the waters from engulfing all the land. God controls the waves. He regulates how high and how far each wave rolls. A deadly tsunami cannot encroach a millimeter more than the Lord's decreed barrier!

Even though God sent a worldwide flood during the time of Noah, He made a covenant that there would never again be such a flood (Genesis 9:11). Waves cannot cross over God's barrier to cover the earth (Psalm 104:9). Since the Lord restrains the oceans, He certainly had the power to hold back the Babylonian invaders.

Parents usually set boundaries for their children. When my wife and I took our small daughters to the beach, we set limits on how far they could go into the ocean. One of them ventured a little further, and a wave splashed salt water into her eyes!

Because only the Lord is powerful enough to construct sea borders, the people should have feared Him. Sadly, they did not. In contrast to the oceans, they crossed the moral barriers that God had erected. God had placed barriers to keep them pure, but they gushed over the barricades into impure territories.

The Lord gave Jeremiah some scathing words to describe them. Even though they had eyes and ears, they could neither see nor hear. (The idols they worshipped also saw or heard nothing!) They were foolish and senseless. (5:21).

The Hebrew word translated as "senseless" means "without heart". Jeremiah, the prophet of the heart, was deeply troubled by people who had no heart toward God. He preached that the people had stubborn and rebellious hearts (5:23). They did not confess in their hearts that God is the Lord of nature (5:24).

In addition to controlling the seas, God also sends spring and autumn rains at just the right time every year. He rules over the seasons of harvest. Yet the people did not admit that He is the Lord of the environment (5:24). Do not emulate them!

**What is a specific barrier that the Lord has set up in your life that He does not want you to cross?**

## Day 57

### SIN BARRIER

**Jeremiah 5:25.** *Your wrongdoings have kept these away; your sins have deprived you of good.*

In contrast to the Lord's barriers, the people unwittingly had made their own. They had set up obstacles by their sins. These sin barriers were keeping God's blessings out of their lives.

God sends the needed rain for farmers' crops (5:24), but the Lord had kept back the rain because of their sin (3:3). Jeremiah then described some particular groups of sinners. These were economic, political and religious leaders who had led the whole country astray because of their sins.

Some were like bird catchers hiding in ambush, setting deadly traps for their own people. Their houses were like cages filled with the birds they had caught. They had become rich and powerful through deceit and fraud. (5:26-27).

There was no limit to their evil deeds. They had positions of power, so they could have defended the rights of the poor. They refused to do so. They did not even plead the cause of orphans (5:28).

Even more horrible and shocking were the sins of the religious leaders. The prophets spoke lies. And the priests did not acknowledge God's authority but exercised power only by their own authority. The people loved this religious system (5:30-31).

They had erected thick barriers of sin. People usually give no thought to where their sin will lead them at the end of their days. Unless the sin barrier was removed, they would face grave eternal problems.

Jeremiah asked what they would do at the end (5:31). Another great prophet had asked the same question. What would they do in the day of punishment, to whom would they flee, and where would they leave their wealth (Isaiah 10:3).

What will you do in the end? Will you finish your life with no regrets? Tear down your sin barriers so that He may bless you at the end of your time.

The Lord desires to give His bounty to His people. He has much to give you. Tear down your sin barriers so that He may bless you now.

**What sin is the Lord prompting you to confess (1 John 1:9) so that He may pull you closer to Himself and bless you more? Confess it now!**

## Day 58
### A TIME TO FLEE

**Jeremiah 6:1.** *"Flee for safety, people of Benjamin! Flee from Jerusalem! Sound the trumpet in Tekoa! Raise the signal over Beth Hakkerem! For disaster looms out of the north, even terrible destruction."*

Enemy soldiers were coming from the north to attack Jerusalem, and they would destroy the city. Jeremiah specifically warned his own people, those of the tribe of Benjamin. They should leave the city immediately.

People would soon hear a battle trumpet in Tekoa. An earlier prophet had come from this town (Amos 1:1). The town of Tekoa was close enough to Jerusalem for the city inhabitants to hear the sound of Tekoa's trumpet. The Hebrew words for "sound" and "Tekoa" have the same consonants, so Jeremiah spoke a memorable pun. As the people pondered the pun, they should have prepared to flee from the city.

Besides hearing the trumpet, the people would see the signal over Beth Hakkerem. Beth Hakkerem means the house of the vineyard. The signal they would see would probably be fire and smoke. It was time to flee from the city!

The Lord referred to Jerusalem as the beautiful daughter of Zion. Her beauty would not protect her, for shepherds would come against this delicate woman and surround her with their tents. They would cry out for battle against her. They would attack her at night and destroy her (6:2-5).

Jeremiah preached that the Lord commanded the enemy troops to build siege ramps against the city. His verdict was that oppression had filled Jerusalem. Wickedness, violence and destruction would come upon the city. No one would be able to live there. The city would be like a barren vine that has been picked of all its grapes (6:6-9). Anyone in the city who knew that the attack was coming should certainly flee.

Jeremiah had described the sinful practices of the political and religious leaders (5:26-31). He could not find anyone who practiced justice (5:1-5). All the people were committed to their idols (5:7). Why would anyone with a relationship with the Lord want to stay in a corrupt city like that? The godly should flee.

There are times when you should flee, as you grow in your relationship with the Lord. Run away from immorality (1 Corinthians 6:18), like Joseph fled from Potiphar's wife (Genesis 39:1-12). Flee from idolatry (1 Corinthians 10:14). Run from youthful evil desires (2 Timothy 2:22).

**From what specific temptations and sins must you flee in order to run closer to the Lord?**

## Day 59
### MISSING THE PLEASURE

Jeremiah 6:10. *To whom can I speak and give warning? Who will listen to me? Their ears are closed so they cannot hear. The word of the LORD is offensive to them; they find no pleasure in it.*

Jeremiah had a growing sense that people were not listening to him. The Lord had given him urgent warnings to preach, but they did not want to hear. They did not want to listen because they did not want to be offended.

Jeremiah used a stunning metaphor to describe their hearing problem. The Hebrew word that is translated as "closed" actually means "uncircumcised". Jeremiah had earlier preached that the people had hearts that needed to be circumcised (4:4). They had closed both their hearts and their ears to spiritual reality.

They needed spiritual surgery performed on their ears. They had ears but did not hear (5:21). With closed ears, God's Word offended them. If their ears were opened, the Word would delight them.

Through the decades, the people would continue to ignore Jeremiah. He would finally tell them that he had preached to them repeatedly for twenty-three years, but they had not listened (25:3). How could Jeremiah keep preaching to such an unresponsive audience?

Jeremiah's sermons were from the Lord. He found delight in God's Word (15:16), even though his listeners did not. Jeremiah's delight in God's Word would bring him blessing (Psalm 112:1).

Through the centuries, closed ears continued to be a problem. Jesus told parables to people who listened but did not hear (Matthew 13:13). Stephen told his audience that both their ears and their hearts were uncircumcised (Acts 7:51).

Jesus healed the deaf (Matthew 11:5). He opened a deaf man's ears by sticking his fingers into them (Mark 7:31-37). His physical healing illustrated His power to heal spiritually. Jesus can open uncircumcised ears if people want Him to.

Has Jesus opened your ears so that you have joy when you hear God's Word? Is His Word your supreme pleasure? Delight in His Word, and you will find enjoyment in His relationship with you.

**What portion of God's Word has given you pleasure during the past week? How?**

Day 60

## More than a Minor Scratch

**Jeremiah 6:14.** *They dress the wound of my people as though it were not serious. 'Peace, peace,' they say, when there is no peace.*

The people suffered from a life-threatening gash. Tragically, they did not know they were seriously wounded. They thought it was a flesh wound. They believed that all they needed was a small bandage.

You cannot treat a deadly injury with a Band-Aid! Those who administer such superficial first aid may be trying to save much money on medical expenses! Those who deny that there is a problem are deceivers.

Jeremiah said that the religious leaders were deceiving the people. The prophets and the priests did not care about telling the people the truth. They were merely greedy for financial gain (6:13).

The religious leaders were useless physicians. They ignored the serious skin puncture and simply said, "Peace, peace." They did not tell the people that the wound would bring death if left untreated.

When I was a young child, another young child accidentally hit me in the head with a sharp object. I remember the pain. I am glad my parents took me to the doctor to have my head wound treated and stitched up.

In contrast, the priests and prophets disregarded the spiritual wound. They took no notice of the problem that was far more severe than a break in the skin. There was a deep breach between the people and God. Their relationship with the Lord was severed.

The cause of this breach was sin. The result of the spiritual wound was the Lord's wrath. Jeremiah felt the message of God's wrath within him and he could not keep holding it in. He had to alert all the people, young and old, about the Lord's wrath (6:11). If they ignored the warning, they would lose everything (6:12).

A breach between people and God also exists today. Only Jesus could effectively treat this spiritual wound. His death provided the cure. For those who believe, His wounds healed their wound (1 Peter 2:24).

**Without Jesus, how serious would your wound be?**

## Day 61
### FINDING REST

**Jeremiah 6:16.** *This is what the LORD says: "Stand at the crossroads and look; ask for the ancient paths, ask where the good way is, and walk in it, and you will find rest for your souls. But you said, 'We will not walk in it.'"*

Jeremiah asked the people to imagine that they were travelers. They came to some crossroads and did not know which way to go. Jeremiah preached that they should ask for directions.

They needed travel tips so that they would choose the ancient paths. The old roads were the ways that God had long ago revealed would lead to wise living. Jeremiah wanted them to choose the good way and follow it.

Jeremiah merely paraphrased the same promise that the Lord had given through Moses centuries earlier. God assured His people that His presence would go with them and He would give them rest (Exodus 33:14). The people now needed to choose the way of the Lord's presence.

They chose foolishly. They asserted that they would not walk on the ancient paths. They therefore forfeited the promise that they would find rest for their souls.

"You will find rest for your souls." Centuries later, Jesus quoted Jeremiah's words when He invited weary and burdened people to come to Him and take His yoke upon them. Jesus asked them to learn from Him. Jesus promised to give them rest (Matthew 11:28-29).

Jesus Christ was the fulfillment of the ancient paths. The good way led to Him. Only He had been given everything by God the Father (Matthew 11:27). Only He could give lasting rest to those who were burdened with guilt and weary from life's troubles. Only He had the true yoke of discipleship to offer.

A yoke was a wooden device that kept two animals together. The yoked animals were usually oxen. Their combined strength could plow fields or pull large objects. Both oxen obviously had to do the same task and go in the same direction. When you are yoked to Jesus, you go in His ways and learn from Him. However, Jesus' yoke is different from oxen yokes. Whenever the owner of the oxen decided to yoke them together, the yoke went on. In contrast, Jesus never throws His yoke upon you. Jesus gave an invitation, not an edict. The decision is yours.

**Without Jesus, describe how much unrest you would have.**

## Day 62
### UNACCEPTABLE OFFERINGS

**Jeremiah 6:20.** *"What do I care about incense from Sheba or sweet calamus from a distant land? Your burnt offerings are not acceptable; your sacrifices do not please me."*

Incense was an expensive tree resin from Sheba, a far-away country that is now called Yemen. Calamus was a spice that perhaps came from distant India. Calamus was mixed in oil to anoint the priests and the tabernacle (Exodus 30:23-25). People who offered incense and calamus to the Lord were giving expensive gifts to Him.

The Lord had commanded that certain animals be given to Him as burnt offerings. A burnt offering was a whole animal consumed on the altar (Leviticus 6:9). The Lord also asked for sacrifices, which meant that part of the animal was offered to the Lord.

The people were bringing all these offerings and sacrifices to the Lord. He had established the sacrificial system. Yet He was pleased neither with them nor with their sacrifices. What was the problem?

Sin was their problem. The people had refused to walk on the Lord's ancient paths (Jeremiah 6:16). They did not listen to the watchmen who were the true prophets (6:17). They rejected God's words and His law (6:19).

Jeremiah later preached that the people's sacrifices were so worthless that they should add the meat of their burnt offerings to their other sacrifices and eat it all themselves! The Lord had given more than mere commands about burnt offerings and sacrifices when He made the covenant with Moses. He demanded obedience (7:21-23).

A New Covenant was needed. Jeremiah later revealed the Lord's terms for the New Covenant (31:31-34). The Lord promised total forgiveness.

Jesus became the mediator of the New Covenant (Hebrews 9:15). The church communion cup became a symbol of the new covenant in His blood (1 Corinthians 11:25). His death was the ultimate sacrifice. He offered His body as a sacrifice once for all (Hebrews 10:10). He died for us while we were still sinners (Romans 5:8).

Your belief in Jesus' sacrifice pleases the Lord. His sacrifice means that you no longer need to try to earn His favor through your own sacrifices. You are free to live for Him as a living sacrifice.

**Without Jesus, what kind of sacrifices would you try to offer to God?**

## Day 63
### METAL TESTER

**Jeremiah 6:27.** *"I have made you a tester of metals and my people the ore, that you may observe and test their ways."*

Because of the sin of the citizens of Judah, the Lord would put obstacles before them (6:21). He warned them about how the army from the north would bring terror on all of them (6:22-26). Then He added a clarification about Jeremiah's job description. As prophet to the nations, Jeremiah would be a metal assayer.

An assayer is a person who analyzes the quality of a substance. Jeremiah would evaluate the value of his people. A metal assayer examines ore to determine if precious metals are in it. He heats the ore and mixes it with lead. The heat causes the lead to oxidize. The lead mixes with the impurities and separates from the pure metal (if there is any).

Jeremiah preached the results of his assaying work. His tests showed that all the people were stubborn rebels. Of all possible insurgents, they were the most rebellious. Among their blatant sins was slander. They were corrupt, like cheap bronze and iron (6:28).

When the Lord first called Jeremiah, He told the prophet that he would be as strong as bronze and iron (1:18). The enemy soldiers from the north would also be as strong as bronze and iron (15:12). However, the imagery changed when Jeremiah became a metal tester. He was looking for silver, not bronze or iron.

Jeremiah already had the experience for his task. He had previously studied the people. The Lord had earlier sent him out to look for those who were righteous. He walked up and down every street in Jerusalem. He searched among the poor and the powerful. (5:1-5).

Jeremiah blew his bellows fiercely so that the fire would consume the lead. He finally realized that his work was futile. The lead did not remove what was wicked. No silver was found, so the Lord rejected the ore (6:29-30).

The Lord gives all people the chance to prove themselves valuable. God sends the refining fire to show any silver or gold in each person's life. Sooner or later, the Lord will test you. Trust Him as He produces what is precious.

**How has the Lord tested you recently? What were the results?**

## Day 64
### TEMPLE SERMON

**Jeremiah 7:1-2.** *This is the word that came to Jeremiah from the LORD: "Stand at the gate of the LORD's house and there proclaim this message: 'Hear the word of the Lord, all you people of Judah who come through these gates to worship the LORD.'"*

The Lord routinely gave Jeremiah both the words to preach and the location to preach them. The Lord told Jeremiah to go to the temple gate on a certain day. This day may have been during one of the festivals when many people were present. Large crowds would have heard Jeremiah's words as they entered the temple.

Since the chapters in Jeremiah's book are not in chronological order, this may have been the same temple sermon that the prophet preached early in King Jehoiakim's reign (26:1-6). After Josiah's death, Jeremiah probably did not preach at the temple very often. The hostile reaction to his sermon almost cost him his life (26:7-24). Jeremiah was soon restricted from going to the temple (36:1-5).

The people of Judah had survived some recent political upheavals. King Josiah's death on the battlefield resulted in his son Jehoahaz becoming king. Three months later, Jehoahaz was dethroned by the Egyptians and imprisoned in Egypt. The Egyptians then made Jehoiakim the king of Judah.

In spite of the Egyptians interfering with Judah's politics, the temple remained intact. The temple gave the Judeans a sizeable sense of security. They thought that the temple's glory had protected them from being destroyed by the Egyptians. The Judeans equated the temple with the Lord's presence.

The people thought that no nation could bring down their temple. Many years earlier, Jerusalem was spared from certain destruction during King Hezekiah's reign (2 Kings 19:1-37). They now thought that the temple would stand forever.

They clung to the superstition that the temple was merely a safe house from their enemies. They believed the fallacy that their thoughts, words and behavior had no relevance to the temple's survival. Jeremiah's sermon would shock them out of their Pollyannaish thinking.

What about you? Do you have any safe house superstitions hidden in your heart? If so, allow the Lord to perform spiritual heart surgery on you.

**What false beliefs are you willing for the Lord to remove from your heart?**

## Day 65
### TEMPLE SUPERSTITION

**Jeremiah 7:4. Do not trust in deceptive words and say, "This is the temple of the LORD, the temple of the LORD, the temple of the LORD!"**

Jeremiah stood at the temple gate (7:2) and preached a bold sermon. He had a large audience. All the people of Judah were crowding into the temple courts. Jeremiah chose one of the religious festival days when he knew that thousands would be there. They could not enter the temple without hearing the prophet's harsh message.

Jeremiah warned them that they were trusting in false words. Perhaps they were even chanting repeatedly, "Temple of the Lord!" Perhaps if the temple were small enough, they would have wanted to keep it in their homes. They would have considered the temple to be an idol of good luck! They worshipped a building instead of the Lord.

King Solomon had built this magnificent temple. It had stood there for centuries. King Josiah had cleaned it up and renovated it, and now it was a beautiful structure. However, since the people had deserted the Lord in their hearts, the temple now no longer served any purpose.

Standing in the temple did not make them into godly people any more than standing in a pool would make them into swans! In Jeremiah's opinion, the people were trusting in the temple in lieu of trusting in the Lord. They thought that the temple would last forever.

Later in his sermon, he accused them of breaking at least five of the Ten Commandments (7:9). If they were really depending on the Lord, their lives would display some godliness. But they were godless, trusting in idols.

The people superstitiously believed that the temple would protect them. Their repetitive words were deceptive. Even though they sincerely thought that temple could save them, they were deadly wrong.

It is time for you to rise above those masses that teem into the temple for the wrong reasons. Do not copy those who think an hour of religion will hide them from the consequences of a week of sin. Pray to the Lord, and do not use vain repetitions!

**Name some of the "deceptive words" that are dangers to you.**

Day 66
GOD'S HOUSE

**Jeremiah 7:11. *Has this house, which bears my Name, become a den of robbers to you? But I have been watching! declares the LORD.***

The people were crowding into the temple thinking that they were secure. They did repugnant deeds, and then they trusted that the temple would save them from the Lord's displeasure. Those who stopped to listen to Jeremiah at the temple gate were probably offended. If they had listened with spiritual hearts, they would have known that Jeremiah was right.

Jeremiah preached that the temple had become a den of robbers. Thieves went to their hideout after they stole. Just like the robbers would leave their cave to rob again, so also the people would leave the temple and live detestably.

Hundreds of years later, Jesus Christ confronted another temple problem. He chased the moneychangers and animal merchants out of the temple court. Their monetary gain, under the guise of making sacrifice purchases more convenient for the people, was detestable to Jesus Christ. He used Jeremiah's term, "den of robbers" (Matthew 21:13).

Jesus also used a phrase from Isaiah, "house of prayer". The noises of commerce and animal trafficking were not conducive to prayer! Jesus Christ's actions showed that He believed the temple did not exist for the convenience and profit of the religious leaders. The temple was the Lord's.

The Lord said that the temple bore His name. The Lord had exclusive ownership of the temple. The purpose of the temple was to draw people closer to the Lord. People were supposed to go to the temple so that they could worship God. However, they were ignoring the Lord and worshipping the building and other things.

The Lord said that He had been watching. The Lord always watches. Jeremiah had learned about this attribute of God when the Lord first called him. When Jeremiah saw the vision of the almond tree (1:11-12), he learned that the Lord observes every detail of the tide of history. History flows according to the Lord's words.

The Lord is watching you! Nothing you do escapes celestial scrutiny. Live for the Lord so that you may hear from Him, "Well done, good and faithful servant!"

**Name one area of your worship that you will examine closely this week, to determine if it is genuine and pleasing to God.**

## Day 67
### BANNED PRAYER REQUEST

Jeremiah 7:16. *"So do not pray for this people nor offer any plea or petition for them; do not plead with me, for I will not listen to you."*

Jeremiah's prayers for his people were now forbidden. The Lord commanded him not to pray for them, for He would not listen. You may have difficulty accepting this seemingly harsh divine veto on Jeremiah's prayers for his nation. If so, you should ponder the Lord's rationale.

Through Jeremiah's sermon, the Lord reminded the people about Shiloh (7: 12-15). Shiloh was a city north of Jerusalem where the tabernacle was first located. Because of the peoples' sins, the Lord had abandoned His dwelling place in Shiloh (Psalm 78:56-60). No amount of prayer could now raise Shiloh from the ashes. In the same way, no prayer could save the temple from destruction. Evil deeds brought down Shiloh, and the same intensity of wickedness was bringing down Jerusalem.

Judah's sins were blatant. Entire families were involved with idol worship. Their idolatry harmed themselves and it also brought them under the Lord's wrath (7: 17-20).

Their temple sacrifices were useless, because they had not obeyed the Lord. Obedience was primarily what the Lord wanted from His people. Their evil hearts were leading them further and further into disobedience (7:21-24).

Jeremiah's people were doing more evil than their ancestors had done. Even though the Lord had sent many prophets through the centuries, the people did not listen to God's Word (7:25-26). Since the people would not listen to Him, God would not listen to Jeremiah's pleas for them.

In spite of the prohibitions, Jeremiah continued to pray for his people (18:20). The Lord had to keep reminding Jeremiah not to pray for them (11:14; 14:11; 15:1). Jeremiah could not help but pray, because he loved the people!

The Lord revealed special insight about the future to Jeremiah, so Jeremiah knew that his prayers for the Judeans would be useless. God does not divulge similar information to you and me today. When Jesus Christ came, prayer guidelines changed. Now you are privileged to pray for all people (1 Timothy 2:1).

**Have you given up on praying for certain people? Write their names and resume your prayers for them!**

Day 68

NUMBERED HAIRS

**Jeremiah 7:29.** *Cut off your hair and throw it away; take up a lament on the barren heights, for the LORD has rejected and abandoned this generation that is under his wrath.*

These were not personal words to Jeremiah about cutting off his own hair. The command was not like my seminary professor in the 1970's telling me to get a haircut! The Hebrew verb is a feminine imperative, addressed to the whole city. People today often referred to a city with the pronoun *she.*

"Cut off your hair!" was Jeremiah's message to Jerusalem. The Hebrew word for "hair" is a derivative of the word for "Nazarite." The Nazarites wore their hair long as an illustration of their dedication to the Lord (Numbers 6:28). If a Nazarite were to cut his hair, he symbolically ended his closeness to the Lord. Samson was the classic example of a Nazarite who allowed his hair to be cut (Judges 16:15-22).

The people in Jeremiah's day had little in common with a committed Nazarite. The days of their long hair were numbered. Jeremiah preached that they should cut off their hair as an illustration of their rejection of the Lord. Also, they should cut off their hair as a sign of mourning.

Jeremiah told them to go to the desolate hilltops and sing a lament, because the Lord had rejected them. To respond in any way other than grieving would be irrational. Lamenting on the barren heights was entirely appropriate for these people. They worshipped idols on the barren summits (3:2), the very idols that were the cause of the Lord's wrath against them. They even sacrificed their own children to idols (7:31).

Jeremiah's people considered their hair to be one of the most beautiful parts of their bodies. They considered shaved heads to be humiliating. In fact, if they had taken their own Scriptures seriously, they would have known that the Lord forbade His people from making themselves bald (Leviticus 21:5). Then they would have caught Jeremiah's biting irony. It was a pagan custom to shave one's head and cut one's body.

Jesus said that God knows the number of hairs on each person's head (Matthew 10:30). The Lord cares about even the trivial parts of your body and life. As you grow closer to the Lord, are you honoring Him with every detail of the life that He has given you?

**What is one area of your life where you will focus on honoring God more than you have in the past?**

Day 69

## SOMETHING DETESTABLE IN THE TEMPLE

**Jeremiah 7:30.** *The people of Judah have done evil in my eyes, declares the Lord. They have set up their detestable idols in the house that bears my Name and have defiled it.*

Jeremiah had begun his sermon by exposing the false hope that the people had placed in the temple (7:4). Now he revealed a major problem with the temple. The temple was no longer God's holy residence, because idols currently resided in it.

In former years, the evil King Manasseh filled the Lord's temple with pagan altars. He also put a carved image of Asherah in the temple (2 Kings 21:1-7). Asherah was the goddess of fertility, and worshipping her appealed to the Judeans' perverted sexual desires.

During Jeremiah's earlier years, King Josiah removed the idols from the temple. He burned them outside the city. He also removed the Asherah pole, burned it and ground it to dust (2 Kings 23:4-7). Centuries earlier, the Lord had told Moses' people to tear down Asherah poles whenever they saw them (Exodus 34:13).

Josiah organized workers to make extensive repairs of the temple (2 Chronicles 34:8-11). He went into the temple court to read to the people the newly discovered Scriptures (2 Chronicles 34:29-30). He led a Passover celebration, and the Passover lambs were sacrificed in the temple as the Lord had prescribed centuries earlier (2 Chronicles 35:1-19). Josiah restored the temple to a building that would honor the Lord.

Josiah was now dead, and the idols were back. Ezekiel later reported that there were many idols in the temple. Both men and women were worshipping other gods in the temple courts (Ezekiel 8:3-16). They had defiled the Lord's sanctuary with their detestable images (Ezekiel 5:11).

The argument for having statues of deities in the temple was that they aided the worship of the true God. Pictures and images help make truth clear. Yet the Lord unmistakably loathed them.

The Lord hates idols today. He knows the human temptation to adore the image instead of the reality. A representation will limit people's perception of the Lord God and will compete for their loyalty. Also, worshipping idols corrupts humanity, because men and women take on the likeness of the one they worship (Hosea 9:10).

**Write a prayer to the Lord, asking Him to remove whatever is in your heart that may be detestable to Him.**

## Day 70
### Worship Idea that Never Entered God's Mind

**Jeremiah 7:31. *They have built the high places of Topheth in the Valley of Ben Hinnom to burn their sons and daughters in the fire – something I did not command, nor did it enter my mind.***

Jeremiah's powerful preaching exposed the horrible ultimate end of idolatry. Not only did the people worship gods instead of God, they actually sacrificed their own children at the idolatrous high places in the Valley of Ben Hinnom. This valley was the trash dump outside the city walls.

Such an idea was so atrocious that it never entered God's mind. On at least two other occasions, Jeremiah preached that this hideous ritual did not enter God's mind (19:5; 32:35). Jeremiah emphasized that neither God's words and nor His thoughts ever advocated the killing of children as an act of worship.

How could any idea never enter God's mind? Doesn't God know everything? Yes, He does!

The Bible teaches that God is omniscient. God knows all about all creatures. He knows what they are doing all the time. No one can hide from Him (Hebrews 4:13).

God's thoughts are infinite. He knows and understands every human thought. He is familiar with all the ways of all people (Psalm 139:1-18).

The holy God does not lose His purity when He knows about unholy matters. The Lord knew about the possibility of child sacrifice, and He knew that sinful people would do it. However, God did not command this vile practice as an aid to worshipping Him!

The Judean religious leaders perhaps quoted Scripture to defend child sacrifice. They might have referred to God's command to give the firstborn son to Him (Exodus 22:29). Tragically, they went even further in their misinterpretation and burned their daughters as well!

The Hebrew word translated as "mind" is literally "heart". The Lord said that burning children to other gods "did not rise upon My heart." He knew it would happen, but it was not what His heart wanted for His people. The religious leaders rationalized an alleged command from Him. But they did not know His heart.

**How can you grow closer to the heart of God?**

## Day 71
### DEAD-END IDOLATRY

**Jeremiah 8:2.** *They will be exposed to the sun and the moon and all the stars of the heavens, which they have loved and served and which they have followed and consulted and worshiped. They will not be gathered up or buried, but will be like refuse lying on the ground.*

When King Josiah tried to spiritually reform his nation, he did away with the idolatrous priests. Not only had these priests burned incense to the idol Baal, they had worshipped the sun, moon and constellations (2 Kings 23:5). Josiah also dug up the graves of the deceased idolatrous priests and burned their bones on their own pagan altars (2 Kings 23:16).

Jeremiah preached that an even more widespread grave robbery would happen in the future. The enemy soldiers who would conquer Judah would desecrate the tombs. They would take out not just the bodies of the ungodly priests. They would also remove the bones of the kings, government officials, prophets, and every other person who was buried in Jerusalem (8:1).

The enemy would spread the bones out on the ground and expose them to the elements. The sun would beat down on them during the day, and the moon and stars at night. The bones would disintegrate and become fertilizer for the land.

Before they died, the people had worshipped the sun, moon and stars. And now in death, their bones lay on the ground exposed to their objects of worship. In describing such a disgusting scene, Jeremiah depicted the logical conclusion to a devotion to heavenly idols. The idols could do nothing for them in death. Moreover, the idols had done nothing for the people while they lived!

Jeremiah used five verbs to describe their life long commitment to stellar idols. The people loved, served, followed, consulted and worshipped them. These were tragic epitaphs to wasted lives.

King Josiah had sincerely tried to remove idols from his nation. He thought that removing the idolatrous priests and burning the bones of the dead priests would make an impact on the people. History demonstrates that they were not impressed. The king could not remove the idols from his people's hearts.

The road paved with idols is a dead-end street! Why couldn't the people listen to Jeremiah and learn the truth about astrological idols? Why didn't they worship the Creator instead of His creation?

**What particular part of God's creation are you prone to worship? Confess it to the Creator and grow closer to Him.**

Day 72
## WHAT THE BIRDS KNOW

*Jeremiah 8:7. Even the stork in the sky knows her appointed seasons, and the dove, the swift and the thrush observe the time of their migration. But my people do not know the requirements of the LORD.*

Birds instinctively know their time and what to do in each season. Birds respond correctly to God's created order. When they migrate, they go where they are supposed to go.

Bird watchers today believe that birds navigate by the stars. When the weather is so bad that the birds cannot see the stars, they find their way by the earth's magnetic fields. Both the stars and the magnetic fields are God's design.

Jeremiah was probably a bird watcher. Growing up in a rural town provided many occasions to observe the birds. Jeremiah learned to identify the different species and he watched them come in the spring and leave in the fall. He often used birds as illustrations when he preached.

These four migratory birds instinctively knew God's design for them, but the people of Judah did not! When the Lord asserted through Jeremiah that the people did not know the Lord's order for them, He used a deep Hebrew word for "know". Knowing the Lord's law means much more than having intellectual knowledge. It means to know at the emotional and willful levels. To know the Lord's law means to have His standards so imbedded in your total being that your desire to obey is almost as natural as the birds knowing when to fly.

You can choose to follow the ways that God intended for His people. If you choose not to follow the Lord, Jeremiah taught that you are more foolish than a bird!

When I was a small boy, one of the worst names that my friends would call each other was "birdbrain". Being a birdbrain meant being a dimwit. None of us wanted to be known as a stupid kid with a bird-sized brain!

Do you have less wisdom than a birdbrain? Birds know when to change locations, but do you know that it is now time for you to fly closer to God? The Lord created you to follow Him. Today.

**What is one area of your life where you sense God has specific expectations for you?**

## Day 73
## THEY COULD NOT BLUSH!

**Jeremiah 8:12.** *"Are they ashamed of their loathsome conduct? No, they have no shame at all; they do not even know how to blush. So they will fall among the fallen; they will be brought down when they are punished," says the Lord.*

Jeremiah had already preached these same words about their inability to blush (6:15). They had refused to be ashamed (3:3). Jeremiah wanted them admit their shame over their sin (3:25).

The people had lost their sense of shame. They felt no remorse over their abominable lifestyle. Jeremiah itemized their abhorrent sins.

They had turned away from the Lord (8:5) and had rejected His Word (8:9). They were evil (8:6). They were greedy and deceitful (8:10). They had every reason to be ashamed.

However, they felt no shame. Their sin had become so ingrained that it had seared their consciences. It had blinded them morally. It had hardened their hearts so that they were no longer sensitive to the difference between right and wrong. They had lost all awareness of their wickedness.

Sooner or later, the Lord will put to shame those who feel no shame. Jeremiah used the guild of the wise scribes as an example. These wise men had rejected the very source of their wisdom. They had denied the word of the Lord and they felt no shame about their lack of true wisdom. Consequently, they would be brought to shame in the future (8:8-9).

Many people today are the same way. They try to suppress the blush. What they do not realize is that getting rid of shame in their lives does not eliminate their personal sin. Shame came into the world along with sin and it will remain here as long as there is still sin.

Do you blush? Do not lose your sense of disgrace over ungodly lifestyles that you observe. It is okay to feel shame over the sin of your neighbors as well as for your own. Blush for the Lord!

**Is there anything that you have done that still makes you blush when you think about it? Confess it to the Lord and grow closer to Him.**

## Day 74

### Faint Heart

**Jeremiah 8:18. *O my Comforter in sorrow, my heart is faint within me.***

The Lord had given much to the Judeans, but they had abandoned Him. Now He was taking it all away from them. He used an agricultural illustration. He was going to take away their harvest and remove all the grapes from their vines. All their fig trees would wither and bear no fruit (8:13).

Jeremiah spoke as if he were the Judeans responding to the Lord's judgment against them. He imagined that they would urge each other to flee to the fortified cities and die there. They claimed that the Lord had given them poisoned water to drink. Jeremiah hoped that they would confess that they had sinned against Him (8:14).

The people had hoped for peace and healing. All they received was terror (8:15). Jeremiah said that the enemy could already be heard in the northern region of Dan. The army was so huge that the soldiers' neighing horses were causing earthquakes (8:16).

The Lord compared this fierce enemy from the north with venomous snakes. No snake charmer would be able to stop them (8:17). It was a frightening comparison. One day while walking through a forest in East Texas, I encountered three different species of venomous snakes. I was scared and ran, so they did not bite me! The Judeans, however, would not be able to run.

The whole scene was too much for Jeremiah. He cried out in his sorrow to the Lord. He told the Lord that his heart was faint. In contrast to the Judeans, Jeremiah's heart was sensitive toward both the Lord and the plight of the sinful people. Even though the Lord had told him not to pray for them (7:16), Jeremiah still deeply cared for his people. His heart was weak with sadness.

Jeremiah spoke about the heart many times in his sermons. Often he shared about his own heart. Later he portrayed his heart as broken (23:9). Yet his hope was in the Lord who would someday give him a new heart (Ezekiel 36:26).

Jeremiah brought his faint heart to the Lord, knowing that only He could give full comfort. You have access to His comfort today. Go to Him now and receive His limitless encouragement.

**Describe an incident when you brought your sorrows to the Lord. How did He comfort you?**

## Day 75
### Do Not Wait Until the End of Summer!

**Jeremiah 8:20.** *"The harvest is past, the summer has ended, and we are not saved."*

Jeremiah preached with his prophetic ear toward the future. He could hear the future voices of his people. They used the illustration of their grain harvest ending in spring and their fruit harvest at the end of the summer. They cried out that their opportunity to repent and become part of God's harvest was past. Their summer had ended, and they had no hope of being delivered from God's judgment.

The harvest was supposed to be a time of joy. Moses had told the people to rejoice together at the end of a harvest (Deuteronomy 16:10-11). Another prophet compared the gladness of a harvest with the future happiness brought about by the Messiah's gift of salvation (Isaiah 9:3).

Jeremiah heard his people's cries from a distant land. They were crying that the Lord their King was still in Jerusalem, but they were not with Him. Jeremiah gave them the Lord's reply to their cries. They had incited His anger with their foreign idols (8:19).

Jeremiah saw the future captivity of his people. They were exiles in a foreign country. They could not return to their fields and orchards.

Jeremiah described them as a dejected daughter who cried out hopelessly. His daughter was devastated, and Jeremiah empathized with her. She was broken, and Jeremiah felt the same way (8:21).

Jeremiah wished that he could get some medicine for her pain. He asked if there was any balm in Gilead. Was there no doctor available (8:22)? Many spices, herbs and trees grew in the region of Gilead. For centuries, Gilead had been known as the place to obtain medicinal ointments. The merchants who bought Joseph from his brothers were carrying balm from Gilead (Genesis 37:25).

Not even balm from Gilead could heal the spiritual condition of Jeremiah's people. Their opportunity to return to the Lord was gone. Their summer had ended. They were having a bleak winter.

What about you? Perhaps the Lord has given you opportunities to grow closer to Him. Do not wait until the end of summer!

**What immediate opportunities do you have to grow closer to the Lord?**

## Day 76
### WEEPING PROPHET

**Jeremiah 9:1.** *Oh, that my head were a spring of water and my eyes a fountain of tears! I would weep day and night for the slain of my people.*

Many people identify Jeremiah as the weeping prophet. Certainly he wept, but Jeremiah was much more than a mere teary-eyed sage! Behind his tears was strength. He was just as much an iron pillar prophet (1:18) as he was a weeper.

Jeremiah wished that his eyes were like a reservoir fed by never-ending springs. If only his head were a great lake, always sending water to his eyes. He wanted to continually cry over the tragedy of his people.

A literal translation says that Jeremiah wept for "the slain of the daughter of my people," referring to his people as his only daughter. Jeremiah did not have any children. If he were to imagine that he had a daughter, he knew that she would be the apple of his eye. Jeremiah identified with the feelings of the Lord, who related to His people as a father to his daughter. Sadly, His daughter had totally rejected the relationship.

Jeremiah was weeping with dismay, but he wanted to find a solution. In the previous verse he asked if there was not any balm in Gilead (8:22)? The town of Gilead was famous for its medicinal ointments. Sick and hurting people went there for the ointment to soothe their pain. With a fresh burst of tears, Jeremiah realized that even the ointment in Gilead could not heal the spiritual wound of his people. If there were not sufficient balm in Gilead, he knew that he would find no salve anywhere that could help his people.

He wept, because his rebellious countrymen were under the Lord's judgment. There was no hope for them. Even the balm in Gilead could not relieve Jeremiah's sore eyes. He had wept too much. He loved his people, but he knew that they deserved the coming doom.

Centuries later, Jesus also wept (John 11:35). Jesus lamented over Jerusalem's unbelief, and He wanted to gather the people together just like a hen gathers her chicks under her wings. Sadly, they were unwilling (Luke 13:34).

Are you a weeping believer? Do you cry over unbelieving people's lostness? If so, your tears are a genuine display of love for people who have gone astray.

**How much do you weep over lost people?**

## Day 77
### WILDERNESS WISHES

**Jeremiah 9:2.** *Oh, that I had in the desert a lodging place for travelers, so that I might leave my people and go away from them; for they are all adulterers, a crowd of unfaithful people.*

If Jeremiah had not focused on his calling, he might have started a monastery! He did not actually go into the wilderness to live a monastic life. He merely expressed a desire to escape from the sinful people who were all around him.

People are naturally sinners, but the people in Jeremiah's day were in a special category of sinners. They were unresponsive sinners. They did not respond to Jeremiah's preaching, and they showed no interest in repenting. Their lack of interest was like the attitude of many people today.

Jeremiah used the term "adulterers" to describe his sinful contemporaries. They had committed spiritual adultery by forsaking God and turning to idols. Jeremiah was disgusted with them. He just wanted to go away and have them out of his life.

David had expressed similar feelings about wanting to escape. David wished that he had wings like a dove so that he could fly away. He wanted to go far away and live in the wilderness (Psalm 55:6-7).

Jeremiah's desire for a wilderness retreat reflected the shocking idea that God would soon leave His people. In the near future, God would leave His temple in Jerusalem, and the Babylonians would destroy it. The only future for spiritual adulterers would be severe judgment.

However, God called Jeremiah to stay in the city. Jeremiah remained faithful to this calling. His example inspires all of us who are sometimes tempted to quit our ministries. Jeremiah wanted to quit because his ministry was an apparent failure. He saw no spiritual response from the people to whom he ministered.

The important lesson from Jeremiah's ministry is that the time to quit is not when you feel like a failure. The important issue is faithfulness, not perceived failure. Continue in the ministry to which God has called you. Do not be bothered by unresponsive people. Faithfulness that endures short-term failures will result in long-term spiritual success!

**Write a prayer for your spiritual leaders requesting that they may be kept from being discouraged about unresponsive people.**

## Day 78
### BOW-LIKE TONGUES

**Jeremiah 9:3.** *"They make ready their tongue like a bow, to shoot lies; it is not by truth that they triumph in the land. They go from one sin to another; they do not acknowledge me," declares the LORD.*

Jeremiah preached a memorable metaphor about bow and arrows. The human tongue was like a bow, and the arrows it shot were lies. The people's tongues kept shooting out one falsehood after another. Their dishonesty resulted from ignoring the Lord.

When I was younger, I enjoyed archery. I liked the exhilarating feeling of pulling back my bow and then releasing the arrow to fly toward a target. I wanted to keep shooting one arrow after another.

Telling lies, like shooting arrows, is addictive. The people in Jeremiah's day showed habitual sin patterns because they rejected the Lord from having any influence in their lives. Their lies led to many other sins.

One result of their sin was lack of trust among family and friends. They were cheating and slandering each other. Jeremiah used the Hebrew name for "Jacob" to describe their deceit (9:4).

"Jacob" was a common word in Jeremiah's day to describe a deceiver. Centuries earlier when Jacob was born, he was holding on to his twin brother's heel (Genesis 25:26). His parents named him Jacob ("the Cheater"), because Jacob was trying to cheat his brother out of being the first-born son. Jacob succeeded later (Genesis 27: 1-29).

Jeremiah preached that everyone was deceiving each other. No one told the truth. They had trained their tongues to lie, and their frequent use of this skill had wearied them (9:5).

They were hopelessly entrenched in deceit, and they refused to acknowledge the Lord (9:6). Their decision not to acknowledge Him (9:3) led to a stubborn refusal to know Him. Consequently, they could not stop their tongues from sinning.

I hope you are bridling your tongue better than they restrained theirs! Remember the dangers of the tongue. The human tongue is a restless evil (James 3:8).

**How can the Lord help you to control your tongue?**

Day 79
## ARROW-LIKE TONGUES

**Jeremiah 9:8. *Their tongue is a deadly arrow; it speaks with deceit. With his mouth each speaks cordially to his neighbor, but in his heart he sets a trap for him.***

Jeremiah preached to the people that their speech was deceitful, like a deadly arrow. The deceit was in their friendly words, which they did not really mean. In their hearts they were thinking of ways to trap the same neighbors to whom they spoke warmly.

Jeremiah had preached that the tongue is like a bow (9:3). A bow without the arrows is not an effective weapon. The tongue is both the bow and the arrows so it is remarkably lethal!

Because of their wickedness, the Lord planned to refine the masses of His people like metal in a furnace (9:7). He intended to punish them for their deceitful speech. In response, Jeremiah would mourn for the entire land that God would scorch in His judgment (9:9-10).

The Lord would make the nation into heaps of ruin. The wise men and women would understand why. The catastrophe would happen because the people rejected the Lord. They followed the foolish inclinations of their hearts and gave their loyalty to the idols of Baal (9:11-14).

The Lord would make them eat the bitter food of suffering and drink the toxic water of judgment. He would scatter them among the nations, and warriors would chase them with swords. They might as well call now for the professional wailers so that the women could start singing songs of mourning (9:15-22).

If only they had remained faithful to the Lord so that they could have avoided these disasters! If only they had allowed the Lord to change their hearts so that their words would not be like deadly arrows. If only people would not speak with deceitful arrows today.

What about you? With your one tongue you can both praise God and curse people (James 3:9). Develop the good use of your tongue. Bridle your tongue from speaking evil.

**Describe an approaching situation in which you will especially need the Lord's help in restraining your tongue.**

Day 80

### THE SMART, THE STRONG AND THE SATED

**Jeremiah 9:23.** *This is what the Lord says: "Let not the wise man boast of his wisdom or the strong man boast of his strength or the rich man boast of his riches...."*

People in Jeremiah's day mistakenly believed that having wisdom, power and wealth made people great. Postmodern people apparently have not progressed beyond this attitude. They have not learned that true wisdom, power and riches come only from a person's relationship to the true God.

Jeremiah did not condemn wise, powerful and wealthy people. His message was for the wise not to rely on their cleverness, for the strong not to depend on their toughness, and for the rich not to trust in their portfolios.

Jeremiah had earlier stated that people were practicing idolatry (9:14). The Lord called on those who considered themselves wise to understand why God's judgment was imminent (9:12). The Lord's message to them was that they might as well call the mourners who were skillful (literally "wise" in the Hebrew) in their wailing (9:17). Doom was coming, and the professional wailers should teach others to sing mournfully.

Worldly wisdom is radically different from God's wisdom. Worldly wise people are engrossed in their own selfish lives. In contrast, spiritually wise people seek the wisdom from above and endeavor to live godly lives.

Those who are physically strong and care nothing for God live only for what their strength can achieve for themselves. In contrast, godly people pursue spiritual strength. They understand that nothing is stronger than a moral strength that comes from commitment to the Lord.

Those who are rich in this world and who live solely for the enjoyment of their wealth will sooner or later learn that money is fleeting. People who love money will never be satisfied with their wealth (Ecclesiastes 6:10). In contrast, godly people are preoccupied with spiritual riches and their satisfaction is eternal.

Jeremiah's message to worldly people was for them to turn away from boasting about their dependence on earthly props. Spiritual people must resist bragging about their earthly blessings. Seek God and Him alone.

**In which of these three areas do you need to examine yourself? How can you give this area over to the Lord?**

## Day 81
### SPIRITUAL BOASTING

**Jeremiah 9:24.** *"But let him who boasts boast about this: that he understands and knows me, that I am the LORD, who exercises kindness, justice and righteousness on earth, for in these I delight," declares the LORD.*

Centuries after Jeremiah lived, Paul quoted the prophet's words. Paul wrote that believers should boast only in the Lord (1 Corinthians 1:31). Both Paul and Jeremiah knew that the Lord actively displays His attributes on earth. Specifically, He demonstrates kindness, justice and righteousness. How does He exercise these qualities on earth -- through people like you?

In contrast to boasting about earthly blessings (9:23), Jeremiah called on all the people (not just the wise, strong and rich) to boast about only what is eternally worthy of boasting. They should brag merely about a personal relationship with the Lord, through which they can know and understand Him. Jeremiah had earlier preached about a promise from God about knowledge and understanding. The Lord would send shepherds who would have hearts like His. They would teach the people about true knowledge and understanding (3:15).

The Lord wants you to know and understand Him. He desires for you to intimately experience His faithfulness, justice and righteousness so that you will live according to these qualities. The greatest benefit that the world receives is God's people living according to God's attributes. Sadly, many people will not allow the Lord to shine through their lives and display these attributes.

The Hebrew word "hesed" can be translated as loving kindness, loyal love or faithfulness. God has demonstrated His "hesed" toward His people through the centuries. God has always totally committed Himself to His people, to those who are committed to Him. He desires to show His loyalty to you today.

The Hebrew word "mispot" can be translated as justice or fairness. The word describes the principle by which the Lord always governs the universe. God never wavers from His principles. He always shows fairness to blameless people and gives chastisement to the blameworthy.

The Hebrew word "sedqah" means righteousness. God continuously works according to His righteous standard. God's people in Jerusalem were supposed to operate under this same standard, but they had rebelled.

**What is the area in which you most need to allow the Lord to communicate His attributes through you?**

## Day 82

### INTERNATIONAL ALLIANCE

**Jeremiah 9:26.** "... *Egypt, Judah, Edom, Ammon, Moab and all who live in the desert in distant places. For all these nations are really uncircumcised, and even the whole house of Israel is uncircumcised in heart."*

Jeremiah listed some nations that seemed to form an unlikely coalition. What did Judah have in common with gentile nations such as Egypt, Edom, Ammon and Moab? They shared at least two characteristics.

First, these nations all practiced the rite of circumcision. And secondly, the Lord would punish them all, because they were circumcised yet uncircumcised (9:25). Jeremiah used an oxymoron to emphasize his argument. He said that they were circumcised in uncircumcision!

They had circumcised themselves outwardly, but not inwardly. Jeremiah had already preached that the people of Judah needed to circumcise their hearts (4:4). They were no better than the unbelieving nations that surrounded them.

The Lord had given circumcision as a special sign only to Abraham and his descendants. By the time when Jeremiah lived, many other nations apparently circumcised their males also. Perhaps they used circumcision as a ceremony when their boys entered puberty.

Even though circumcision was believed to be a sign of protection against the Lord's anger, it would not protect them if their hearts were uncircumcised. Jeremiah preached that the Lord would use His power to punish this international alliance. Later, Jeremiah sent messages to Edom, Moab, Ammon and other nations announcing that the Babylonians would conquer them (27:1-7). Even a possible alliance with Egypt would not protect them from the Babylonians.

Centuries later, Paul wrote that trusting in physical circumcision was a useless alliance between a sinner and a rite. He wrote that the value of circumcision is only for the person who obeys God's Law. However, a person who sins against the Law, his circumcision becomes uncircumcision (Romans 2:25).

Do you have a useless alliance with a religious ritual? Is that formality blocking the possibility of a more intimate relationship with the Lord? Are you a member of the most powerful international coalition, the alliance between Jesus Christ and His people?

**Describe how your relationship with the Lord is a spiritual alliance.**

## Day 83
### GOD'S INCOMPARABILITY

**Jeremiah 10:6.** *No one is like you, O LORD; you are great, and your name is mighty in power.*

The people in Jeremiah's day wanted gods they could see. They cut trees, carved idols and lavished them with silver and gold. Prior to this verse, Jeremiah described the making of idols (10:3-4). Then he ridiculed them (10:5).

If you do not secure them with nails, the idols will topple. If you want your idols moved to different locations, you must carry them. If you seek a word from the gods, you will wait a long time. In fact, you will never hear from the idols. They cannot speak. They cannot help you in any way. The best that you can say about idols is that you need not fear them!

The Lord is unlike any idol. There is absolutely no comparison. You need to know that one of the true descriptions of God is His incomparability. The Lord is unique. He is in an exclusive category of One. No other being in any other religion comes close to qualifying for a comparison with Him.

The Lord is great. You must realize that the Lord sets the standard for true greatness. God is perfectly majestic. If you choose to call others great, you are merely stating that they are greater than most people. But they are not in the same league of magnitude as the Lord.

Not only is the Lord incomparable and great, His name is mighty. God's name is the same as His character. His power is unlimited. In contrast to idols that cannot move themselves, the Lord can move mountains. He can unleash powers beyond your imagination.

The Lord desires to communicate His might to people. Later Jeremiah preached that the Lord would let the people know about His mighty power so that they would know that His name is the Lord (16:21). The entire Bible, from beginning to end, is about God's communication about Himself to you and me. From the Genesis creation of heaven and earth to the Revelation formation of a new heaven and earth, the Lord revealed His power.

As you meditate on these wonderful truths about the Lord, you should realize how much you need Him today. Draw near to the incomparable, great, powerful God.

**How does God's greatness affect your need for Him?**

## Day 84
### KING OF ALL NATIONS

*Jeremiah 10:7. Who should not revere you, O King of the nations? This is your due. Among all the wise men of the nations and in all their kingdoms, there is no one like you.*

Russia and the United States have the same King. Unfortunately, most of their citizens do not acknowledge Him. They think that only their human government is overseeing them. Sooner or later, they will know the truth.

Throughout history, a few nations have willingly submitted to His rule. Most have not. The Lord is King over every nation, willing or unwilling, that has ever existed. The kings of ancient Babylon had to learn this lesson. Jeremiah repeatedly warned the people that the Babylonians would destroy them. He also preached that the king of Babylon, Nebuchadnezzar, was merely God's servant (25:9)!

Later, Nebuchadnezzar learned this lesson for himself. He learned from Daniel that God is the Lord of kings (Daniel 2:47). Nebuchadnezzar learned that God is ruler over human kingdoms and He bestows them on whomever He wishes (Daniel 4:25). He learned that God is sovereign over human governments and He personally selects all the kings and governors (Daniel 5:21).

In contrast, King Belshazzar did not learn this lesson during his lifetime (Daniel 5:22-23). (He has learned it in eternity under God's judgment!) Belshazzar was the last Babylonian king before Babylon was conquered. Jeremiah predicted that Babylon would come to an end after seventy years (25:12). As the King of kings, the Lord sets up and brings down nations.

The Lord has always ruled over all the nations, and He continues to do so. In contrast to not fearing idols (10:5), everyone should fear the King of all nations. Sadly, the people in Jeremiah's day did not revere Him (5:22). They showed Him no respect at all.

Because He is the sovereign King, God is worthy of your highest honor. He deserves your reverence of Him. The Lord is your King. Through Jesus Christ, you can be a citizen of His kingdom. Live like a citizen of the King today!

**What specific perspective on life does God's kingship give you?**

## Day 85
### THE ONLY TRUE GOD

**Jeremiah 10:10. *But the LORD is the true God; he is the living God, the eternal King. When he is angry, the earth trembles; the nations cannot endure his wrath.***

Jeremiah preached an unmistakable contrast between God and idols. Jeremiah had described idols as useless. Idols had to be carried because they could not walk on their own (10:5). In contrast, the Lord is true, living and eternal.

Idols were false, but the Lord is true. Any truth that the idolaters perceived in their idols was strictly illusionary. The Lord and everything about Him is true. All of God's words are true (Psalm 119:160). It is impossible for God to tell any falsehoods (Hebrews 6:18).

Fortunately, it is possible to turn to God from idols and serve the true and living God, like the Christians in Thessalonica did (1 Thessalonians 1:9). The new believers learned that their idols were dead, but God is alive. Their idols were a lie, but God is true. He was true not just for them, but also for everyone.

Jeremiah knew why idols were so appealing. Many of them were made of silver and gold. They were clothed with purple, the color of royalty. Skilled craftsmen made these idols into beautiful works of art (10:9).

Idols had beauty, but they were dead! In contrast, the Lord is living. Moses knew that God is living because he heard the voice of the living God (Deuteronomy 5:26). Jeremiah had earlier described God as the spring of living water (2:13). God's Word is living (Hebrews 4:12).

Idols were momentary, but the Lord is everlasting. The Lord is the eternal God and He is the perpetual King. Moses sang that the Lord would reign forever and ever (Exodus 15:18). A psalmist wrote that the Lord is King forever and ever (Psalm 10:16). David wrote that the Lord sits as King forever (Psalm 29:10). All other kings have come and gone. Only the Lord surpasses time.

In addition to describing God as true, living and everlasting, Jeremiah wrote a fourth characteristic of God. In contrast to idols that pose no threat (10:5), God displays His anger. Entire nations cannot bear God's anger. His wrath is directed toward sin, and toward those who reject the God who is true, living and everlasting. People who will not listen to the Lord and will not obey Him will be overcome by His wrath.

**Why does God show His angry toward nations?**

## Day 86
### UNIVERSAL MEMO

**Jeremiah 10:11.** *"Tell them this: 'These gods, who did not make the heavens and the earth, will perish from the earth and from under the heavens.'"*

This is the only verse of Jeremiah's writings that was not written in Hebrew. Jeremiah wrote it in Aramaic, which was the international language of his day. Peoples of all nations would be able to understand the Lord's condemnation of idolatry.

The message was simple. Idols had no role in creating the earth. Idols will vanish from the earth in the future.

Jeremiah summed up in Aramaic what he wrote in Hebrew in the verses that followed. God made the heavens and earth (10:12). The Lord continues to display His power through His creation (10:13).

In contrast, idols are deceitful gods (10:14). Idols are worthless and will pass away (10:15). Idols are not in the same religious league as God, for He is the Lord Almighty and Maker of everything (10:16).

Perhaps Jeremiah penned this verse in Aramaic so that the future exiles would be able to repeat this simple phrase to their captors. The exiled people could explain in Aramaic why they would not participate in idol worship. They could even help the Babylonians escape from the futility of idol worship. The exiles could help them understand that idols had done nothing to create the earth, and idols will eventually pass away from the earth.

When the exiles entered Babylon, they saw hundreds of temples to pagan idols. God's Word through Jeremiah would help them not be overwhelmed by all the idols. Idols could not harm them, because idols made nothing and will become nothing. Perhaps the people reminded each other, "Did you get Jeremiah's memo about the idols?"

An idol is a fanciful substitute for eternal reality. A person who knows the true God will never want a worthless substitute. An idol is nothing more than a powerless replacement for the omnipotent Lord. An idol neither creates nor lives.

Jeremiah was preparing God's people to become God's witnesses to all the nations. They had a message. You also have a message, and perhaps there are idolaters living near you!

**Which idols tempt you to draw away from the Lord?**

## Day 87
### GOD'S POWER THEN

**Jeremiah 10:12. *But God made the earth by his power; he founded the world by his wisdom and stretched out the heavens by his understanding.***

Only the Lord could have created the universe. Only He has the wisdom and power to do so. In contrast to idols who did not make heaven and earth (10:11), the Lord alone is the supreme creator.

Jeremiah repeated this verse in his sermon of judgment against Babylon (51:15). Jeremiah contrasted the truth about God as Creator with the excessive idolatry in Babylon. There was absolutely no comparison between God's power and the power of the Babylonian idols. The same power with which God created the earth would bring down the greatest empire on the earth.

Jeremiah briefly described God's creative work in three parts. He used three different Hebrew words for "earth", "world" and "heavens". The prophet wrote that God made the earth, set up the world and extended the heavens.

First, God made this planet by His power. In contrast, the idols have no power. Idols do not even have the strength to move themselves!

Jeremiah compared idols to scarecrows in a cucumber field (10:5)! A scarecrow does nothing. An enlightened person is not afraid of the scarecrow. How could an idol have anything to do with creating the earth?

Secondly, God set up the world by His wisdom. In contrast to the secular evolutionist's belief that impersonal cosmic forces brought the world into existence, we can rejoice that God's wisdom established the world. The world is not here by accident or chance. God gave meaning, purpose and direction to the world.

Thirdly, God spread out the heavens by His understanding. The expanse of the universe is larger than any of us can comprehend. The hugeness of the universe frightens those who do not know the true God. They feel small and alone.

In contrast, true believers take great comfort in the vastness of the cosmos. They know that God is even bigger than what He created! And you can relate to the immense God today!

**In what ways does the fact that God is greater than all He created bring encouragement to you?**

Day 88

## GOD'S POWER NOW

**Jeremiah 10:13.** *When he thunders, the waters in the heavens roar; he makes clouds rise from the ends of the earth. He sends lightning with the rain and brings out the wind from his storehouses.*

Both Jeremiah and one of the psalmists wrote that God brings out the wind from His storehouses (Psalm 135:7). This picture helps us see that the Lord is so great that He even controls weather patterns.

You could not see the demonstration of the Lord's power when He created the universe. You were not there, but you can see continuing evidence of God's power today. The same God whose strength created the cosmos shows His might today.

You can see God's power in a thunderstorm. The thunder, rain, lightning and wind are all displays of the Creator's might.

Even though thunderstorms frighten many people, I tend to enjoy storms. If the rain is not pouring down too heavily, I like to go outside to watch and feel the tempest. I especially enjoy watching a storm as it approaches.

I like to watch the dark clouds move across the sky and feel the increasing wind against my face. I take pleasure in watching the distant lightning. Since I live in an often-parched area in Texas, I am glad the storm is coming!

Jeremiah implied that thunder represents God's voice. Nature is part of God's general revelation to people, so certainly God's voice is in the thunder. God speaks generally in storms, communicating His power. God speaks specifically in the Bible and communicates His salvation.

In contrast to God's voice, idols cannot speak (10:5). The idolaters had a storm god named Baal. They should have known that Baal had no power. Storms came and went and terrified many people. So they worshipped Baal. They thought that the storm idol could do something about the storms. Baal never did anything!

God is in every storm. He made it, He controls it, and He has purpose in every storm. Because of God's power over storms, you can let the Lord use the next storm to pull you closer to Himself.

**How can displays of God's power draw you closer to Him?**

## Day 89
### DIRECTOR OF STEPS

**Jeremiah 10:23.** *I know, O LORD, that a man's life is not his own; it is not for man to direct his steps.*

The Lord is the director of steps. He lays out each journey that individuals must travel, and then He guides each person in the walk of that life. People are incapable of wisely directing their own destinies. Only fools resist God's claims of owning them.

Centuries earlier, Solomon wrote a proverb about the director of steps. People should indeed plan their lives as responsibly as they can. Yet the Lord determines what actually happens to their plans. God orders their daily steps (Proverbs 16:9).

Jeremiah prayed and acknowledged that God is the director of steps in response to what the Lord had revealed to him. The Lord was going to bring distress on Jerusalem by putting the city under siege. God was planning to fling the inhabitants of Judah out of their land (10:17-18).

Jeremiah identified himself with the brokenness of his people. He felt the pain of their imminent destruction. He told the Lord that he accepted his suffering and he would bear it (10:19).

Jeremiah identified himself with Jerusalem. He described the city as his destroyed tent. All the tent ropes were broken and all his children had left the tent. No one was available to repair the tent (10:20).

Jeremiah accepted the steps that the Lord directed for him. Centuries later, Paul told Timothy to accept the life of suffering that the Lord had given them both (2 Timothy 2:3). They both followed the steps that the Lord laid out for them as loyal soldiers to their commander Jesus Christ.

Believers no longer own their own lives. Jesus Christ bought them at an enormous price. Their bodies have become temples of the Holy Spirit (1 Corinthians 6:19-20).

Are you in total agreement with the Lord's ownership of you? Are you accepting the steps that He is making for you? Are you allowing Him to direct your steps?

**Describe a recent incident in which it was clear that the Lord directed your steps.**

## Day 90
### CORRECTION

**Jeremiah 10:24. *Correct me, LORD, but only with justice—not in your anger, lest you reduce me to nothing.***

Jeremiah knew that the Lord was the God of justice. He also knew that the Lord had absolute anger toward sin. Jeremiah was pleading for a bit of divine mercy so that the Lord would not diminish his nation into nothingness.

Jeremiah prayed on behalf of his people. He knew that they needed correction, but he did not want them to be annihilated. Jeremiah knew the difference between the Lord's justice and His anger. God in His wrath could totally destroy them. God in His justice would not allow the Babylonians to obliterate them, because the Babylonians themselves would fall under divine justice.

Jeremiah had preached that the Lord shows His justice on the earth (9:24). Centuries earlier, David sang that Lord makes Himself known by His justice (Psalm 9:16). God loves righteousness and justice (Psalm 33:5).

Because of the reality of God's justice, Jeremiah called the leaders of his nation stupid. They were like shepherds whose flocks were scattered. They would have nothing, because they had not sought the Lord. They deserved God's anger (10:21).

Because they ignored God, an uproar would come to them from the north. A hostile army would empty the cities. Only wild animals would live in them (10:22).

Jeremiah prayed that Lord would pour His wrath on nations that did not know Him. Jeremiah had Babylon specifically in mind. The Babylonians would devour Judah, and Jeremiah wanted the Lord to judge those nations that invaded his nation (10:25).

Jeremiah did not have a vengeful spirit. Instead, he had a strong sense of God's justice and he wanted Him to display His justice on all the earth. The Lord is the maker of all nations, so He certainly has the right to judge them.

The Judeans needed correction, and you do also. You should welcome the ministry of divine correction in your life. The Lord will correct you both with His mercy with His justice.

**Describe any difficulties you may have in fully believing in God's justice. Bring those difficulties to Him in prayer.**

## Day 91
### A PREACHING TOUR

**Jeremiah 11:6.** *The LORD said to me, "Proclaim all these words in the towns of Judah and in the streets of Jerusalem: 'Listen to the terms of this covenant and follow them....'"*

Jeremiah did not just preach in the temple courtyard once a week. He did not wait for people to come to the temple to hear him. He went to them. He preached to them in the city streets and in the towns throughout Judah. Jeremiah was an itinerant prophet.

His message was simple. He preached about the terms of the Lord's covenant. The Lord is a covenant maker and a covenant keeper. The people were neither.

Jeremiah told them that the Lord had given a solemn warning to their ancestors when He brought them out of captivity in Egypt. The Lord continued warning them through the centuries. The Lord still warned them on the very day that Jeremiah preached to them (11:7). There had been a persistent problem. The people did not listen to the Lord or pay any attention to Him. They followed the pigheaded preferences of their own wicked hearts! Because the people had not obeyed the terms of His covenant with them in the past, the Lord brought on them all the punishments specified in the covenant (11:8).

Jeremiah preached that those who disregarded the Lord's covenant would be cursed (11:3). He based his sermon on Moses' book. Moses had recorded the same warning about the consequence of failing to heed God's covenant. A person is cursed if he or she disobeys God's law (Deuteronomy 27:26).

Centuries later, another man quoted Moses' words about the curse. He deduced that everyone who tries to live under Moses' law is under a curse. The reason everyone is cursed is because the law cannot justify anyone before God (Galatians 3:10-11).

The good news is that Jesus Christ redeemed us from the curse of the law. He did this by becoming a curse for us. His death on the cross took away the curse from those who believe in Him (Galatians 3:13).

Jeremiah brought the news of God's curse to every town in Judah and every street in Jerusalem. (He would later preach the good news of the new covenant.) Today, the good news about redemption from the curse should be even more widespread. Perhaps many preachers today should go on tour and preach the truth.

**What is the Lord prompting you to do to help circulate the Gospel?**

Day 92

CONSPIRACY

**Jeremiah 11:9. *Then the LORD said to me, "There is a conspiracy among the people of Judah and those who live in Jerusalem...."***

The Lord revealed to Jeremiah some information about a conspiracy. The Judeans were involved in a subversive plot. What was this intrigue all about?

A conspiracy is a group effort. One person cannot commit a conspiracy alone. The Lord implied that a great many people in Judah and Jerusalem were conspiring. Countless people had been involved in the secret planning. Now, because the Lord revealed it to Jeremiah, the conspiracy was public knowledge.

Conspiracies are often against governments. Apparently, these people were planning to undo King Josiah's spiritual reforms. Josiah had torn down many altars to idols. Tragically, the idols remained in people's hearts.

They outwardly followed Josiah's restructuring of the nation's religion. They knew their king enforced his laws. However, inwardly they resisted Josiah's spiritual policies. They longed for their idols. Perhaps they waited patiently for a new king who would rebuild the altars!

Their conspiracy was not merely against the government of King Josiah. It was against the Lord Himself! Josiah tried to bring back God's Word to the nation, but the people wanted to keep their sinful lifestyles.

They returned to the same evil that some of their ancestors had committed. Instead of following the Lord, they pursued other gods. They broke the covenant that the Lord had made with their nation (11:10).

The Lord would bring judgment on them because they forsook Him. They would cry out to Him, but it would be too late. Then they would cry to their idols and burn incense to them. However, their gods would not save them from the coming disaster (11:11-12).

When God is silent, you should patiently wait for Him. You should not look for help from other sources, especially idols! Only the Lord is your true and reliable helper.

**Describe a recent incident in which your help could only have come from the Lord.**

## Day 93
## TOO MANY "GODS"

**Jeremiah 11:13.** *You have as many gods as you have towns, O Judah; and the altars you have set up to burn incense to that shameful god Baal are as many as the streets of Jerusalem.*

Many years before Jeremiah's day, the evil King Ahaz built idol altars in every city of Judah. He burned incense on them to other gods (2 Chronicles 28:25). The worship of Baal became even more deeply ingrained in their culture during Manasseh's reign (2 Kings 21:3). Finally a man became king who followed the Lord.

In the twelfth year of his reign, Josiah began tearing down some of the altars to Baal (2 Chronicles 34:4). In Josiah's thirteenth year, Jeremiah began his ministry as a prophet (Jeremiah 1:2). Jeremiah boldly preached against idols while Josiah kept smashing them!

In Josiah's eighteenth year (2 Chronicles 34:8), the king began restoring the temple. The high priest found a copy of the Scriptures in the temple during the repairs. This exciting discovery was like a probable situation today of finding long-forgotten dusty Bibles in a church building where God's Word is no longer taught!

After reading the Scriptures publicly, Josiah began a second demolition of idols (2 Kings 23:4-20). Because Josiah had read God's Word to all the people, they knew the terms of His covenant. When Jeremiah preached that the people had broken the Lord's covenant (11:3-8), they would understand what he meant.

King Josiah tried to change the heart of his nation by tearing down altars to Baal. He wanted to replace false religion with worship of the true God. He repaired the temple, read the Scriptures, and brought back the Passover celebration.

Then Josiah died. Evil kings reigned after him. The idols again prospered.

Jeremiah had earlier preached that the people of Judah had as many gods as they had towns (2:28). Now he added that their gods outnumbered the streets in Jerusalem. The large numbers indicated the quantity of gods in their hearts.

Do you have too many gods? Even if you have only one in addition to the Lord, that is one too many! Grow closer to the Lord and shun the idols.

**How can your relationship with the Lord remove your attraction to idols?**

## Day 94
### OLIVE TREE

**Jeremiah 11:16. *The LORD called you a thriving olive tree with fruit beautiful in form. But with the roar of a mighty storm he will set it on fire, and its branches will be broken.***

The Lord described Jeremiah's nation as a healthy olive tree with many olives. Tragically, a lightening storm caused a fire that burned the tree down. Every one of the olive branches was broken.

Why did God send the storm to destroy the tree? Jeremiah kept preaching and explained that the Lord had planted the olive tree. Now He would burn it, because it had burned incense to Baal (11:17).

During a two-week teaching assignment in Jordan, I stayed in a building next to some wonderful olive trees. I enjoyed walking under the thick foliage of those trees every day. The trees bore many olives that were not yet ripe. I regretted having to miss those olives when they were ready to be eaten!

The olive tree plays a prominent role in God's Word. From Genesis to Revelation, the Lord revealed truth by using the actual tree or metaphors of it (Genesis 8:11; Revelation 11:4). Arguably, the most compelling use of an olive tree illustration is in Paul's letter to the Romans.

Like Jeremiah, Paul wrote that Israel was like an olive tree. Some of its branches were broken off. These broken branches represented the Jews who did not believe. They no longer had a place on the olive tree. Those believers who were not Jews were like wild olive branches, but God miraculously grafted them onto the cultivated tree. Paul had strong hopes that his fellow Jews would come to faith in Jesus and be grafted back into their olive tree (Romans 11:17-24).

As one olive tree, both Jewish believers and Gentile believers have the same root. The root is holy (Romans 11:16). Paul warned the Gentile believers not to be arrogant about their position on the tree. They should be humbled by their gratitude to Israel, which provided the root. Jesus taught that salvation comes from the Jews (John 4:22).

You should not be presumptuous about your inclusion in the olive tree. If you are a true olive branch, it is only by God's grace. Grow closer to the One who planted the tree.

**How has the Lord recently kept you humble about your relationship with Him?**

## Day 95
### LIKE A GENTLE LAMB

**Jeremiah 11:19.** *I had been like a gentle lamb led to the slaughter; I did not realize that they had plotted against me, saying, "Let us destroy the tree and its fruit; let us cut him off from the land of the living, that his name be remembered no more."*

Jeremiah had exposed a popular conspiracy against God's covenant (11:9). Then he learned that the conspiracy had become personal! Their plot included the elimination of Jeremiah!

Their code name for Jeremiah was "the tree and its fruit". They did not know that Jeremiah would never marry and that he would not have the "fruit" of children (16:2). They wanted to kill the tree before its fruit budded so that Jeremiah's name would be forgotten. The tree's fruit could also refer to Jeremiah's ministry. Jeremiah's enemies did not like the prophet's words. They wanted to permanently silence the preacher and get rid of his ministry.

Jeremiah's foes were in his own hometown. His fellow villagers were seeking to kill him (11:21). Jeremiah had grown up with them and did not suspect that they would turn against him.

Jeremiah felt like he was a gentle lamb being led to the slaughter. He was oblivious to his neighbors' plot against his life until the Lord revealed the danger to him. The Lord made known to Jeremiah their evil plan (11:18).

Jeremiah had preached about the futility of evildoers bringing sacrifices to the Lord's house (11:15). Lambs were animals that were sacrificed in the temple. Jeremiah saw himself as an innocent sacrificial lamb.

An earlier prophet had used the same lamb illustration (Isaiah 53:7). Jeremiah's feelings about his imperiled life were a prophetic picture of a future lamb. Every Easter, my wife bakes a cake in the form of a lamb. The perfect gentle lamb who went to the slaughter was Jesus Christ (Acts 8:32-35).

Jeremiah's enemies threatened that they would cut him off from the land of the living. The Messiah's enemies would do the same to Him (Isaiah 53:8). They crucified Jesus, but He gave up His own life (John 19:30). Jesus Christ was truly the Lamb of God who took away the sin of the world (John 1:29).

**What are some tangible ways in which the name "Lamb of God" helps you in your relationship with Him?**

Day 96

## Heart Tester

**Jeremiah 11:20.** *But, O LORD Almighty, you who judge righteously and test the heart and mind, let me see your vengeance upon them, for to you I have committed my cause.*

As a child, I first became aware of personal enemies when someone slit the tires on my bicycle. But I have never experienced enemies like Jeremiah did. Jeremiah learned that his enemies were plotting to kill him! He felt like a gentle lamb on the way to its slaughter. He was totally unaware that some people wanted both him and his ministry eradicated (11:18-19)!

In response, Jeremiah prayed. He praised the Lord for being the righteous judge who examined all human minds and hearts. He asked for God's vengeance on his enemies. Jeremiah was not asking for his own revenge. People who want vengeance are thinking primarily about themselves. Jeremiah wanted God to carry out His retribution.

God's vengeance is not based on His need for revenge. He has no need for revenge. He has no needs at all, in contrast to the many needs of humans. His vengeance occurs entirely from His justice.

Jeremiah was concerned about defending the Lord's honor. The reason Jeremiah had enemies was because he spoke for God. Those who threatened Jeremiah had chosen to become God's enemies. He wanted the Lord to deal justly with His enemies.

Jeremiah saw himself as standing in the Lord's courtroom. Jeremiah had a legal case to bring before the Judge. He knew that he stood before a perfect Judge who tested everyone's heart and knew everyone's thoughts and motives. The Lord was testing the heart of Jeremiah as well as his enemies' hearts. Some men in Jeremiah's hometown were threatening to kill him if he did not stop preaching (11:21). The Lord's answer was that He would indeed punish those men (11:22-23).

When Jesus Christ came, He raised the standards on prayer for enemies. He taught His followers to love their enemies (Matthew 5:44). Paul wrote that believers should never avenge themselves, but they should leave all vengeance for the Lord to carry out (Romans 12:19).

What about you? Have you recently asked God to test your heart? Have you asked Him to search your thoughts?

**Describe any reluctance you may have against the Lord testing your heart.**

## Day 97
### WHY DO THE WICKED PROSPER?

**Jeremiah 12:1.** *"You are always righteous, O Lord, when I bring a case before you. Yet I would speak to you about your justice: Why does the way of the wicked prosper? Why do the faithless live at ease?"*

Some men from his hometown were threatening Jeremiah's life. They were rejecting his prediction of the destruction of Jerusalem. They believed that if you do not like the prophecy, then you should kill the prophet!

Jeremiah did well to turn to his God in prayer. Even though he was anxious about being murdered, he began by praising the Lord. He praised the Lord for being righteous. Whatever else Jeremiah prayed, his core belief was that the Lord did everything right. Jeremiah did not question the correctness of the Lord's actions.

Jeremiah did wonder about the Lord's timing in judging the wicked. Jeremiah was especially concerned about the bad men whom he knew in his hometown. Why was the Lord delaying judgment on evil people?

Jeremiah thought that he knew the Lord well enough so that he could boldly complain. He had grown in his relationship with the Lord. He could openly ask Him for answers to questions about life apparently making no sense.

His question continues to form on the lips of people today. Why are wicked people so happy? Why don't bad things happen to bad people?

The Lord did not give an immediate intellectual answer to Jeremiah's query. We must remember that the Lord does not owe us any philosophical explanations. Jeremiah's basic question was not philosophical. It was personal. He was crying to God for help.

The Lord would answer Jeremiah's cry. God would continue to help him as Jeremiah sought to live righteously, because the Lord is always righteous.

Perhaps you also are struggling with the problem of the prosperity of evil people. Ponder Jeremiah's prayer and the Lord's response to it. Remember that the Lord will certainly judge the unrighteous, because He is righteous. It is just a matter of time. Amazingly, the unrighteous still have time to turn to the Lord.

**How does Jeremiah's bold prayer and God's patience with him, help you as you pray to the Lord today?**

## Day 98
### GALLOPING WITH HORSES

**Jeremiah 12:5.** *"If you have raced with men on foot and they have worn you out, how can you compete with horses? If you stumble in safe country, how will you manage in the thickets by the Jordan?"*

These words from the Lord must have encouraged Jeremiah in a powerful way. They can lift your spirits, too. Jeremiah's problems in his small hometown were like footraces with other men. The Lord had even greater plans for the young prophet. Jeremiah would run with the horses in the city of Jerusalem. Jeremiah was weary from his footrace with men. The Lord understood this fatigue, but He wanted the prophet to think about horses.

Even though I am a native Texan, I am not a cowboy! I have never owned a horse. Yet, I think that horses are among the most beautiful animals that God created. I especially enjoy watching the way horses run – powerfully, yet gracefully. However, I have never seen a man or woman running with horses! It is impossible. Horses run too fast. How could Jeremiah possibly expect to compete with the horses?

Racing with horses is a vivid way of describing the best way to live. It means living to one's fullest potential. It describes a person of faith who lives courageously and selflessly. This person runs far ahead of the many who settle for personal safety and mediocre lives.

How did Jeremiah respond to these words from the Lord? How did he live the rest of his life? Did he accept God's unique plan for his existence?

Jeremiah had a difficult life, just like perhaps you do. He faced persecution, discouragement and humiliation. He was misunderstood, slandered and ignored. But the prophet decided to trust God with his destiny. He lived the rest of his life in obedience to God. He did not let hostile people deter him from following the Lord. He consistently did what was right, regardless of the results. Jeremiah achieved the exceptional life that his enemies would never have.

The Lord can also give you the ability to run with the horses. Competing with horses is challenging, tough and painful, but it is the most fulfilling way to live. Live by faith in Jesus, and have a life that is certainly not easy. But it is the best life!

**Will you accept the Lord's challenge to gallop with the horses? In what area of service to Him is He asking you to consider this challenge today?**

## Day 99
### HAVING JORDAN ADVENTURES

Jeremiah 12:5b. *"If you have raced with men on foot and they have worn you out, how can you compete with horses? If you stumble in safe country, how will you manage in the thickets by the Jordan?"*

I have occasionally wondered what my life would have been like if I had stayed in my hometown all my life. I think I would have had a relatively safe and predictable life, but I would have missed out on serving the Lord in difficult countries. I would not have ridden trains across the icy Soviet Union or motorcycles through sweltering Vietnam!

Up until now, Jeremiah had lived in a peaceful land. The good king Josiah had ruled a nation that was safe for godly people. The government encouraged Jeremiah's ministry. Jeremiah easily grew in his faith while in a secure environment. However, the Lord did not want Jeremiah to trust Him only during times of peace. The Lord warned Jeremiah that he would not remain in safe country indefinitely. The Lord had plans for him to work in riskier territory. He warned him about the thickets by the Jordan.

What exactly would Jeremiah face by the Jordan? Various possible translations from the Hebrew include "the swelling of the Jordan" and "the thickets by the Jordan." Both translations imply danger. Perilous floods resulted when the Jordan River overflowed its banks. The thickets by the Jordan were the haunts of ferocious beasts!

Lions inhabited the Jordan thickets. These were not tame animals! Whenever people walked down to the Jordan jungle, they took massive risks. The Jordan was a symbolic name for every future menace that Jeremiah would experience. The Lord had precarious places planned for Jeremiah. However, He had promised Jeremiah when He first called him that He would rescue him. Every risk that Jeremiah would take would strengthen his faith as he experienced the Lord's protection.

Running with the horses and surviving the Jordan were the answers that the Lord gave to Jeremiah's prayer. The prophet had asked God why the wicked were prospering (12:1). The Lord knew that Jeremiah did not need a philosophical answer. Jeremiah needed personal spiritual strength.

The Lord's words should challenge you. If you cannot deal with a minor job, how will you manage a really demanding one? If small incidents dishearten you, how will you handle the precarious moments? If you want to forever avoid the unsafe turf, what will your life amount to in the end? Think of all the adventures you would miss!

**How does Jeremiah's adventurous life challenge you?**

## Day 100
### BETRAYAL

*Jeremiah 12:6. Your brothers, your own family—even they have betrayed you; they have raised a loud cry against you. Do not trust them, though they speak well of you.*

I grew up in a good family with nice relationships with all my siblings and cousins. Jeremiah's family experience was different. The Lord revealed to Jeremiah that members of his own family had turned against him. Like a mob ready to lynch someone, they were crying loudly behind his back. Even though they spoke agreeably to him, the Lord warned Jeremiah not to trust them. Perhaps they praised Jeremiah's ministry with their tongues while they were plotting against him in their hearts!

The original Hebrew used the word "even" three times in this verse to emphasize the degree of scandal. Even Jeremiah's own brothers, even they had betrayed him. Even they cried loudly against him.

Some of his family joined others from Jeremiah's village that plotted to take his life. The Lord promised that He would punish them (11:21-23). Jeremiah's family and his neighbors were included with the many that the Lord would abandon (12:7).

Jeremiah was learning difficult lessons about trusting people. Those whom he trusted most were betraying him. Jeremiah would experience the additional pain of being falsely accused of betraying his own nation (37:13-14). When the Lord first called him, He warned Jeremiah that many people would be against him (1:18-19).

The Lord helped Jeremiah see that his betrayal was a symptom of a much more serious spiritual problem. Jeremiah's brothers' betrayal of the prophet was an illustration of the whole country's betrayal of the Lord. Like a lion in the forest, the nation had roared against God (12:8).

Jeremiah later preached about the dangers of trusting in men. Trusting in men brings hardship, but trusting in the Lord results in blessing (17:5-8). Every person that you know is a potential betrayer. Your response to betrayers should be to grow closer to the Lord.

Have you ever felt betrayed? If so, you are in the best of company. One of His own disciples betrayed Jesus Christ. Jesus understands betrayal and He can help you during heartbreaking times. He will not abandon you when you suffer betrayal.

**How can your relationship with the Lord help heal you of hurt feelings caused by people who betrayed you?**

## Day 101
### SPECKLED BIRD

**Jeremiah 12:9.** *Has not my inheritance become to me like a speckled bird of prey that other birds of prey surround and attack? Go and gather all the wild beasts; bring them to devour.*

Jeremiah grew up in a small village, so he had numerous opportunities to observe birds. He used bird illustrations in his sermons on many occasions. For example, he had preached that the land would be so devastated that even the birds would be gone (12:4).

The Lord would bring about this devastation because He had abandoned His people. He had left them because they, like a roaring lion, had turned against Him. He now hated them (12:7-8).

How could the God of love hate the people of Judah? They were like a speckled bird among many drab birds. Judah was different from all the other nations because of the covenant relationship with God. How could He hate His own people?

The Lord does not hate in the same way that you or I might hate. If I hate my neighbor, I sin. The Lord's hate is much different. The Lord withholds blessings of His love from those who snub Him. The Lord is always the God of love, but many people reject His love. Those who live under the absence of His love consequently experience the opposite of His love.

Because Judah had rejected God's love, Jeremiah compared the nation to a vineyard that would be made into a wasteland. The land would become so desolate that sowing wheat on it would only reap thorns. The Lord would uproot Judah from the land. However, He would later have compassion on the people (12:10-17).

All this would happen because the Judeans reneged on being God's special bird. Like many drab birds attacking a colorful one, many people would attack Judah because the nation was so different from all the others. Judah had tried to be like other nations by worshipping those nations' idols. Jeremiah wanted Judah to know that idolatry would not protect her. The birds and beasts (other nations) would destroy her.

Are you like a speckled bird? Do you stand out among others because of your relationship with the Lord? If so, Jeremiah has a warning for you. Do not become a speckled bird that tries to be just like the ungodly birds of the world. Forget about what others may think of you. Be a speckled bird for the Lord.

**In what ways has your relationship with God made you different from other people you know, like a speckled bird surrounded by plain birds?**

Day 102

JEREMIAH'S "BELT"

**Jeremiah 13:1.** *This is what the Lord said to me: "Go and buy a linen belt and put it around your waist, but do not let it touch water."*

Visual images linger after words are forgotten. People chose to ignore Jeremiah's sermons, but their curiosity riveted them toward his new linen garment. What piece of clothing did Jeremiah purchase?

The Hebrew word is not precise. He bought either a belt or – underwear! If it was a belt, everyone would notice it as he walked down the street. His normal attire was probably a coarse cloth tunic or robe, and a bright linen belt around his waist would turn people's heads.

People in Jeremiah's day used the fibers from flax plants to weave linen clothing, which was worn by the wealthy. Linen was also the material that priests wore. Jeremiah's wearing linen would symbolize the nation of priests that God had intended Judah to be. The Lord wanted His people to be close to Him, as close as a belt around His waist.

Possibly Jeremiah bought a linen loincloth instead. If so, he would wear it next to the private part of his body. It would illustrate the intimacy of God's relationship with His people.

God told Jeremiah to keep his new garment out of water. This command enriched the symbolism. When a piece of clothing gets wet, it loses its store-bought newness. It is no longer a "virgin" garment. The Lord wanted to prevent His people from drowning in the waters of other gods. He wanted to keep His men and women exclusively for Himself.

Washing the linen was exactly what the people had done. They wanted to live their own lives and not stay committed to the new linen. Their attitude was sinful pride. The Lord would judge the great pride of Jerusalem (13:9).

The God whom Jeremiah knew still seeks intimacy with His people. If you are one of His, your relationship with Him can be remarkably close. Cling like linen to Him today!

**Is your relationship with God as intimate as you know He wants it to be? What steps will you take to become closer to Him this week?**

## Day 103
### TRAVEL TIME

*Jeremiah 13:3-4. Then the word of the LORD came to me a second time: "Take the belt you bought and are wearing around your waist, and go now to Perath and hide it there in a crevice in the rocks."*

The Lord told Jeremiah to take his newly purchased garment to a certain location and to bury it under the rocks. The Lord used this act of linen burial to illustrate that His relationship with His people was changing. However, the Lord did not desire to change the relationship. The people did. They had chosen to leave Him. In the symbolic act, Jeremiah represented God. His belt stood for the people. Because the people had forsaken Him, the Lord would remove them from Himself and His protection.

Like Jeremiah's linen, the people would hide themselves. They would try to avoid God's instruments of judgment, the Babylonians. They would not succeed.

Where did Jeremiah hide his garment? Did he travel all the way to the Euphrates River, or did he go the short distance to a village called Perath? In the Hebrew language, the word for "Perath" is usually translated as "Euphrates". Some Bible scholars argue that since the word "river" is not found after in Jeremiah 13, and since the Euphrates River was hundreds of miles away, the nearby village was the more reasonable destination.

However, the longer journey to the Euphrates River would make a more intense impression on the people. Also, the long journeys to Babylon and back would keep Jeremiah away from the evil King Jehoiakim, who reigned for eleven years. Jeremiah was almost put to death at the beginning of his reign (26:1-24), and the prophet finally hid from the king (36:26).

Traveling from Jerusalem to Babylon would take several months. Ezra's journey from Babylon to Jerusalem took four months (Ezra 7:9). Then Jeremiah would need another three or four months to return. Later he would make the same journey again (13: 6-7). Such a long trip merely to perform a symbolic act seems excessive today and probably raised eyebrows back then.

No extravagant effort is wasteful if done in obedience to the Lord. As you seek to know Him better, you will sense His divine shuffling of your schedule. Giving your time and your life to the Lord is the most sensible gift in the universe that you can offer!

**Describe a recent incident in which you sacrificed your time to the Lord.**

## Day 104
### RUINED AND USELESS

**Jeremiah 13:6-7. *Many days later the LORD said to me, "Go now to Perath and get the belt I told you to hide there." So I went to Perath and dug up the belt and took it from the place where I had hidden it, but now it was ruined and completely useless.***

Jeremiah had a fascinating ministry. The people most likely paid special attention to his symbolic performances. They probably long remembered the times when he wore a yoke (27:2), broke a pot (19:1-3), bought some land (32:9) and invited teetotalers to drink wine in the temple (35:1-6)!

Jeremiah's longest performance was the saga of his belt. He bought it, wore it, kept it unwashed, traveled with it, removed it and hid it. He put it in a rock crevice near the Euphrates River. A long time later, he dug it up. His drama ended with the belt decomposed.

Jeremiah acted out such interesting dramas because the Lord spoke to him about the symbolic acts. Each show was God's idea. Jeremiah listened to the Lord every time.

In contrast, the people had dismissed God's Word. Their hearts became stubborn. They had gone after idols to serve and worship them. Therefore, they would become just as worthless as Jeremiah's ruined belt. The Lord would destroy their pride (13:9-10).

Over a period of time, the Judeans became just like that decayed belt. They corrupted themselves from the idolatry imported from other nations. Their spiritual lives rotted, just like the belt. Even though they would try to hide from the Babylonians, the waters of God's judgment would still find them.

The Lord had wanted His people to hug Him tightly, just like the linen belt clung to Jeremiah's body. Instead, they removed themselves from Him. They became ruined and useless because they stopped listening to Him (13:11). In his earliest preaching, Jeremiah told the people to hear the Lord's Word (2:4). Tragically for them, they refused to pay attention to God.

As long as you are still on the earth, the Lord plans for you to be valuable and useful to Him. Do not become like the ruined and useless Judeans. Listen to the Lord and thrive.

**In what areas of your life have you resisted listening to God? How can you correct your reluctance to listen to Him?**

Day 105

## HAZARDS OF HAUGHTINESS

**Jeremiah 13:15.** *Hear and pay attention, do not be arrogant, for the LORD has spoken.*

Pride produces perils. Haughtiness has hazards. Arrogance always acquires adversity!

Jeremiah was preaching about pride. His symbolic performance with his belt warned the people that the Lord would wipe out their pride (13:9). He alerted them to the urgency of giving glory to God before He brought darkness on them (13:16). If their pride kept them from listening to the Lord, Jeremiah would weep for them (13:17).

Jeremiah used an illustration of wineskins. He said that every wineskin should be filled with wine. He knew he would draw their attention by mentioning their favorite drink, and he knew they would think his statement was obvious. Of course every wineskin should have wine (13:12)!

They were not listening. They were merely thinking about wine. They missed Jeremiah's point. Instead of drinking from the wineskins, they themselves were the wineskins. They were filled with the wine of God's wrath and the Lord would smash them against each other (13:13-14).

Jeremiah preached because there was still time for them to start listening and avoid God's judgment. If only they would not be too proud to hear! If only they would heed God's Word!

Are you listening? You should always be alert to what the Lord says to you through His Word. Maintain an attitude of hearing Him.

Are you arrogant? You might not publicly admit your pride, but privately you must examine yourself for any hints of haughtiness. Arrogant people think that they can manage their lives better than God can. Proud people do not think clearly. They are selfish with their possessions and they look condescendingly on others.

Do you know that the Lord has spoken? You probably think that He has, or else you would not be reading this. Do you know that His Word is forever true? Listen to Him today.

**What area of your life is becoming dangerously arrogant? Humbly bring it to the Lord.**

Day 106

GOODBYE KING

*Jeremiah 13:18-19. Say to the king and to the queen mother, "Come down from your thrones, for your glorious crowns will fall from your heads." The cities in the Negev will be shut up, and there will be no one to open them. All Judah will be carried into exile, carried completely away.*

During his lifetime, Jeremiah ministered under five Judean kings. He prophesied that one of them, along with the king's mother, would lose his power and go into exile. Which king was it?

Jeremiah had taken two trips to the Euphrates River (13:3-7). The length of time required for these journeys would have kept him away from King Jehoiakim for several years. Jehoiakim had wanted to arrest him (36:26). After Jehoiakim died, Jeremiah could again prophesy openly. Jeremiah directed his words toward the next king, who was only eighteen years old when he came to the throne. The youthful King Jehoiachin would have needed his mother to help him rule.

Of the five kings under whom Jeremiah lived, only Jehoiachin's mother was called the queen mother. As Jeremiah predicted, Jehoiachin and the queen mother went into exile (29:2). Most of the people in Jerusalem went with them. The cities in the Negev were shutting their gates in preparation for the Babylonian invasion. The Negev was the dry area in southern Judah. None of the walled cities would be able to withstand the Babylonians and eventually the whole nation of Judah went into exile.

Jehoiachin was a "goodbye king". He reigned for only three months, and then he left Jerusalem never to return. He lived in exile much longer than he had been a free man in Jerusalem. After thirty-seven years in exile, Jehoiachin was finally released from prison. He continued to live in Babylon the rest of his days (52:31-34).

Did Jeremiah stand in the street and wave goodbye to King Jehoiachin as the Babylonians carried him off? Did Jeremiah wave to the ten thousand others who left the city as captives? Maybe.

While he was king, Jehoiachin did evil in the sight of the Lord (2 Chronicles 36: 9). He paid the price for his sin. He apparently had not pondered the fact that each of his actions would bring corresponding results. He pushed the Lord out of his life, so the Lord pushed him out of his land. He did not seriously believe that he would always reap what he sowed. If only the king had planted seeds that pleased God!

**What specific seeds are you now sowing that will please God?**

Day 107

## Naked Prisoner

**Jeremiah 13:22. *And if you ask yourself, "Why has this happened to me?" – it is because of your many sins that your skirts have been torn off and your body mistreated.***

Jeremiah gave the people a question that they would ask themselves in the future. "Why has this happened to me?" He had just told them the terrible things that would transpire, and he knew that they would ask why.

Jeremiah had prophesied that an army from the north would carry Judah into exile. All the people would experience tremendous pain. Jeremiah personified Jerusalem as a woman, and he spoke to her about the coming disaster (13:19-21).

The words Jeremiah said to Ms. Jerusalem in this verse were literally, "It is because of your many sins that your skirts have been exposed and your heels have been violated." The ancient Hebrew language apparently had no specific words for the private parts of the human body. The Hebrews used inoffensive words to describe nakedness.

"Skirts" referred to what was under the skirts. And "heels" was a veiled term for something other than the literal feet. If skirts were removed, much more than heels would be exposed! Ms. Jerusalem would be stripped, completely from head to heels! She would not be treated like a lady. Everything would be taken away from her. She would become a prisoner of war.

In an earlier time, the Lord told Isaiah to go naked and barefoot as a prophetic picture of people going into captivity. Rather than going totally nude, Isaiah may have worn a loincloth. In any case, prisoners of war were led away with their buttocks uncovered (Isaiah 20:1-4).

Many people today will suffer just as much shame as those prisoners being led away naked. They are now prisoners of the devil (2 Timothy 2:26). They are not aware of their captivity because the god of this world has blinded them to the truth (2 Corinthians 4:4).

Jesus Christ came to set prisoners free (Luke 4:18). Following Jesus will give you confidence that you are truly liberated. Follow Him today. He will guard you from future humiliation.

**How can the Lord enable you to overcome feelings of shame that still linger from your past?**

Day 108
## CAN YOU CHANGE?

**Jeremiah 13:23.** *Can the Ethiopian change his skin or the leopard its spots? Neither can you do good who are accustomed to doing evil.*

Jeremiah was not a racist! He was not suggesting that black people should try to change their skin color. Black skin is beautiful.

Also, Jeremiah was not proposing that a leopard would be more improved without its spots! The spots and the black skin illustrated how some situations could never change. Even though scientists today can change a person's skin pigmentation, even the bravest scientist is not going to try to remove a live leopard's spots! Jeremiah's point was that chronic evildoers could not start suddenly doing good deeds. Unless they turned to the Lord, habitual sinners had no hope of changing.

The Hebrew word that is translated as "Ethiopian" is "Cushite". Cushites were tall and smooth-skinned people (Isaiah 18:2). They lived in the area that currently forms the African nations of Ethiopia and Sudan.

Jeremiah and his people had probably seen very few Cushites. Jeremiah knew a certain Cushite named Ebed-Melech (38:7-13). The Cushites' black skin would make a memorable example for the people of what could not change.

The people would not allow themselves to be changed, even though the warnings about God's judgment were unmistakable. Jeremiah alerted them that the enemy would come from the north and would inflict much pain. The enemy would humiliate them so that they would be as shamed as a woman whose skirt is stripped off (13:20-22).

The Lord would scatter them like straw in the wind, because they had chosen to forget Him. They stubbornly trusted in idols and lies. The Lord considered them to be detestable and unclean (13:24-27).

However, they would not change. They could not change. What about you?

Can you alter yourself? Do you have any particular embedded evil tendencies that you have tried to change and have failed? Do not give up. Reposition yourself closer to the Lord. He can permanently transform you for good.

**What specific moral qualities do you wish to change about yourself? Express this desire to the Lord.**

Day 109

SHAME

*Jeremiah 13:26. I will pull up your skirts over your face that your shame may be seen ....*

Jeremiah had earlier preached that the people of Jerusalem would be like a stripped female prisoner of war. Her skirts were torn off because of her many sins (13:22). The prophet used the skirt metaphor again, this time to reveal two of her major sins.

The city that Jeremiah personified as Ms. Jerusalem was guilty of adultery and prostitution. These sexual sins occurred on the hills (13:27). Since idol altars were on the hills, Jeremiah accused Ms. Jerusalem of spiritual adultery as well as physical. The people had forsaken the Lord God to worship gods. Jeremiah used this shocking punishment as a metaphor for God's judgment of those who were involved with spiritual adultery.

Ms. Jerusalem had sinned greatly. Many nations that formerly honored her would soon despise her. They would have seen her nakedness (Lamentations 1:8).

Public humiliation of prostitutes and adulteresses was an ancient custom. Other prophets explained this method of exposing the shame. All previous lovers of the guilty woman were gathered, and her nakedness was exposed to all of them (Ezekiel 16:37). Her skirts were lifted over her head (Nahum 3:5).

Another prophet wrote about this public humiliation. He was actually married to an unfaithful woman. The adulteress was stripped naked (Hosea 2:3, 10), and eventually became a slave. As an illustration of God's love, Hosea bought her back from the slave market (Hosea 3:1-2).

Many people today are like Hosea's adulterous wife and Jeremiah's Ms. Jerusalem. However, they can have hope of being purchased out of the slave market of their sins. Jesus Christ paid the price of their sins and redeemed them when He died on the cross.

Shame will come later to everyone who shamelessly rebels against God now. Those prostitutes who enjoyed displaying their nakedness will suffer disgrace when the Lord reveals their bareness. Only through Jesus, who endured the cross and scorned its shame (Hebrews 12:2), can you become free from future shame.

**Explain how Jesus' shameful death on the cross can release you from your personal struggles with shame.**

Day 110
DROUGHT

**Jeremiah 14:1.** *This is the word of the LORD to Jeremiah concerning the drought ....*

The people had not seen any rain for many months. They wept for their dried up land. The drought affected every city in Judah (14:2).

They found no water in their cisterns, so they covered their heads in grief. The farmers lost all their crops in the parched land. All the animals suffered also. The deer deserted their young because there was no grass to eat. Wild donkeys panted desperately because they could find no pasture (14:3-6).

Because of the drought, the people found themselves pleading to the Lord for help. Even though they confessed that they had sinned and backslid, they accused God of being like a stranger in the land. They presumptuously expected the Lord to come to their rescue whenever they needed His help. They accused Him of being like a confused man and a powerless warrior for not relieving the drought (14:7-9).

Even though they said words of confession, the Lord knew that they did not pray with repentant hearts. They constantly wandered from Him to other gods. Consequently, the Lord did not accept their insolent prayers. Even though they fasted and brought sacrifices to the temple, the Lord was not pleased with their superficial rituals. The drought was just the beginning of their troubles. The Lord would also bring sword, famine and plague (14:10-12).

Jeremiah tried to intercede on behalf of the people by telling the Lord that other prophets were misleading the people. These prophets preached that they would have peace and would not suffer from war or famine. The Lord answered Jeremiah by revealing that these prophets were lying. The Lord had neither sent nor spoken to them. Though they claimed to have visions from God, they preached from their deceptive hearts (14:13-14).

Drought brings famine. Even though famine is a terrible condition, spiritual famine is far worse. Spiritual famine was the concern of a true prophet who lived before Jeremiah's time. The prophet explained that a spiritual famine was a shortage, not of food, but of hearing the Lord's words (Amos 8:11).

Do not slip into a spiritual famine. Keep listening to God's Word. Paying attention to Him will keep you from worrying when a drought comes.

**What is your personal plan to prevent spiritual famine in your life?**

## Day 111
### TEARS

*Jeremiah 14:17. Speak this word to them: "Let my eyes overflow with tears night and day without ceasing; for my virgin daughter—my people—has suffered a grievous wound, a crushing blow...."*

A typical day for Jeremiah included hours of weeping for his people. When he had sleepless nights, he wept. He cried for both the current sins and the future disasters of his people.

The false prophets, who predicted that there would be no war or famine, ironically would die from war and famine. And all who had listened to their false prophecies would suffer from these two tragedies. No one would be left to bury them (14:15-16).

Those Judeans who lived in the country would die by the sword. Those who fled to the cities would die of famine. The false prophets and priests would live in exile in an unfamiliar land (14:18).

Jeremiah recorded the people's insincere prayers. They blamed God for their wound. They asked the Lord why He hated Jerusalem. They waited for the Lord to give them peace, but they claimed that He had given them only terror. They pleaded with Him not to annul His covenant with them (14:19-21).

However, they were the ones who had broken the covenant. Jeremiah therefore wept over the wound of his people. They had a spiritual injury that was terminal. They had fatally wounded themselves by rejecting God and chasing idols. Jeremiah sobbed for them.

As Jeremiah wept, it became clear that God Himself was weeping. God's heart of unlimited compassion went out to His people. He referred to His people as His virgin daughter.

How could the Lord have this attitude toward Judah, whose sins had made the nation into a prostitute? Judah was like a harlot as she pursued idols (2:20), so how could the nation now be a virgin?

Jeremiah saw Judah the way the Lord intended her to be. God had desired for the nation to be His bride (2:2). God could even recreate Judah into a virgin (31:21), but Jeremiah's people refused to cooperate. As the Lord's representative, Jeremiah wept.

**During those times when you are especially close to the Lord, what brings tears to your eyes?**

## Day 112
## RAIN

**Jeremiah 14:22.** *Do any of the worthless idols of the nations bring rain? Do the skies themselves send down showers? No, it is you, O LORD our God. Therefore our hope is in you, for you are the one who does all this.*

The Lord is the only rain sender. None of the idols had any power to send rain. Not even Baal, the storm god, could launch one drop of water from the heavens.

Sadly, Jeremiah's people thought otherwise. They brought sacrifices to the Baal idols. They believed that Baal was their chief rainmaker. Their hope should have been in the Lord.

Jeremiah preached often about the dangers of worshipping Baal. Most of the prophets spoke in the name of Baal, which was completely unprofitable to everyone (2:8). Those who sacrificed to Baal were also guilty of theft, murder, adultery and lying (7:9). Worshipping Baal caused the people to forget about the Lord (23:27). The people even burned their own children as sacrifices to Baal (19:5).

The people should have remembered their national history. Elijah had proven the powerlessness and uselessness of Baal. During a severe drought, Elijah told the evil King Ahab to bring 450 prophets of Baal to Mount Carmel. The prophets of Baal had already proven themselves incapable of producing rain, and Elijah challenged them to beg Baal to bring fire. They shouted, danced and cut themselves all day, but Baal was silent. Then Elijah drenched his altar with water and prayed to the Lord. The Lord sent fire. After eliminating all the false prophets, Elijah then prayed for rain. The Lord sent a downpour (1 Kings 18:17-46).

Jeremiah's people had forgotten about the failures of Baal. Jeremiah prayed what he wished that they would pray. He acknowledged their wickedness to the Lord, perhaps hoping that they too would confess their sin. He pleaded with the Lord to remember His covenant with the people (14:19-21).

Jeremiah confessed to God the worthlessness of idols on behalf of his people. He wanted them to acknowledge that only the Lord sends showers. What about you? Are you convinced that the Lord totally monitors the weather? Do you grow closer to the Lord during storms?

**Describe in precise detail how your hope in the Lord can increase when you observe your next rainstorm.**

## Day 113
### MOSES AND SAMUEL

**Jeremiah 15:1.** *Then the LORD said to me: "Even if Moses and Samuel were to stand before me, my heart would not go out to this people. Send them away from my presence! Let them go!"*

Moses and Samuel were two of the greatest interceders who ever lived. They both prayed for an entire nation, and the Lord listened to their prayers. Jeremiah had hoped that God would hear his prayers for the descendants of the people of Moses and Samuel. Jeremiah would be severely disappointed.

If the Lord would not give His heart to Jeremiah's people, then they were in hopeless trouble. Jeremiah would not become the powerful intercessor that Moses and Samuel were. Nobody's prayers could help.

Jeremiah was the opposite of Moses. The Lord told Jeremiah to let the people go away from His presence. In contrast, the Lord had told Pharaoh through Moses to let His people go away from their oppression in Egypt (Exodus 5:1). Jeremiah would later tell the people to put themselves under the yoke of Babylon (27:12), but the Lord used Moses to break the yoke of Egypt (Leviticus 26:13).

Jeremiah was also the opposite of Samuel. Jeremiah's people were not on record for asking Jeremiah to pray for protection from the Babylonians. The Lord had told Jeremiah not to pray for these people (7:16). In contrast, the Israelites asked Samuel to pray continually for their deliverance from the enemy. The Lord answered and saved the people from the Philistines (1 Samuel 7:8).

Jeremiah became both the Anti-Moses and the Anti-Samuel! However, the Lord's rejection of Jeremiah's people did not occur until after Jeremiah had preached for more than twenty years. Remember that Jeremiah's writings are not in chronological order. The Lord's absolute rejection of His people probably happened shortly after the fourth year of King Jehoiakim, when Jeremiah had already been preaching for twenty-three years (25:1-3). During the fourth year of King Jehoiakim, the Lord still gave the opportunity to repent and receive His forgiveness (36:1-3).

Now it was too late for Jeremiah's people. The Lord had given them many chances. They had not turned away from following the evil practices that King Manasseh (15:4) had started decades earlier. God's judgment had begun. It was too late.

**What issue do you need to settle with the Lord today, before it is too late?**

## Day 114
### THE CONTENDER

**Jeremiah 15:10.** *Alas, my mother, that you gave me birth, a man with whom the whole land strives and contends! I have neither lent nor borrowed, yet everyone curses me.*

I cringed when I heard a preacher call Jeremiah a whiner! He claimed that Jeremiah whined all the way through his book. I hope this preacher will use *Jeremiah's God* in his daily devotions and learn the truth about Jeremiah!

Jeremiah was a contender, not a complainer. He challenged everyone in his country to forsake their idols and turn back to the Lord. Unfortunately for them, they did not want to hear his message. So their attitude toward him was contentious. They, not Jeremiah, were ultimately responsible for the strife.

As Jeremiah cried out to the Lord about his frustration, he spoke imaginatively to his mother. Mothers especially feel the pain that their children feel. Jeremiah wished that he had not been born in order to spare her the pain.

Jeremiah had just preached that many mothers would lose their children in the future Babylonian destruction (15:7-9). Then he thought of his own mother. Knowing what her pain must have been because of his suffering was more than he could bear. Later he would curse the day of his birth (20:14).

The Lord first called Jeremiah when he was still in his mother's womb (1:5). Wishing that he had never been born was the same as rejecting God's plan for his life. Jeremiah had faithfully preached God's words, but the results were painful to him. Jeremiah felt like everyone was cursing him.

Jeremiah was neither a lender nor a borrower. He did not loan money at high interest rates, nor did he borrow money and make it difficult for creditors to collect. There were no economic reasons why everyone should hate him. The reasons were spiritual.

Do you sometimes feel like you are a contender with those around you? If so, is it because you are following the Lord, and they are not? Even if they curse you, remember that Jesus said you would be blessed if they persecute you because of Him (Matthew 5:11).

**Describe some recent contentions with other people that you wish to bring before the Lord now.**

Day 115

GOD'S GOOD PLANS

*Jeremiah 15:11. The LORD said, "Surely I will deliver you for a good purpose; surely I will make your enemies plead with you in times of disaster and times of distress."*

After Jeremiah poured out his heart to the Lord about how everyone was cursing him (15:10), the Lord answered him. The Lord encouraged him, which was exactly what Jeremiah needed.

There are several ways to translate and interpret this verse from the Hebrew. In the context, it seems that God answered Jeremiah directly about his situation. Even in the midst of disaster and distress, Jeremiah would manage well. The Lord encouraged Jeremiah in two areas. God promised that He would deliver him, and He promised that Jeremiah's enemies would beg him for help.

The Lord reminded Jeremiah about His promises when He first called him to be a prophet. The Lord had been forthright with Jeremiah about the difficulties that he would face. The Lord had promised him twice that He would deliver him out of his troubles (1:8, 19).

The Lord also had promised Jeremiah that his enemies would not overcome him (1:19). Jeremiah would have many enemies. They would include kings, priests and the people of his own nation (1:18).

Not only would these enemies be unable to defeat Jeremiah, they also would come pleading for assistance. For example, the evil Zedekiah asked Jeremiah for help on several occasions. He sent messengers to ask Jeremiah to pray that the Lord would cause the Babylonians to withdraw from their attack on the city (21:2). He sent messengers again to simply ask for prayer (37:3). Later, Zedekiah personally met with Jeremiah and asked him for any helpful information (38:14).

After the Babylonians destroyed the nation of Judah, a rebellious remnant of Judeans was left in the land. They came to Jeremiah to ask him to pray for them. They wanted the Lord's guidance about whether they should go to Egypt (42:1-6). They went to Egypt anyway, in disobedience to the Lord's command that Jeremiah gave to them (43:1-7). The Lord continued to display His faithfulness to Jeremiah even as Jeremiah continued to have problems.

**What difficulties are you facing today? How can God's good plans for you encourage you in the midst of your troubles?**

## Day 116
### FOUR PRAYER REQUESTS

*Jeremiah 15:15. You understand, O LORD; remember me and care for me. Avenge me on my persecutors. You are long-suffering—do not take me away; think of how I suffer reproach for your sake.*

Jeremiah's emotional tensions seemed to explode as he demanded four things from the Lord in quick succession. His attitude, however, was one of faith. He trusted the Lord to honor his prayer.

Jeremiah was in distress. He wanted the Lord to remember him, to care for him, to avenge him and to not take him away him. Jeremiah's four prayer requests were (1) remember, (2) care, (3) avenge and (4) protect.

First, Jeremiah prayed that the Lord would remember him. He wanted to remind the Lord that he had suffered much because of the ministry God had given him. Jeremiah was experiencing many difficulties in his life, and he felt like the Lord had forgotten him.

Secondly, Jeremiah prayed that the Lord would care for him. Jeremiah wanted the Lord's attention. He wanted God to take notice of his situation and to nurture him.

Thirdly, Jeremiah wanted the Lord to take vengeance on his enemies. He wanted God to pay back those who had been persecuting him. Divine revenge on enemies was a common prayer request throughout the Old Testament. Men like Jeremiah considered their foes to be God's enemies. They considered God's revenge to be important for His own reputation. Centuries later, Jesus changed the believers' prayer for vengeance when He said to love your enemies and pray for your persecutors (Matthew 5:44).

Fourthly, Jeremiah asked that the Lord would protect him. He prayed that the Lord would not take away his life. He did not want his enemies to kill him. Jeremiah had endured their many insults and threats, all for the Lord's sake.

Jeremiah told the Lord that he was suffering reproach for His sake. This was exactly what David prayed in Psalm 69:7. Both David and Jeremiah knew that their pain was directly linked to their obedience to God's calling.

Do you have some prayer requests to bring before the Lord today? You can trust Him that He understands what you need. Ask Him.

**What four prayer requests will you bring before the Lord today?**

Day 117
### JEREMIAH'S JOY

**Jeremiah 15:16.** *When your words came, I ate them; they were my joy and my heart's delight, for I bear your name, O LORD God Almighty.*

In the midst of an emotional prayer in which he lashed out about his difficult life, Jeremiah remembered the basis of his joy. Even though your life may never be as agonizing as Jeremiah's, you may have already experienced major loss. You may have lost what you felt was most dear to you. If so, you can avoid despair by letting the source of Jeremiah's joy be yours.

His joy was God's Word. He remembered the thrill of first hearing the news about the discovery of the Scriptures in the temple. He recalled the Lord's words when God first called him into ministry. Those were exhilarating moments. Jeremiah was trying to think back to those moments to help him deal with his current frustration.

God's Word was his joy because he received, ate and digested it. He let the Word transfuse his heart so that it affected his entire intellect, emotions and will. His experience was like the psalmist who wrote that God's words tasted sweeter than honey to him (Psalm 119:103).

Another reason why God's Word was Jeremiah's joy was because Jeremiah bore the Lord's name. Jeremiah often wrote that the temple bore the Lord's name. This was the only time that he referred to himself as bearing the Lord's name.

When Jeremiah preached his famous temple sermon, he said that the house that bore the Lord's name had become a den of robbers (7:11). Hundreds of years later, Jesus Christ quoted part of this verse when He chased the moneychangers out of the temple.

The quality of temple activities was extremely important, because the temple bore the Lord's name. Bearing the Lord's name meant that it belonged to God. God owned the temple. Jeremiah knew that God also owned him. It was this sense of divine ownership that brought Jeremiah great joy.

Do you ever have times when you think that you have every reason to have joy, but you simply do not feel joy at that moment? That is the tension that Jeremiah felt. Jeremiah chose to remember the joy even when he did not feel it. The joy was there, and sooner or later the feelings would return. Remember the joy!

**What specifically brings joy to your life, and how does your joy reflect God's love for you?**

Day 118

**DECLINING THE PARTIES**

*Jeremiah 15:17. I never sat in the company of revelers, never made merry with them; I sat alone because your hand was on me and you had filled me with indignation.*

Jeremiah did not go to parties. The people at these parties were those whose idea of a good time was to ridicule the Lord. Since Jeremiah was a true prophet of the Lord, they also made fun of him and mocked his message

Jeremiah was not by nature antisocial. He liked being with people. He wanted people to accept him. They didn't. He was probably wondering if there was any honor connected with being a prophet. Ever since his call to the ministry, Jeremiah had experienced much isolation from his own people. Each day was filled with loneliness. He prayed about his feelings of being isolated from people

Jeremiah complained that the Lord had filled him with indignation. No one wants to invite an angry man to a party! His indignation was caused by his message of judgment that he faithfully preached. Jeremiah was so close to the Lord that he felt the same anger that the Lord did toward people's sins. Jeremiah could not sit with blatantly evil people and laugh at their jokes!

The Lord's hand was on Jeremiah. Jeremiah knew that. However, he did not think that the Lord's hand felt like it should. The Lord is spirit. The Lord does not have literal hands. Like a strong hand forcing Jeremiah to stay where he was, the Lord impressed on Jeremiah's mind the importance of avoiding godless parties.

The Lord intended for Jeremiah's life to be different from those of most other people. Jeremiah would pursue his life apart from normal social activity. The prophet would follow the Lord's guiding hand.

There are times when the Lord calls you to be alone. Times of loneliness are a part of God's plan for you. However, you are never truly alone because God is always with you.

The Lord has a unique plan for each believer. He has a distinctive plan for you. Follow His guidance today.

**What are your current thoughts about God's unique plan for you?**

## Day 119
### JEREMIAH'S PAIN

**Jeremiah 15:18.** *Why is my pain unending and my wound grievous and incurable? Will you be to me like a deceptive brook, like a spring that fails?*

The land was experiencing a drought (14:1). The Lord had withheld rain, and the brooks were drying up. In his prayer, Jeremiah accused God of being like a deceptive brook. In other words, he called God a liar! Jeremiah's attitude was wrong!

I understand about deceptive brooks in Texas. Texans call them creeks. After a heavy rain, a Texas creek can overflow with water. If I go back to the creek a month later, it often is dried up. The creek is supposed to have water, but it deceived me.

Jeremiah felt like the Lord had been like a deceptive creek to him. He had relied on the Lord for help, but he saw no water in the celestial stream. He felt like God was an undependable resource of strength. Jeremiah had faithfully preached about God's power to others, but he was not experiencing it in his own life.

Jeremiah was expressing his most inward feelings to the Lord. He complained about his pain. Jeremiah used a Hebrew word for pain that is used only five other times in the entire Old Testament. The word is used twice in the book of Job to describe the extreme pain that Job experienced. The word means an extremely agonizing form of hurting.

Jeremiah also told the Lord about his wound. His wound was caused by identifying with the wound of the rest of his people. Jeremiah had used the Hebrew word for "wound" many times in his preaching. He preached that the people had a serious wound because they had a deadly spiritual problem. The wound also referred to all the catastrophic results of their spiritual rebellion against God.

Jeremiah certainly was honest with his feelings, but he went too far. The Lord reproved Jeremiah for his disrespectful prayer (15:19). You should not call God a deceptive brook! Jeremiah should have known better. He himself had preached that the Lord is the spring of living water (2:13).

Everyone feels pain, but you should not allow your suffering to shape your perception of who God is. God gives you living water through Jesus Christ (John 4: 10-14), and no amount of pain will dry it up!

**How can God's living water help you in your pain?**

Day 120

JEREMIAH'S CHOICE

**Jeremiah 15:19.** *Therefore this is what the LORD says: "If you repent, I will restore you that you may serve me; if you utter worthy, not worthless, words, you will be my spokesman. Let this people turn to you, but you must not turn to them."*

Jeremiah had accused the Lord of deceiving him, and now Jeremiah needed to repent. If he repented, God would restore him and continue to use him in the ministry to which He had called him. The very word that Jeremiah often used in his messages – 'repent' – was the word the Lord now directed toward Jeremiah himself.

The Lord told Jeremiah not to be like the rest of the people. The ungodly people around him had apparently influenced Jeremiah's attitude, and Jeremiah needed to repent of that attitude. Jeremiah had to learn that he must never compromise his message in order to make living among the people easier for him. He must wait for the people to turn to him, and wait for the people to turn to the Lord.

Jeremiah wrongly uttered worthless words to the Lord. He felt like he needed to tell God what he was feeling. As Jeremiah expressed his feelings, the Lord brought him to repentance and corrected his wrong thinking. After going through this experience, Jeremiah would speak worthy words even more powerfully in the future.

Worthy words are words that are precious and valuable. They are not false words of peace and security that people want to hear. The Lord had given true words to Jeremiah, but Jeremiah had grown weary from the opposition to these true words.

Words. Words are your primary communication tools. You certainly do not want to say worthless words to other people, and this is why your prayer life is so important. As you pour your heart out to the Lord in prayer about your personal pain, you might possibly say some worthless words to Him. It is better to say worthless words to God than to the people to whom you are ministering! The Lord can take your sincere and frustrated words to Him and bring about changes in your life.

If you utter worthless words to the Lord, He will likely deal with you in the same way He dealt with Jeremiah! The Lord rebuked Jeremiah (15:19), but then He gave Jeremiah some promises (15:20-21). By giving him the promises, the Lord answered Jeremiah's prayer about his pain. The Lord will also deal with you in gracious ways.

**When might you be tempted to speak worthless words?**

## Day 121
### LIKE A WALL

Jeremiah 15:20. *"I will make you a wall to this people, a fortified wall of bronze; they will fight against you but will not overcome you, for I am with you to rescue and save you," declares the LORD.*

The Lord did not give Jeremiah new promises. He repeated the promises that He gave when He first called Jeremiah. However, the Lord gave these promises to Jeremiah in a fresh way. He reminded Jeremiah of certain promises at just the right time when Jeremiah needed them.

The Lord reminded Jeremiah about His "wall" promise to him. He had promised to make Jeremiah like a bronze wall when He called him (1:18). God was still in the process of making Jeremiah into this hard wall that no one would be able to penetrate. The people were increasing their opposition to him, but they would not be able to batter the wall down. The Lord had promised that they would not be able to overcome him (1:19).

Even though he would be like a wall, Jeremiah's enemies would still attack him. He would find himself in painful and difficult circumstances. The Lord assured him that He would rescue him out of every predicament. The Lord had given Jeremiah this same promise when He first called him (1:8,19).

In addition, the Lord promised to be with him. The Lord had promised to be with him when He first called Jeremiah (1:8,19). The Lord's personal presence with His people is one of His most fantastic promises. Believers are never alone! Jesus Christ told His followers that He would be with them always (Matthew 28:20).

Like He did with Jeremiah, the Lord gives you promises that He has already given. He reminds you of a certain promise in the Bible at just the time when you need it. His promise then becomes fresh, relevant and personal. God's promises can give you confidence that you can grow closer to Him.

The Lord was with Jeremiah. If you are a follower of Jesus Christ, He is with you also. Today you face the same issue that Jeremiah did. The Lord was with Jeremiah, but was Jeremiah really with the Lord? The Lord is with you, but are you with Him? Are you aware that even though He is with you, He does not force Himself on you without your approval? Choose to be with Him today.

**In what ways is the Lord with you?**

## Day 122
### DELIVERANCE FROM EVIL

**Jeremiah 15:21.** *"I will save you from the hands of the wicked and redeem you from the grasp of the cruel."*

When the Lord first called Jeremiah, He promised the young man that He would rescue him (1:8,19). The Lord now specifically applied this promise to Jeremiah's situation. Rescuing Jeremiah meant saving him from the clutches of cruel men.

In order to be rescued, a person must first be a captive. Jeremiah would face arrest, prison and torture. During much of his life, Jeremiah's life would be in danger from ruthless men. They thought that Jeremiah's life was easily disposable. God would prove them wrong. The Lord would deliver Jeremiah every time.

Throughout his life, Jeremiah encountered many cruel people among his own Judeans. Pashhur the priest had him beaten and put in stocks (20:2). Priests and prophets under King Jehoiakim seized him and wanted to kill him (26:8). Officials under King Zedekiah lowered him into a cistern and left him to die (38:6). The Lord rescued him every time.

The ultimate deliverance would come during the Babylonian conquest. Forty years after the Lord called Jeremiah, the Babylonians destroyed Jerusalem. They killed or captured almost every Judean. Jeremiah escaped from both sword and exile, because the Lord delivered him.

God also delivered two of Jeremiah's friends. God promised both Baruch (45:5) and Ebed-Melech (39:17-18) that He would spare their lives during the Babylonian disaster. God kept His promise.

However, these were specific promises only to Jeremiah, Baruch and Ebed-Melech. The Lord does not promise long lives on earth to all of His people. Some of the most godly men and women die while they are young. The world is not worthy to have believers who live by faith in their relationship with the Lord (Hebrews 11:38).

Through Jesus Christ, God offers a greater deliverance. When Jesus taught His disciples to pray, He told them to ask the Father to deliver them from evil (Mathew 6:13). The Apostle Paul knew that God would deliver him from every evil deed and bring him safely to heaven (2 Timothy 4:18). If you are one of God's people, He will deliver you.

**From what danger do you need the Lord to deliver you today?**

Day 123
## Missing Marriage

**Jeremiah 16:1-2. *Then the word of the LORD came to me: "You must not marry and have sons or daughters in this place."***

Most people look forward to getting married. They want to experience life-long intimacy with another human being. Many want to have children.

Jeremiah's life would be different from his contemporaries. The Lord's plan for him was for Him to remain single his entire life. For a godly person like Jeremiah, singleness meant both celibacy and childlessness.

The Israelites highly valued marriage and children. At the beginning of human life on earth, God said it was not good for man to be alone (Genesis 2:18). A family with many children was considered a blessing (Psalm 127:3-6). Jeremiah's bachelorhood sharply diverged from the Judean culture and would attract widespread attention.

Jeremiah's singleness was a compelling illustration for a major theme of his preaching. By remaining unmarried, Jeremiah would escape the grief of losing a wife and children to the cruel Babylonian warriors. Jeremiah preached that entire families would die from disease, famine or the sword (16:3-4).

His singleness also became a prophecy illustration for the Messiah. Jesus Christ did not get married. Many people thought that Jesus was Jeremiah raised from the dead (Matthew 16:14).

Throughout history during certain distressing times, it has seemed wise not to marry and have a family. For example, Jesus predicted a horrible future event when many people would die. Jesus said that childless women would be the blessed ones (Luke 23:29). Also, the Apostle Paul wrote about a current distress that might cause people to avoid getting married (1 Corinthians 7:26).

Has the Lord called you to remain single? Has God prevented you from having children of your own? Do you sometimes feel like you are missing out on major happiness? Follow the Lord and His unique calling of you and you will find the deepest joy possible in this life.

**Whether single or married, how might you be encouraged about your marital status as you grow closer to the Lord?**

## Day 124
### FORGETTING FUNERALS

**Jeremiah 16:5.** *For this is what the LORD says: "Do not enter a house where there is a funeral meal; do not go to mourn or show sympathy, because I have withdrawn my blessing, my love and my pity from this people," declares the LORD.*

Jeremiah's actions caused his words to be embedded in people's minds. When Jeremiah did not attend funerals, the people wondered why. They then listened to him more attentively.

Jeremiah's lack of sympathy was a prophetic picture of future devastation. So many people would die that they would not be buried. The few who remained alive would not mourn or try to comfort each other (16:6-7). God would not grieve either.

The evil King Jehoiakim also became a prophetic illustration of Judah's bleak future. Jehoiakim died eleven years before the Babylonians destroyed Jerusalem. There was no royal funeral for him.

Jeremiah predicted that no one would lament Jehoiakim's death. Jeremiah knew that he certainly would not. He would not sing a lament for Jehoiakim like he did at Josiah's funeral. Instead, the people would throw Jehoiakim's body outside the city gates. King Jehoiakim would have a donkey's burial (22:18-19)!

Not having funerals would be a terrible way to suffer. A wise king had observed that funerals are more significant than birthdays because of what wise people can learn at them (Ecclesiastes 7:1-2). I remember that the funeral for my dad was an important time for my family and me to grieve, remember and reflect. His funeral was our final opportunity to honor his life.

If only King Jehoiakim and the rest of the people had returned to the Lord! Perhaps then God would not have withdrawn His compassion. Maybe the Lord would not have removed His peace and His blessings.

The Lord predicted that these immense losses would happen. During the days of Moses, God warned about the severe consequences of disobedience (Deuteronomy 28:15). However, Jesus Christ's death for sin changed these outcomes. Now, nothing can separate a believer from God's love (Romans 8:38-39).

**Describe how important it is for you to believe that the Lord will never remove His love.**

## Day 125
### BOYCOTTING BANQUETS

**Jeremiah 16:8.** *"And do not enter a house where there is feasting and sit down to eat and drink."*

Jeremiah did not attend dinner parties. His avoidance of banquets was another lifestyle illustration that supplemented his messages. People would ask him why he was absent from happy social gatherings, and he would tell them God's words.

Jeremiah preached that God would soon eliminate all joyful feasts from Judah. Even weddings would cease (16:9). No one would be left in Judah to celebrate anything.

The people would then ask Jeremiah why the Lord would do such a horrible deed to them. They seemed oblivious to their guilt. They asked Jeremiah what sin they had committed (16:10).

Jeremiah would answer that their ancestors committed two major sins. They forsook the Lord and His law and they followed other gods. Jeremiah's contemporaries were even more evil than their ancestors. They allowed their wicked hearts to affect every part of their lives. They did not listen to the Lord at all (16:11-12).

Their sin would have grave consequences. The Lord would send them out of their land. They would become exiles in a foreign nation famous for its multitude of gods. There they would have opportunities to serve other gods day and night (16:13).

While Jeremiah still had their attention, he would also give them a message of hope. In a future day, the Lord would bring His people back to the land. Their return from the nation in the north would replace the exodus from Egypt as the popular story to tell (16:14-15).

Restoration! At the time of his choosing, God always reestablishes His people. He often restores within a short period of time. When I traveled alone in the Soviet Union, I longed to leave that country and be restored to my family. I did and I was!

However, many reunions will not occur until after life on earth ends. Jeremiah's joyful feasting did not resume until heaven. You can rely on the Lord of all restorations, either for the short term or the distant future.

**What do you trust the Lord to restore for you in the future?**

Day 126

## WHAT GOD SEES

**Jeremiah 16:17.** *My eyes are on all their ways; they are not hidden from me, nor is their sin concealed from my eyes.*

The God whom Jeremiah knew sees everything. If people try to hide themselves, God still sees them (23:24). The Lord clearly observes all the deeds of every person on earth (32:19).

God saw the sin of the Judeans, and He knew that they had littered His land with vile idols (16:18). So He sent for enemy armies who would be like fishermen and hunters. The fierce foreign soldiers would fish for the Judeans and then they would hunt for them. They would hunt for them in every mountain, hill and crevice (16: 16).

God is spirit (John 4:24), so He does not have literal eyes. But He sees absolutely everything. My young grandchildren used to think that covering their eyes with their hands made it impossible for anyone else to see them! They had to learn that God always sees them.

Because God knows all, Jeremiah could trust Him to be his refuge during times of distress. God sees each time of distress before it comes, and He can provide sufficient protection. Jeremiah could depend on the Lord to be his strength and his fortress (16:19).

Because God sees everything, He knows about each idol. In Jeremiah's day, God saw the thousands of gods that the Judeans made. He asked a rhetorical question about whether people make their own gods. The answer was "yes", but the things they made with their hands were not really gods (16:20).

Because God sees everything, He knows exactly what to teach everyone. Jeremiah preached that the Lord would teach His people about His power. Knowing about His power would convince them about the greatness of His name (16:21).

God not only sees what you see, He also sees everything that you cannot see. The Lord sees everything in your future, so there is no need for you to consult astrologers, futurists or seers. Do not turn to gods that are not really gods! God not only knows everything about your future, He also will be your fortress as you face the challenges of the future.

**How does the fact that God sees everything affect the intimacy of your relationship with the Lord?**

## Day 127
### UNGODLY GODS

**Jeremiah 16:20.** *"Do men make their own gods? Yes, but they are not gods!"*

Jeremiah preached against idols throughout his long career. By using both a rhetorical question and an emphatic exclamation, he summarized two important points about idols. (1) Idols are man-made. (2). Idols are useless.

Jeremiah's generation probably excused their idolatry in the same way that people do today. "The idols make me feel so much better." "The idols help me think about God." "Using idols, I can worship God better."

It is also tempting to dismiss idols as mere distractions from all that is real. They can entertain us and give us a break from the hardships of life. No! Idols are extremely dangerous. Idols keep people from knowing God. The Scriptures warns against having foolish thoughts about idols.

Everyone who trusts in idols will also become like them (Psalm 135:14-18). Idols can be easily destroyed (Isaiah 37:19). Idols see nothing and understand nothing (Isaiah 44:18). God's anger burns against idols (Hosea 8:4-6).

In the context of Jeremiah's uncomplicated statement about gods, he said that the Judean people had polluted the land with their vile images. They had filled God's land with repugnant idols. Ironically, these false gods did them no good (16: 18-19).

Because of their idolatry, Jeremiah preached that Judah's sin was engraved with a flint point on their hearts. One particular idol that they worshipped was the Asherah pole. If called upon to be witnesses against their parents, the children would remember the poles. They would remember climbing the high hills with their parents to worship this goddess (17:1-2). If the people in Jeremiah's day had kept centennial celebrations, they might have commemorated eight hundred years of having the goddess Asherah in their culture! Eight hundred years before Jeremiah, Moses had warned the people about Asherah (Exodus 34:13).

Many centuries after Jeremiah lived, idol makers heard the Apostle Paul teach that gods made by human hands were not gods at all. The idol makers' careers were at stake! They claimed that their profession would lose its good name (Acts 19:26-27)!

**Name a present-day idol that could give you economic prosperity. Ask the Lord for strength to reject that idol.**

Day 128

SHRIVELED

*Jeremiah 17:5-6. This is what the LORD says: "Cursed is the one who trusts in man, who depends on flesh for his strength and whose heart turns away from the LORD. He will be like a bush in the wastelands; he will not see prosperity when it comes. He will dwell in the parched places of the desert, in a salt land where no one lives...."*

Jeremiah preached extensively about the spiritual condition of the human heart. He grieved over people whose hearts turned away from the Lord and trusted only in human beings. The best that Jeremiah could say about such people was that they were like a shriveled bush in the desert. Far worse, such people fall under the Lord's curse.

How sad that the hearts of the Judeans turned away from the Lord! Jeremiah had warned that the Judeans' sin was engraved on their heart (17:1). He cautioned that the heart is deceitful and incomprehensible (17:9). Only the Lord can search the heart and judge each person's deeds (17:10).

When I traveled around the Dead Sea in Israel, I saw nothing but bleak desert. Vegetation could not grow in the salty land. Those plants that tried to grow were shriveled bushes.

The salty wasteland near the Dead Sea would remind Jeremiah's listeners of Sodom and Gomorrah. The Dead Sea was the location where these cities once existed. The citizens of these cities were examples of people who looked to man for strength.

The Lord judged these cities by raining down burning sulfur. Everyone in Sodom and Gomorrah died. Even the plants were destroyed. Lot's wife looked back at the ruins of Sodom and Gomorrah and she became a pillar of salt (Genesis 19: 24-26). That area became known as the salt land.

The Hebrew word for the desert bush is similar to the word for "curse". Those who listened to Jeremiah would easily remember this wordplay every time they saw a shriveled shrub. They would remember that the bush illustrated God's curse on those who depend on man for strength.

Do not be like a shriveled bush in the wilderness! Guard your heart so that you do not turn your trust toward what humankind can do for you. Trust in the Lord and He will give you unlimited strength.

**What specific changes should you make immediately in order to avoid a shriveled life?**

Day 129
HAPPY TRUST

**Jeremiah 17:7.** *But blessed is the man who trusts in the LORD, whose confidence is in him.*

People wonder if Jeremiah was a happy man. Did he receive the Lord's blessing even as he gave this promise of blessing to others? Could the weeping prophet also be the happy prophet?

Certainly Jeremiah trusted in the Lord, living by faith amidst an ungodly culture. He did not depend on his society to give him happiness. The Lord was his delight.

One way that the Lord blessed Jeremiah was by giving him friends. His friends shared his devotion to the Lord and they helped him during times of difficulty. Among his friends were King Josiah, loyal Baruch, courageous Ebed-Melech and the influential Ahikam.

Also, Jeremiah was blessed because he knew his life purpose. He knew what God had called him to do. The Lord blessed him by giving him a long life so that he could fulfill his God-given goals.

Jeremiah had a fascinating life. His ministry took him on extensive journeys throughout his nation of Judah. (One of the ways that the Lord has blessed me is my extensive travel throughout Texas!) Jeremiah probably traveled to Babylon. He spent the last years of his life in Egypt. In the city of Jerusalem where he lived much of his life, he knew every street and every landmark.

Above all, God blessed Jeremiah by giving him a close relationship with Himself. In contrast to his own life, Jeremiah observed the disastrous results when his political leaders did not trust the Lord. Kings Jehoiakim and Zedekiah placed their confidence in earthly powers. King Jehoiakim rebelled against Babylon (2 Kings 24: 1) while trusting that Egypt would send help. He died in dishonor. King Zedekiah also trusted in Egypt's help against Babylon. He discovered that Egypt was a useless ally.

Jehoiakim and Zedekiah proved to be fools for not trusting the Power over all powers. They lost the chance to be blessed. They never knew true happiness.

What about you? Does your walk with God bring you assurance that He is blessing you? Would you describe yourself as a happy person?

**In what specific ways is your current level of trust in the Lord bringing you happiness?**

Day 130

FRUITFUL

**Jeremiah 17:7-8.** *"But blessed is the man who trusts in the LORD, whose confidence is in him. He will be like a tree planted by the water that sends out its roots by the stream. It does not fear when heat comes; its leaves are always green. It has no worries in a year of drought and never fails to bear fruit."*

Jeremiah preached that all those who trust in the Lord will be blessed (17:7). Those who place their confidence and hope in Him are like trees. These trees have been transplanted to a new location by a river bank so that their roots can reach deep into the water. These trees are unworried by heat or drought. Their leaves remain green and the trees bear fruit.

Jeremiah's people needed to hear this message. Jeremiah warned them that they had forsaken the Lord, who is the fountain of living water (17:13). They associated trees with their pagan altars on the high hills (17:2). Jeremiah wanted to change what a tree symbolized for them. He wanted them to trust in the Lord and be like a tree that is rooted in the living water.

The symbol of a tree is similar to the one in Psalm 1. The psalmist described the daily activity of a person who trusts in the Lord. That person meditates on His law day and night (Psalm 1:2). Sadly, the Judeans in Jeremiah's day had rejected the Lord's law.

The land was in drought (14:1-6), so the people would be interested in hearing about water. Jeremiah had experienced his own spiritual drought when he prayed that he felt that the Lord had been like a deceptive brook to him (15:18). Jeremiah now testified that he was trusting in the Lord. He was again experiencing the fountain of living water. Jeremiah was like a sturdy tree looking forward to being fruitful.

The tree produces fruit in its appointed time (Psalm 1:3). When I studied forestry in college, I learned that different species of trees have different periods of time during which they yield fruit. A certain pine tree produces its seeds only every two years and it does not yield any fruit at all during its early years.

Jeremiah did not experience much fruit from his ministry for many years. He preached for twenty-three years and the people did not pay attention to him (25:3). The appointed time for his fruit had not yet arrived. The fruit of Jeremiah's life now includes many centuries of believers who have matured because of his writings.

**In what ways are you like a fruitful tree in your relationship with the Lord?**

Day 131
## HEART PROBLEM

**Jeremiah 17:9.** *The heart is deceitful above all things and beyond cure. Who can understand it?*

Jeremiah's words shatter the popular belief that human beings are basically good. His words crush the concept that people are essentially decent and moral. His words should cause you to wonder about people who say that they speak to you from the bottom of their heart!

Jeremiah was a prophet, not a physician. He did not preach about the specific organ that pumps blood to the rest of the body. He preached about the inner spiritual life. The heart represents all that a person really is. The heart directs all words and actions that a person says and does. From the heart flow the springs of life (Proverbs 4:23).

Jeremiah knew that the human heart is the most devious thing on earth. He admitted that his own heart needed healing (17:14). He preached that the heart of the entire nation was hardened with sin (17:1). This sin problem causes hearts to turn away from the Lord (17:5).

Centuries later, Jesus Christ also spoke about the depravity of the human heart. He said that deceit comes from within a person. He taught that dishonesty comes out of a person's heart. Along with deceit, every other evil thought and deed originates in the human heart (Mark 7:20-23).

A deceitful heart is a heart that tells lies to you. Dishonesty is deeply imbedded in the human heart. People feel great pain when they are misled and betrayed by their own hearts.

The heart's deception is a terminal condition. Lies and deception keep feeding on themselves and increasing. The heart's sin leads to death (Romans 6:23).

The heart is incurable. No human therapy can heal it. Only the Lord can permanently help the human heart.

You do not know your own heart. Do not trust it. Look to the Lord and seek Him with all of your heart. Allow God to change your deceitful heart.

**How are you allowing the Lord to deal with your deceitful heart?**

## Day 132
## WHAT GOD KNOWS

**Jeremiah 17:10.** *"I the LORD search the heart and examine the mind, to reward a man according to his conduct, according to what his deeds deserve."*

Jeremiah had asked a question about the human heart, and the Lord immediately answered it. Jeremiah had asked, "Who can understand it?" The Lord answered that He alone comprehends the heart.

The Lord knows everything that you do everyday. The Lord also knows everything that you think as you do everything you are doing. You can hide your thoughts from everyone but God.

There is even more that the Lord knows. He knows everything that you have the potential to think and do. That is what it means for the Lord to examine your heart. He knows your motives as you think and speak and act. The Lord knows all about your individual self. He will give to each one according to what that person has done. He will either commend or condemn you and me.

The public has such a fixation on tolerance today. The god they are creating in their own image is a tolerant one. Their god could never condemn anyone. Tolerance is easy for a god who is ignorant of all the facts!

Jeremiah's God never remained in ignorance or passive tolerance. Jeremiah kept warning the people that the Lord would bring decisive judgment on their city. The coming disaster would be a completely merited sentence on them.

Human judges and courts deal with many evil deeds, but they cannot accurately discern human hearts. You must never judge another's motives. Only God knows that person's heart and intentions.

The fact that the Lord knows all of your thoughts, words and deeds should gravely disturb you! However, the true believer who by grace through faith has escaped the coming judgment will see a positive point. The Lord will give rewards according to what a believer has done. Today, do your thoughts, words and deeds reflect your faith in the true God? If so, you are having another day that will give you confidence when you see the Judge!

**Describe your level of confidence in standing before God the Judge in the future.**

## Day 133
### THRONE OF GLORY

**Jeremiah 17:12.** *A glorious throne on high from the beginning is the place of our sanctuary.*

Jeremiah's life was difficult and he knew that he needed a sanctuary. A sanctuary is a place where one goes to find protection and peace. The best sanctuary is a place where a person can come close to God.

Jeremiah believed that his sanctuary was a throne. When he prayed, he went to God's throne. He knew that he went directly into God's presence.

One of the best known verses about prayer in the Bible is Hebrews 4:16, which encourages believers to go before the throne of grace. When the Righteous Branch came and died for the sins of the world, God's glorious throne became available to all believers. Today, believers can kneel before the throne of grace and glory.

The word *glory* is best suited to describe only the Lord. Jeremiah's God is the God of glory. One characteristic of His glory is brightness. Even the brilliant Texas sunshine that I enjoy pales in comparison to the splendor of God's radiant throne of glory.

God's throne is *on high.* Even though God's throne in the temple was on "the high mountain of Israel" (Ezekiel 20:40), the glorious throne is even higher. Jeremiah preached that the Lord would bring judgment from on high (25:30).

God has been on His throne from the beginning. God's throne existed long before Moses constructed the throne on the Ark of the Covenant, and long before that throne was put into the tabernacle and later into the temple. Even before time began, the Lord has ruled from His glorious throne.

Today, the believer's sanctuary is Jesus Christ. Jesus replaced the temple as the sanctuary for His people (John 2:19-21). Jeremiah knew that God would replace the temple.

The residents of Jerusalem considered the temple to be their only sanctuary. Later, they would be devastated when their temple burned to the ground. They should have listened to Jeremiah, whose sanctuary was higher. Bow now before that glorious throne.

**How should your relationship with God involve His throne?**

## Day 134
### MOCKING THE PROPHET

**Jeremiah 17:15.** *They keep saying to me, "Where is the word of the LORD? Let it now be fulfilled!"*

Jeremiah preached clearly and often that armies from the north would conquer the nation of Judah. Where were these enemy soldiers? They were not even on the horizon! Since Jeremiah's prophecy had not happened, the people ridiculed him by asking, "Where is the word of the Lord?"

They implied that Jeremiah was a false prophet. The Lord had given Moses the standard for measuring true and false prophets. Moses wrote that if what a prophet says does not come true, it proves the Lord has not spoken through him (Deuteronomy 18:21-22).

Jeremiah took this untrue criticism to the Lord. He told God about how the people were mocking him. He was like the sons of Korah, who heard the jeers, "Where is your God?" (Psalm 42:3)

He had praised the Lord for being his hope and his fountain of living water. He told the Lord that everyone who renounced Him would be shamed. Those who turned away from Him would be written in dust (17:13). He prayed for healing and praised God (17:14). He described to the Lord how faithful he had been (17:16).

Jeremiah's self-appointed critics did not wait long enough before they started their derision. They finally stopped ridiculing Jeremiah when Nebuchadnezzar became king of Babylon. From then on, they knew for certain that the Babylonians were a threat.

During his first year as king, Nebuchadnezzar attacked Jerusalem and captured some of the most gifted young men (Daniel 1:1-4). The Babylonians came back eight years later and took captive ten thousand citizens of Jerusalem (2 Kings 24:14). They came back eleven years after that, and they totally destroyed Jerusalem (2 Chronicles 36:17-20).

Jeremiah's prophecy came true. He knew it would, but the mocking was still painful for him. Mockers deride true prophecies even today. Scoffers especially ridicule the promise that Jesus Christ will come again (2 Peter 3:3-4).

**How can ridicule from others draw you closer to God?**

## Day 135
### DIVINE SHELTER

**Jeremiah 17:17.** *Do not be a terror to me; you are my refuge in the day of disaster.*

Persecution was taking its toll on Jeremiah. People were questioning whether Jeremiah was a true prophet (17:15), even though he faithfully served as the spiritual shepherd that the Lord called him to be (17:16). Greatly anguished, he took his problems to the Lord in prayer.

The people doubted Jeremiah's prophecy about the future day of disaster. He had said that the whole nation would be devastated (4:19). They preferred to listen to all the other prophets who preached peace (6:13-14).

He asked the Lord not to be a terror to him. He knew that when the time of the great disaster on his nation arrived, he would be in grave danger. Jeremiah pleaded with the Lord to spare him on that terrible day.

Jeremiah feared that God would leave him defenseless before his enemies. He wanted the Lord to send terror instead to his persecutors (17:18)! He had asked the Lord to bring shame on all those who had forsaken Him (17:13).

There is no record of God's response to this prayer. Jeremiah asked the Lord not to be a terror to him, and the Lord was silent. God's people today also experience His silence. We ask Him for help, and we hear nothing. Sometimes we feel like the psalmist who begged God not to remain quiet (Psalm 83:1).

During times of God's silence, we can reflect on what God has already said. The Lord had previously promised Jeremiah that He would deliver him from his persecutors (1:19). Jeremiah could only trust that the Lord would also rescue him from the foreign armies on the day of disaster.

Jeremiah had earlier affirmed that the Lord was his refuge in time of distress (16:19). The Psalms give continuous testimony of God being a refuge for His people. David took refuge in the Lord (Psalm 11:1). God was both refuge and strength for the sons of Korah (Psalm 46:1).

The Lord can be your refuge also. He can shield you from danger and rescue you from peril. He can be your shelter in time of need, which is quite often!

**In what ways has the Lord been your refuge during the past month?**

## Day 136
### SABBATH DAY

*Jeremiah 17:21. This is what the LORD says: "Be careful not to carry a load on the Sabbath day or bring it through the gates of Jerusalem."*

People and donkeys were carrying many selections of food and merchandise through the city gates. Even though this was the Sabbath day, the crowds were just as large as any other day. Everyone was thinking about buying and selling, except for one man. One man was only observing. Then he began preaching.

Jeremiah told the people that the Sabbath day should be kept holy, just like the Lord had commanded their ancestors. Keeping the Sabbath meant not carrying any loads out of their houses. It meant not doing any work on the Sabbath day (17:23).

One of the reasons that the Lord commanded His people to keep the Sabbath was so that they would remember that He had freed them from slavery in Egypt (Deuteronomy 5:6). Of the Ten Commandments, the command to keep the Sabbath was the only one that emphasized that the Lord had commanded it (Deuteronomy 5:12). Therefore, keeping the Sabbath became a symbol for keeping all of God's laws.

If only the people of Judah in Jeremiah's day had kept the Sabbath! Their obedience would have brought blessing to their city. Future kings and many people would always go through the city gates. Instead of bringing merchandise for their own financial gain, they would bring sacrifices to the Lord (17:25-26).

Centuries later, the religious leaders of Jerusalem went to the opposite extreme. They had added their own rules to the Sabbath command. Jesus spoke against these human-made rules. He said that God had made the Sabbath for the people's benefit (Mark 2:27).

Jesus Christ claimed to be the Lord of the Sabbath (Matthew 12:8). The issue for you is the same as it was for Jeremiah's people – obedience. They were obligated to obey the Sabbath law. You must obey a higher law, the law of Christ. Jesus rose from the dead on the first day of the week, not on the Sabbath day. Most believers today meet to worship Him on Sunday, not on the Sabbath. Are you worshipping and obeying the Lord of the Sabbath?

**How would you describe the level of your obedience to the Lord during the past week?**

## Day 137
### VISITING THE POTTER

**Jeremiah 18:1-2.** *This is the word that came to Jeremiah from the LORD: "Go down to the potter's house, and there I will give you my message."*

Jeremiah probably had made other plans for his day. He had not intended to visit the potter's shop. But when the Lord spoke, Jeremiah listened. The prophet began his day by walking down to see the potter. The Lord wanted Jeremiah to think about potters and pots that day.

The potter's house was in a lower part of the city. Jeremiah had to walk down to it. One of the lower city gates was called the potsherd gate, which led to the valley of Ben-hinnom (19:2). Ben-hinnom was the city dump where broken pottery was discarded.

Ben-hinnom was also the location of pagan altars where people burned their children (7:31). It was a horrible place for a spiritually sensitive person like Jeremiah to go near. As he went to the potter's house, he walked down metaphorically as well as geographically.

For now, Jeremiah ignored the child sacrifices and concentrated on the potter's work. The ancient Palestinians produced plenty of pots. These pots keep many archaeologists employed today!

The potters contributed an invaluable product for Jeremiah's people. Clay pots enabled them to store food and drink and to transport it when necessary. However, the potters were more than mere container suppliers. They were artists. They made pots of beauty as well as usefulness.

When Jeremiah arrived at the potter's house, the Lord spoke to him further. He compared the clay in the potter's hand to Jeremiah's people. The people were in His hand (18:6).

You also are like clay in the Lord's hand. You are like a clay pot that the Master Potter made. If you are a believer, you are an earthen vessel that holds the treasure of the gospel (2 Corinthians 4:7). The Lord plans to give you a hope and a future (29:11). He will complete the good work that He began in you (Philippians 1:6). As you respond positively to Him, He will patiently shape you according to His superb plan.

**What is a specific way that God has shaped you during the past month to give you hope?**

## Day 138
## ON THE POTTER'S WHEEL

*Jeremiah 18:3-4. So I went down to the potter's house, and I saw him working at the wheel. But the pot he was shaping from the clay was marred in his hands; so the potter formed it into another pot, shaping it as seemed best to him.*

When Jeremiah went down to the potter's house, the potter was busy working at his wheel. The wheel was made of two stones. The potter formed the clay on a flat upper stone. A vertical pole connected this stone to a lower stone, which the potter pushed with his foot. As the wheel turned, the potter shaped the spinning clay into a pot.

The potter was not merely relaxing with a ceramic hobby! He was working. He had vocational purpose as he labored to produce pottery.

The potter had high standards for his work. As Jeremiah watched, the potter was not satisfied with the way his clay pot was turning out. So he mashed the clay into a lump and started over. What went wrong? Jeremiah did not mention the exact problem. The clay possibly had impurities and the potter decided to make a less pretentious pot.

As Jeremiah kept watching, the potter re-shaped the pot. The potter finally created exactly what he wanted. He had total control over what he did with the clay. He had made pottery during his entire lifetime. He knew his trade.

Like the potter and his clay, the Lord has absolute control over His people. If the Lord is grieved over the impurities of some of His human beings, He can mash them into lumps and re-shape them.

God was the original potter. He formed the first man out of the dust of the earth (Genesis 2:7). The Hebrew word for "form" is the verb of the word for "potter". The Lord shaped the first man like a potter shapes his clay. Jeremiah heard this same word when the Lord first called him. The Lord had formed Jeremiah in his mother's womb (1:5). He gave Jeremiah an image to remember the rest of his life. The Master Potter had shaped Jeremiah into the unique person that the Lord wanted him to be.

The potter is not equal with the clay (Isaiah 29:16). God is the potter and you are the clay (Isaiah 64:8). The Lord made you and fashioned you, so you should pray to Him for understanding about Him and you (Psalm 119:73).

**In what ways is God shaping you into His vessel?**

## Day 139
### GOD'S REPENTANCE AND YOURS

**Jeremiah 18:7-8.** *"If at any time I announce that a nation or kingdom is to be uprooted, torn down and destroyed, and if that nation I warned repents of its evil, then I will relent and not inflict on it the disaster I had planned."*

Jeremiah had earlier preached that God does not change His mind (4:28). God in His sovereignty perfectly planned His programs before the beginning of time. God has no need to make any changes to His purposes.

Yet, an amazing phenomenon happens when a person repents to the Lord. Even though God had already planned to punish, He withholds His punishment. It would seem that when a person repents, God then repents.

Repentance is a human attribute. The Lord used other human attributes to help people know Him better, but He unmistakably used human descriptions in a figurative way. For example, Jeremiah saw the Lord's hand reach toward his mouth (1:9). Obviously the Lord does not have hands or any other human anatomy parts, because God is spirit (John 4:24).

The Lord has never done any evil and never will. He does not repent in the way that He invites nations and individuals to do. God has nothing from which to repent (Numbers 23:19).

When God repents, He does not change His values or standards. He is unchanging in all of His attributes. The Lord's repentance involves His consistent response to changes in a nation or individual. If people continue in their disobedience, the Lord sends judgment. If they choose to obey Him, the Lord sends grace. The Lord is the consistent Judge and the unswerving Grace Giver. People choose which attribute of His that they experience.

The Lord told Jeremiah at the outset of his ministry that he would announce uprooting and destruction as well as building and planting (1:10). The Lord uproots and destroys in His holy justice, but He builds and plants in His gracious love. Jeremiah was giving His nation a clear choice. Judah could still choose to repent.

You also have a choice. Are you living with the God of grace and growing closer to Him? Or do you need to repent of recent disobedience?

**In your own words, what does God do when people repent?**

## Day 140
### CHANGE

**Jeremiah 18:11.** *Now therefore say to the people of Judah and those living in Jerusalem, "This is what the Lord says: Look! I am preparing a disaster for you and devising a plan against you. So turn from your evil ways, each one of you, and reform your ways and your actions."*

God told Jeremiah to preach a message of repentance. Because of their wicked living, the people were on the receiving end of an approaching disaster from the Lord. The Lord was in opposition to them.

The Lord was preparing a catastrophe for them. The Hebrew word that is translated as "preparing" literally means "shaping". It is from the same root word that is translated as "potter". Jeremiah's pun reminded that people that the Master Potter can do as He wishes with the clay of Judah.

When the Lord called Jeremiah into the ministry, one of the first words He spoke to Jeremiah was the "potter" word. As the divine potter, the Lord told Jeremiah that He knew Jeremiah even before He "shaped" Him in his mother's womb (1:5). Jeremiah's experience was that God continued to shape him during his entire life.

Jeremiah chose to let the Potter continue to form him. He wanted the people to make the same decision. They needed to repent from their sinful idolatry and turn to the Potter who would make them into godly people.

This sermon, which began with Jeremiah's walk to the potter's house (18:2), was one of Jeremiah's most forceful messages. However, even the most powerful sermon does not automatically change human hearts. The Lord cautioned Jeremiah about how the people would respond.

The Lord warned Jeremiah that the people would stubbornly continue to live according their own plans. The people of Judah wanted to live independently from God's ways. Their hearts were evil (18:12).

If the people would change their ways, they could avert the approaching calamity sent by the Judge. Their reforms would need to be radical. What about you? Do you need to change?

**As you grow closer to the Lord, what does He want you to change about your way of life?**

## Day 141
### SLANDER

**Jeremiah 18:18.** *They said, "Come, let's make plans against Jeremiah; for the teaching of the law by the priest will not be lost, nor will counsel from the wise, nor the word from the prophets. So come, let's attack him with our tongues and pay no attention to anything he says."*

Jeremiah faced opposition and persecution throughout his life. He knew that he had indispensable words from the Lord, but his enemies claimed that Jeremiah was unnecessary. They spread lies about him.

The city already had an ample number of priests, sages and prophets. The priests were experts in the Scriptures. The sages were popular advisers on quality living. The prophets (who were false) gave alleged words from the Lord that the future was looking progressively better. So the people thought they had no need for Jeremiah.

The people had placed inflated confidence in their religious institutions. They thought that the law could never leave the priests. They believed that wisdom could never depart from the wise men. They insisted that words from the Lord could never disappear from the prophets. They considered Jeremiah's words to be divisive and threatening to their institutions. So they tried to destroy Jeremiah's career by slandering him. They attacked him with their tongues. They spoke untrue and unkind words about Jeremiah. His persecutors words must have hurt Jeremiah deeply.

I too felt pain when a man in my church told lies about me. I did not know how to deal with his tongue and with the other people whom he was influencing. One day I realized that he was just like Diotrephes.

Diotrephes was a church member who had a pride problem. He rejected the words of the Apostle John. Diotrephes even said evil and accusing words against John (3 John 9-10).

Diotrephes apparently did not realize that his only future was church discipline. Many churches today have a Diotrephes. Do not be surprised if a Diotrephes says wicked words about you, especially if you are actively serving the Lord.

Jeremiah did not record all the slanderous words against him. These words have been lost forever, as they deserved to be. If you are living for the truth, others will probably tell lies about you. Their lies will not endure eternity. Ignore the lies and grow closer to the God of truth.

**How does the Lord help you when you are slandered?**

## Day 142
### SMASHED

**Jeremiah 19:1-2.** *This is what the LORD says: "Go and buy a clay jar from a potter. Take along some of the elders of the people and of the priests and go out to the Valley of Ben Hinnom, near the entrance of the Potsherd Gate. There proclaim the words I tell you .…."*

Jeremiah had collected many illustrations for his preaching by watching a potter at work (18:1-2). The Lord told Jeremiah to return to the potter and make a purchase. Jeremiah's symbolic actions were beginning to cost him money! Later he would pay seventeen silver shekels for some seemingly worthless land (32:9).

Jeremiah took some of the political and religious leaders with him. After buying a clay pot, he led them out of the city through the Potsherd Gate. Once they were in the Valley of Ben Hinnom, Jeremiah began preaching to them.

Jeremiah warned that the Lord would soon bring terrible ruin on their nation. Why? They had turned their backs on the Lord and had embraced foreign gods. They had built altars to these gods and even sacrificed their children to them (19: 3-5).

As Jeremiah preached to them in the Valley of Ben Hinnom, the Judeans saw his message vividly illustrated for them. Perhaps they actually saw a child being sacrificed. The Valley of Ben Hinnom was where they had built the pagan altars on which they burned their children (7:31).

Jeremiah predicted that the valley's name would be changed. Its new name would be the Valley of Slaughter, because many would die there by the swords of enemy soldiers. So many people would die that they would not be buried. Birds and beasts would eat their bodies (19:6-9).

Then, while the leaders watched him, Jeremiah broke his new clay jar. He told them that their nation and their city would also be smashed beyond repair. The Lord would smash every house in which people worshipped idols (19:10-13).

Jeremiah then left the valley and returned to the city. He went to the temple court where more people could hear his message. He explained that the reason the Lord would destroy their city was because they were stiff-necked and disregarded His words (19:14-15). The Lord would smash a nation in order to rebuild a people who would seek Him.

**What has the Lord smashed in your life to bring you closer to Him?**

## Day 143
### IN THE STOCKS

*Jeremiah 20:1-2. When the priest Pashhur son of Immer, the chief officer in the temple of the Lord, heard Jeremiah prophesying these things, he had Jeremiah the prophet beaten and put in the stocks at the Upper Gate of Benjamin at the Lord's temple.*

Pashhur had the credentials of an esteemed religious leader. He was second only to the high priest. He was the top security officer in the temple. Everyone trusted him to keep the peace in the courts of the Lord's house. However, Pashhur's true character exploded when he heard Jeremiah preach.

Pashur heard Jeremiah say that God would bring calamity on the city. In Pashhur's mind, this message was intolerable! Pashhur then unleashed his hysterical anger toward Jeremiah. Jeremiah the prophet was punched and beaten.

Pashhur's persecution of Jeremiah was a direct result of Jeremiah's preaching. Pashhur should have responded to the prophet's sermon with a priest's heart. He should have reacted with a warm godly heart and recognized Jeremiah's words as from the Lord. Instead, he responded foolishly. He attacked God's spokesman viciously.

Pashhur persecuted Jeremiah by an entrance to the Lord's temple that faced toward the land of the tribe of Benjamin. The Upper Benjamin Gate faced north. Ironically, the Babylonians would come from the north (1:14-15) and take Pashhur into captivity (20:6).

Pashhur put Jeremiah in the stocks. Jeremiah felt the pain. He was still hurting from the beating when he felt his body wrenched to fit into the tortuous stocks. His neck, legs and arms were tightly confined in this barbaric device. Perhaps he remembered that his ancestor Joseph had his neck and feet bound in shackles (Psalm 105:18). Hundreds of years after Jeremiah's day, religious leaders violently assaulted Jesus Christ (Matthew 26:67).

To be persecuted by those who claim to be religious leaders is emotionally painful. Jeremiah still bore the pain when he later prayed and lamented to the Lord (20:7-18). Have you experienced persecution pain? You can endure like Jeremiah did. When you find yourself twisted into the stocks of life, pray candidly to the Lord who can comfort you.

**How can the Lord encourage you during times of persecution?**

## Day 144
### RIDICULE

**Jeremiah 20:7.** *"O Lord, you deceived me, and I was deceived; you overpowered me and prevailed. I am ridiculed all day long; everyone mocks me."*

Jeremiah earlier prayed that the Lord had deceived His people (4:10). However, it became clear that the false prophets were the ones who were deceiving. Jeremiah had also accused the Lord of being like a deceptive brook, and the Lord told him to repent from these worthless words (15:18-19). Therefore, it is odd that Jeremiah would again accuse the Lord of deception.

It is probable that Jeremiah was not accusing the Lord of deceiving him. Jeremiah used a different Hebrew word from the one that he used to describe the Lord as a deceptive brook. The word he used in this verse can be translated in other ways. Other possible translations of the word are "persuade", "seduce" and "entice".

Jeremiah was referring to the time when the Lord called him to be a prophet. The event of his call should help determine the best meaning of the word he used in this prayer. The Lord did not deceive Jeremiah when He called him. God explained to him what his ministry would be (1:7-10) and how extensive the opposition would be to his ministry (1:18).

Jeremiah voiced his doubts about God's call (1:6), but the Lord powerfully answered his objections. As Jeremiah thought back to his call, he felt like the Lord took advantage of his youthfulness. The Lord "enticed" him to become a prophet.

The people opposed Jeremiah, just like the Lord said they would. However, Jeremiah was not prepared for their intense and prolonged ridicule. They had a new name to add to their list of derogatory names for Jeremiah. They now called him "Terror on Every Side" (20:10).

This was too much for Jeremiah to bear, and he correctly brought the matter to the Lord. He had faithfully preached the Lord's message that Pashhur would be called "Terror on Every Side" (20:3). The people now mocked Jeremiah with this name.

It hurts to be ridiculed. I remember being deeply wounded when people called me "naïve" for trusting God! The ridicule did not stop Jeremiah from serving the Lord. After he prayed, Jeremiah grew stronger.

**How have you been ridiculed in the past? If you are still in pain from this, pray now to the Lord about it.**

## Day 145
### JEREMIAH'S GREATNESS

*Jeremiah 20:8. Whenever I speak, I cry out proclaiming violence and destruction. So the word of the Lord has brought me insult and reproach all day long.*

The reason that Jeremiah preached violence and destruction was because he faithfully preached the words that God gave him. Jeremiah's people had rejected the Lord, and Jeremiah was telling them the truth about their future. Jeremiah had to suffer the consequences of his preaching. The people rejected and insulted him.

No one likes a steady diet of insults and criticisms. When Jeremiah had all he could take, he turned to the Lord in prayer. He did not pray out of weakness, grumbling about his reproach. No. He brought his problems to the Lord and trusted that God would strengthen him.

You should not call Jeremiah merely "the weeping prophet". His life was much more than mere tears. He was not weeping when he prayed about his own problems. He wept for his people, not for himself.

Also, Jeremiah was not a whiner. A whiner is someone who complains in a high-pitched, childish, annoying way and doesn't stop. Jeremiah was no whiner! He brought his complaints to the Lord, but then he went out to face the people again.

In addition, Jeremiah was not effeminate, which is how the author of a book I read described him. Jeremiah prayed often, but praying is not just an activity for women. The more Jeremiah prayed, the tougher he became as a man.

Jeremiah was one of the great men in the Old Testament, because he was faithful. Many people seem to forget that Jeremiah was not a fictional cartoon character. Jeremiah was not an eccentric found in the comic strips! He was a real man who is now with the Lord. You will meet him in heaven.

I have a warning for those of you who may have told others that Jeremiah was nothing more than a weeping, whining woman-like weakling! Someday when we are together in heaven, I am going to introduce you to my friend Jeremiah. And Jeremiah will look at you with his penetrating eyes and ask, "Now what was that you said about me?"

**What changes do you need to make in the words you say about other believers, since you will meet all of them when they are with the Lord in heaven?**

## Day 146
### FIRE IN MY BONES

**Jeremiah 20:9. But if I say, "I will not mention him or speak any more in his name," his word is in my heart like a burning fire, shut up in my bones. I am weary of holding it in; indeed, I cannot.**

Jeremiah had complained that the Lord overpowered him (20:7). Jeremiah realized the reason why. He had internalized the Lord's words, and now he knew that the Lord had overpowered him through His Word.

Many people today think that the Lord's words are a product of fanciful and imaginative tradition, with no reality behind them. In contrast, Jeremiah knew the reality of God's Word. The fire was not his imagination. He really knew the fire of God's Word!

God's Word is the communication from the only true Lord of the universe. Jeremiah had received this Word, and it blazed within him until he preached it to others. He could not keep quiet.

The Lord had earlier told Jeremiah that He was making His words that were in Jeremiah's mouth into fire (5:14). Jeremiah's fire was a glaring distinction from the wordless winds of the false prophets (5:13). He knew that God's word was like a fire (23:29). Jeremiah knew that the Lord had sent fire into his bones (Lamentations 1:13).

Many of God's people have experienced the burning of His Word in their hearts. When the resurrected Christ talked to two of His disciples on the road to Emmaus, their hearts were burning. They said that their hearts burned within them while Jesus spoke with them on the road and explained the Scriptures to them (Luke 24:32).

They had intense feelings as they heard God's Word from the lips of Jesus. I also have had certain moments when I felt that certain portions of the Bible were like fire within me. His fire changed me.

What about you? Is God's Word in your heart? Do you have fire in your bones?

**How much of God's Word do you have in your heart?**

## Day 147
### LIKE A MIGHTY WARRIOR

Jeremiah 20:11. *"But the LORD is with me like a mighty warrior; so my persecutors will stumble and not prevail. They will fail and be thoroughly disgraced; their dishonor will never be forgotten."*

In Jeremiah's day, many boys wanted to be warriors when they grew up. The same is true today. Even when my son was very young, he wanted to be in the military. He told me that he wanted to defend his country against evil in the world.

As Jeremiah prayed, he thought of the Lord as a warrior. God was his powerful champion. God was his hero at the front of the battle line. God was the one who terrified Jeremiah's enemies.

Jeremiah undoubtedly remembered that Moses had told God's people that the Lord would fight for them (Exodus 14:14). Moses led the people in singing that the Lord is a warrior (Exodus 15:3). The Lord went before them and fought for their benefit (Deuteronomy 1:30).

Jeremiah remembered the simple words "with me." The Lord was not on a distant battlefield, He was right there with Jeremiah. When the Lord first called Jeremiah, He had promised to be with him (1:8). The Lord promised to deliver Jeremiah from those who would fight against him (1:19). None of Jeremiah's enemies could successfully battle a prophet who had the Mighty Warrior on his side!

Jeremiah had confidence that the Lord would disgrace his enemies. In fact, the Lord did bring dishonor to Jeremiah's persecutors. Some of their names are recorded, and Bible readers have remembered their shame for more than 2500 years!

Who can forget the disgrace of Pashhur, who had Jeremiah beaten and put in the stocks? The Lord renamed him "Terror on Every Side" (20:1-6). Or who can forget the dishonor of Hananiah, who falsely predicted the exile would be for only two years. Jeremiah predicted that Hananiah would die that very year. He did (28:17)!

If you are a true believer, you are in a battle. You are fighting against the devil (Ephesians 6:11), the evil system of this world (1 John 2:15) and even your own sinful nature (Galatians 5:24). You cannot fight alone. God is with you like a mighty warrior.

**Describe how you are using God's armor (Ephesians 6:10-18) in your current spiritual warfare?**

## Day 148
### SMUG

**Jeremiah 21:1-2.** *The word came to Jeremiah from the LORD when King Zedekiah sent to him Pashhur son of Malkijah and the priest Zephaniah son of Maaseiah. They said: "Inquire now of the LORD for us because Nebuchadnezzar king of Babylon is attacking us. Perhaps the LORD will perform wonders for us as in times past so that he will withdraw from us."*

Jeremiah did not arrange his writings in chronological order. He wrote here about an incident that happened during the last two years of Judah's last king. Jeremiah gave an example of how the Lord answered his prayer about his shameful situation.

Jeremiah had poured out his heart to the Lord about how he spent all his time in shame (20:18). Jeremiah told the Lord that everyone cursed him (15:10). The Lord changed Jeremiah's circumstances. Now under King Zedekiah, Jeremiah had the respect that he deserved.

The king regarded Jeremiah as a godly prophet. He sent a politician and a priest to ask Jeremiah to pray. The king wanted an accurate report of what Jeremiah said, so he sent an evil politician and a good priest. Pashhur the politician was evil because he later persuaded the king to put Jeremiah in a cistern (38:1-6). Zephaniah the priest had been sympathetic to Jeremiah as false prophets attacked Jeremiah (29:21-32).

What did King Zedekiah want from Jeremiah? The king wanted Jeremiah to pray that the Babylonians would retreat. Zedekiah knew that it would take a miracle, but he was desperate. His advisors probably reminded him that the Lord had rescued His people many times in the past by doing amazing wonders.

Jeremiah gave the two messengers the Lord's answer. The Lord Himself would fight against Zedekiah and his people. A terrible plague would kill many people and animals in the city. The Babylonians would capture King Zedekiah and all those who survived the famine and the war (21:3-7).

Poor Zedekiah! He did not receive the word from Jeremiah that he wanted. Zedekiah was an evil king who did not humble himself before Jeremiah. He hardened his heart against the Lord (2 Chronicles 36:12-13). The king had so much pride that he did not even come to Jeremiah himself. He sent two messengers. Zedekiah was smug. You can be better!

**How can your relationship with God prevent you from being smug?**

## Day 149
### SHALLUM'S LEGACY

**Jeremiah 22:11.** *For this is what the LORD says about Shallum son of Josiah, who succeeded his father as king of Judah but has gone from this place: "He will never return."*

Jeremiah's message of judgment became personal. A specific king named Shallum would be carried off into exile. He would never return to his homeland.

King Shallum was also known as Jehoahaz. The people of Judah made Jehoahaz king when his father Josiah died. Jehoahaz was twenty-three years old when he became king. He reigned in Jerusalem for only three months. The king of Egypt removed him from power and imposed a heavy tax on the land. The Egyptian king then made Jehoahaz's brother king over Judah and took Jehoahaz as a prisoner to Egypt (2 Chronicles 36:1-4).

Jehoahaz died in Egypt (2 Kings 23:34). It was a sad ending for a man who could have carried on the same spiritual reforms that his father Josiah had done.

What legacy can a man leave if he has only three months? Three months was plenty of time for King Jehoahaz to stir up mischief. The Lord's evaluation of him was that he did evil in His sight (2 Kings 23:32).

Jehoahaz's mother's name was Hamotol. She was the daughter of another Jeremiah (2 Kings 23:31). Perhaps Jehoahaz's mother and grandfather were named because they were the ones who influenced him to sin.

Jehoahaz was not Josiah's first-born son (1 Chronicles 3:15). When Josiah died, the people from the surrounding countryside favored Jehoahaz more than his older brothers and made him king (2 Kings 23:30). Perhaps they saw some admirable traits that were lacking in Josiah's other sons. Jehoahaz would disappoint them.

Jeremiah's ministry began eighteen years before Jehoahaz became king. Jehoahaz would have heard about Jeremiah and his preaching since the age of five. If only he had listened to Jeremiah!

Jehoahaz was an evil king who reigned for only three months. In contrast to Jehoahaz, how can you live in the next three months to leave a mark for good? Three months of intimacy with the Lord is the best way to spend ninety days.

**How can Jehoahaz's legacy be a warning to you?**

Day 150
JOSIAH'S LEGACY

Jeremiah 22:15-16. *"Does it make you a king to have more and more cedar? Did not your father have food and drink? He did what was right and just, so all went well with him. He defended the cause of the poor and needy, and so all went well. Is that not what it means to know me?" declares the LORD.*

In contrast to his evil sons, the good King Josiah governed with justice. While his evil son Jehoiakim spent lavish sums on cedar for his palace, the good King Josiah's economic priorities had been helping the poor and needy.

After Josiah had been king for thirteen years, the Lord called Jeremiah into ministry (1:2). During Jeremiah's early years of ministry, he saw all of Josiah's religious reforms. The reforms were impressive.

Josiah insisted that the temple be repaired. During the restoration, a copy of Moses' law was discovered. Shaphan the scribe read the book to King Josiah. Josiah tore his clothes in response, because he knew that his people had disobeyed God's words. Then Josiah called a public meeting in the temple courtyard for all the people. He read the Scriptures to them. Josiah made a covenant before the Lord that he would obey Him. All the people also agreed to the terms of the covenant.

Josiah then tried to change his nation's culture by tearing down the idols. He took all the idolatrous priests off of the government parole. He went down to the Valley of Hinnom where children were sacrificed. This was the wicked ancient equivalent of abortion! The king shut down the altars. Then Josiah reinstated the Passover. The Passover feast commemorated the death angel's passing over the Hebrew houses in Egypt, because of the lamb's blood on the doorposts. Keeping the Passover would help Josiah's people look forward to the coming Lamb of God.

The day that Josiah died was a tragic date in Judah's history. He was killed in a battle with the Egyptians. All the people of Judah and Jerusalem mourned Josiah's death. Jeremiah composed laments for him. It became customary for all the male and female singers to sing Jeremiah's lamentations in honor of Josiah (2 Chronicles 35: 23-25).

What is your spiritual legacy? How will you be remembered on earth after you leave? If you leave behind an honorable spiritual legacy, people will know that your relationship with the Lord was genuine and intimate.

**In what specific ways are you building a spiritual legacy?**

Day 151

JEHOIAKIM'S LEGACY

*Jeremiah 22:18. Therefore this is what the LORD says about Jehoiakim son of Josiah king of Judah: "They will not mourn for him: 'Alas, my brother! Alas, my sister!' They will not mourn for him: 'Alas, my master! Alas, his splendor!'"*

Jeremiah's words about Jehoiakim's fate did not bode well for the king. No one in Jerusalem would grieve for him. They would feel no sadness for their king's death. Jeremiah had written a lament for King Josiah's funeral, but there would be no lament for Jehoiakim.

There was no hope for King Jehoiakim. The Lord knew that Jehoiakim would never turn back to Him. Jeremiah prophesied that Jehoiakim's death would be downright dishonorable. His funeral would be like a donkey's! His body would be dragged away and thrown outside the gates (22:19). In contrast to the enduring mourning for Josiah (2 Chronicles 35:25), no one would lament Jehoiakim's passing.

What was so bad about Jehoiakim that he would have such a sub-human burial? The answer is clear when you accept the Lord's evaluation of him. Jehoiakim did evil in the sight of the Lord (2 Kings 23:37). He committed horrible sins (2 Chronicles 36:8). Jeremiah endured eleven years of Jehoiakim's wicked reign. He preached that Jehoiakim always looked for ways to increase his wealth by dishonest means. Jehoiakim's heart was set only on fraud, oppression and murder (22:17).

Jehoiakim built a lavish palace for himself, with cedar panels and spacious upper rooms, by forcing his people to work for him as slaves. He did not pay them for their labor (22:13-14). With such an expensive palace, perhaps he was trying to be like King Solomon! Sadly, he lacked Solomon's wisdom. He deprived his own people of their basic human rights. King Jehoiakim's political agenda could be summarized in one word. Injustice!

Jehoiakim killed a godly prophet named Uriah (36:23). Later he tried to arrest Jeremiah (36:25). Jehoiakim showed his contempt toward God by burning a scroll that contained God's words (36:22-24).

You can learn from this example of a bad man. You can avoid being like Jehoiakim by rejecting the evil tendencies that he had. You can grow closer to the Lord whom Jehoiakim rejected.

**What can you learn from Jehoiakim's evil life?**

Day 152
## FALSE SECURITY

**Jeremiah 22:20.** *"Go up to Lebanon and cry out, let your voice be heard in Bashan, cry out from Abarim, for all your allies are crushed."*

In the midst of prophecies against kings Jerusalem, Jeremiah gave a warning to the entire city. He invited all the citizens of the city to go with him on an imaginary trek. He wanted them to climb and shout from three different regions of Palestine.

Jeremiah told them first to go up north to Lebanon. Beautiful forests grew on the mountains of Lebanon. Centuries earlier, King Solomon had built the temple using cedars from Lebanon (1 Kings 5:2-6). Solomon also used the trees from Lebanon to build his own palace (1 Kings 7:1-2).

After Lebanon, Jeremiah told the city people to go to Bashan and to cry loudly there. Bashan was also rich in natural resources. Its pastures fed many sheep, goats and cattle (Deuteronomy 32:14). Many oak trees grew in Bashan (Ezekiel 27:6).

The third place from which Jeremiah told the people to shout was Abarim. Moses had climbed one of the mountains of Abarim, Mount Nebo, so he could view the promised land. He died on that mountain (Deuteronomy 32:49-50).

When I traveled to Jordan, I also stood on the peak of Mount Nebo. I saw the same magnificent panorama that Moses saw. Unlike Moses, I did not die there!

Why did Jeremiah tell the people to cry out from these three locations? From Lebanon and Bashan in the north and from Abarim in the south, they were to lament the loss of their lovers. They would soon lose every political ally and every foreign idol that they kept in Jerusalem.

They relied on alliances and idols instead of the Lord. They depended on economic prosperity, symbolized by Lebanon and Bashan. They trusted in their religious history, revering Moses when he stood on the mountain in Abarim. They relied on the security of their own city, described as Lebanon nested in the cedars (22:23). They trusted in everything except God. Do not misplace your trust as badly as they did!

**How can you trust totally on the Lord and keep from hoping in false securities?**

## Day 153
### REJECTED RING

**Jeremiah 22:24.** *"As surely as I live," declares the LORD, "even if you, Jehoiachin son of Jehoiakim king of Judah, were a signet ring on my right hand, I would still pull you off."*

Jeremiah had prophesied about King Jehoiakim's death and burial (22:18-19). Now the prophet spoke about Jehoiakim's son. The son would be the next king, but he would not be encouraged by Jeremiah's words about him!

Jehoiakim's son was known by three different names. His royal name was very similar to his father's. The son was called Jehoiachin. King Jehoiachin was also known as Jeconiah and also as simply Coniah.

As king of God's people, Coniah was supposed to be like a signet ring on the Lord's right hand. A king would use his signet ring to show his authority and to stamp official documents. Lamentably, Coniah proved useless as God's ring.

He was worthless because he chose to do evil in the sight of the Lord (2 Kings 24:8-9). Therefore, the Lord would give Coniah over to the very people whom he feared. The Babylonians would make him their captive (22:25).

He would spend the rest of his life in Babylon. The Lord would toss both Coniah and his mother into Babylon, almost as easily as I throw a rotten apple into our compost pile! Coniah would never return to his beloved nation of Judah (22:26-27), even though the false prophets said he would. One false prophet claimed that Coniah would return within two years, along with all the other exiles (28:1-4).

The false prophets were wrong. Coniah was a rejected ring that would be hurled into Babylon to stay. God is the Heavenly Heaver! He pitches people from one nation to another, but He throws them tenderly. Coniah did not die during his forced march to Babylon.

Has the Lord hurled you into a place you do not like? Are you learning the lessons that He is teaching you in that place? As you learn, you can be confident that He is with you both in your Jerusalem and in your Babylon.

**What did the Lord teach you during a time when you were in a place where you did not want to be?**

## Day 154
### DISCARDED DISH

**Jeremiah 22:28.** *"Is this man Jehoiachin a despised, broken pot, an object no one wants? Why will he and his children be hurled out, cast into a land they do not know?"*

The Lord called King Coniah an unwanted piece of pottery. Why was Coniah undesirable? He was like a broken bowl, a marred mug, a damaged dish, a vitiated vase! He was useless as king over God's people.

Small fragments of pottery occasionally surface in our yard, after lying forgotten and unnoticed for many years. My wife and I collect the pieces as we find them. I picked up a potsherd recently and said, "This is Coniah!"

A broken pot is the opposite of powerful royalty. After a short three-month reign, Coniah would never again sit on the Jerusalem throne. He would never see his palace again.

Is this man Coniah a despised pot? Many people in the land of Judah would have answered, "No." They did not considered Coniah to be undesirable pottery. They wanted Coniah to be their king even after the Babylonians took him away.

So Jeremiah tried to get their attention by exclaiming, "O, land, land, land, hear the word of the Lord (22:29)!" They needed to hear about God's judgment of Coniah. Jeremiah pleaded with men and women of the land to learn from Coniah's fate.

Coniah would never return to be king, and neither would any of his sons. Because he would have no royal heirs, Coniah as a king would be childless (22:30), even though he eventually had seven sons (1 Chronicles 3:17-18).

Imagine yourself as one of the people of the land. Would you have listened to Jeremiah's ardent plea? Even though the Lord had been with King David and his many descendants, He was now withdrawing His fellowship from Coniah. Divine fellowship was gone, because Coniah had abandoned the Lord in his heart. Would you have followed Coniah?

**Explain how Coniah's doom is a warning to you about your relationship with the Lord?**

## Day 155
### THE RIGHTEOUS BRANCH

**Jeremiah 23:5.** *"The days are coming," declares the Lord, "when I will raise up to David a righteous Branch, a King who will reign wisely and do what is just and right in the land."*

After living under series of evil kings, Jeremiah received some encouraging news from the Lord about an upcoming king. A future descendant of King David would finally rule with wisdom and justice. He would be the righteous Branch.

The evil kings had been like irresponsible shepherds. They had destroyed and scattered the sheep entrusted to them. They had been "anti-shepherds"! The Lord would punish all those evil shepherds (23:1-2).

At the end of the exile (and at the end of all exiles), the Lord Himself will gather His flock. He will bring them back from every country where they had lived as exiles. Also, the Lord will choose good shepherds to take care of them. God's people will then live fearlessly and not be scattered again (23:3-4).

When this righteous Branch finally reigns, the people will live in safety. The entire nation will be saved. The Branch will be called "The Lord our Righteousness" (23:6).

Ironically, the evil King Zedekiah's name meant "The Lord my righteousness". Zedekiah was unrighteous, so his name was a sham. Only the Branch would have the authentic righteousness from God.

Who is the righteous Branch? Who is the one who is called God's servant the Branch (Zechariah 3:8)? Who is the Lord's servant who will bring justice to the nations (Isaiah 42:1)? Who is the one called David's horn (Psalm 131:17)? Who is the Seed of the woman (Genesis 3:15)? Who is the King whom God the Father called "Son" (Psalm 2:6)?

Jesus Christ! Jesus is the root and offspring of David (Revelation 22:16). Only Jesus is the Righteousness from God (1 Corinthians 1:31). Only Jesus makes your relationship with God possible.

**Why would you not be able to have a relationship with God without the righteous Branch, Jesus Christ?**

## Day 156
### BROKEN HEART

*Jeremiah 23:9. Concerning the prophets: "My heart is broken within me; all my bones tremble. I am like a drunken man, like a man overcome by wine, because of the LORD and his holy words."*

Jeremiah shared about his broken heart. Like countless others (perhaps including you) who have experienced broken hearts, Jeremiah was emotionally devastated. Because he loved his people so much, he was overcome by too much pain. He was like a drunken man as he thought about his spiritually-wayward people. He felt weak. His bones shook.

The people strayed from God because they followed the false prophets. These prophets were adulterous in their neighborhoods and wicked in the temple (23:10-11). Their messages came, not from the Lord, but from false gods named Baal (23:13).

Because they followed the false prophets, the people would suffer. Indeed, they were already suffering. Everything in their land had withered from the drought (23:10).

Jeremiah felt like his bones were as dry as the land! He suffered with his people. Yet he knew that the drought was merely a token of the coming judgment on his people. God would punish them by sending darkness and disaster (23:12). Jeremiah was heart-broken because the people would not listen to the Lord's holy words of judgment.

When I was a young man, I heard a 20th Century Jeremiah named Francis Schaeffer speak about being broken-hearted. He warned against the false prophets of our day. He talked sadly about our ungodly culture.

Then he suddenly looked at all of us and asked, "Why aren't you weeping!?" He said that this was a time for tears. He sharply reminded us that our lost world was under divine judgment.

What about you? Are you heart-broken over the disorientation of your society? Are you dismayed over the popularity of the false prophets?

**What teachings of the false prophets of today are breaking your heart? How can their teaching steer you closer to the true Lord?**

## Day 157
### SODOM AND GOMORRAH

**Jeremiah 23:14.** *"And among the prophets of Jerusalem I have seen something horrible: They commit adultery and live a lie. They strengthen the hands of evildoers, so that no one turns from his wickedness. They are all like Sodom to me; the people of Jerusalem are like Gomorrah."*

The religious leaders had utterly failed in their ministry, and Jeremiah had the task of exposing them. They were adulterers, meaning that they were unfaithful both to God and to their wives. They were liars. They preached lies and lived their entire lives in deceit. And they encouraged evildoers instead of helping these bad people turn away from sin.

What would the Lord do with religious leaders like these? Through Jeremiah, the Lord gave His judgment of them. He considered them to be as bad as the people of Sodom and Gomorrah.

How terrible were the people who lived in Sodom and Gomorrah? One of Jesus' disciples wrote that the people of Sodom and Gomorrah were perverted and sexually immoral ( Jude 7). Jesus Himself referred to the day that the Lord rained down fire and sulfur and judged the residents of Sodom for their sin (Luke 17:29).

In Jeremiah's day also, Sodom and Gomorrah were bywords for the worst sins and the severest judgment. The pages of Scripture vividly describe the lives and deeds of the inhabitants of Sodom and Gomorrah. Abraham's nephew Lot had chosen to live in Sodom.

Two angels in the form of men came to Sodom one evening, and Lot greeted them and invited them to his house. That night, all the men of the city surrounded the house. They called out to Lot and insisted that he bring out his two guests so that they could have sex with them. Lot refused and even offered his two daughters to them. The men of the city then threatened Lot with bodily harm (Genesis 19: 1-9).

Do not live in deceit and unreality as you seek closeness with God. You can never have intimacy with the Lord if you are trying to live in sexual intimacy with anything or anyone other than your husband or wife. Flee from the thought patterns of Sodom and Gomorrah!

**How does Satan tempt you to immorality and what action will you take to protect yourself from this evil?**

Day 158

THE GOD WHO TRANSCENDS

**Jeremiah 23:23-24.** *"Am I only a God nearby," declares the Lord, "and not a God far away? Can anyone hide in secret places so that I cannot see him?" declares the Lord. "Do not I fill heaven and earth?" declares the Lord.*

The prophets who opposed Jeremiah did not understand God. They seemed to follow the popular thinking that the Lord was localized. They thought that the Babylonian gods lived in Babylon and the Lord's place was in Jerusalem.

Jeremiah's enemies were wrong about God. They claimed to be prophets, but God had never spoken to them. They kept teaching that God would bring peace. Their life style should have tipped the people off that their words were false. They were unfaithful to their wives and they supported evil programs. A true prophet would not have ignored God's commandments.

The Lord spoke clearly about Himself by asking a series of questions. The Lord did not design the questions to be answered merely with "yes" or "no". The questions can stretch your perception of God, if you let them. The first question inquired about the nearness and distance of God. Was God only the national deity of Judah? Or was God also in remote areas where Judeans would never set foot?

God is far beyond the theological ideas of small thinkers. God is personal, but He is also worldwide. He is close-by, but He is also transcendent. He is with His people, but He is also above and beyond the universe.

The Lord asked a second question. Think about it. Have you ever tried to hide from God? Does God always know where you are? Is there anything that God does not know about you? Do you have secret places where you try to forbid God from entering?

The Lord asked a third question. Ponder the implications. Is God really everywhere? Is there any place that is outside His dominion? Are there places where His presence is somehow limited? Do "heaven and earth" include all possible space in which God exists?

God is not a computer disk that you can activate when you need Him! The Lord is not your employee to whom you can dictate your plans! He occupies the heavens, which includes everything out there that you can both see and not see!

**How does the fact that God fills heaven and earth help you trust Him with your problems?**

**Day 159**

**FIRE AND HAMMER**

**Jeremiah 23:29.** *"Is not my word like fire," declares the Lord, "and like a hammer that breaks a rock in pieces?"*

The Lord's Word is like a fire. This fire performs two actions. It refines the good and consumes the evil. Fire purifies by separating the valuable from the worthless. God's Word would divide Jeremiah's messages from the dreams of the false prophets.

Pray that your pastor today will take courage in the refining work of the Word. Pray that preachers and teachers today will deliver Biblical messages. Pray that the Lord will eliminate their vain chatter and leave only His pure word in the listeners' minds.

Jeremiah himself had encountered this truth. He had experienced God's Word blazing in his heart. God's Word also consumes what is evil. God's Word would burn up all the false words said in opposition to Jeremiah.

Where are the sermons of the false prophets? What has happened to the messages of Hananiah, Shemaiah, and Ahab son of Kolaiah? I suppose the sermons of the false prophets finally smoldered into ashes under the scorching Babylonian sun.

The Lord's Word is also like a hammer. Do not think of a small tack mallet! Imagine a heavy sledgehammer that can crack boulders. God's Word breaks everything that is against Him. In contrast to the false prophets' calming words, God's Word shatters all tolerance toward sin. The Word of the Lord smashes pretension and self-centeredness. It pulverizes deception.

When I was a boy, I came home from school one afternoon to find huge piles of concrete slabs in our yard. My dad had ordered truckloads of rubble from a torn-up street. His plan was to use broken pieces of concrete to landscape our yard. He even bought a new sledgehammer for me to use to help him with this project. I was not happy!

Every afternoon and on weekends I got my sledgehammer and pounded on our concrete piles. Gradually the piles grew smaller. Now I smile as I remember those rock piles. My dad and I took the broken concrete and built beautiful terraces.

Let the Lord's Word be your personal stonecutter. Allow God to hammer on your stony character. He can break you and then use you to landscape His kingdom!

**How are you responding to God's refining process in your life?**

## Day 160
### PLAGIARISM

**Jeremiah 23:30.** *"Therefore," declares the LORD, "I am against the prophets who steal from one another words supposedly from me."*

The prophets were not preaching words from the Lord. They were preaching their own ideas based on what they thought the people wanted to hear. However, many prophets were not even preaching their own ideas. Instead of working to compose their own false words, they were stealing false words from their colleagues!

The false prophets were racing each other down to the lowest part of the pit of spiritual darkness. Rejecting the true Lord had put them on the road to the bottom. Plagiarizing untrue words about the Lord was as foolish as false ministry gets!

In contrast, Jeremiah's sermons were completely true. He did not compose his messages in order to pander to what the people wanted to hear. Nor did he steal words from those false prophets who did. Jeremiah preached the same thoughts as the true prophets who preceded him.

Much of what God told Jeremiah to preach had already been preached. Many of Jeremiah's words were the same as God's words to Moses. Jeremiah quoted extensively from what Moses wrote in Deuteronomy. Jeremiah also used some of Hosea's sermons in his messages.

Was Jeremiah the same as the false prophets, plagiarizing from other prophets? No! The Lord repeated three times that He was against those prophets (23:30-32). Not only did they steal words from others, they also falsely claimed that the words were from the Lord. The false prophets were not helping the people in any way. They were unprofitable prophets!

The only reason that Jeremiah was a professional prophet was because God called him. At the time of the call, God told Jeremiah that he would speak those words that the Lord commanded (1:7). God put His words in Jeremiah's mouth (1:9). He promised to be with Jeremiah and to deliver him from all who opposed him (1:19).

Using material from the Bible is not plagiarism. The Lord intends for His words and ideas to be communicated world-wide. Use His words freely and relentlessly today.

**Which of God's words is He bringing to your memory today that He wants you to abundantly use in your life?**

## Day 161
### Two Baskets of Figs

**Jeremiah 24:1.** *After Jehoiachin son of Jehoiakim king of Judah and the officials, the craftsmen and the artisans of Judah were carried into exile from Jerusalem to Babylon by Nebuchadnezzar king of Babylon, the LORD showed me two baskets of figs placed in front of the temple of the LORD.*

It was a bleak day in Jerusalem when the Babylonians banished thousands of its residents. After seeing such a massive captivity, Jeremiah must have been especially sensitive to the vision the Lord showed him. Jeremiah saw two baskets of figs. One basket contained gorgeous figs, ready to be eaten. The other basket was filled with rotten figs, fit only for the compost pile!

The figs were in front of the temple, apparently as an offering to the Lord. Perhaps instead of a vision, Jeremiah saw real figs as he walked past the temple. If so, the basket of rotten figs was a commentary on the low level of attitudes toward worship. No true worshipper would offer God the very worst!

After showing him the baskets, the Lord then explained to Jeremiah that the figs symbolized two groups of people (24:5-8). The good figs were the thousands of people whom Nebuchadnezzar deported from Jerusalem. They were on their way to Babylon, where the Lord would make them good in His sight. In Babylon they would turn to the Lord.

However, those who stayed behind were like the bad figs. They could still go to the temple, but they did not really care about the Lord. They liked to stand in front of the temple, just like the basket of rotten figs!

My wife and I have a fig tree in our garden. For many years, it did not produce figs. One year the tree had only two figs. One fig looked ripe, so we picked it. To our horror we saw that dozens of ants were in it! We could not eat such an awful fig. We did everything we could to keep ants off of the other fig.

We finally picked the good fig. My half of the fig was the tastiest imaginable. After waiting for so long, we highly valued that one good fig.

Live in the basket of the good figs. Allow others to value what you can give them. Only the Lord can make you into a good fig. Let Him ripen you today.

**How do you determine the kind of fig you are becoming?**

Day 162

GOOD FIGS

**Jeremiah 24:5.** *"This is what the Lord, the God of Israel says: 'Like these good figs, I regard as good the exiles from Judah, whom I sent away from this place to the land of the Babylonians....'"*

When our fig tree was mature enough to produce abundant figs, my wife and I sadly observed that birds pecked and ate most of them. After several seasons of lost figs, we finally covered the tree with a net. The birds could not get through the net to eat our figs.

We saw the figs on our tree as good, and we wanted to protect them. In the same way, the Lord saw His people living as exiles as good. He wanted to shield them from the harmful "birds" of life.

The first step toward the Lord's protecting the "good fig" people was His removal of them from Judah. Jerusalem and Judah were under God's judgment. The Lord took them from harm's way to the shelter of the Babylonian empire.

The Lord would look out for them while they were exiled in Babylon. Using the same metaphors that God gave Jeremiah when He first called him (1:10), God would plant them and build them up. He would eventually bring them back to the land (24:6).

Using one of Jeremiah's favorite words, "heart", the Lord promised to give the good figs a heart to know Him. They would return to the Lord with their whole heart (24:7). God would use the exile to correct their spiritual heart problem.

Jeremiah preached often about problematic hearts. Their hearts were stubborn and evil (3:17). They had rebellious hearts (5:23). Their hearts kept them from obeying the Lord (11:8).

Solving the heart issues would enable the people to grow close to the Lord. God's intention for the good figs was having a close relationship with them. He would be their God and they would be His people (24:7).

Most of the people were not good when they went into exile. Once they were in Babylon, they had the opportunity to become His good people. Likewise, you were not good when you came by faith to Jesus Christ. He is in the process of making you good.

**How is your relationship with the Lord consistent with His intentions for the good figs? What aspect do you wish to ask Him for help?**

Day 163
Bad Figs

**Jeremiah 24:8.** *"But like the poor figs, which are so bad they cannot be eaten," says the Lord, "so will I deal with Zedekiah king of Judah, his officials and the survivors from Jerusalem, whether they remain in this land or live in Egypt...."*

Our fig tree grew too large, and I had to prune the branches. I cut too many branches, and now we have no figs at all. But in my opinion, no figs are better than bad figs! The Lord's perspective was different. He allowed the bad figs to keep living for a while.

The bad figs that remained in Jerusalem were opposed to Jeremiah's visual sermon about the two kinds of figs. The people in Jerusalem considered themselves to be the good and lucky ones. They thought that the exiles in Babylon could not have relationships with God. They could not worship in the Lord's temple in Jerusalem.

The bad figs left in Jerusalem thought they were safe. They were wrong. Jeremiah named King Zedekiah specifically as a bad fig. He and all who remained in Jerusalem would meet their demise. Trying to flee to Egypt would not save them.

Even though the bad figs remained in the land that the Lord had given to their ancestors, their stay was temporary. God would do away with them. He would send the sword, famine and plague against them (24:10).

Instead of defeating the bad figs then, the Lord gave them ten more years. Why? Why were ten more years of bad figs better than no figs?

The answer is grace. The Gracious Lord would give the bad figs another chance. Ten years later, Jeremiah gave Zedekiah an opportunity to become a good fig.

Jeremiah said that anyone who decided to leave Jerusalem and go over to the Babylonians would live (38:2). He told Zedekiah specifically that his life would be spared if he surrendered to the Babylonians. If he surrendered, his whole family would live. If he surrendered, the Babylonians would not burn the city (38:17).

Sadly, even though the Lord kept giving him occasions to repent, Zedekiah chose foolishly. Do not choose foolishly like he did. Consider yourself a good fig and allow the Lord to continue working in your heart.

**What specific lessons can you apply to your life from the example of the bad figs?**

Day 164

PERSISTENCE

**Jeremiah 25:3.** *"For twenty-three years – from the thirteenth year of Josiah son of Amon king of Judah until this very day – the word of the Lord has come to me and I have spoken to you again and again, but you have not listened."*

It has now been twenty-three years since the year when the Lord first called Jeremiah (1:2-5). Ominously, this twenty-third was the first year of King Nebuchadnezzar of Babylon (25:1). Nebuchadnezzar would later lead Babylon to conquer Judah. Jeremiah's message from the beginning had been that the Lord would use a conquering army from the north to bring judgment on His people (1:14-16)

For twenty-three years, Jeremiah faithfully preached the messages that God had given him, but there had been a problem. Jeremiah's audience had been totally unresponsive. I understand how Jeremiah must have felt. During a certain period of my life, I thought that no one had listened to me!

How could Jeremiah keep doing a ministry under these conditions? The answer to this question is what Jeremiah told the people in this verse. "The word of the Lord has come to me."

Could you keep doing the same job for twenty-three years if no one affirmed you and no one paid you? Could you speak the same words to the same people who never listened to you – for twenty-three years? What if those people mocked you? Even the mockers would have to admit that you were persistent.

Reflect on the past twenty-three years of your own life. Think of all your ministries beginning with that distant year twenty-three years ago. Think of all the ways you have tried to serve the Lord and live for Him. Now imagine that you have seen absolutely no positive results from all your efforts. That is how it was with Jeremiah.

Jeremiah's persistence was not the same as stubbornness. He had godly reasons for his tenacity. Jeremiah's persistence was a spiritual resolve to continue obeying God regardless of the outcome. Even after twenty-three years, he had the absolute certainty that the Lord would prevail.

You also can be persistent like Jeremiah. Do not be bothered by discouraging results of your efforts. Cling to the unconditional conviction that God will prevail. Your perseverance can grow when your faith is tested ( James 1:2-4).

**How can the Lord help you develop perseverance?**

## Day 165
### BEGINNING OF THE 70 YEARS

*Jeremiah 25:11-12. This whole country will become a desolate wasteland, and these nations will serve the king of Babylon seventy years.*

Seventy years was considered the normal human life span even back in those ancient times. Moses wrote that the days of a human life total seventy years, but they add up to eighty years for those who are strong (Psalm 90:10). Jeremiah preached God's message that a whole generation would live as captives of Babylon for seventy years. He later repeated his prophecy of seventy years in a letter to the exiles in Babylon (29:10).

After Daniel was in Babylon more than sixty-five years, he meditated on this prophecy about the seventy years (Daniel 9:2). Daniel apparently understood that Jeremiah meant a literal seventy years. Daniel perhaps thought that he might still be alive to see the end of the exile. Daniel's prayer (Daniel 9:3-19) and the Lord's answer (Daniel 9:20-27) anticipated the finish of the seventy-year captivity.

When did the seventy years begin? There are at least two possibilities. From the time that Daniel and the first group were taken to Babylon (Daniel 1:1) to the time of when the first group of freed exiles arrived back in Jerusalem (Ezra 1:1-4) was a time of seventy years. Also, from the year that the Babylonians destroyed the temple (Jeremiah 52:12-13) to the year the freed exiles rebuilt the temple (Ezra 6:15) was a period of seventy years.

The seventy years were sabbatical years (2 Chronicles 36:21). The Lord had told His people that the land would have its Sabbath rests while they were away from it because of their sins (Leviticus 26:43). The Lord had commanded them to leave the land unplanted every seventh year (Leviticus 25:3-5). Since the time of Moses, the number of failures to comply with these Sabbath years was seventy.

Judah would not be the only captive of Babylon. Many other nations would also live under Babylonian rule. Jeremiah listed them later in his sermon (25:19-26). They would serve the Babylonian kings for seventy years.

Seventy years was a long time. It took seventy years for the Lord to purify His people under Babylon before they were spiritually ready to serve Him back in the land. The Lord's cleansing of your life also takes time. It has begun. Be patient like Daniel who waited seventy years.

**Why does it seem to take so long for the Lord to purify your life?**

Day 166

FACING THE JUDGE

**Jeremiah 25:31.** *"The tumult will resound to the ends of the earth, for the LORD will bring charges against the nations; he will bring judgment on all mankind and put the wicked to the sword," declares the LORD.*

As the perfect and eternal Judge, God can bring lawsuits against people. The Lord is both the Judge and the prosecuting attorney. He needs no jury. No defense attorneys are available to you. There is no court higher than God's to which you can appeal His verdicts!

Jeremiah had warned his people that the Lord was bringing two major charges against them. First, they had turned their hearts away from Him. The second charge was that they had turned to idols (2:9-13).

An earlier prophet had given the same warning. The Lord was bringing a charge against the Israelites. The Lord saw no love or faithfulness in the land. The nation did not acknowledge God (Hosea 4:1). Another prophet called on the mountains to be witnesses of the Lord's legal case against His people (Micah 6:2).

However, the Lord's lawsuits went far beyond Israel and Judah. The Lord had legal charges against every nation on earth! Jeremiah preached in detail about the Lord's litigation against Egypt, Babylon and seven other nations (46:1-51:64).

God's charge is a universal one that continues today. There is only one Lawgiver, and there is only one Judge (James 4:12). God the Father and Jesus Christ will judge the living and the dead (2 Timothy 4:1). No one is righteous and no one seeks God (Romans 3:10-11). Everyone has sinned and has fallen short of God's glory (Romans 3:23).

I recently received an official jury summons. I was "hereby summoned to appear" before a district courtroom on a certain date. On that day I joined about fifty other potential jurors. The judge finally walked in and told us we were not needed, because the two parties had settled their dispute out of court.

The wisest spiritual decision that anyone can make is to settle with God outside of His court of judgment. You can settle out of court with Jesus. Coming to Jesus the Savior will settle the issue of heaven or hell. Walking daily with the Lord Jesus as your Master will settle the issue of a spiritually productive life. Walk with Him today.

**As you grow closer to the Lord, how do you relate to Him as your Judge?**

## Day 167
### PREACHING TO MULTITUDES

**Jeremiah 26:2.** *"This is what the Lord says: Stand in the courtyard of the Lord's house and speak to all the people of the towns of Judah who come to worship in the house of the Lord. Tell them everything I command you; do not omit a word...."*

Jeremiah did not choose the career path that led to his being a prophet and a preacher. The Lord chose him, and the Lord chose the path. God called Jeremiah to be an exceptional servant of His during Judah's most difficult years.

Jeremiah's life became more stressful the year that Jehoiakim became the next king of Judah. Jehoiakim proved to be an evil man who cared nothing about God's Word. Under King Jehoiakim, Jeremiah began to experience more intense persecution. The abuse began after one of Jeremiah's sermons. At the beginning of Jehoiakim's reign, the Lord gave a tough message to Jeremiah to preach (26:1).

If Jeremiah had always wanted to preach to large crowds, the timing was excellent. The Lord told him to go to the temple courtyard when the city was crowded. Unlike my young grandchildren who thrive on talking to large groups of extended family members, speaking before multitudes was not necessarily Jeremiah's aspiration! But God called him to do it.

Many Judeans were coming to Jerusalem from every part of the nation. They all came to worship in the temple. However, Jeremiah knew that they came to worship *the temple* in the temple! They did not come to sincerely worship the Lord.

In another sermon, perhaps it was the same sermon, Jeremiah warned against trusting in deceptive words about the temple. The false prophets had deceived the people into believing that the Lord would never destroy His own house. They taught the people how to chant repeatedly, "This is the temple of the Lord (7:4)."

Throngs would hear Jeremiah speak that day. The Lord told him not to omit any word from the sermon. The crowds must hear the entire message.

Are you a people-pleaser who is impressed by the influence you have over multitudes? Are you inclined to exclude certain words of truth so as to not offend anyone in the crowd? Remember the Lord's words to Jeremiah. Do not omit a word.

**How can you suppress the temptation to omit certain words from God's Word because you do not want to offend other people?**

## Day 168
### AVOIDING DISASTER

**Jeremiah 26:3.** *Perhaps they will listen and each will turn from his evil way. Then I will relent and not bring on them the disaster I was planning because of the evil they have done.*

At the beginning of Jehoiakim's reign, the Lord told Jeremiah to preach to the crowds in the temple courtyard (26:1-2). The Lord gave him a message that He knew the people would reject. He gave Jeremiah a sermon about imminent disaster.

"Listen, and turn from evil!" This was how the Lord wanted the people to respond to the looming calamity. These words were so simple and clear that even my two-year-old grandson can understand them. He knows what his parents mean when they tell him to listen and stop being bad!

If the people of Judah refused to listen and turn from their wickedness, they would lose their temple and their city. Jeremiah preached that Jerusalem would become unpopulated (26:9). The temple would become like Shiloh (26:6).

What had happened to the town of Shiloh? Shiloh was the original location of the tabernacle in the promised land (Joshua 18:1). The tabernacle was the precursor to the temple. Shiloh continued to be central worship place through the time of Eli and Samuel (1 Samuel 1:9). The people removed the ark of the covenant from the tabernacle in Shiloh when the Philistines threatened them (1 Samuel 4:1-4). The Philistines defeated the Israelites in battle (1 Samuel 4:10) and captured the ark (1 Samuel 5:1). The Philistines probably destroyed Shiloh during this time. A psalmist later wrote that the Lord had abandoned His home in Shiloh, because of the people's sins (Psalm 78:56-60).

Jeremiah's point about Shiloh was that the town was destroyed in spite of its rich spiritual history. The Judeans took personal offense to the reference to Shiloh. They resented any threats against their temple and city. They rejected Jeremiah's message. Consequently, they would suffer disaster.

Have you experienced personal disasters in your life because you did not heed the Lord's guidance? Put those disasters behind you. Turn from your foolish ways and follow the light toward God's grace. If you listen and turn, the Lord will not let loose His wrath on you!

**How do you know that the Lord will not angrily send misfortunes into your life?**

## Day 169
### Unpopularity

**Jeremiah 26:8. But as soon as Jeremiah finished telling all the people everything the LORD had commanded him to say, the priests, the prophets and all the people seized him and said, "You must die!"**

Jeremiah had just barely finished saying all the Lord had commanded him to say. Suddenly he was mobbed. Many hands seized him. He heard everyone shouting at him, "You deserve to die!"

The priests, prophets and all the people had misarranged priorities. They considered their city to be more important than God's Word. They totally disregarded Jeremiah's words from the Lord.

These words came at the beginning of King Jehoiakim's reign. The Lord had told Jeremiah to stand in the temple courtyard and preach to all the people. The main idea of his message was that the people had a choice: obedience or judgment. The people needed to heed the exhortations of God's true prophets, whom they had historically ignored. If the people did not finally decide to obey the Lord, then He would destroy the temple and make the city an example to be used in curses by people from all nations (26:1-7).

Arguably, Jeremiah was the most unpopular man in the whole city. Much of the city's population opposed him. The religious leaders were clearly against Jeremiah. They did not like Jeremiah's preaching, so they wanted him to die.

They knew that they could not just kill Jeremiah themselves. If they did, they would be in severe trouble with the government. So they brought Jeremiah to the government officials and hoped for the death penalty (26:11).

"You must die" are some of the most terrifying words that a person can hear! Moses wrote that a prophet who does not speak the Lord's truth must surely die (Deuteronomy 18:20). The people falsely accused Jeremiah of being a false prophet. Jeremiah's future looked bleak, but that did not matter to him. He boldly preached the same message to the officials that he had given to all the people (26: 12-13). He could be bold because he knew his fate was in the Lord's hands, not the government's.

Are human authorities threatening you? Follow Jeremiah's example. Live boldly, and live intimately with the Lord.

**What must you do when you face persecution for being true to what you know God wants you to do?**

## Day 170
### REFORM AND OBEY

**Jeremiah 26:13.** *"Now reform your ways and your actions and obey the LORD your God. Then the Lord will relent and not bring the disaster he has pronounced against you...."*

Jeremiah boldly told the government and the people to change their ways. He dared to do this because of his confidence that the Lord had sent him. He clearly presented the Lord's two-step requirement.

The people first needed reformation. The Lord commanded them through Jeremiah to reform both their general lifestyle and their specific deeds. They needed to change.

They also needed to go a second step. Jeremiah told them to obey God. They had slipped into dreadful disobedience, ignoring the fact that God was their God. After a radical surgery of reformation, they needed daily healing of obedience.

It was not too late. Even though the Lord had pronounced a death sentence on their city, the people could still avert catastrophe. The choice was theirs. If they would reform and obey, the Lord would change His mind about them.

How could God do this? People often change their minds about people and events. In contrast, God holds His resolve perfectly. How could God give in?

The Bible teaches that God faithfully does what He says. God does not change, either in His justice or in His mercy. People are the ones who change. When they rebel, God launches His judgment. When they reform and obey, God pours His compassion. God's message of judgment is conditional.

The Lord Himself does not change, but neither does He stand still! He constantly activates His word, like He did through Jeremiah. People can then choose either to respond to or reject the Lord.

Have you been lax in your desire to reform your life and obey the Lord? If so, you need to amend your ways and you need to start today. Change your attitude toward God, and you will find His unchanging love.

**In what areas do you need to amend your ways?**

Day 171
ANOTHER PROPHET

**Jeremiah 26:18.** *Micah of Moresheth prophesied in the days of Hezekiah king of Judah. He told all the people of Judah, "This is what the Lord says: 'Zion will be plowed like a field, Jerusalem will become a heap of rubble, the temple hill a mound overgrown with thickets.'"*

As Jeremiah stood trial, some of the leaders remembered a similar case involving another prophet. The prophet Micah lived about one hundred years before Jeremiah's time. Remarkably, Micah had prophesied the same doom for both Jerusalem and the temple that Jeremiah now preached.

This was the same Micah whose prophecies are recorded in the Bible book of his name (Micah 1:1). Micah lived in a small village southwest of Jerusalem. He lived and ministered during the same time as Isaiah. Isaiah was the great prophet in Jerusalem, while Micah lived in the rural area of Judah. Yet Micah spoke to all the people, including those who lived in Jerusalem.

The elders cited one verse from Micah's prophecies. They reminded the people that Micah had predicted that Jerusalem would become a pile of ruins (Micah 3:12). Micah used three different terms for the same city – Jerusalem, Zion and the temple hill. No one doubted which city faced doom.

Micah's warning had shocked Hezekiah and the people. They turned to the Lord, and the Lord averted the disaster. One hundred years later, God's people had grown complacent. They responded to Jeremiah's warning in the opposite way. They threatened the prophet with death (26:11).

Humanly speaking, a few elders controlled Jeremiah's destiny that day. As they deliberated the implications of Micah in Jeremiah's trial, we can wonder what Jeremiah was thinking. He preached the same message about Jerusalem that Micah had. Micah was honored by his king's positive response, but Jeremiah faced imminent demise.

Jeremiah had the same divine calling that Micah had. He faithfully spoke God's words like Micah had done. However, Jeremiah knew that the opposition to his own ministry was not an invalidation of his calling. He continued to follow his calling, regardless of the results. Can you do the same? Can you continue to do what God has called you to do even when hostile people oppose you?

**How can you avoid comparing your dismal circumstances with those of another prophet like Micah, whose circumstances were much better than Jeremiah's?**

## Day 172
## ANOTHER KING

**Jeremiah 26:19.** *"Did Hezekiah king of Judah or anyone else in Judah put him to death? Did not Hezekiah fear the Lord and seek his favor? And did not the Lord relent, so that he did not bring the disaster he pronounced against them? We are about to bring a terrible disaster on ourselves!"*

Unlike the newly crowned King Jehoiakim, King Hezekiah had been a godly man. He did right in the sight of God. Hezekiah trusted in the Lord more deeply and consistently than any other Judean king. He consistently clung to the Lord. Because of Hezekiah's faith, the Lord was with him (2 Kings 18:1-6).

Even though the prophet Micah had prophesied against the city that Hezekiah ruled, Hezekiah did not put the prophet to death. Nor did the king allow anyone else to harm Micah. King Hezekiah believed the prophet's message of doom.

Hezekiah humbled himself and entered the temple to pray. He begged the Lord to show favor rather than judgment. The Lord listened to Hezekiah and postponed the disaster.

Jeremiah was now predicting the same disaster. Some of the elders saw the remarkable similarity. Having learned from history, they cautioned against putting Jeremiah to death.

In contrast to Micah being *another prophet* like Jeremiah, Hezekiah was most certainly not *another king* like Jehoiakim! Unlike Hezekiah, Jehoiakim had already put to death a good prophet. King Jehoiakim had killed the prophet Uriah. Uriah was murdered because he preached against the nation just like Jeremiah was now doing (26:20-23).

The same fate could be Jeremiah's, if King Jehoiakim had his way. Perhaps some of the elders longed for another king. They were nostalgic for a king like Hezekiah.

Hezekiah had been dead for a long time. Josiah, another godly king of Judah, had recently died. The nation of Judah would have no more good kings.

Do you also wish for another king? Are you weary of the injustices of many of the current world political leaders? It is okay to be wistful for a Perfect King.

**How are you consciously living under the Perfect King today?**

## Day 173
### Don't Be Like Uriah!

**Jeremiah 26:20.** *Now Uriah son of Shemaiah from Kiriath Jearim was another man who prophesied in the name of the Lord; he prophesied the same things against this city and this land that Jeremiah did.*

Jeremiah was not alone in his view of God and the world. Jeremiah was not a totally lone voice as he preached an unpopular message. There were others who were also faithful to God. One of them was Uriah.

This was not the same Uriah who was the husband of Bathsheba during King David's reign. This Uriah lived (and died) during Jehoiakim's reign. He probably had a calling from the Lord similar to Jeremiah's. One does not normally risk his life to preach unless he has a clear call!

King Jehoiakim wanted to kill Uriah because he did not like the prophet's preaching. Uriah quickly left the country, but the king's men pursued him. They brought him back to the king who sliced him with a sword (26:21-23).

King Jehoiakim was a foolish man! He believed too highly in his own political power. The king thought that he could silence the prophecy by slicing the prophet. The prophecy still lived through Jeremiah's preaching. The Lord can always call more prophets who will be true to His word.

The Bible does not record Uriah and Jeremiah spending time together. They probably knew each other and possibly encouraged each other as they faced increasing hostility. The murder of Uriah showed that Jeremiah's life also was in eminent danger. Uriah's death was also an example of the nation's murder of many prophets about which Jesus Christ later preached (Luke 11:47-51).

However, Uriah made a fatal error. He fled in fear to Egypt. The Lord had specifically commanded the people not to seek help from Egypt (2:18). If they did, they would be put to shame (2:36).

Going to Egypt symbolically means trusting in the world instead of in the Lord (Ezekiel 23:27). Egypt is a moniker for the world system that is opposed to God (Revelation 11:8). Do not be like Uriah and go to Egypt to try to escape from your difficulties. Be like Jeremiah and trust in the Lord to bring you through the trouble.

**How do you know when you are depending on the world instead of on the Lord?**

## Day 174
### FRIEND IN GOVERNMENT

*Jeremiah 26:24. Furthermore, Ahikam son of Shaphan supported Jeremiah, and so he was not handed over to the people to be put to death.*

The government leaders decided in favor of Jeremiah. They told the priests and prophets that he should not be sentenced to death. A particularly persuasive government official was named Ahikam. His opinion saved Jeremiah.

Ahikam was a friend in high places just when Jeremiah needed him. Ahikam recognized that Jeremiah spoke in the name of the Lord, the same God whom Ahikam followed.

A godly father named Shaphan had raised Ahikam. Both father and son had served under King Josiah. Shaphan had two other sons who also would later help Jeremiah. And one of Ahikam's sons would later serve as governor of Judah and show kindness to Jeremiah. The whole family was Jeremiah's friend.

Ahikam had observed his father's remarkable life and career. Shaphan was one of King Josiah's most trusted officials. Evidently Josiah sensed that Shaphan followed the Lord because he sent Shaphan to oversee the repairs of the temple (2 Chronicles 34:8). During the temple cleanup, a copy of some Scripture was discovered. The Lord's word had been ignored and forgotten in His own temple!

Shaphan personally read the Lord's words to the king (2 Chronicles 34:18). Josiah responded in humility and started reforming his country. Shaphan and his son Ahikam helped the king bring about national spiritual reformation.

Ahikam held a key government post because the Lord had placed him there. And the Lord used Ahikam to keep the promise that the Lord had given to Jeremiah years earlier. The Lord had promised to rescue Jeremiah from kings, priests and the people of the land. The Lord kept His promise. Ahikam delivered Jeremiah.

You have the chance today to draw closer to this keeper of divine promises. If you are one of His, the Lord has promised to never leave you. Until the appointed time for you to enter heaven, He will rescue you from every danger. He might even use a man like Ahikam to deliver you. Trust the Lord's faithfulness today.

**Describe how the Lord has been faithful to you in recent days.**

Day 175

WEARING A YOKE

**Jeremiah 27:2. *This is what the LORD said to me: "Make a yoke out of straps and crossbars and put it on your neck...."***

Heads turned and people murmured when Jeremiah walked into their midst one day. He was wearing a wooden yoke strapped to his neck. It was a yoke that oxen normally wore.

Perhaps many of the locals were embarrassed by Jeremiah's latest symbolic act. He wore the yoke to a meeting of distinguished international visitors. Jeremiah appeared before the envoys of the kings of five nations who had come to Jerusalem to meet with the Judean king, Zedekiah (27:3). Their purpose was probably to form an alliance against Babylon.

As he wore the yoke, Jeremiah preached to them that they should accept the yoke of Babylon. The Lord was going to give all the nations over to King Nebuchadnezzar. All would be under the power of Babylon (27:6).

Jeremiah preached that those nations who try to resist the yoke of Babylon will be punished. The Lord will bring war, famine and plague. Nations that rebel against Babylon will be destroyed (27:8).

Unfortunately, each nation had its own false prophets, diviners, mediums and sorcerers. They were all telling their own people that they would not serve the king of Babylon. Jeremiah warned that they were prophesying lies (27:9-10).

Those nations that rejected the lies and did submit to Babylon would survive. The Lord would allow them to remain in their own land. They would be able to cultivate their own fields (27:11).

Then Jeremiah wore his yoke and spoke to King Zedekiah (27:12-13). Jeremiah next preached his yoke sermon a third time. He spoke to the priests and to all the people who gathered around them (27:16-22).

Jeremiah was courageous and obedient as he wore that yoke. The yoke symbolized Jeremiah's servitude to the Lord. Would you have worn the yoke?

**How does Jeremiah's yoke sermon help you accept the difficult situations in which God places you?**

## Day 176
### THE OVERPOWERING GOD

**Jeremiah 27:5.** *With my great power and outstretched arm I made the earth and its people and the animals that are on it, and I give it to anyone I please.*

When the Lord made the planet and its inhabitants, He created everything by His mighty power. God described His great strength as being like an extended arm. Jeremiah saw God's power in the form of an outstretched hand (1:9).

Jeremiah's sermons often emphasized the Lord's enormous might. God displayed His power in the past through creation. Jeremiah specified three features of the Lord's creation. These three were the earth, the people and the animals.

When the Lord created the earth, He made an instrument through which people would be able to see His eternal power and divine nature (Romans 1:20). When He created people, He fashioned men and women in His own image (Genesis 1: 27). When He made the animals and the entire environment, He intended for all of nature to praise Him (Psalm 148:7-10).

The Lord displayed His power in the past through creation. One way that He shows His power now is through His authority over government (Romans 13: 1-7). When the Lord first created humans, He told them to rule over His creation (Genesis 1:28). Human governments now, wittingly or unwittingly, carry out this divine command and manage sections of the planet.

Nations attempt to control the earth, lead the people and use the animals. The Lord gives this governmental power to whomever He chooses. People cannot understand the mind of God in His appointment of political leaders.

In Jeremiah's day, the Lord was preparing to hand over power to King Nebuchadnezzar of Babylon. Nebuchadnezzar would govern over much of the earth. The Lord would even make all the wild animals subject to him. Nebuchadnezzar would be the Lord's servant (27:6).

Even though he was a pagan, Nebuchadnezzar was God's servant in the sense that God used him to accomplish entirely what the Lord wanted. In the same way, the government officials under whom you live today are God's servants (Romans 13:4). Honor His servants today as you live with Him and for Him.

**List several ways in which you can show honor to God's servants in government?**

## Day 177
### EVEN THE WILD ANIMALS

*Jeremiah 27:6. Now I will hand all your countries over to my servant Nebuchadnezzar king of Babylon; I will make even the wild animals subject to him.*

After hearing Jeremiah's yoke sermon, the people of Judah should have known that they had no hope as a nation. King Nebuchadnezzar would conquer them and he would defeat every other nation as well. Even the wild animals would fall under Nebuchadnezzar's control. If the wild animals could not escape, how could the Judeans?

Jeremiah had preached that the Lord created the earth and all the people and animals on it (27:5). So, certainly the Lord had the power to give the animals to whomever He wished. God chose Nebuchadnezzar to be the human power over the animals.

Jeremiah lived to see the fulfillment of these words. The Lord gave to Nebuchadnezzar all the beasts of the field (28:14). Along with the animals, God gave the birds of the sky to the Babylonian king (Daniel 2:38). It was as if King Nebuchadnezzar owned a global zoo!

Because of certain children's stories, my young grandchildren are afraid of wild animals. They especially fear untamed bears, hungry weasels and big, bad wolves! They think they can forget about their fears when they ask me to pretend like I'm a wild animal!

Nebuchadnezzar himself also became known as a wild animal. Jeremiah knew that the king of Babylon was like a vicious lion (50:17). However, the Lord would eventually bring Babylon's ferociousness to an end.

During the years of the Babylonian empire, even the wild animals served Nebuchadnezzar. Today, all animals are subject to God. In the future, no animal will threaten you as Jesus Christ eradicates all residual effects of sin. With no more sin on earth there will be no more untamed animals.

The wolf and the lamb, the leopard and the goat, and the young lion and the calf will all live peacefully together. The lions will no longer devour flesh. The lions will eat straw like the ox (Isaiah 11:6-7).

**Describe your level of confidence in the belief that the Lord has all the wild animals under His control.**

Date 178

POWER SHIFT

*Jeremiah 27:7. All nations will serve him and his son and grandson until the time for his land comes; then many nations and great kings will subjugate him.*

God appointed a time when the Babylonian rule of the world would end. All the nations would not serve King Nebuchadnezzar permanently. Nor would the nations be under an unending dynasty of Nebuchadnezzar's descendants.

The length of Babylon's world domination was seventy years. The end of Jerusalem's ruin would mark the beginning of Babylon's punishment. After seventy years, the Lord would bring judgment on the Babylonians for their cruelty against His people (25:12).

Even though God used the Babylonians as His servants, they were guilty for their own actions. The Babylonians brutally destroyed the Lord's people, temple and city. For their excessive brutality, they would receive God's condemnation. The Lord would destroy their nation. Then, another empire would arise in Babylon's place.

Jeremiah had already seen one major power shift during his lifetime. During King Jehoiakim's fourth year, the Babylonians defeated the Egyptians in a pivotal battle (46:2). Jeremiah saw world dominance change from Egypt to Babylon.

Changes in world leadership can cause global instability and personal anxiety. I remember feeling especially anxious when a certain person became the next President of the United States! In the same vein, Daniel was alarmed by the revelation that King Nebuchadnezzar would lose his throne and live like an animal in the fields (Daniel 4:19-25).

The nation in which you live has a limited duration. Your country as you know it will not last. You will probably see a major power shift within your lifetime. Do not worry. The final power shift will result in the perfect Messiah ruling as King.

You can look forward to the day when strangers will no longer enslave God's people (30:8). The days are coming when the righteous Branch will reign wisely as King (23:5). You can live calmly in anticipation of the righteous King.

**What specific truths from the Lord can give you calmness when you see political turmoil in the world?**

Day 179
OPTIMISTIC LIES

**Jeremiah 28:1-2.** *In the fifth month of that same year, the fourth year, early in the reign of Zedekiah king of Judah, the prophet Hananiah son of Azzur, who was from Gibeon, said to me in the house of the LORD in the presence of the priests and all the people: "This is what the LORD Almighty, the God of Israel, says: 'I will break the yoke of the king of Babylon...".*

Hananiah was a popular religious speaker. People liked listening to him, because he did not preach the messages of doom for which prophets like Jeremiah were known. Hananiah assured that people that the Lord would soon defeat the king of Babylon.

Four years earlier, the Babylonians had taken into exile King Jehoiachin and thousands of others. Hananiah said that they all were going to return to Jerusalem within two years. Also, the Lord would bring back all the articles in the temple that the Babylonians had stolen (28:3-4).

Hananiah told the people what they wanted to hear. They liked his positive message, and they believed him because he claimed to be a prophet of the Lord. Even the meaning of his name appealed to them. Hananiah means, "The Lord shows grace." However, Hananiah undoubtedly used his name to promote his bogus ministry.

In contrast, another man named Hananiah really knew the graciousness of the Lord. He was one of Daniel's three friends in Babylon. The Babylonians changed his name from Hananiah to Shadrach (Daniel 1:7).

While the prophet Hananiah preached peace, Jeremiah preached sword, famine and plague (27:13). Hananiah claimed that the exile would be short, but Jeremiah prophesied that the Judeans would be slaves of Babylon for three generations (27:7). Hananiah claimed that the temple articles would soon be returned, but Jeremiah asserted that the rest of the temple vessels would be carried to Babylon (27:21-22). Hananiah talked about Judah's success, but Jeremiah warned about the nation's evil deeds (26:3).

Hananiah was a false prophet. He may have sincerely believed what he was preaching, and he may have been preaching from his heart. However, Jeremiah warned against those prophets whose messages were from their hearts. Prophets who prophesy about visions from their hearts were not speaking words from the Lord (23:16).

**How can the Lord help you not believe the messages of today's false prophets?**

Day 180
## JEREMIAH'S RESPONSE TO OPTIMISTIC LIES

**Jeremiah 28:5. *Then the prophet Jeremiah replied to the prophet Hananiah before the priests and all the people who were standing in the house of the LORD.***

Even though Hananiah preached cheerful sermons, he was a false prophet. Jeremiah confronted him in the courtyard of the temple. Jeremiah exposed Hananiah before the priests and all the people.

Jeremiah began by agreeing that what Hananiah preached was desirable. Jeremiah said "amen" to the Lord's bringing the temple vessels and all the exiles back from Babylon back to Jerusalem. Jeremiah certainly wished that this could and would happen (28:6).

Jeremiah said the prophets in preceding generations prophesied the same depressing situations. The great Biblical prophets who lived before Jeremiah's day did not preach peace like Hananiah did. They predicted war, disaster and plague (28:7-8).

For example, Hosea preached that the people of Israel would be destroyed because they ignored God's law (Hosea 4:6). Isaiah prophesied that the Lord was rising to judge the people (Isaiah 3:13). Men would fall by the sword (Isaiah 3:25).

These prophets still preached hope. Even in the midst of war, disaster and plague, God had a good plan for His people. However, their messages, like Jeremiah's, called for repentance.

Jeremiah and Hananiah could not both be right. Jeremiah proposed a test. The prophet of peace proves himself true if the peace really happens (28:9).

Then Hananiah took the yoke off Jeremiah's neck and broke it. Hananiah said that the Lord would break the Babylonian yoke from all the nations within two years. Without further confrontation, Jeremiah walked away (28:10-11).

Hananiah's sense of timing and theatrics probably won the temple audience over to him that day. He was still a false prophet. Jeremiah wisely walked away from Hananiah's game. It was needless to continue the confrontation. Jeremiah would speak again, but only after the Lord gave him the words.

**Describe a recent incident in which the Lord helped you keep silent and walk away from an unnecessary confrontation.**

## Day 181
### HANANIAH'S FAME ENDS

*Jeremiah 28:12-13. Shortly after the prophet Hananiah had broken the yoke off the neck of the prophet Jeremiah, the word of the LORD came to Jeremiah: "Go and tell Hananiah, 'This is what the LORD says: You have broken a wooden yoke, but in its place you will get a yoke of iron....'"*

Even though Hananiah was a common name, all the people in Jerusalem seemed to know about him. They knew him as the prophet from Gibeon (28:1). Many of them believed him instead of Jeremiah.

Soon after Hananiah broke Jeremiah's yoke, Jeremiah returned to Hananiah. Jeremiah gave him some fresh words from the Lord. His message to Hananiah was that the Babylonian yoke was now iron, not wooden. It was now many yokes, not just one. All the nations would wear iron yokes and would serve King Nebuchadnezzar. Even the wild animals would be under his control (28:12-14).

The Lord was using King Nebuchadnezzar to judge the nations. So the people needed to accept the inevitable and learn to live in the difficult times ahead of them. Jeremiah was trying to help them do this.

Hananiah had the wrong message, the wrong attitude and a wrong sense of timing. The people would indeed return from Babylon. However, the return would be after seventy years, not after two. Infinitely worse than his poor sense of timing, Hananiah was a preacher of rebellion against the Lord. He persuaded the nation to trust in lies. Before the end of one year, the Lord would take his life (28:15-16).

Hananiah did not live long enough to see if his predictions came true. If he had lived for another two years, he would have known that he was wrong. What would he have done then? Because of his popularity, he probably would have persuaded the people to believe another lie.

Hananiah's popularity ended the day that he died. He was famous for his optimistic message about a short exile. He was literally dead wrong!

Hananiah died in the seventh month of that same year (28:17). Jeremiah's short-term prophecy about Hananiah's death came true. Now there was additional evidence that Jeremiah was a true prophet of the Lord.

**How does the timing of Hananiah's death strengthen your conviction that every word of Jeremiah is from the Lord and therefore relevant to your life?**

## Day 182

### SURVIVORS

*Jeremiah 29:1. This is the text of the letter that the prophet Jeremiah sent from Jerusalem to the surviving elders among the exiles and to the priests, the prophets and all the other people Nebuchadnezzar had carried into exile from Jerusalem to Babylon.*

One of the ways in which Jeremiah preserved his words for future generations was to write a letter. He wrote to a certain group of people in a specific situation, but his message to them was one that people need to hear today. The prophet's letter is like the letters in the New Testament, which are timeless.

The postmark on Jeremiah's letter was Jerusalem. The Babylonians had recently attacked Jerusalem and captured the talented and the educated. Among these was Ezekiel the prophet. The ones left behind in Judah were mostly the poor, who would be a burden on Nebuchadnezzar's empire. The king wanted only those who had skills to help build his magnificent city of Babylon.

This was not the final assault on Jerusalem. The utter destruction of the city would come ten years later. Jeremiah now lived in a city populated by the impoverished and the disadvantaged.

Jeremiah knew that the hope of his people lay in distant Babylon. The captives from Jerusalem were in the place where they would cry out to the Lord. Many would express their dependence on Him. Jeremiah had a message from the Lord for these displaced people, but he knew he could not personally travel to Babylon. He sent a letter to the exiles.

Death certainly came to some during that seven hundred mile forced march from Jerusalem to Babylon. Jeremiah wrote to those who had survived. He referred to the leaders as the surviving elders. The horror of walking in chains to a pagan land would have devastated many of the elderly. But some survived.

Jeremiah's God has a message for you. You are probably in some sense a survivor yourself. You can perhaps think of a time when you had a serious accident, a severe disease or a vicious persecution and you could have died. You did not. You survived. Draw nearer to the God who made you a survivor for a reason.

**Describe yourself as a survivor for God.**

Day 183

MEGA EXILE

Jeremiah 29:2. *(This was after King Jehoiachin and the queen mother, the court officials and the leaders of Judah and Jerusalem, the craftsmen and the artisans had gone into exile from Jerusalem.)*

The king of Babylon was building the next superpower. He wanted the finest people from every nation to help him do it. He found some superb human assets in Jerusalem and the surrounding countryside of Judah. He brought clever politicians, skilled craftsmen and experienced smiths to Babylon.

It was a gigantic exile. The total number of prisoners from Judah was 10,000 (2 Kings 24:14)! One year earlier, the Babylonians had taken away 3,023 adult males (Jeremiah 52:28).

Instead of killing King Jehoiachin, the Babylonian king exiled him as one of his trophies. The Babylonians also deported the officials of Jehoiachin's court. They even carried away Jehoiachin's mother. Jeremiah had earlier prophesied that the royal mother and son would be flung into another country and die there (22:26).

Jehoiachin's mother's name was Nehushta. She was the daughter of Elnathan, who had lived in Jerusalem. He may have been the same Elnathan who served under Jehoiachin's father. If so, Jehoiachin's grandfather caused the death of a godly prophet (29: 22-23), but he later tried to stop the king from burning God's Word (36:25).

Included among the thousands of exiles was a priest named Ezekiel (Ezekiel 1: 1-3). Jeremiah did not mention Ezekiel by name, probably because God did not call Ezekiel to become a prophet until five years after the exile.

Ezekiel was an example of how the Lord spiritually provided for His exiled people. Babylon did not have a Biblical library where the people could read or hear God's Word! If the people were truly seeking the Lord, they could hear His words through prophets like Ezekiel.

Do not fall into the deceptive trap of thinking that you lack the spiritual resources to know the Lord. Even if you are feeling like you are exiled, you still can find access to Him through His Word. Seek Him.

**How does God's Word provide closer access to Him?**

## Day 184
### RELIABLE PEOPLE

**Jeremiah 29:3. *He entrusted the letter to Elasah son of Shaphan and to Gemariah son of Hilkiah, whom Zedekiah king of Judah sent to King Nebuchadnezzar in Babylon.***

When Jeremiah sent the letter to the exiles in Babylon, the Judean government paid for the delivery! The king of Judah sent an envoy to the king of Babylon, probably as an attempt to keep some sort of peace between the two nations. Jeremiah gave his letter to two men in this official delegation before they left for Babylon. The temporary peace arrangements are forgotten, but Jeremiah's letter is still read today.

Jeremiah's letter was extremely important. He would need to give it to those whom he trusted. He gave the letter to Elasah and Gemariah. We would know nothing else about Elasah or Gemariah if their fathers' names were not given to us. The fact that their fathers were Shaphan and Hilkiah helps us understand why Jeremiah trusted them.

Shaphan and Hilkiah served in the administration of a previous king, the good King Josiah. Josiah was king while Jeremiah was growing up. Josiah is best remembered as a godly king who attempted to bring spiritual reformation to his nation. During Josiah's reign, Hilkiah discovered a copy of the Scriptures that had long lain neglected in the temple.

Hilkiah gave the Scriptures to Shaphan, who was Josiah's "secretary of state". Shaphan read the scroll, and then he read it to King Josiah. As a result, the king did even more to spiritually reform the country.

Hilkiah was also the name of Jeremiah's father, who was a different Hilkiah. Because of the understood parallel with Shaphan, it is most likely that Gemariah's father was the Hilkiah who found the scroll in the temple. Otherwise, Gemariah would have been Jeremiah's brother, to whom Jeremiah made no other reference.

Apparently, Elasah and Gemariah followed in their fathers' professional and spiritual footsteps. Even though the current king of Judah cared nothing about spiritual values, he trusted the competence of Elasah and Gemariah to negotiate with the Babylonians. And Jeremiah trusted them with his letter.

Are you also counted among the trustworthy? You do not need to wonder whether you have this trait if your relationship with the Lord is close. Allow the trustworthy God to grip you today!

**What are the traits of a trustworthy person, and are you developing these traits in yourself?**

Day 185
DIVINE EXILE

**Jeremiah 29:4.** *This is what the LORD Almighty, the God of Israel, says to all those I carried into exile from Jerusalem to Babylon….*

Jeremiah's letter to the exiles had divine authority. He wrote to them exactly what the Lord said. Even though the Babylonians forced their captives to live far from their nation, the God of their homeland still cared enough to speak to them.

Nebuchadnezzar's military had carried off more than ten thousand residents of Judah. He would get everyone else ten years later. Going into exile was a traumatic event. Jeremiah's letter shocked them with the assertion that the Lord Himself had taken them into exile!

Nebuchadnezzar was certainly the one who brought the captives from Jerusalem to Babylon (29:1). However, the Babylonian king was merely a servant of the Lord (25:9). The phrase "Nebuchadnezzar, God's servant" is not an oxymoron! Whatever the Lord wants, He brings it about by using people of His choosing.

Nebuchadnezzar had exiled the Judeans in order to strengthen Babylon and weaken Judah. However, Jeremiah specifically called the Lord "the God of Israel". God had not changed His political allegiance from Israel to Babylon! The Lord planned to use the exile to bless His own people. He sent them into exile in order to give them a hope and a future (29:11).

Jeremiah emphasized that they were in a divinely controlled exile, because he wanted to help them accept their fate. If they understood that God had sent them into exile, they would more likely heed God's words about how He wanted them to live while in exile.

When you take your mind off the Lord, you might ascribe your unpleasant circumstances to oppressive people or bad luck. At times you may feel like you are living in exile, away from familiar surroundings and likable people. However, no banishment occurs behind the Lord's back. God personally oversees every upheaval.

If the Lord has placed you in a situation you do not like, you must cleanse your attitude. Your conditions will change sooner or later. For now, patiently accept the location where God has planted you.

**How is the Lord helping you accept your current location?**

## Day 186
## BUILD AND PLANT!

**Jeremiah 29:5.** *Build houses and settle down; plant gardens and eat what they produce.*

Jeremiah wrote his letter in response to those exiles who believed that they would soon return home. No, they were going to live in Babylon for a long time. So they might as well build houses and plant their vegetable gardens.

Build and plant! These two words reverberated in Jeremiah's call from the Lord many years before. Not only would Jeremiah preach judgment to the nations, he would also speak of times to build and plant (1:10). The Lord is always in the process of building and planting His people.

The exiles who read Jeremiah's letter had a choice. They could respond positively to the Lord's words and thrive where the Lord planted them. Or they could reject Him and become no better than their disobedient ancestors who became like useless wild vines (2:21).

Perhaps many of the exiles would plant fig trees in their gardens. They themselves were the good figs about whom Jeremiah had preached (24:5). In Babylon, the Lord would make them good.

Ezekiel was one of the exiles (Ezekiel 1:1-3). He was an example of one who had settled down in Babylon. He lived in his own house (Ezekiel 8:1).

The Babylonians did not keep the exiles in chains. They gave them freedom to build their own families and lives. The exiles were free to contribute to the society where they found themselves. Even so, some exiles would never consider themselves to be true citizens of Babylon. They had a higher citizenship. They were resident aliens, like believers are today.

If you are a true follower of the Lord, your citizenship is in heaven. The Lord who sent the exiles to Babylon, and who would send their descendants back to the land, will send you to heaven when He wishes. Meanwhile, plant a garden! And are you planting and harvesting in the spiritual realm while you wait for God's call to come home?

**What does it mean to you to have a citizenship in heaven?**

## Day 187
### POPULATION GROWTH

**Jeremiah 29:6.** *Marry and have sons and daughters; find wives for your sons and give your daughters in marriage, so that they too may have sons and daughters. Increase in number there; do not decrease.*

The Lord had exiled His people from Jerusalem to Babylon. They would remain in Babylon for a long time. God wanted them to marry and start families. His command in Jeremiah's letter was for them to be fruitful and multiply.

Many of the exiles probably thought differently. The Babylonians had uprooted them from everything they knew, and the exiles felt tremendously unsettled. They perhaps thought that Babylon was no place to get married and have children.

Trying to have families during distressful times can be painful. The Lord ruled out marriage and family plans for Jeremiah. Jeremiah's single life would illustrate the future grief of many parents who would lose their children to the Babylonians, and to famine and disease (16:1-4). However, life in Babylon would be different for the surviving exiles.

After seventy years (29:10), the Lord would lead them from Babylon back to the promised land. It would be just like a new exodus. In their early history, the people had multiplied their population while they were slaves in Egypt. When the Hebrew men finally numbered 600,000 (Exodus 12:37), Moses led their exodus from Egypt into Canaan.

God's people were in Egypt for four hundred years before their numbers were large enough to leave and become a nation. The exiles in Babylon would have only seventy years. They needed to have their weddings soon!

Jeremiah had predicted that the Babylonian invasion of Judah would be like a reversal of creation (4:23). In contrast, the seventy years in Babylon would be like a reenactment of creation. It would be similar to the Lord telling the first man and woman to be fruitful and multiply (Genesis 1:28).

What about you? Do you want to see more believers get married and have children today? Does your surrounding culture, or the Lord, influence your thinking?

**How is your relationship with the Lord shaping your attitudes toward children?**

## Day 188
### PRAY FOR BABYLON!

*Jeremiah 29:7. Also, seek the peace and prosperity of the city to which I have carried you into exile. Pray to the LORD for it, because if it prospers, you too will prosper.*

The exiles from Judah did not want Babylon to prosper. They did not want to contribute anything toward the welfare of Babylon. Babylon was their political, military and moral enemy.

Jeremiah's letter gave the exiles seemingly radical commands from the Lord. All their lives they had worked toward the peace of Judah. Now they were supposed to seek the peace of Babylon. Furthermore, they were to pray for Babylon!

The Lord wanted the exiles to be upright Babylonian citizens. He wanted them to work hard to make Babylon a better place in which to live. The Lord wanted them to both work and to pray that Babylon might thrive. He wanted them to be salt and light in the Babylonian culture.

Jeremiah's letter prohibited the exiles from withdrawing into their own secure ghetto. The Babylonians brought them in as captives. Now the Lord would make them into prayer warriors and witnesses.

Jeremiah's words from the Lord set a standard of living for believers that would be reinforced throughout the rest of the Bible. Jesus said to pray for those who persecute you (Matthew 5:44). Paul wrote that if possible, so far as it depends on you, you should live peaceably with all people (Romans 12:18).

Peter wrote that you should maintain good conduct among non-Christians. Even if the unbelievers slander you as wrongdoers, they will see your good deeds and glorify God when He appears (1 Peter 2:12). Peter also wrote that believers should honor all people, love other Christians, fear God and honor the king (1 Peter 2:17).

The exiles could work hard and have a successful life in Babylon. But they longed to be back home. In the same way, believers today often yearn to be in their heavenly home. Until heaven, you are living in temporary exile somewhere in the world. You live in your own Babylon. Pray for your Babylonian community.

**How does your relationship with the Lord motivate you to pray for lost people?**

## Day 189
### FALSE HOPE

**Jeremiah 29:8. *Yes, this is what the LORD Almighty, the God of Israel, says: "Do not let the prophets and diviners among you deceive you. Do not listen to the dreams you encourage them to have."***

Living in exile was incredibly difficult for these people. They had not chosen to live in a foreign country. The Judeans did not want to be with the people of Babylon. They wanted to be back home, where they understood the language, and where they enjoyed the food, and where they could go to the temple of their Lord.

Even though many of these exiles did not follow the Lord, they still loved the temple. They knew that Solomon's Temple was their religious heritage. They undoubtedly missed everything about their old way of life. They wanted someone to tell them that they would soon leave Babylon and go home.

Among those who survived the exile were the false prophets. These bogus forecasters were ready to tell the people what they wanted to hear, even if it was not true. Jeremiah wrote a letter, similar to what future apostles of Jesus Christ would write, to warn against false teaching.

The reason that the exiles in Babylon were listening to the false prophets was because they were searching for hope. There were rumors of weaknesses in the Babylonian Empire. People hoped that another nation would conquer Babylon, and then the exiles could go home.

The prophets and diviners kept feeding this hope to the exiles. Diviners? What were diviners doing there? The Lord gave His people priests and prophets, but not diviners! All the other nations had diviners, who were specialists in knowledge about the future. So the people of Judah, in their rebellious attitude toward the Lord, wanted their own diviners.

Do not try to replace God with your own diviners and daily horoscopes! Only God knows the future, and He is keeping most of it hidden from you. Trust Him for your future. Live confidently today, because knowing God is more important than knowing about the future. God is the Lord of both the present and the future.

**Why would you trust the possibility of a great economic future instead of trusting God?**

Day 190

## SHOCK OF THE 70 YEARS

**Jeremiah 29:10.** *This is what the LORD says: "When seventy years are completed for Babylon, I will come to you and fulfill my gracious promise to bring you back to this place."*

Before receiving Jeremiah's letter, the exiles did not want to settle down in Babylon. They thought the captivity would last a short time, maybe for a couple of years. One of the prophets in Jerusalem had predicted that the exile would end within two years (28:1-4). Imagine their shock when they heard about a seventy-year exile!

Most people can endure two years. When my family and I moved overseas to a foreign city, I had a two-year commitment with the mission. After about six weeks, culture shock hit me severely, and I did not like being there. However, a thought occurred to me on one unusually sunny afternoon. I thought that I could live there, or just about anywhere, if I knew it was for only two years! (As it turned out, we lived there considerably longer.)

As the full impact of Jeremiah's words sank in, the exiles must have despaired at first. "Seventy years! In seventy years we will all be dead! We will never see Jerusalem again!"

If they remembered the previous section of Jeremiah's letter, they could lift themselves from despair. Jeremiah had told them to build houses and start families. He told them specifically to marry and have sons and daughters. He wrote that they should find wives for their sons and let their daughters get married so that they too could have sons and daughters.

The exiles and many of their children would not live to see the end of the seventy years, but their grandchildren would. The exiles could hope in the promise that their own grandchildren would return to Jerusalem. So now was the time to get married and start having families!

Jeremiah assured them that God would fulfill His good word to them. Throughout the Scripture, the Lord has given many gracious promises. He will keep them all. The all-powerful gracious God is the only one who gives gracious promises that are certain. He is the God whom Jeremiah knew. Are you growing in your gracious relationship with Him?

**What promises from God are you claiming?**

## Day 191
### A HAPPY ENDING

**Jeremiah 29:11.** *"For I know the plans I have for you," declares the LORD, "plans to prosper you and not to harm you, plans to give you hope and a future...."*

God knows what will happen to you in the future. God had revealed to Jeremiah what would happen to Jerusalem and Judah. Many false prophets were saying that the exile would soon end. They knew nothing about the Lord's plans, even though they pretended to know.

None of them could have imagined how superior the Lord's plan was to what they falsely preached. They experienced what seemed to be a huge calamity. They had no idea about the great plans that the Lord had formulated. God's purposes were for the eventual success of His people.

This is a clear promise from the Lord about the restoration of His people to their promised land. The consistent character of God is behind this promise. Not only did the Lord know the plans He had for Judah, but also He knows what He has planned for each one of His people living today. He plans to give each one a hope and a future, which means He gives each believer a hopeful end. God plans to give to each believer's life story a happy ending.

When I was young, my mother read children's stories to me. All of the stories had happy endings. The people in the stories lived happily ever after. However, one night she read a story that had a sad ending. The story was about a little boy and his dog. At the end of the story, the dog died. I cried because I wanted a happy ending!

As much as you would like to, you cannot write your own joyful finish to your life. The Lord is the supreme planner. He is the master of happy endings. His plan for you is far beyond your capacity to imagine, if you are a believer.

Only true believers have a future and a hope. Unbelievers are no better off than were those idol worshippers in Jerusalem whom the Lord would soon judge.

Are you confident that your life will have a happy ending? Are you aware of the unsearchable spiritual riches that the Lord gives through His righteous Branch, Jesus Christ? Are you allowing your beliefs to affect your attitudes today?

**How do your beliefs about God affect your attitudes?**

Day 192

THE LISTENING LORD

**Jeremiah 29:12.** *Then you will call upon me and come and pray to me, and I will listen to you.*

Jeremiah had earlier preached the bad news about God not listening. The Lord would not listen to Jeremiah's prayers for his people (7:16). God would not listen to Jeremiah's people when they call out to Him in the midst of disaster (11:14).

Why wouldn't the Lord listen to them? Isn't He the God who hears? Doesn't He eagerly welcome people's prayers that are directed toward Him?

The people were hopelessly rebellious and headed toward judgment. No prayer could modify their destiny. They had already chosen to worship their gods instead of the one God. They would not reconsider their foolish decision to reject the Lord and embrace idols.

Jeremiah wrote that the prayer situation was changing. The Judeans who were now in Babylon were the "good figs". They would return to the Lord with all their heart (24:7). God would listen to them.

The Lord's listening ability is perfect. His hearing far surpasses mine, even when I am listening to my wife! God does not have the limitations of human ears.

God hears while people are still in the process of speaking to Him (Isaiah 65:24). Not only does the Lord listen to prayers, He also hears before the prayer is said. The Lord knows what people need even before they ask Him (Matthew 6:8). He listens to every unspoken prayer before it is spoken.

King Solomon prayed about the future possibility that the people would be taken captive and taken to another country. If they were to repent, Solomon prayed that the Lord would hear their prayers (1 Kings 8:46-53). He asked God to hear their prayers even while they were in a foreign nation. Solomon understood that the Lord did not limit his listening only to those prayers uttered in the temple.

You do not need to be in a church building or a chapel in order for God to listen to you. Jeremiah was imprisoned in the courtyard of the guard when the Lord told him to call to Him and He would answer (33:3). Wherever you are today, call to Him. He will listen.

**Describe your level of confidence in the Lord's listening to you today.**

## Day 193
### SEEKING GOD

**Jeremiah 29:13. *You will seek me and find me when you seek me with all your heart.***

The exiles had no temple, no sacrifices and no holy land. They had no religious props with which to bolster their relationship with God. They could no longer worship God in the way in which they were accustomed. Jeremiah assured them that they could know God simply and directly. He invited them to seek God with all their heart.

Centuries earlier, Moses wrote the same evangelistic invitation. Moses predicted that the Lord would scatter His people among nations that worshipped idols. Even in the midst of idolatrous people, God's people could seek Him. They could seek the Lord from where they were. They would find God if they sought Him with all their heart and soul (Deuteronomy 4:27-29).

Searching for God with all your heart means seeking Him with both your mind and your will. You must seek the Lord both intellectually and volitionally. You must seek Him through prayer and worship. God promised that as you seek, you will find Him.

The fact that God can be found means that He is accessible. God is nearby and reachable. He will never move away and neglect to leave a forwarding address! God is available to you, if you want to know Him.

Centuries after Jeremiah lived, Jesus Christ also taught about seeking. He promised His people that if they seek, they will find. If they knock, He will open the door (Matthew 7:7-8).

A reality exists that far surpasses your search for God. This reality is that God is seeking you! God promised to give His people a new heart. Then they would return to the Lord with all of their heart (24:7). One of the hymns that I remember singing as a new believer was called "I sought the Lord". I sang, "I sought the Lord, and afterward I knew He moved my soul to seek Him, seeking me. It was not I that found, O Savior true. No, I was found of Thee."

Everyday you should seek the Lord. As you grow closer to Him, you will realize that you have absolutely no reason for spiritual pride. You found the Lord only because He first found you.

**What particular thoughts, ambitions or habits keep you from seeking the Lord always?**

Day 194

PHONY PROPHETS

**Jeremiah 29:15.** *You may say, "The LORD has raised up prophets for us in Babylon...."*

The exiles in Babylon kept clinging to a false hope. They had their own prophets with them in Babylon whose messages were always positive. However, one of Jeremiah's letters exposed these prophets as fake.

Jeremiah wrote what the Lord really had to say about the king and those who still lived in Jerusalem. Contrary to the rosy predictions of the phony prophets, Jeremiah wrote that the Lord would bring war, starvation, and disease on the people in Jerusalem. The Lord would treat them like figs that are so rotten that they cannot be eaten. He would make all the kingdoms of the earth disgusted and horrified at Jerusalem's fate. (29:16-18).

The Lord would do this to the people who were still in Jerusalem because they had not heeded what He said to them through His servants the prophets. The Lord had sent them true prophets over and over again, but they had not listened to them. The exiles had not paid any attention to the true prophets either (29:19-20).

There were two fake prophets in Babylon about whom Jeremiah warned. The Lord had a specific message for the false prophets Ahab and Zedekiah. These were not the same men as the former King Ahab and the current King Zedekiah, although they had similar bents toward evil. These so-called prophets were telling lies and claiming the Lord's authority to do so. The Lord consequently would hand them over to King Nebuchadnezzar who would put them to death in front of the exiles (29:21).

All the exiles of Judah in Babylon would then use the names of Ahab and Zedekiah as examples whenever they put a curse on anyone. The exiles would call on the Lord to treat their enemies like Zedekiah and Ahab whom the king of Babylon roasted in a fire (29:22).

These two bogus prophets committed adultery with their neighbors' wives. They spoke words that the Lord did not give to them. They acted foolishly (29:23).

Not everyone who claims to speak words from God is actually doing so. Beware of the false prophets who speak today. Evaluate their words biblically, and then shun them. You have no time for fake prophets, because you want to grow closer to the Lord.

**How should you respond to false teachers?**

Day 195
SHEMAIAH'S LETTER

**Jeremiah 29:29.** *Zephaniah the priest, however, read the letter to Jeremiah the prophet.*

Zephaniah the priest in Jerusalem received a letter from one of the exiles in Babylon. The exile's name was Shemaiah. Shemaiah's letter was critical of Jeremiah.

Shemaiah's letter put pressure on Zephaniah the priest. He wrote that the Lord had placed Zephaniah in the leadership of the Lord's temple. In Shemaiah's mind, the Lord had made Zephaniah responsible for controlling any crazy person who pretended to be a prophet. Zephaniah's duty was to put any such person in the stocks. Shemaiah wanted to know why the priest had done nothing about Jeremiah (29:26-27).

Shemaiah then summarized the letter that Jeremiah had sent to the Babylonian exiles. He claimed that Jeremiah had written that the exiles would be in Babylon for a long time. He charged that Jeremiah instructed the exiles to settle down and build houses. He told them to plant gardens and eat what they produce (29:28).

Jeremiah had indeed written these instructions to the exiles (29:5, 10). The critical issue was whether Jeremiah had written his letter as a true spokesman for the Lord. Or was Shemaiah the true prophet? After Zephaniah read Shemaiah's letter to Jeremiah, the Lord spoke to one of the men. He spoke to Jeremiah.

The Lord told Jeremiah to give a message to Shemaiah. The Lord exposed Shemaiah as a false prophet. On his own initiative Shemaiah had sent letters, not just to Zephaniah, but also to all the other priests and to all the people in Jerusalem (29:24-25).

The Lord told Jeremiah to send another letter to the exiles in Babylon. The Lord wanted Jeremiah to expose Shemaiah as a phony prophet to all the exiles. Jeremiah wrote that the Lord did not send Shemaiah as a prophet and that Shemaiah was giving them false assurances. Shemaiah had counseled rebellion against the Lord. So the Lord was going to punish Shemaiah and his whole family. There would not be any of them left to experience the Lord's blessings (29:30-32).

Shemaiah had implied that Jeremiah was a madman (29:26). Shemaiah's letter could have ruined Jeremiah's day. You may have days when you receive letters like this. When you do, consider the source of the letter. If the letter is from someone like Shemaiah, then do not be discouraged. Just keep living closer to the Lord.

**How should you react when you are falsely accused?**

Day 196
BOOK OF HOPE

**Jeremiah 30:1-2. *This is the word that came to Jeremiah from the LORD: "This is what the LORD, the God of Israel, says: 'Write in a book all the words I have spoken to you....'"***

The Lord told Jeremiah to write a book of His words. Under God's direction, Jeremiah also wrote other Scripture. During King Jehoiakim's reign, he dictated to Baruch some other words from the Lord. Baruch wrote them on a scroll (36:4). Later, Jeremiah wrote a scroll containing God's words about Babylon (51:60). These and other writings eventually became the Bible Book of Jeremiah.

When Jeremiah wrote a letter to the exiles in Babylon, he told them that the Lord planned to give them hope and a future (29:11). Then the Lord revealed the specifics of His plan to Jeremiah and instructed him to write these words in a book. God's plan for the welfare of His people is detailed in the next four chapters (30-33).

The Lord gave these words to Jeremiah to write in order to give His people hope. Many believers refer to these four chapters as Jeremiah's Book of Comfort. Jeremiah wrote that Israel and Judah would be restored (30:3). The Lord would make a new covenant with the two nations (31:31-34). Their hearts would be changed (32:39-40). A descendant of David would bring justice and righteousness to the earth (33:15).

Before Jeremiah's time, the Assyrians had conquered the nation of Israel. Jeremiah prophesied repeatedly that Judah would also go into captivity. Undoubtedly, Jeremiah longed to have some good news to share! The Lord's good news was that the captivity would end. The people would return to their land. These promises would give Jeremiah and his people real hope.

Jeremiah needed hope. Jeremiah had preached for years that judgment was coming. His own people rejected both his message and him. Instead of listening to the truth, they placed their faith in false hopes. Jeremiah needed a word from the Lord that would lift him up.

You need hope, too. Even if you face gloom today, you need to know that the Lord will someday reign. He will reward you for your perseverance as you serve Him for years and even decades. You need to know that there is hope.

**As you face this day that the Lord has given you, what specifically is giving you hope?**

## Day 197
### RESTORATION

**Jeremiah 30:3.** *"'The days are coming,' declares the LORD, 'when I will bring my people Israel and Judah back from captivity and restore them to the land I gave their forefathers to possess,' says the LORD."*

After seventy years of Babylonian captivity, the Lord did indeed restore the nations of Israel and Judah. However, He did not bring the people back to the land in their previous condition. The Lord returned people who were better.

They came back to the land as different people from their ancestors. They were no longer idolaters. The Judeans who lived during Jeremiah's time had worshipped idols (1:16). Even when God first formed the nation of Israel under Moses, the people tended to adore idols (Deuteronomy 32:21). From Moses to Jeremiah, the people pursued idols.

Seventy years in Babylon purged them of their idolatrous habits. The change was permanent, even throughout successive generations. When Jesus Christ preached against the sins of the Pharisees hundreds of years later, He never mentioned idols. He said that the Pharisees were hypocrites. They were not idolaters. When the Lord restores, He makes people better.

Jesus' disciples recognized His power to restore. After His resurrection, they asked Him if He was going to now restore the kingdom to Israel (Acts 1:6). (The answer was no.) The disciples believed that Jeremiah and other prophets spoke of a more glorious restoration than the return after the Babylonian captivity, and they believed that it had not yet happened. God promised a future permanent restoration. The people would never be uprooted from their land again (Amos 9:15).

Through Jesus Christ, believers can experience restoration now. They can restore relationships with each other. Spiritual believers should restore those who have fallen into sin (Galatians 6:1). When Christians are in different locations, they can pray that God would restore them to each other. Philemon had prayed that Paul would be restored to him (Philemon 22). The author of the Letter to the Hebrews asked for prayer that he would be restored to them soon (Hebrews 13:19).

Jeremiah's God is the God who restores. The Lord promised to restore His people to spiritual health. He promised to restore their city, their honor and their community (30:17-20). He will restore you, through Jesus Christ.

**What are you especially praying that the Lord will restore for you?**

Day 198

## Men in Labor

*Jeremiah 30:6. Ask and see: Can a man bear children? Then why do I see every strong man with his hands on his stomach like a woman in labor, every face turned deathly pale?*

Jeremiah did not have a wife. If he had, I can imagine what she might have said in reaction to his illustration of a woman in labor. "What does a man know about the pain of giving birth? A man can never know what it is like!"

Jeremiah, like every other man, did not have the personal experience of bearing children. Yet the Lord chose this vivid comparison as He revealed to Jeremiah the degree of future pain. Jeremiah had used this illustration of labor pains in previous sermons. He preached that the city of Jerusalem would be gasping for breath, like a woman in labor (4:31). He predicted that when the Babylonian armies came to Jerusalem, the Judeans' pain would be like a woman in childbirth (6:24).

Jeremiah particularly warned those in the royal palace in Jerusalem. He described them as safely nested in the Lebanon cedars, which was what the palace was built with. However, even the royal family would not be safe. They would groan like a woman in childbirth (22:23).

Jeremiah was not the only one who used this illustration. Isaiah and Micah did too. When Jesus preached about the end times, He said that war, famine and earthquakes would be just the beginning of birth pains (Matthew 24:7-8). Paul continued this metaphor when he wrote to the Thessalonians. He wrote that the day of judgment would come suddenly. Suffering would come on people like labor pains on a pregnant woman (1 Thessalonians 5:1-3).

What happens after a woman gives birth to a child? According to Jesus, the joy she has over her baby is greater than all the pain she experienced (John 16:21). Pain comes first, but pain is not the end.

Jesus, Jeremiah and the other prophets used this illustration of labor pains to give us hope. In the great tribulation of the future, unimaginable suffering will give birth to Christ's kingdom. Before that happens, each of us goes through our personal "tiny trib". In light of eternity, our pain is just for a moment. God will use all of our sufferings to give birth to something better.

**In what exact ways can your relationship with the Lord help you endure pain?**

## Day 199
### TROUBLE

**Jeremiah 30:7.** *How awful that day will be! None will be like it. It will be a time of trouble for Jacob, but he will be saved out of it.*

At the beginning of the Book of Hope, the Lord gave Jeremiah some bad news. Before the glorious restoration, a time of trouble would occur. It will be the worst disaster that the world has seen.

The time of trouble was not the Babylonian destruction of Jerusalem. After that event, as terrible as it was, Daniel wrote that a time of distress like none other would still happen in the future (Daniel 12:1). Hundreds of years later, Jesus Christ spoke of a future great tribulation. Its destruction would be greater than anything else that has ever occurred (Matthew 24:21).

Forty years after Jesus' death, Jerusalem was destroyed again, this time by the Romans. This again was not the worst time of trouble. Far greater atrocities against humanity and against Jews in particular were committed in the 20th Century.

In the 1st Century after the Romans sacked Jerusalem, the Apostle John wrote that the time of trouble was still in the future. Included with the disasters will be a great earthquake. It will be more destructive than any other earthquake that people have ever seen (Revelation 16:18).

The good news about the time of trouble is that Jacob will be saved out of it. Jacob is another name of Israel. God will rescue His people from the terrifying tribulation. In ways that are incomprehensible to us, the Lord uses suffering and evil to bring about good.

For Jeremiah's contemporaries who experienced the Babylonian holocaust, theological debates about a future great tribulation were not pertinent. Jeremiah's people were already suffering. They suffered in more ways than any of their ancestors. Many of them died brutally and painfully. Those who lived saw their nation die.

Perhaps you have already experienced greater distress than you could bear. Maybe you will suffer greatly in the future. If so, even if you cannot think about it in the midst of your pain, you can know that our good God will use your suffering for good.

**How can you see God's use of distress in your life to produce something better?**

Day 200

FREEDOM

*Jeremiah 30:8. "'In that day,' declares the LORD Almighty, 'I will break the yoke off their necks and will tear off their bonds; no longer will foreigners enslave them....'"*

Desire for freedom has persisted throughout human history. Jeremiah's people remembered that their ancestors had been slaves of Egypt (34:13). They did not want to face slavery in their generation.

Jeremiah preached for years that slavery indeed awaited them. He wore yokes and bonds to illustrate his message (27:2). He told the king of Judah to put himself under the yoke of the Babylonians (27:12).

The Judeans would be slaves of Babylon for seventy years (29:10). Finally the Lord would break the Babylonian yoke and the people could return to their land. Sadly, their descendants would become slaves again to other powerful nations. What happened to the Lord's promise that foreigners would no longer enslave them?

Centuries later, Jesus taught the Judeans' descendants about true freedom. He told them that by becoming disciples of His, they would then know the truth. And this truth would set them free (John 8:31-32).

The Judean's descendants objected to Jesus' teaching about freedom. They told Jesus that they were Abraham's descendants. They claimed that they had never been enslaved to anyone (John 8:33).

What were they thinking?! At the very moment that they were telling Jesus that they had always been free, they were under the power of the Roman government. And had they forgotten the many years of their ancestors' slavery under the Babylonians?

Jesus was not speaking about political freedom. He told the Jews that slavery to sin was His topic. The problem with this type of slavery is that a sinner cannot become free by his or her own strength. Even though they were sons of Abraham, they had no possibility of being truly free. Jesus Christ claimed to be the Son who could make them free from sin. Then they would be free indeed (John 8:34-36).

The Lord planned for His people to be free to serve. They would have spiritual freedom from their sins. Then they could use their freedom to serve the Lord.

**Explain how you have freedom in your relationship with the Lord.**

Day 201

SERVING THE KING

**Jeremiah 30:9. *Instead, they will serve the Lord their God and David their king,
whom I will raise up for them.***

Jeremiah prophesied that the Lord would set His people free in the future (30:
8). Their freedom would have a focus on service. Whom would they serve? At
first glance, Jeremiah seemed to say that they would serve both the Lord and a
resurrected King David!

Will believers serve King David, the father of Solomon, in the future Kingdom?
Some Bible teachers think so. They teach that a literal David is in harmony with a
literal interpretation of the Bible.

However, Jeremiah closely coupled "the Lord their God" with "David their
King". No resurrected ruler other than Jesus will come close to being equal with
God in being worthy of service from believers. David's name is closely aligned
to the promised Messiah in many Scripture verses. Jeremiah preached that the
Messiah would be the branch of David (23:5). When Jesus rode into Jerusalem on
a donkey, the crowds recognized His fulfillment of Messianic prophecy and called
him the son of David (Matthew 21:9). John wrote that Jesus is David's descendant
(Revelation 22:16).

Jesus can be called the last David, in the same sense that Paul called Jesus the
last Adam (1 Corinthians 15:45). Jesus fulfilled the words about the Messiah being
the Lord's servant David (Ezekiel 37:24). The royal title of David is another way to
describe the Kingship of Jesus.

Hundreds of years before the time of Jeremiah, the Lord made a covenant with
King David. The Lord promised that David's throne would be set up to last forever
(2 Samuel 7:16). This promise has been fulfilled in Jesus Christ. The angel Gabriel
promised Mary that God the Father would give David's throne to Jesus (Luke 1:
32-33).

Even though the Lord referred to Nebuchadnezzar king of Babylon as His
servant (25:9), the king of Babylon would inevitably become one of the strangers
(30:8) from whom believers would be set free. After the Second Coming, there will
be no more pagan kings to serve. Believers will serve only the Lord their God and
the King of kings.

Are you preparing to serve the King forever? Begin by serving Him now. Work
hard for Him and not for yourself.

**In what specific ways will you serve the Lord during the next week?**

## Day 202
### SECURITY

**Jeremiah 30:10.** *"'So do not fear, O Jacob my servant; do not be dismayed, O Israel,' declares the LORD. 'I will surely save you out of a distant place, your descendants from the land of their exile. Jacob will again have peace and security, and no one will make him afraid....'"*

Jeremiah's words from the Lord would uplift believers in Babylon for seventy years. While they were in exile, the Lord did not desire for them to be afraid or depressed about their circumstances. God promised to rescue them from the far away land where they were deported.

Jacob's descendants would be the Lord's servants. They would have nothing more to fear. The testimony of the Bible is that the Lord has richly provided for His servants through the ages. He will give ultimate and permanent security to His servants in the coming Kingdom.

Through these hopeful words about security, the Lord was preparing Jeremiah for His revelation about the New Covenant. The Lord would soon give Jeremiah the terms of the New Covenant. For now, He wanted Jeremiah to comprehend some of the results of the New Covenant.

After the complete implementation of the New Covenant, all God's people will live in peace. They will finally have security at all levels of their lives. No enemy will ever disturb them again.

Jeremiah preached these same words in the midst of his sermon of judgment against Egypt. He prophesied that God would use the Babylonians as instruments of judgment against Egypt (46:26-27). Egypt had been one of the persistent enemies of Israel and Judah. Hearing promises of security for God's people at the end of a message about God's judgment of Egypt would have especially heartened the Jews. God's defeat of all their enemies would guarantee their security.

As well as encouraging the believers during the seventy year exile in Babylon, words from the Lord about security continue to cheer believers today. Through Jesus Christ, you can be secure in God's love. Through Jesus Christ, absolutely nothing can separate you from His love (Romans 8:38-39).

**How has your security in the Lord affected your daily choices during the past month?**

## Day 203
### GOD WITH YOU

**Jeremiah 30:11. "'I am with you and will save you,' declares the LORD. 'Though I completely destroy all the nations among which I scatter you, I will not completely destroy you. I will discipline you but only with justice; I will not let you go entirely unpunished.'"**

When the Lord called Jeremiah, He promised twice to be with him and save him (1:8,19). He later repeated the promise again to Jeremiah (15:20). This was the Lord's assurance to the prophet so that he could be bold as he carried out his ministry.

The Lord gave this same promise to one of the men who helped to fulfill this promise to Jeremiah. After Ebed-Melech saved Jeremiah from the cistern, God promised to save Ebed-Melech from his enemies. The Lord would rescue him because he trusted in Him (39:17-18).

Now the Lord significantly expanded the number of recipients of this promise. God promised to be with an entire nation and to save them. However, He would discipline the people of His chosen nation before He would complete His salvation of them.

The Babylonian captivity would be part of the disciplinary process, but the discipline is not yet finished. This promise to the entire nation extends far into the future. The complete fulfillment of this promise will come only after the Lord destroys all nations. This has not happened yet. Nations today are thriving. And God's people are still scattered.

God continues to discipline His people today, but only with justice. God always disciplines His children only when they need it. As long as they live on earth, believers will never outgrow their need for God's discipline. God can use painful circumstances to teach them His ways.

A sinning believer can expect to receive God's cosmic spanking! This is a partial answer to the difficult question of why there is suffering in the world. You do not always know the reason for a particular distress. When a new hurt comes, you can draw nearer to God to try to sense if He is disciplining you. You can be sensitive to what He wants you to learn. God promises to be with His people and to save them. He is with you today. Are you with Him?

**Describe specifically how you can be confident that the Lord is with you today.**

## Day 204
### JOY AND HONOR

**Jeremiah 30:19.** *From them will come songs of thanksgiving and the sound of rejoicing. I will add to their numbers, and they will not be decreased; I will bring them honor, and they will not be disdained.*

If you could experience never-ending joy and honor, you would have the best possible life. The Lord promised both to His restored people. Jeremiah undoubtedly received major encouragement from this verse.

During much of his ministry, Jeremiah knew that each day would bring him sorrow and dishonor. He wept for his people, yet they continued in their sins. He honored God by obeying Him, yet the people did not honor him for being the Lord's prophet.

However, Jeremiah knew that future joy and honor would come. This knowledge enabled him to endure his difficulties. He knew that God would later restore His people (30:18). He also knew that the Lord would punish every oppressor of His people (30:20).

Knowing that he would experience future joy and honor, Jeremiah could experience present joy in the midst of all his problems. He found great joy from God's Word. The Lord's words were the delight of His heart (15:16).

Also, later in life he began to receive the honor that was due him. The Babylonians showed him much respect and honored him with gifts (40:5). Long after his death, Jeremiah was honored by being compared with Jesus Christ (Matthew 16:13-14).

I have slowly learned that I should not seek honor for myself. I used to joke that I was working on my honorary doctorate degree! I have now given up that pursuit. I believe God's promise that He will honor those people who honor Him (1 Samuel 2:30).

God continues to increase the number of people to whom He will give joy and honor. Constantly adding to the population of His people will increase the amount of joy and honor on earth. The Lord has not yet established on earth His perfect Kingdom of joy and honor, because He is giving more people opportunities to come to Him (2 Peter 3:9).

**To what extent do you trust the Lord for the joy and the honor that He has promised?**

## Day 205
### HOME-GROWN AND PRIESTLY

**Jeremiah 30:21.** *"'Their leader will be one of their own; their ruler will arise from among them. I will bring him near and he will come close to me, for who is he who will devote himself to be close to me?' declares the Lord"*

The Lord revealed a tremendous promise to Jeremiah about the future leader of His people. He told Jeremiah that the ruler would have two characteristics. These two features would have especially encouraged the prophet. The future prince would be (1) a native Judean and (2) would be qualified to be close to God.

The fact that the future ruler would be from his own nation would hearten Jeremiah. Jeremiah knew that Judah would be under the dominance of Babylon for seventy years (25:11). The Lord gave Jeremiah additional hope that someday his nation would not serve foreign monarchs. Actually, the Lord had given this promise many centuries earlier. In Moses' time, God promised that the future king would come from among their brothers (Deuteronomy 17:15).

The second feature would also cheer Jeremiah. After enduring a succession of ungodly men on the throne in Jerusalem, Jeremiah would welcome the promise of a godly ruler. This leader would have an intimate relationship with the Lord.

God described this future ruler's closeness to Him in such a way that only a priest could fit this description. Jeremiah knew that only a priest could draw near to God and represent the people before Him. Since Jeremiah's father was a priest, Jeremiah was especially sensitive to this fact.

Not even kings could draw near to God on behalf of the people. Before Jeremiah's time, some kings had tried to perform priestly roles. King Jeroboam tried to set up a system of sacrifices outside the temple, but the Lord rebuked him through a prophet (1 Kings 12:26-13:6). King Uzziah arrogantly burned incense in the temple, and the priests opposed him. Uzziah immediately came down with leprosy (2 Chronicles 26:16-21).

The future leader would be a native-born king (30:9) as well as a priest. None of Abraham's descendants met this description until Jesus. Jesus Christ was born in Bethlehem, Judah. God the Father called Jesus to be a high priest (Hebrews 5:4-6). Only Jesus could be the fulfillment of the home-grown and priestly ruler.

**How does Jesus as the fulfillment of the priestly ruler enable you to grow closer to God?**

## Day 206
### THE LORD'S FIERCE ANGER

**Jeremiah 30:24.** *The fierce anger of the LORD will not turn back until he fully accomplishes the purposes of his heart. In days to come you will understand this.*

I still remember seeing the anger on the face of my earthly father when I was a young boy. I knew that I deserved his anger, because I had disobeyed. In the same way, I realized later in life that I also deserved God's anger.

However, many people today do not like to think of the Lord as angry. They certainly do not like the concept of His anger being fierce! They want God to be like a gentle grandfather in a rocking chair "upstairs"!

People in Jeremiah's day had the same attitude. They did not want to believe that God in His wrath would judge them. They wanted to believe the false prophets who preached that they would have peace.

In contrast to the false prophets, Jeremiah warned about a specific unleashing of the Lord's fierce anger. A destroyer of nations would come from the north. The land of Judah would be ruined (4:6-8).

Jeremiah lived to see the results of God's anger. The Lord used the Babylonians to judge Jeremiah's city. Even the Babylonian commander of the guard understood that the Judeans had brought this destruction on themselves by sinning against the Lord (40:2-3).

It would take a longer time for the Judeans themselves to understand. Jeremiah said that they would understand "in days to come". Long after the city lay in ruins, the people began to comprehend the Lord's anger.

People today are even slower to understand. Many do not realize that all unrighteous people are under God's wrath (Romans 1:18). They are also oblivious to the fact that everyone is unrighteous (Romans 3:8).

The way to escape God's fierce anger is clear. In His love, God sent Jesus Christ to die for you (Romans 5:8-9). By His blood, you can be saved from His wrath.

**Briefly explain how you have personally escaped from the Lord's fierce anger.**

## Day 207
## THE GOD OF ALL

**Jeremiah 31:1.** *"At that time," declares the Lord, "I will be the God of all the clans of Israel, and they will be my people."*

The clans of Israel were scattered, weak and disorganized. The northern ten tribes of Israel were already in exile when Jeremiah was born. Jeremiah lived to see the day of the exile of the southern two tribes, when the Babylonians conquered Judah. It appeared as if the Lord was no longer the God of *any* of the clans of Israel.

However, the Lord gave Jeremiah tremendous hope in this section of the book (chapters 30-33). It would be obvious in the future that the Lord truly was the God of all of Israel and Judah. The Lord made His New Covenant with both Israel and Judah (31:31). The Lord would be God of all.

Also, all of Israel would be His people. The Lord had revealed to Jeremiah that they would be His people and He would be their God (30:22). The relationship would be two-way.

In another sermon, Jeremiah preached that this two-way relationship had been God's intention from the beginning. In order for this two-way relationship to work, the people had to obey God's commands. Obedience was the key (7:23).

When God made the first covenant with Moses, He promised this two-way relationship (Exodus 6:7). The Lord promised that He would walk among them and be their God, and they would be His people (Leviticus 26:12). The people failed to obey, but God kept His two-way relationship promise by making the New Covenant (31:31-34).

Jesus Christ became the mediator of the New Covenant (Hebrews 8:6). Anyone can now be one of God's people through Jesus Christ. It does not matter whether that person is a Jew or Gentile. All believers in Jesus Christ receive the promise of the two-way relationship.

In the future, the God of all Israel will truly be the God of all people everywhere. Yes, your relationship with the Lord is very personal. But you must remember that your relationship with God is not exclusive. In the future, everyone will bow and confess that Jesus is Lord (Philippians 2:9-11). Your God is the God of all.

**How does the fact that the Lord is God of all affect your relationship with Him?**

Day 208
### LONG-LASTING LOVE

**Jeremiah 31:3. *The LORD appeared to us in the past, saying: "I have loved you with an everlasting love; I have drawn you with loving-kindness....."***

Jeremiah's life was tough and painful, but he knew that God loved him. In this stunning verse about God's love, there is a Hebrew word that can refer to either time or distance. The word can be translated as either "in the past" or "from afar". Either translation correctly describes the fullness of God's love.

Jeremiah knew that the Lord had appeared to his people in the past. When the Lord appeared to Moses, He said that He would show love to those thousands of people who would love Him (Exodus 20:6). The Lord loved the people who followed Moses and expressed that love by bringing them out of Egypt (Deuteronomy 7:8). The Lord chose to love them (Deuteronomy 10:15).

The Lord loved them in the past, but He would also love them from afar. In a far off land He would express His affection for them. As the people went into exile in Babylon, the Lord's love for them would be just as intense as if they were in Jerusalem. They would be ejected from the Lord's city, but not be rejected from His love.

The Lord's love is unchangeable. He loved His people from the beginning, because He chose to do so. Even when they disobeyed Him, He waited patiently and lovingly for them to return to Him. Jeremiah's generation was like the prodigal son in the parable that Jesus told. God was the loving Father who waited for them to return. He wanted to shower them with His inexplicable love as soon as they came back to Him.

Jeremiah described God's love as active. God had "drawn" His people to Himself. The Lord's strong love pulls men and women into relationships with Himself. Later, this same Hebrew word was used to describe Jeremiah's rescue from the cistern. Jeremiah's friends "pulled" him out of the cistern (38:13).

Are you aware of the strong pull of God's love? God's love is like the strong pull of a father rescuing his child. When I was a young boy in the ocean for the first time, a wave knocked me down and water covered my head. I did not know which direction the shore was. I then felt my father's hands and he pulled me out of the water.

The powerful pull of God's love is perpetual. Jeremiah knew that God loved him continually. The Lord has loved even before time began. God's love will never end.

**Describe your level of awareness of how much God loves you.**

## Day 209
### LOVE FROM AFAR

*Jeremiah 31:3. The LORD appeared to us in the past, saying: "I have loved you with an everlasting love; I have drawn you with loving-kindness...."*

The Lord was Jeremiah's closest friend. When Jeremiah felt like everyone was cursing him (15:10), he knew that he could still depend on the Lord for comfort. When he learned that even his own family members had turned against him (12:6), he nonetheless knew that the Lord still loved him and would protect him.

The Hebrew literally says, "The Lord appeared to *me*." But the pronoun "you" in "I have loved you," refers to the nation, as the next verse makes clear. The Lord's personal message to Jeremiah was that He loved the people of Jeremiah's nation.

The Hebrew word translated as "in the past" can also mean "from afar". If the Lord appeared to Jeremiah from afar, His appearance confirmed what Jeremiah had preached about God. Jeremiah had explained that the Lord was more than the God who was near. He was also the God who was far off (23:23).

Jeremiah's friendship with God was based on knowing both that the Lord was near him all the time and also that God was far off. God was bigger than Jeremiah could imagine. Jeremiah could not fully understand God's immensity, but he knew that the Lord was not confined to the temple in Jerusalem. He knew that the Lord's throne was in heaven. He knew that the Lord lived in a high and holy place (Isaiah 57:15).

The Hebrew word for "drawn" can also be translated as "continued". This word is translated as "continue" in Psalm 36:10, where David prayed that the Lord would continue His loving kindness to those who knew Him. Believers do not need to pray this prayer any longer. Through Jesus, God's everlasting love continues.

Jeremiah also preached about God's loving kindness at other times. Jeremiah knew that God exercised loving kindness, justice and righteousness on the earth (9:24) He knew that the Lord shows His loving kindness to many people (32:18).

God's love is an everlasting love, and the fact that God continues to love gave Jeremiah double confidence that God's love toward him was permanent. God loves you in this same double lasting way. The Lord wants His relationship with you to be immersed in His eternal love.

**Describe in your own words how God's love to you is everlasting.**

## Day 210
### DISTANT AND VULNERABLE

*Jeremiah 31:8. See, I will bring them from the land of the north and gather them from the ends of the earth. Among them will be the blind and the lame, expectant mothers and women in labor; a great throng will return.*

From the day that the Lord called him, Jeremiah knew about the land of the north. He knew that a nation from the north would conquer Judah. He also knew the reason why. The Judeans had forsaken the Lord and had turned to worship idols (1:14-16).

Much later in Jeremiah's career, the Lord revealed some good news about the land of the north. The captives would be freed from Babylon and be able to return to their land. However, the Lord's promise went much further than Babylon. God promised to bring His people from the most remote spots on the earth.

I have been in far-flung areas in foreign countries where I felt like I was in the outer extremities of civilization! I prayed that God would bring me back to familiar territory! He did. The Lord's point to Jeremiah was that no one would be so far away that the Lord could not restore that person.

Have you felt distant from the Lord? Do you sense that He is not close enough to restore you? Remember that God is nearby as well as far away (23:23).

The Lord would also restore those who felt the most vulnerable. The blind, the lame, expectant mothers and those actually in labor would doubt that they could travel back to the land. The blind would not see the road. The lame, as well as women in labor, would not be able to walk on the road.

The Lord has special provisions for the disadvantaged. In His kingdom, the eyes of the blind will be opened and the lame will leap like a deer (Isaiah 35:5-6). Jesus healed the blind and the lame during His ministry on earth. Jesus' mother had God's help as she traveled to Bethlehem carrying Him in her womb. Women in labor cannot journey at all. They are among the ones that the Lord will carry in His arms.

The Lord will gather His lambs and carry them close to His heart (Isaiah 40:11). Even the most vulnerable people could still travel on that road back from captivity. Their weaknesses would not hold them back, and yours need not either!

**What feelings of inadequacy seem to be holding you back from traveling on the road toward intimacy with God? How can you overcome these and grow closer to the Lord?**

Day 211

STREAMS

*Jeremiah 31:9. They will come with weeping; they will pray as I bring them back. I will lead them beside streams of water on a level path where they will not stumble, because I am Israel's father, and Ephraim is my firstborn son.*

After being released from captivity, the people would follow the Lord back to the promised land. They would pray, expressing their dependence on Him. And they would weep, shedding both tears of repentance and tears of joy.

As the streams of tears flowed down their cheeks, the Lord would lead them near streams of water. God's streams would replace the tear streams on their faces. Centuries earlier, David had written that the Lord would shepherd His people beside quiet waters (Psalm 23:2).

This group of weeping and praying men and women would include many more people than just the Judeans returning from the Babylonian captivity. There would also be a large number of Israelites from the long-banished northern kingdom. The Israelites would come back also, because the Lord said that He was Israel's father.

The Lord also said that Ephraim was His firstborn son. Ephraim was another name for Israel. Ephraim was originally the name of one of Joseph's sons, who was blessed as the firstborn by Joseph's father (Genesis 48:13-14). Even though Joseph was not a firstborn son himself, he received the birthright of the firstborn because of his older brothers' sin (1 Chronicles 5:1-2).

So neither Ephraim nor his father Joseph was physically a firstborn son. Yet they both received the rights of firstborns. Later, the entire nation of Israel took on the name of Ephraim. However, it appeared as if the nation lost any firstborn benefits when it went into captivity.

Through Jeremiah, the Lord reaffirmed that the nation was still His dear son. Ephraim was the child in whom God delighted. The Lord would show Ephraim His mercy (31:20).

The Lord in His compassion would lead the captives to freedom by the streams of water. Jeremiah had preached that the Lord is the fountain of living waters (2:13). God would lead them back to Himself. He still leads needy people to His streams today.

**How can your relationship with the Lord be as refreshing as streams of water?**

## Day 212
## JOY

**Jeremiah 31:13.** *Then maidens will dance and be glad, young men and old as well. I will turn their mourning into gladness; I will give them comfort and joy instead of sorrow.*

Jeremiah was not a prophet of gloom and doom his entire life! He knew about joy and happiness. He preached some of the most optimistic words in the entire Old Testament.

In this one verse, a form of the word "joy" is used three times. First, the people will have joy as they danced. Second, God will turn their mourning into joy. Third, God will replace their sorrow with joy.

The Lord promised that He would give joy to men and women of all age groups. God had promised that sorrow would be permanently eliminated (31:12). Jeremiah had earlier preached that the people should put on sackcloth on ashes and mourn over their situation. Destruction was in their future (6:26). Now God revealed that He was reversing human sadness.

The Lord had told Jeremiah that his people would take up their tambourines and dance with joyous people (31:4). They would sing loudly with joy (31:7). And they would shout for joy on top of Zion (31:12).

People who have joy have an expectation of future goodness. They can live happily in the present by living moment by moment for the Lord. The Lord has given many promises about joy for His people.

Jesus Christ had joy. The most amazing fact about the joy that Jesus had was His joy on the cross. For the joy set before Him, He endured the cross (Hebrews 12:2). Jesus certainly did not enjoy the pain of suffering. He had joy because He looked beyond His crucifixion. Jesus saw what His suffering would accomplish. Jesus looked forward to sharing His joy with all those people who would be in heaven because of their faith in what His death accomplished for them.

Jeremiah had joy because He believed God's promises and looked toward the future. Jeremiah's people would have unending joy in the future. They would have a permanent gloom reversal. It was enough for Jeremiah to have this glimpse into the joyous kingdom, so that he could live his remaining days with hope.

**What thoughts about your future give you the most joy?**

## Day 213
### SATISFACTION

**Jeremiah 31:14.** *"I will satisfy the priests with abundance, and my people will be filled with my bounty," declares the LORD.*

All God's people will be satisfied in the future. Even fleeting moments of dissatisfaction will cease to exist. God's goodness in its limitless glory will constantly fill everyone in His Kingdom.

Jeremiah wrote that the priests especially would experience satisfaction. As a priest's son, he probably took note of the Lord's mention of this religious class of people. The priests in his day were deceitful (6:13) and godless (23:11), but Jeremiah anticipated a time when every priest would trust in the Lord.

The "abundance" that the Lord would give to the priests is literally "fatness" in Hebrew. The Hebrew term was used to describe the part of the animal sacrifices that the priests could eat (Leviticus 7:31-36). Since all the people would have bounteous food, they would bring many more offerings to the priests. So the priests would share in the abundance.

Why will there priests in the coming Kingdom? Doesn't the high priesthood of Jesus Christ make the Jewish priests obsolete? Because Jesus gave Himself once for all as the perfect sacrifice for sin, how can there be any more need for priests and their inferior sacrifices?

When the church began in Jerusalem after Jesus' resurrection, many of the priests became believers (Acts 6:7). Apparently, these and numerous other priests will serve the Lord in the future Kingdom. They will not make sacrifices for sins. Their offerings will be memorials for the sacrificial work of Jesus Christ.

The provisions for the believer priests to serve throughout eternity are a cue to all believers. In the coming Kingdom, the Lord will provide His richest bounty for all believers so that they can serve them in their distinctive ways. They will be satisfied servants.

What about you? Are you feeling satisfied as you serve the Lord now, anticipating the coming Kingdom where you can serve Him forever? Are you trusting Him to meet your needs for the purpose of serving Him more faithfully?

**How can God's promise of future satisfaction help you be satisfied today?**

## Day 214
### WEEPING MOTHER

**Jeremiah 31:15.** *This is what the Lord says: "A voice is heard in Ramah, mourning and great weeping, Rachel weeping for her children and refusing to be comforted, because her children are no more."*

Rachel was the wife of Jacob, and she had two children. Their names were Joseph and Benjamin. Joseph's descendants eventually lived in the Northern Kingdom of Israel. Sadly, they had been taken then into exile 100 years before Jeremiah's time.

Benjamin's descendants lived in the Southern Kingdom of Judah, where Jeremiah lived. Jeremiah had preached for years that Benjamin's descendants would also go into exile. If Rachel had been alive, she would have wept for both of her sons.

Rachel had died while giving birth to Benjamin. She named him "Ben-oni" which means "son of my sorrow". The Lord wanted Jeremiah to imagine that Rachel still lived. He wanted the prophet to see Rachel as an illustration. He used Rachel's sorrow as she gave life to Benjamin to represent the death of many of her descendants. The Babylonians would take Jeremiah and many other captives to Ramah (40:1), where Jeremiah undoubtedly heard much weeping.

Rachel's weeping became a far-reaching prophecy. Shortly after Jesus' birth, more of Rachel's descendants were slaughtered. Matthew quoted Jeremiah 31:15, one of the saddest verses in the Bible, to describe Herod's slaughter of all the babies in the Bethlehem area (Matthew 2:13-18). However, there would be hope even in the midst of all the tears. Joseph took Mary and Jesus to Egypt, and Jesus was spared from Herod's massacre. The Messiah lived to become a Man, and He chose to die for the world's sins. Consequently, grieving parents can have hope that their babies are alive with Him!

Jeremiah also could preach hope to his contemporaries who faced exile. They should restrain from weeping and wipe away their tears. The Lord promised that their work would be rewarded and that their descendants would return from the land of the enemy. Jeremiah said that there was hope for their future (31:16-17).

Even if you are experiencing a time of weeping, remember that there is still hope for your future. David wrote that weeping may linger for a night, but shouts of joy come in the morning (Psalm 30:5). Maybe you feel like you are having nights of weeping. You can know that a joyful morning is coming!

**What is your expectation of having a future "morning of rejoicing"?**

Day 215
WILD CALF

**Jeremiah 31:18.** *"I have surely heard Ephraim's moaning: 'You disciplined me like an unruly calf, and I have been disciplined. Restore me, and I will return, because you are the LORD my God....'"*

Like untamed calves, the people had strayed from the Lord. Like a mighty rancher, the Lord had caught and disciplined the wild calves. Like Rachel weeping for her children (31:15), the Lord had a heart of compassion as he dealt with the calves.

God gave Jeremiah the words that the people of Ephraim would say in the future. They would confess that they were rebellious and that the Lord had disciplined them. Then they would pray that the Lord would restore them, and they would return to Him.

An earlier prophet compared the people of Israel to a stubborn heifer (Hosea 4: 16). They were like a trained heifer that farmers used to thresh grain. However, the Lord would put a yoke on that young cow (Hosea 10:11).

Unruly calves had to be trained so they would carry yokes. The Lord's yoke is easy and is in the calf's best interests. However, because of their rebellion against the Lord, the people of Ephraim were cruelly yoked by the Assyrians and taken away as captives.

The words that Jeremiah put in the mouth of Ephraim were literally in Hebrew, "Turn and I will return." If God turned to the people of Ephraim and accepted them, they would turn to Him. As a humbled people, they wanted to return to the Lord. They would embrace the Lord as their God.

Do you still sometimes behave like a wild calf? If you belong to the Lord, He will keep taming and disciplining you. However, He no longer looks upon you as a calf.

Through Jesus Christ, God sees all of His people as His own sons and daughters. He disciplines them as human parents would punish their own children. Often human parents discipline as seems best to them, but God always chastises in ways that are best for His children. Human parents carry out discipline for a short time, until their children grow older. The Lord will discipline His children during their entire earthly lives (Hebrews 12:5-11)!

**In what ways has the Lord disciplined you like His own child during the past year?**

## Day 216
### GUIDEPOSTS

**Jeremiah 31:21. "Set up road signs; put up guideposts. Take note of the highway, the road that you take. Return, O Virgin Israel, return to your towns ...."**

The final exile to Babylon would definitely happen. Jeremiah advised the captives to plan to set up guideposts as they were taken to Babylon. These markers along the roads would help their descendants find their way back to Jerusalem. The road signs would help keep the returning people from wandering in the desert.

Guideposts were small heaps of rocks that caravans used to mark their way through the deserts. Sometimes the travelers made small stone pillars. It was understood that no one would tamper with the guideposts.

The Babylonians probably did not allow their captives to set up literal road marks. Jeremiah spoke figuratively. His point was that the future return from Babylon was inevitable. The Judean prisoners should plan their itinerary back even as they went to Babylon.

Jeremiah's great prophetic predecessor, Isaiah, wrote about this highway. It would be called the Highway of Holiness (Isaiah 35:8). Those who traveled back to the land on this road would be singing loudly and joyfully (Isaiah 35:10). God would lead them as they went on the right road (Isaiah 42:16).

Jeremiah had earlier preached that the Lord wanted His people to walk on the ancient paths. They refused (6:16). Their ancestors followed the ways of the Lord, but they did not. Their future descendents would.

The Lord would give His people a new beginning when they returned from Babylon. He called His people "Virgin Israel". It would be like a prostitute turning back the years and becoming a virgin again. A nation of idol worshippers would become one that was faithful to the Lord. Only the Lord could make this transformation.

If you know the Lord, He has given you a new beginning. He desires to bring you along the road from captivity to freedom. The Lord wants you to follow the road from the ensnarement of the world back to His heart. The road to God's heart is lined with guideposts to show you the way toward intimacy with Him.

**What particular guideposts do you think that the Lord wants you to notice this week? Why?**

## Day 217
## No More Wandering

**Jeremiah 31:22.** *"How long will you wander, O unfaithful daughter? The LORD will create a new thing on earth—a woman will surround a man."*

The Lord gave Jeremiah some harsh words to describe His people. They were unfaithful wanderers. They had drifted away God and had no relationship with Him. They used to be like a faithful woman whom the Lord called His virgin of Israel (31:21). Now they were like a daughter who had radically strayed. They needed to return to Him.

In the future they will return. It will be permanent. The Lord will be like a faithful husband to His people forever and they will genuinely know Him (Hosea 2:19).

The new thing that the Lord will create is their total return. They will come back from all the nations that had enslaved them (29:14). Not only will they return to their land, they will return to the Lord with all their hearts.

In the future, Israel will be like a woman who sets out to find her Husband again. She will be focused in her pursuit, not like the wanderer that she used to be. When she finds Him, she will "surround" Him.

This Hebrew word for "surround" can also mean "protect". The word described how the Lord took care of His people in the wilderness after they left Egypt. He encompassed them and guarded them. He protected them like an eagle shields her young (Deuteronomy 32:10-11). Through the years God continued to protect His people from the nations that threatened them. Godly men like David used the word for "surround" to express how the Lord's protection is unfailing (Psalm 32:7). Finally, the Lord withdrew His protection when His people left Him. They wandered away from Him.

In Jeremiah's day, a man always protected a woman. A woman surrounding a man was a complete role reversal of men and women. The role reversal illustrated how different everything will be in the future.

In the future, God's people will surround the Man. They will embrace the one true Lord, Jesus Christ. They will never again be wanderers. They will be worshippers forever.

**Do you ever see yourself as a spiritual wanderer? How can this verse help you be more resolute for the Lord?**

## Day 218
## VIGOR

**Jeremiah 31:25.** *"I will refresh the weary and satisfy the faint."*

The Lord gave a promise that has encouraged believers ever since Jeremiah's day. First, God gave assurances that He would restore land and cities to both farmers and shepherds (31:23-24). Then He spoke to their personal needs for refreshment and strength.

Farmers and shepherds must have strength in order to do their jobs. In the future Kingdom, the King will give them and everyone else the energy they need. He will give vigor to all Kingdom citizens.

Jeremiah certainly had days when he felt weary and faint. He undoubtedly longed for refreshment and satisfaction. After receiving this particular promise in a dream, Jeremiah awoke from a pleasant sleep (31:26).

This promise for vigor helped introduce Jeremiah to the New Covenant. After promising that Israel and Judah would be restored (31:27-30), the Lord revealed the terms of the New Covenant (31:31-34). The Lord's restoration and forgiveness would bring permanent rejuvenation.

Under the New Covenant, the Lord would write His law on their hearts. This law would not be the same law that Moses had given, because the New Covenant would be different from the old. The New Covenant law is what Paul called the law of Christ (Galatians 6:2). Jesus invited people who were weary and burdened to come to Him. (Matthew 11:28). Then Jesus quoted from Jeremiah that they would find rest for their souls (6:16).

The Lord had earlier disclosed to Jeremiah that His people would never languish again in the coming Kingdom (31:12). Many years before Jeremiah's day, the Lord promised that those who placed their hope in Him would gain new strength. (Isaiah 40:31). Centuries after Jeremiah, Jesus Christ made it possible for believers to do everything through Him who gives strength (Philippians 4:13).

The Lord gives refreshment and satisfaction to His people today. They then have the strength to always abound in the work of the Lord (1 Corinthians 15:58). They then can be strong in the grace that is in Christ Jesus (2 Timothy 2:1)

**Write a prayer to the Lord in which you ask Him for strength for a certain situation that faces you in the immediate future.**

## Day 219
### SLEEP

**Jeremiah 31:26. *At this I awoke and looked around. My sleep had been pleasant to me.***

When you think about Jeremiah's life, you do not need to take antidepressants! The Lord gave him some enjoyable experiences. One such experience occurred when Jeremiah enjoyed a satisfying sleep.

He had a pleasant sleep that night. He awoke feeling refreshed. Jeremiah experienced what would become permanent for God's people – everlasting refreshment. Just before he awoke, he heard that the Lord would refresh His weary people (31:25).

Jeremiah was weary from years of preaching to both the hostile and the apathetic. He was emotionally exhausted by the threats on his life. He probably had many sleepless nights. However, one night he slept deeply and dreamed divine promises.

After all the distresses that Jeremiah experienced throughout his ministry, the Lord gave him a night of a pleasant sleep. Jeremiah dreamed about the glorious future of his nation. God revealed His plans through Jeremiah's dream.

I have not received revelation like the New Covenant in a dream, but I do know what Jeremiah meant by having a pleasant sleep. However, I occasionally have a sleepless night. After praying for sleep and then realizing that I will not get it, I remind myself that there will be a time when I will sleep again!

When the Lord withholds slumber, He has a purpose. You often do not know the reason, but you can trust that the Lord knows why. Even though sleep is a basic universal experience, you should never treat it as an entitlement! Sleep is a gift.

Even if you do not take God seriously, He still gives you the gift of sleep. He also gives you many other undeserved blessings. God sends the sunrise for both the godly and the indifferent. He sends rain on the just and unjust (Matthew 5:45).

God revealed His great plans to Jeremiah while the prophet slept. When he awoke, he immediately remembered his dreams. He remembered that the Lord would bring His people back from captivity and enrich them. God desires to bless His people. Carry these pleasurable thoughts with you today.

**Express thanks to the Lord for those times that He has given you pleasant sleep.**

Day 220
## SOUR GRAPES

**Jeremiah 31:29-30.** *"In those days people will no longer say, 'The fathers have eaten sour grapes, and the children's teeth are set on edge.' Instead, everyone will die for his own sin; whoever eats sour grapes – his own teeth will be set on edge...."*

When I was a young child, one of my teachers read to us the Aesop's fable about the fox and the grapes. The fox could not reach the grapes, so he despised them. "Sour grapes" came to be known as a person's hatred toward whatever he or she cannot have. However, Jeremiah's sour grapes were different the grapes in Aesop's fable.

Have you ever eaten a sour grape? I have! The sour grape caused me to tighten my lips and set my teeth on edge! I now choose my grapes carefully before I eat them. When I accidentally ate the sour grape, it affected only me. It did not set my daughters' and my son's teeth on edge. The ancient proverb about sour grapes probably began with a family whose children watched their father eat a sour grape. The children were most likely so disgusted that they set their own teeth on edge!

The proverb expressed a common belief that God would punish children because of their parents' sins. Children were blaming their parents for their problems and denying their own guilt. However, their Scriptures were clear that people are responsible for their own sin. Moses wrote that fathers must not be put to death for their children's sin, or children for their fathers' sin. Each person must be punished for his own sin (Deuteronomy 24:16). Perhaps this sour grape proverb had arisen from the Lord's words to Moses that the fathers' sins would bring divine punishment to future generations. If so, Jeremiah was announcing that the situation was changing.

The Lord promised that in the future no one would even consider quoting a proverb like this. Everyone would know the truth that God judges each person with perfect justice. The Lord would unfasten the link between the sins of ancestors and future experiences. He would do this through the New Covenant that He would now reveal to Jeremiah (31:31-34). The issue would no longer be who was guilty, but who was forgiven. The emphasis of the New Covenant is on forgiveness (31:34). The blaming of each other can now end. Both parents and children can find long-term forgiveness.

Forget about sour grapes! Do not try to guess who should be blamed for your misery. The Lord is offering total forgiveness through Jesus Christ, who is the mediator of the New Covenant (Hebrews 9:15). Live as a forgiven person today and give your problems over to the Lord.

**Why is it sometimes difficult to live as a forgiven person?**

## Day 221
### NEW COVENANT

**Jeremiah 31:31.** *"The time is coming," declares the LORD, "when I will make a new covenant with the house of Israel and with the house of Judah...."*

In the New Covenant, God will do everything. A New Covenant was needed because the people had broken God's covenant with Moses. At Mount Sinai, the key phrase was "If you..." The key phrase in the New Covenant is God's promise of "I will."

Count the number of times that God says, "I will"! *I will* make a new covenant... *I will* make it with the house of Israel and Judah... *I will* put My laws into their minds... *I will* write them upon their hearts... *I will* be their God... *I will* forgive... *I will* remember their sins no more (31:31-34).

The Lord takes the initiative in every phrase of the New Covenant. Therefore, the terms of the New Covenant are absolutely successful. God's agreement with you through the New Covenant should give you absolute confidence in your life with Him.

In contrast, the key phrase in the Old Covenant was "If you..." The Old Covenant was conditional upon the people's obedience. Sadly, the people under the Old Covenant did not obey God.

When God made the first covenant, He made it with Moses and the Israelites. God did not make the first covenant with Pharaoh and the Egyptians. Nor did God intend for the covenant to be with Buddha and his people!

Likewise, the New Covenant is intended for a very specific people group – the house of Israel and the house of Judah. Hundreds of years before Jeremiah lived, Israel had split into two nations. The northern kingdom continued to be called Israel, and the southern kingdom was called Judah. However, the Lord did not exclude any descendant of the people who originally followed Moses. He included everyone in the New Covenant that had formerly been under the old one.

So where does this leave you and me? I do not belong to either the house of Israel or to Judah! Even though God did not originally make the New Covenant with gentiles, the New Covenant includes believers of all nationalities. The New Covenant started when Jesus Christ died (Luke 22:20). Through faith in Jesus Christ, the Messiah of Israel, you too can participate in the blessings in the New Covenant.

**Which of the "I will" promises the New Covenant are especially encouraging to you today as you seek to grow closer to the Lord? Why?**

## Day 222
### INCLUSIVE

**Jeremiah 31:31.** *"The time is coming," declares the LORD, "when I will make a new covenant with the house of Israel and with the house of Judah...."*

When Jesus Christ became the mediator of the New Covenant, this covenant then excluded everyone who did not believe in Jesus. Jesus clearly stated that He was the only way to God (John 14:6). Only believers in Christ can experience the blessings of the New Covenant.

However, the New Covenant is largely inclusiveness. The Lord intended to include many, many people in the New Covenant. He planned to include not just the people of Judah. Even though the people of the Northern Kingdom of Israel had gone into exile because of their sins a century earlier, God intended to include Israel's descendants also.

The early Jewish Christians like Paul looked forward to the time when all Israel will be saved. They believed that the Lord would remove all ungodliness from the nation sometime in the future. All the people of Israel would recognize that Jesus is their Messiah. This anticipation of the early Jewish Christians was based on the New Covenant (Romans 11:26-27).

A major New Testament message is that Gentiles as well as Jews can receive the blessings of the New Covenant. The gospel invitation goes out to everyone. "Whoever will call on the name of the Lord will be saved," is quoted three times in the Bible.

Joel prophesied it (Joel 2:32). Peter preached it (Acts 2:21). Paul wrote about it in the context of there being no difference between Jew and Greek. Everyone who calls on the name of the Lord will be saved (Romans 10:13).

In addition to all Israel being saved and the gospel invitation being given to everyone, there is a third reason why the New Covenant is inclusive. The Lord told Jeremiah that every believer from the least to the greatest would know Him (31:34).

Under the New Covenant, the very young as well as the very old would know the Lord. The poor as well as the wealthy, the laborers as well as the PhD's, the oppressed as well as the powerful – there would be no distinctions. All would know the Lord equally.

**In what specific ways is your relationship with the Lord helping you see other people as equal in His sight?**

Day 223

BETTER

**Jeremiah 31:31.** *"The time is coming," declares the LORD, "when I will make a new covenant with the house of Israel and with the house of Judah...."*

I cannot seem to find ample words with which to express the utmost significance of God's revelation of the New Covenant to Jeremiah. These four verses (31:31-34) contain the most important ideas in the entire Book of Jeremiah. The author of the Letter to the Hebrews quoted these four verses in their entirety (Hebrews 8:8-12). These four verses became the longest Old Testament quotation found in the New Testament.

"Testamentum" is the Latin word for covenant. Within 150 years after Christ's death and resurrection, the Christians were distinguishing Old and New covenant Scriptures as either Old Testament or New Testament. Jeremiah's passage on the New Covenant became the bridge between the Old and New Testament.

God revealed only to Jeremiah the name, New Covenant. God gave revelation to Isaiah and Ezekiel about the covenant, but He told them it would be called an "everlasting covenant" (Isaiah 55:3; Ezekiel 37:26). Jeremiah also knew it would be an everlasting covenant (32:40).

Of all the prophets, only Jeremiah received from the Lord all the specific terms of the New Covenant. Only Jeremiah received revelation that Judah and Israel (31:31) would become united as Israel (31:33). Only Jeremiah witnessed Jerusalem's total destruction and thus experienced the urgent need for a New Covenant.

During the Last Supper with His disciples, Jesus said that the cup which was poured out for them was the New Covenant in His blood (Luke 22:20). He said that His blood of the covenant would be poured out for the forgiveness of sins (Matthew 26:28). When Jesus died, He became the mediator of the New Covenant (Hebrews 9:15).

Paul quoted Jesus' words about the New Covenant when he instructed the church about remembering Jesus' death in each communion service (1 Corinthians 11:25). Jesus' followers became servants of the New Covenant (2 Corinthians 3:6).

The New Covenant is better (Hebrews 8:6). It promises complete forgiveness, a changed heart and a direct relationship with the Lord. The New Covenant is for you!

**Explain how the New Covenant is crucial for your relationship with the Lord.**

Day 224
BROKEN

**Jeremiah 31:32.** *"It will not be like the covenant I made with their forefathers when I took them by the hand to lead them out of Egypt, because they broke my covenant, though I was a husband to them," declares the LORD.*

Jeremiah learned that the New Covenant would be clearly distinct from the covenant with Moses. Sadly, the people under the first covenant failed to remain faithful. They broke the covenant with Moses and became broken people. They did not continue in God's covenant, so God was not obligated to continue the relationship.

However, God in His love did not just give up on them. God wrote a New Covenant so that He could restore the relationship. Rather than doing a makeover of the first covenant, the Lord instituted an entirely new one.

The Lord gave Jeremiah two beautiful illustrations that depicted how much God loved the people to whom He gave the first covenant. He loved them both as a parent and as a husband. Like a faithful husband, the Lord had stayed with His people. Even when they were rebellious toward Him, He continued to love them like a husband loves his wife. Now the Lord was instituting a New Covenant, so the Lord could demonstrate a husband's love toward His people even more completely.

And like a parent, God had taken those people by the hand and led them out of Egypt. One of the ways that a human parent loves his small child is by holding his hand to keep his child from stumbling. I remember holding my children's hands tightly when they were young. At times their feet would be in mid-air as I clung to their hands to keep them from falling!

Like a loving parent, God constantly helped those children of Israel. God led them in the same way that a father takes his child by the hand when there are rocks over which he might stumble. God miraculously led them out of Egypt and persistently protected them.

Children grow up, and they do not want their parents to hold their hand any more. But even as adults, believers are still God's children. Even though you are no longer under the covenant with Moses, you need God to hold your hand even now. If today brings you more trouble than you would care to have, remember that God wants to hold your hand. He can keep you from falling!

**In what ways do you consider yourself a child in your relationship with the Lord?**

## Day 225
### HEART-ENGRAVING

**Jeremiah 31:33.** *"This is the covenant I will make with the house of Israel after that time," declares the LORD. "I will put my law in their minds and write it on their hearts. I will be their God, and they will be my people...."*

The people under the New Covenant will truly be God's people. They will be His men and women. He will be their God, and nothing will ever change this relationship.

Under the New Covenant, the Lord will finally have a people who will be totally faithful to Him. This faithfulness will be inside each person. The New Covenant will be internal. God will write His law on people's hearts.

It will be a different law from what God gave to Moses. The law given to Moses was external. It was written on stone. The success or failure of the Old Covenant depended on the behavior of Moses and his people. The success of the New Covenant will never be questioned, because it is based on God's forgiveness and on people's changed hearts.

God's law includes much more than the Old Covenant law. Hundreds of years before God gave the stone tablets to Moses, Abraham's relationship with the Lord was based on his obedience to God's laws (Genesis 26:5). The Apostle Paul wrote about believers being under the law of Christ (1 Corinthians 9:21).

When the Lord revealed to Jeremiah that He would write His law on people's hearts, Jeremiah probably remembered a severe problem with human hearts. Their hearts already had something else written on them. Jeremiah had written that the sin of Judah was engraved with an iron stylus on the tablet of their heart (17:1).

A scribe would use an iron stylus to write a permanent record. Through their own choices, the people of Judah had marked their hearts permanently with sin. Their hearts were morally useless. They needed new hearts.

God promised through Ezekiel that He would give them a new heart. He also promised that He would put His Spirit within them (Ezekiel 36:26-27). Through His Spirit, God would put His law into His people's minds, and He would engrave His law on their new hearts. The Lord is the heart-engraving God.

**What specific parts of God's law do you sense that He has recently been engraving on your heart?**

Day 226

KNOWABLE

**Jeremiah 31:34a.** *"No longer will a man teach his neighbor, or a man his brother, saying, 'Know the LORD,' because they will all know me, from the least of them to the greatest," declares the LORD.*

Under the New Covenant, the Lord is knowable. Under the Old Covenant, the people of Israel knew God in a limited way. They did not know Him fully. They often forgot about Him. Under the Old Covenant, only the educated scribes could teach the rest of the people about God's law. But under the New Covenant, there would be no special class of spiritual gurus who alone must teach the rest of us about God's law.

Having God's law written on your heart enables you to then know the Lord. The emphasis of the New Covenant is not on knowing the law. The emphasis is on knowing the Lord.

Knowing the Lord must be on His terms, not your terms. The Lord had already revealed to Jeremiah how He wanted people to know Him. Knowing God means knowing what is on God's heart, and God is especially interested in exercising kindness, justice and righteousness on earth (9:24). God implements these qualities on earth through people who know Him.

Knowing the Lord includes remembering with Him what He has done. When I spend time with my wife or with other family members, we talk a lot about what we have done together in the past. In a similar way, when we know the Lord, He likes to hear us talk to Him about what He has done. That is why much of the Bible is repetitive. The Lord delights in hearing from His people about His deeds.

Sadly, the religious leaders in Jeremiah's day did not think about what God had done. They did not know the Lord (2:8). God had to remind them through Jeremiah's sermons that the Lord had brought them out from slavery and led them into a fruitful land (2:6-8).

To really know God, intimately and deeply, means that you never forget about Him. In this life, there may be times when you do not even think about God. Those times of forgetting the Lord can be fewer and fewer the more you grow to maturity.

In the future, when the New Covenant is completely fulfilled, believers will know God perfectly. You will never know Him perfectly in this life. You can, however, grow in your intimacy with Him day by day.

**In specific terms, how intimately do you know the Lord?**

## Day 227
### FORGIVING

**Jeremiah 31:34b.** *"For I will forgive their wickedness and will remember their sins no more."*

The forgiving Lord gave the New Covenant. Believers have permanent forgiveness under the New Covenant. God will forgive all sins of His people for all time, because God will no longer remember them. Other prophets besides Jeremiah also emphasized how God's forgiveness seemed to totally eliminate sin.

According to David, the Lord can remove sin from us as far as the east is from the west (Psalm 103:12). The prophets wrote that God throws all of our sins into the depths of the sea (Micah 7:19). God casts our sins behind His back (Isaiah 38:17).

When the Lord finally revealed the terms of the New Covenant to Jeremiah, He described His forgiveness in the boldest terms that one could imagine. Not only will the Lord forgive you, He will also no longer remember your sin. God will forget all your sins!

Unlike my faulty memory (I am always forgetting people's names), God has a perfect memory. How can God forget your sins? Within His perfect love, He can choose to remember your sins no more. If your sins are gone, there are then no sins for Him to remember. The only way you can be acceptable to God is for your sins to be wiped out. The only way for your sins to be eradicated is through Jesus, who took away your sins when He died (Hebrews 9:28).

The Lord does not ignore or overlook sins. Many people outside the church today believe that God "winks" at our sins. No! His holiness demands that there be a penalty for our sins. He provided a Substitute as a sacrifice to take that penalty for us. Jesus Christ was that sacrifice (Hebrews 10:10), and He was also the priest who offered that sacrifice (Hebrews 4:14). ]

Do you really believe that the Lord will remember your sins no more? Do you still feel like you have to do something in order to persuade the Lord to forgive your sins? Do you think that a free gift of forgiveness is too good to be true? Actually, God's forgiveness is so good that it has got to be true! Unconditional forgiveness is available to anyone who comes to the Lord through faith in Jesus Christ.

**Describe how your relationship with the Lord is based on permanent forgiveness.**

Day 228

ASKING, "WHO?"

**Jeremiah 31:35.** *This is what the LORD says, he who appoints the sun to shine by day, who decrees the moon and stars to shine by night, who stirs up the sea so that its waves roar—the LORD Almighty is his name:*

I cringe every time I hear meteorologists attribute the cause of storms to Mother Nature. I know that the reporters of weather cannot hear me, but I always ask them, "Who!?" Who really stirs up the sea and produces tropical storms and hurricanes?

Mother Nature is an imaginary goddess. People who use her name probably feel uncomfortable about saying the name "Lord". In contrast, Jeremiah said the name of the Lord as often as he could. Jeremiah knew that God was the only causer of storms.

The Lord mentioned the shining sun, moon and stars and the stirred-up sea in order to give authority to His New Covenant. He had given the terms of the covenant to Jeremiah (31:31-34). However, the covenant could be useful only if some descendants of Israel survived to inherit its blessings.

The Lord assured Jeremiah that Israel will have descendants as long as the skies kept shining and the seas kept roaring. As long as God's fixed order for the cosmos continued, there would definitely be Israelite offspring (31:36). Jeremiah had no doubts that God would always keep His universal decrees about His creation.

Jeremiah undoubtedly knew the Scriptures about God's creation and His maintenance of the universe. God created the sun, moon and stars (Genesis 1:16), and He continues to regulate them. Jesus said that God causes His sun to rise on both evil and good people (Matthew 5:45). Also, God created the seas (Genesis 1:9-10). He continues to stirs up the seas and make their waves roar (Isaiah 17:12). Those who sailed the seas in ships saw how the Lord sent winds that lifted up the waves (Psalm 107:23-25). God sent the storm the threatened the ship on which Jonah rode (Jonah 1:4).

When the sun shines on you during the day and when you look at the moon and stars at night, and when you go to the beach and hear the waves, you should keep asking the question, "Who?" You need to keep reminding yourself that the answer to the question is the great Creator. His name is the Lord Almighty, the Lord of Hosts. Only He created the oceans and the universe. Only He keeps them going.

**How does your observation of the bright sun, shining moon, twinkling stars or ocean waves keep you encouraged in your relationship with the Lord?**

## Day 229
### UNMEASURED

**Jeremiah 31:37.** *This is what the LORD says: "Only if the heavens above can be measured and the foundations of the earth below be searched out will I reject all the descendants of Israel because of all they have done," declares the LORD.*

God promised to use His powers to preserve the descendants of Israel, just like He now uses them to regulate the universe. Then the Lord went a step further to guarantee the existence of future descendants of Israel. He told Jeremiah that as long as the universe cannot be measured, and as long as the foundations of the earth cannot be explored, God's people will have a future.

Even though astronomers have measured a small part of the universe, most of it is still a mystery. Only the Lord can measure the skies above (Isaiah 40:12). Only He has counted the number of stars (Psalm 147:4).

"Foundations of the earth" refer to the depths of the sea. The people in Jeremiah's day believed that the foundations of the earth were the bottoms of the mountains beneath the ocean that held up the dry land. What we would call the ocean floors were the foundations of the earth. Human beings can barely begin to explore the foundations of the earth. The Lord reminded Job that only He set the measurements of the earth's foundation (Job 38:4-7).

The Lord certainly anticipated the rise of modern science, but He knows His creation better than anyone else. He staked the future of the New Covenant on the idea that no one else can measure it. If scientists can solve all the mysteries of the universe, Israel's offspring have no future. If the descendants of Israel have no future, then God's power does not really back up the New Covenant. If the New Covenant is not really in operation under God's power, then we are still lost!

Because Jesus Christ came to earth and put the New Covenant into effect with His blood, we can know for sure that we are not lost. Scientists should certainly work hard to explore the heavens and earth, but they should remain humble. No astronaut will ever measure the universe. No oceanographer will search out all the depths of the oceans.

God's creation cannot be completely measured and explored. This reality reveals an important fact about God Himself. You cannot measure God. As you seek to have a closer relationship with Him, remember that He is far beyond your calculations.

**What does the fact that God's creation cannot be measured teach you about God Himself and about His relationship with you?**

Day 230
CITY TOUR

**Jeremiah 31:38-40.** *"The days are coming," declares the LORD, "when this city will be rebuilt for me from the Tower of Hananel to the Corner Gate. The measuring line will stretch from there straight to the hill of Gareb and then turn to Goah. The whole valley where dead bodies and ashes are thrown, and all the terraces out to the Kidron Valley on the east as far as the corner of the Horse Gate, will be holy to the LORD. The city will never again be uprooted or demolished."*

Jeremiah had preached for many years that the Babylonians would destroy Jerusalem. The day finally came. The Babylonians burned the palace and all the houses and broke down the walls (39:8). Jeremiah saw the fulfillment of his message of uprooting and destruction. Before this happened, Jeremiah received God's promise that someday the city would be restored. However, people would not rebuild the city for themselves. Jerusalem would be rebuilt for the Lord.

The Lord invited Jeremiah to visualize a tour of the new city under construction. He wanted the prophet to start at the Tower of Hananel, which was on the north side of the city wall. Following the north wall toward the west and south would have led Jeremiah to the Corner Gate. Neither Gareb nor Goah are mentioned anywhere else in the Bible, but they probably refer to points along the western wall, because the Lord led Jeremiah next to the valley where ashes and bodies are thrown. This valley is the Valley of Hinnom, where ungodly people sacrificed their babies to idols (7:31). Now Jeremiah imagined walking east toward the Kidron Valley, then north to the horse gate.

Perhaps Jeremiah wondered about why the two valleys were included in the new walls. To defend the city against enemy soldiers, the valleys would need to be outside the walls. Then Jeremiah saw the point. His Jerusalem was filled with unholy people, so the Lord brought the Babylonians to destroy the city. But the new city would be secure because it would be holy. The Lord would make even the unclean valleys holy. The city would be holy, because the people would have intimate relationships with the Lord. The city would never again be overthrown.

It is possible that, even as Jeremiah thought about this wonderful future for his city, he walked through the ruins of Jerusalem after the Babylonians destroyed it. Jeremiah felt the extreme pain of seeing his devastated city. But like the people in the future Jerusalem would have, Jeremiah had a close relationship with the Lord.

**How do you resolve this tension: God's glorious promises of the future and your experience now of living in the "ruins"?**

## Day 231
### Locked Up

**Jeremiah 32:2.** *The army of the king of Babylon was then besieging Jerusalem, and Jeremiah the prophet was confined in the courtyard of the guard in the royal palace of Judah.*

The Judean king's government was coming to an end. The Babylonians were surrounding his city. Jeremiah's predictions about the city's destruction were coming true. For decades he had warned that Babylon would be God's means for bringing down the city. The people in the city deserved this punishment because they had turned away from the Lord.

The king hated the message, so he locked up the messenger. As he peered beyond the walls and saw Babylonians everywhere, he saw proof that Jeremiah's prophecy was from the Lord. Events were happening like Jeremiah said they would. But the king did not like what was happening, so he acted irrationally. He imprisoned the prophet to try to change what God would do!

Perhaps the king thought that Jeremiah was demoralizing the military. Jeremiah had said clearly that they could not win against the Babylonians. Maybe the king himself felt disheartened. Jeremiah had told the king that he would definitely become a captive of the Babylonians.

Few people believed Jeremiah during all those years when he prophesied that disaster was coming. Now everyone could see that disaster encircled the city. The future looked hopeless, but Jeremiah would now preach a message of hope. Again, few would believe him.

The people did not believe Jeremiah because they knew neither God's love nor His severity. God's judgment of their city was worse than they could accept. And God's promises of future blessings were too good to be true.

Imprisoning the messenger did not affect the message. The king could not hush the prophet. Jeremiah freely preached God's Word even while he was locked up.

In your current situation, are you feeling in some sense like you are a prisoner? Grow closer to the Lord. His Word is never incarcerated!

**How does the Lord comfort you when you are physically or emotionally locked up?**

## Day 232
### JEREMIAH'S COUSIN

**Jeremiah 32:7.** *"Hanamel son of Shallum your uncle is going to come to you and say, 'Buy my field at Anathoth, because as nearest relative it is your right and duty to buy it.'"*

Jeremiah was a prisoner. The Judeans had locked him up because his words were demoralizing the citizens of Jerusalem. He still preached that the Lord was going to hand Jerusalem over to the king of Babylon. He had preached this message for forty years.

The Lord spoke to Jeremiah about a future land purchase. Possibly through a dream, the Lord told Jeremiah that his cousin was coming from Anathoth, Jeremiah's hometown. The Lord told him that his cousin would offer some land for Jeremiah to buy.

Then Hanamel, the son of Jeremiah's uncle, really came to visit Jeremiah in prison. Perhaps you have a relative who, like Hanamel, has the worst sense of timing! Jeremiah's cousin was one of the most insensitive prison visitors in the world! The city was under siege, Jeremiah was in prison, and the cousin had a fabulous land deal that was just right for Jeremiah!

Perhaps Jeremiah thought briefly about how humorous the situation was! Even if Jeremiah was not amused, he knew that the Lord wanted him to buy the land from his cousin. The Lord told Jeremiah that his cousin would come with the land offer. When the cousin actually came, Jeremiah knew what he must do.

Hanamel asked Jeremiah to buy the land for himself because the prophet had the right as his cousin's closest relative to take possession of it. Hanamel was referring to a provision in Moses' Law. If a family member became impoverished, his nearest relative could buy his land (Leviticus 25:25). Hanamel probably had no children, so Jeremiah was his closest family. Hanamel perhaps had become so poor that he was about to lose his land.

Hanamel's field was in Anathoth. Possibly Hanamel had been one of Jeremiah's hostile opponents in Anathoth (11:21). If this were the case, Hanamel may have been testing the prophet. The cousin wanted to see if Jeremiah literally believed, with his own money, that God would restore His people to the land.

What about you? Does your use of your money reflect your faith? Is your relationship with the Lord more important than your money?

**How does your use of your money reflect your faith?**

Day 233

17-SHEKEL BARGAIN

**Jeremiah 32:9.** *So I bought the field at Anathoth from my cousin Hanamel and weighed out for him seventeen shekels of silver.*

We do not know the market price of real estate in the sunset years of Judah. Nor do we know the value of seventeen shekels of silver at that time. However, we do know that the Babylonians surrounded Jerusalem (32:2), it was the tenth year of King Zedekiah (32:1), and it was just a matter of months before the Babylonians would control all of Judah.

Jeremiah knew that his land purchase would be worthless to him. However, he obeyed the Lord and paid his own money for the property. His land purchase became a compelling lesson for all subsequent generations of believers.

After Jeremiah bought the land, he signed the deed of purchase and sealed it. Some men served as witnesses to the purchase. Jeremiah weighed out the silver for his cousin on a scale. One copy of the deed of purchase contained the order of transfer and the conditions of purchase. It was sealed. The other copy was left unsealed (32:10-11).

Jeremiah took both copies of the deed of purchase and gave them to Baruch, in the presence of his cousin Hanamel. The witnesses who had signed the deed of purchase, and all the Judeans who were housed in the courtyard of the guardhouse observed the transfer of the deed (32:12).

In the presence of the people, Jeremiah gave Baruch the instructions that the Lord had given to him. Baruch was to take the both the sealed copy of the deed of purchase and the unsealed copy and put them in a clay jar. In this way the documents would be preserved for a long time to come (32:13-14).

The Lord then explained the reason for preserving the deeds of purchase. They were object lessons of a promise. The Lord promised that houses, fields, and vineyards would again be bought in the land (32:15).

After the Babylonian captivity, the Lord would bring His people back into the land that He promised. In the same way, the Lord will keep all of His promises to you, sooner or later. Do not be impatient and crave the fulfillment of His promises sooner than He planned. As you walk closely with the Lord, you will realize that later is fine.

**What might cause you to doubt God's promises? How can you overcome these doubts?**

Day 234

## A PERPLEXED PROPHET'S PRAYER

**Jeremiah 32:16. *"After I had given the deed of purchase to Baruch son of Neriah, I prayed to the LORD...."***

The Babylonians were overrunning Judah. Perhaps they were roasting meat on the very land that Jeremiah bought! Jeremiah was wondering why God told him to buy a field that would be lost to the enemy. So he took his confusion to the Lord in prayer.

Jeremiah knew the symbolic meaning of his land purchase. After the deed was signed, Jeremiah told the meaning to the people. He explained that the Lord promised that Judean real estate would again be bought in the future (32:15).

Jeremiah proclaimed God's promise confidently in public. Then he prayed about his questions in private. He still had qualms about the worthless land he had bought for seventeen shekels of silver. He wanted the Lord to reassure him, so that he could convince the people about the wonderful future for all Judean lands.

First Jeremiah praised the Lord for His attributes and wonderful deeds (32:17-23). Then he "reminded" God that it was inevitable that the Babylonians would conquer the city. They had already built siege ramps, and the people in the city were suffering from hunger and disease (32:24-25).

The prophet's perplexity dissipated when he heard God's answer. Yes, land would indeed be bought and sold in the future. This would be possible because the Lord would bring the people back to the land (32:37).

However, God's plans were infinitely grander than mere land. The people who would buy and sell fields would be His people. The Lord would give them one heart to always revere Him. Through His everlasting covenant with them, He would always be good to them. With all His heart He would plant them back in the land (32:38-41).

Are you perplexed? Are you still waiting for clarity from the Lord about puzzling situations in your life? You must bow before the Lord who will shower His goodness on His people. Wait patiently for the showers to come.

**What is causing the greatest confusion in your life at this time, and what is your prayer to the Lord about it?**

## Day 235
### MIGHTY

**Jeremiah 32:17.** *"Ah, Sovereign LORD, you have made the heavens and the earth by your great power and outstretched arm. Nothing is too hard for you...."*

Jeremiah was a great human being because he prayed often to the magnificent Creator. He knew that there was indeed an almighty Maker whose strength no one can comprehend. The Lord used His mighty power to produce every aspect of nature.

God made the earth and all that is on it and in it. God created the rocks and the trees and the ox and the seas. He supplied sufficient food and water on the planet for you to survive. He even made the air with the exact percentage of oxygen so you can breathe.

God also made the heavens. From your vantage point on earth you can see the breathtaking universe that He created. David wrote that the heavens publicize the Creator's glory (Psalm 19:1). As you gaze into the sky day or night and see the vastness and the beauty, you know that God made it.

Jeremiah emphasized God's sovereignty and God's power in his prayer. The Lord does not have a literal outstretched arm that you can see, but His strength is superior to the most muscled arm in the world. Since there are no limits to His sovereignty and power, Jeremiah could confidently pray that nothing was too difficult for the Lord.

Jeremiah's prayer was in the historical context of the Babylonians' final siege of Jerusalem. Jeremiah had just bought some land from his cousin, but the conquering Babylonians would make the land worthless. After signing the two copies of the deed of purchase, Jeremiah preached about the meaning of his symbolic act. He proclaimed that houses, fields and vineyards would someday in the future again be bought and sold by God's people.

How could this be? The Babylonian captivity would stretch from years into decades, and the exiles would still remember Jeremiah's land purchase. They would also remember his prayer. The sovereign Creator of the heavens and the earth can certainly deal with the Babylonians. He would keep His promise.

Nothing is too difficult for the Lord. He created the massive universe, and He made miniscule you. In fact, He has not finished making you. You still have some rough edges that He can smooth out with grace and beauty. Allow Him to complete the wonderful work that He began in you.

**Describe how you are comforted by the fact that nothing is too difficult for the Lord.**

## Day 236
### LOVING

**Jeremiah 32:18.** *"You show love to thousands but bring the punishment for the fathers' sins into the laps of their children after them. O great and powerful God, whose name is the LORD Almighty...."*

How can God love while at the same time punish children for their father's sins? Didn't the Lord reveal to Jeremiah that the sour grape proverb was obsolete (31:29-30)? Didn't the Lord disclose to Moses that children should not be put to death for their fathers' sin (Deuteronomy 24:16)?

Jeremiah's prayer was remarkably similar to God's words to Moses after he received the Second Commandment. The Lord explained that He shows loving faithfulness to the thousands who choose Him and obey Him. However, He responds to the sins of the fathers by doling out penalties to their offspring. The Lord punishes the third and fourth generations of the people who reject Him (Deuteronomy 5:9-10).

Jeremiah added that the Lord's punishment goes into the "laps" of succeeding generations. A lap was the fold in the waist of a robe that could be used like a pocket. The lap of his robe was where Moses put his hand at God's command, and his hand was leprous when he pulled it out (Exodus 4:6). The Lord immediately healed his hand, but the lap became known as a symbol of the Lord's judgment. A man's grandchildren and even his great grandchildren often inherit his specific sinful tendencies. Therefore, they also deserve the Lord's punishment for their sins.

However, when the Lord revealed to Jeremiah the terms of the New Covenant (31:31-34), He overruled the principle of third and fourth generation retribution. Jesus Christ is the mediator of the New Covenant (Hebrews 9:15). Jesus can break the cycle of your inherited sinful inclinations.

Jesus not only broke the cycle, He totally reversed it. Now, His grace can affect the third and fourth generations. The Lord can work through you to influence future generations.

Is your lap filled with His grace, "pressed down, shaken together, running over" (Luke 6:37)? Are you counted among the thousands on whom the Lord showers His devoted love? His love is eternally forceful. Responding to His love makes you a new person.

**What are some specific things that cause you to praise God for His love?**

## Day 237
## JUST

**Jeremiah 32:19.** *"…great are your purposes and mighty are your deeds. Your eyes are open to all the ways of men; you reward everyone according to his conduct and as his deeds deserve…."*

Jeremiah continued his prayer that he began after his land purchase. His purpose for purchasing the land seemed foolish, especially to real estate agents! However, the Lord's purposes are always great.

The Lord had a mighty purpose for Jeremiah's land purchase, just like He does for everything else. The Hebrew word for "purpose" can also be translated as "counsel". It is the same word that described the counsel of the wise (18:18). The Lord's counsel is incomparable to human advice. The Lord's counsel is wonderful and His wisdom is magnificent (Isaiah 28:29).

Jeremiah also praised the Lord for His performance of mighty deeds. He remembered the impressive deeds that God did when leading Israel out from Egypt (32: 20-22). Do not forget that the Lord has power to do miracles at the time and place of His choosing!

Jeremiah acknowledged that the Lord sees everything that people do. He even knows what they will do before they do it. He also knows what is in their hearts that motivates them to do what they do. Because the Lord can see all, He is qualified to be the Almighty Judge. He has gathered enough evidence from what He sees to give faultless verdicts on each person.

Jeremiah's prayer showed that he knew the Lord rewards all people for how they live and for what they do. The Lord's recompense to each individual is perfectly fair. The righteous God always does what is right. Those who respond to His love will receive His grace. Those who do not will receive His judgment.

The Master gives rewards to all of His people. He gives salvation as a free gift to those who believe in Jesus (Ephesians 2:8-9), and He gives heavenly recompense to believers based on how they lived on earth (1 Corinthians 3:12-15). The way you live today has eternal implications. You may think you are too spiritual to be motivated by rewards. You may claim that your only desire is to love God and people. However, consider this: The rewards that The Lord gives will enable you to love Him and others even more! Love the Lord today.

**What are some specific ways in which the Lord rewards His people?**

## Day 238
### FAMOUS

**Jeremiah 32:20.** *You performed miraculous signs and wonders in Egypt and have continued them to this day, both in Israel and among all mankind, and have gained the renown that is still yours.*

God is the most famous Person in all of history. He is not famous in the way that many people today are well known. Many celebrities have not done anything noteworthy. They are famous simply for being famous!

God's fame is infinitely higher. His miracles are among the reasons that God is renowned. Jeremiah mentioned specifically the signs and wonders that God did in Egypt in the days of Moses. The miracles themselves have become almost as eminent as the Lord who performed them.

Jeremiah's ancestors in Egypt started out as few in number. They became numerous and grew into a powerful nation within the borders of Egypt. The Egyptians mistreated them and caused them to suffer under hard labor. Jeremiah's ancestors then cried out to the Lord. The Lord brought them out of Egypt with His great power. He brought them out with miraculous signs and wonders. God brought them to a rich land, which He described as a land flowing with milk and honey (Deuteronomy 26:5-9).

In Egypt, the Lord miraculously sent many plagues to torment the Egyptians for their cruelty toward His people. From the first miracle of turning water into blood to the miraculous climax of all the Egyptian wonders – the death of all Egyptian firstborns – God displayed His power over His creation. His signs and wonders in Egypt allowed His people to leave.

As His people traveled from Egypt, other nations heard about the signs and wonders. Because of the greatness of the Lord's strength, terror fell upon all the inhabitants of Canaan. The people of Philistia, Edom and Moab panicked when they heard about the miracles done in Egypt (Exodus 15:14-16).

Those signs and wonders in Egypt had a lasting effect, even on the people in Jeremiah's day. Sadly, many people today do not believe in miracles. They have accepted the skepticism of ungodly intellectuals. They have believed the lie that belief in miracles is irrational. Consequently, they have rejected a major reason why God is famous.

**How does the Lord's fame affect your relationship with Him?**

## Day 239
### THE GOD OF ALL FLESH

**Jeremiah 32:26-27.** *Then the word of the LORD came to Jeremiah: "I am the LORD, the God of all mankind. Is anything too hard for me?..."*

The Lord answered Jeremiah's prayer by beginning with the same words that Jeremiah used. Nothing is too difficult for the Lord (32:17). Nothing is beyond God's ability. God reassured Jeremiah by accepting his prayer and restating His promises.

There was, however, a difference between how Jeremiah began his prayer and how the Lord began His answer. Jeremiah knew that nothing was too difficult for the Lord, because God created the heavens and the earth by using His great power (32:17). In His answer, the Lord gave another reason.

Nothing is too difficult for the Lord, because He is the God of all flesh. He decides where all people are and what they do, regardless of whether they are believers or unbelievers. He is Lord over all those people who do not want Him to be Lord over them. They themselves decide their final destiny, but the Lord uses them as He pleases as long as they live on earth. In the future, everyone will clearly see that God is the Lord of all.

The God of all flesh is especially Master over His own people. When Sarah laughed at the promise that she would give birth to a son, the Lord asked, "Is anything too difficult for the Lord?" The following year, Sarah had her baby boy (Genesis 18:13-14).

When Moses reported to God that there were 600,000 men who needed food, the Lord asked (Numbers 11:23), "Is the Lord's arm too short?" The Lord provided all the food that they needed. He fed them in the wilderness for forty years.

The patriarch Job knew that the Lord could do all things and that none of His plans could be stopped (Job 42:2). In Zechariah's day, many people doubted God's promises about a glorious future. The Lord asked, "If it was too difficult for those people, would it also be too difficult for Him" (Zechariah 8:6)?

The angel Gabriel told Mary that nothing was impossible with God (Luke 1:27). Jesus said that all things are possible with God (Matthew 19:26). God is obviously the God of all flesh.

**In your own words, describe how nothing is too difficult for the Lord in your life.**

## Day 240
### Worship Idea that was Deplorable

*Jeremiah 32:35. They built high places for Baal in the Valley of Ben Hinnom to sacrifice their sons and daughters to Molech, though I never commanded, nor did it enter my mind, that they should do such a detestable thing and so make Judah sin.*

On at least two other occasions, Jeremiah preached against this hideous practice of child sacrifice (7:31; 19:5). The Lord had no intention of ever commanding His people to do this. Child sacrifice was an example of all the evil that the people were doing to provoke the Lord to anger (32:32).

The people sacrificed their children to idols. Jeremiah mentioned two of these gods by name – Baal and Molech. The Judeans built the pagan altars to Baal and they burned (7:31) their children to Molech.

Jeremiah preached against Baal and Molech in other sermons. He accused the people of being like female camels in heat as they chased after Baal (2:23). The stubbornness of their hearts caused them to pursue the Baal idols (9:14). Even the false prophets committed themselves to Baal (2:8).

The people of Judea had imported Molech from another nation. Molech was the god of the Ammonites (49:1). The Judeans should have looked to their own Lord for spiritual direction instead of to pagan nations. Any worship that includes any god other than the true god is a deplorable idea!

As I think about my own three children, I am completely baffled by parents who would sacrifice their children to an idol. My wife and I loved our children dearly even before they were born. Killing one's own children is absolutely contrary to God's first command in the Bible to be fruitful and multiply (Genesis 1:28).

Growth of the earth's human population continues to be God's desire. The Lord especially wants an increase in the number of people who worship Him. Jeremiah wrote to the exiles in Babylon to get married, to have sons and daughters, and to encourage their sons and daughters to get married and have children (29:6).

Burning children to idols, as well as today's abortions and infanticides, are ideas directly from the realm of spiritual darkness. God's people in particular should encourage population growth in families of believers. Nurture in your heart the attitude that Jesus had toward children (Luke 18:16).

**How has your relationship with God affected your attitude toward children?**

## Day 241
### UNENDING GOODNESS

**Jeremiah 32:40.** *I will make an everlasting covenant with them: I will never stop doing good to them, and I will inspire them to fear me, so that they will never turn away from me.*

The Lord had revealed to Jeremiah His terms for a New Covenant (32:31-34). Not only would the covenant be new (in contrast to Moses' old covenant), but it would also be everlasting. In contrast to the conditional and temporary covenant made with Moses, the New Covenant would never end.

Of all the prophets, Jeremiah was the one to whom God gave the specific provisions of the everlasting New Covenant. Only Jeremiah knew it as a New Covenant. The Lord gave some information about this covenant to both Isaiah and Ezekiel, but they knew it only as the everlasting covenant.

The Lord told Isaiah that the everlasting covenant would be based on the promises that God gave to King David (Isaiah 55:3). The Lord had promised David that his throne and kingdom would be everlasting (2 Samuel 7:16). In addition, the man on David's throne would give the people everlasting peace (Isaiah 9:7).

The Lord also revealed to Ezekiel that the everlasting covenant would be a covenant of peace. God promised that His sanctuary would be in their midst forever. He would be their God, and they would be His people (Ezekiel 37:26-27).

Jeremiah mentioned the everlasting covenant in another of his sermons. When he preached about God's judgments on Babylon, Jeremiah announced the release of the Babylonian captives. The freed prisoners would ask for the way back to Zion, and they would join the Lord in an everlasting covenant (50:5).

Jeremiah knew that the everlasting covenant would release unending goodness. The Lord would never stop doing good to His people under the New Covenant. God's everlasting goodness enables His people to have absolute satisfaction with their lives.

David understood about God's eternal goodness. He referred to God's goodness as great. God has stored up His goodness for His people (Psalm 31:19). In other words, we can never exhaust God's supply of goodness!

After I became a believer, one of the first verses I learned was Jesus' promise of an abundant life (John 10:10). I continue to trust Him for a life filled with His goodness now, and I look forward to uninterrupted abundance in the future. What about you?

**To what extent do you trust the Lord's provision of His goodness, both now and for the future?**

## Day 242
### CONFIRMATION

*Jeremiah 33:1-2. While Jeremiah was still confined in the courtyard of the guard, the word of the Lord came to him a second time: "This is what the Lord says, he who made the earth, the Lord who formed it and established it—the Lord is his name...."*

Jeremiah was detained in the courtyard of the guard when the Lord spoke to him about buying a field (32:1-6). Now the Lord spoke to him a second time about the wonderful future of his nation. The Creator who designed the planet certainly had the ability to restore the nation of Judah!

When the Lord's word came to Jeremiah the first time, Jeremiah praised Him for being the sovereign Lord who made the universe (32:17). Now the Lord reassured the prophet that He was indeed the supreme Maker of the world. The Lord used three words to describe His creation work – "made", "formed" and "established".

Throughout history, at least one other option has been available for people to believe about the creation of the world. The popular belief today is the theory of evolution. When I was a young man, I believed the evolutionists when they taught that the universe came together as the result of impersonal forces. God remained distant from me until I acknowledged that only the Lord is the cosmic Creator.

God as the Creator was one of Jeremiah's favorite preaching ideas. When the prophet spoke against the idols, he compared them with the Creator. God the Creator had made the universe using His extensive power and wisdom (10:12), but the idols had done nothing. Also, Jeremiah gave the same description of the Creator in the midst of His sermon of judgment against Babylon (51:15).

After purchasing land from his cousin, Jeremiah began his prayer to the Lord with praises for Him as the Creator. Jeremiah acknowledged that the Lord had made the universe by His enormous power. To Jeremiah, God's creation was proof that nothing was too difficult for the Lord (32:17).

Jeremiah occasionally needed confirmation about divine truth. So do you. The Lord confirmed His words to Jeremiah by reminding him that He was the Creator. The Lord repeats some of His truths throughout the Bible in order to confirm in your mind that these truths are true!

**How does the Lord's confirmation of some of His truths by repeating them help strengthen your relationship with Him?**

Day 243
MIGHTY TRUTHS FROM GOD

**Jeremiah 33:3.** *"Call to me and I will answer you and tell you great and unsearchable things you do not know."*

People want to know about the future. Jeremiah's contemporaries wished for assurance that the enemy would not conquer their city. Their future appeared bleak as the Babylonians laid siege to Jerusalem. Many were perhaps asking, "Where is God in all this?"

God had not moved from His position as the architect of history. God promised Jeremiah the truth about the future. The truth about what will happen is beyond human insight. The Lord described this knowledge by using the same word that many Judeans had used as they thought about their city. Many hoped that Jerusalem was mighty, impregnable, and inaccessible. It was not.

Mighty men can break through walls, but they can never storm God's fortresses through their own strength. They have to ask for God's information about the future. Jeremiah had to call to the Lord for answers. Then the Lord revealed to him what would happen.

The Lord would demolish the city, but later He would rebuild and restore. There would be short-term misery, but gladness would be the ultimate lot of God's people. The key to their positive future would be the promised righteous Branch of David. The Branch would bring lasting justice, righteousness and restoration (23:5-6).

Jeremiah did not know how the Lord could save His people. How could the Lord pardon His people from all sin? How would He give them everlasting peace? These were great and unreachable issues that only the Lord could explain. Answers could come only if a person stood in the Lord's council.

Jeremiah had preached about the council of the Lord. He asked who has stood in the Lord's council to see or hear His Word. Few people had (23:18).

The Lord revealed the answers to Jeremiah. The answers are available today to anyone who calls out to the Lord. Among the most important answers are salvation and spending eternity with the Lord. Call on the name of the Lord and be saved (Acts 2:21).

**What inaccessible questions are you anticipating being answered, either in this life or the next, as you grow in your relationship with the Lord?**

## Day 244
### CLEANSING AND FORGIVENESS

**Jeremiah 33:8.** *"I will cleanse them from all the sin they have committed against me and will forgive all their sins of rebellion against me."*

The word of the Lord about His people's wonderful future came to Jeremiah a second time (33:1). In this second part of the Book of Comfort, the Lord confirmed His glorious promises about the New Covenant. Central to this covenant was God's cleansing of His people from sin.

All sins are forms of rebellion against God. Jeremiah emphasized the Lord's words that the people had sinned "against Me!" Since the sins are against God, only God can forgive them.

In the immediate context of these wonderful words, God promised to restore and rebuild both Judah and Israel. He would heal the formerly wicked city of Jerusalem. He would fill the city with peace and truth (33:5-7). Peace and truth are the supernatural results of God's forgiveness.

Receiving God's forgiveness is the only way to have these abundant blessings. That is why the New Covenant emphasizes the Lord's forgiveness (31:34). God's forgiveness of Israel in the future will be so complete that an intense search for sins will uncover nothing (50:20)!

To be cleansed from sin means that all guilt for all sins is no longer in your life. Where does the Lord put all those sins that He cleanses from you? He throws them in the depths of the sea (Micah 7:19).

The only time that my wife and I went deep-sea fishing was when we were first married. When our boat was so far from shore that we could not see any land, I accidentally dropped a paper cup into the ocean. Our guide told me not to worry about it. He said that the sea destroys everything.

If your sins are in the sea, they are destroyed! If your sins are at the bottom of the ocean, there is nothing that you or anyone else can try to retrieve! You are without guilt if you believe that the Mediator of the New Covenant (Jesus Christ) has cleansed you with His blood.

**How can God's forgiveness strengthen you during the coming week?**

Day 245

FUTURE JOY

**Jeremiah 33:10-11.** *"This is what the LORD says: 'You say about this place, "It is a desolate waste, without men or animals." Yet in the towns of Judah and the streets of Jerusalem that are deserted, inhabited by neither men nor animals, there will be heard once more the sounds of joy and gladness, the voices of bride and bridegroom, and the voices of those who bring thank offerings to the house of the LORD, saying, "Give thanks to the LORD Almighty, for the LORD is good; his love endures forever." For I will restore the fortunes of the land as they were before,' says the LORD."*

Jeremiah gave two illustrations of life situations where people experience intense joy. At weddings, people hear gladness in the voices of the bride and groom. And believers experience joy when they collectively give thanks to the Lord.

Jeremiah foresaw the day when this joy would return to Judah. He happily prophesied this good news. He predicted that the Lord would restore the fortunes of his nation.

Earlier, the Lord had compelled Jeremiah to preach bad news to his nation. Jeremiah prophesied repeatedly that the Lord would end the sound of joy in the voices of bride and groom (7:34; 16:9; 25:10). The nation would become a desolate waste, without people or animals (33:9). There would be no joy for the people under judgment.

But the joy would return. The Lord would forgive their sins (33:10). Then they would bring thank offerings to the Lord's house. They would joyfully give thanks to the Lord, because they knew the Lord was good. They knew that they could depend on His love, not only for the rest of their lives, but forever.

The Lord tears down in His judgment, but He rebuilds in His goodness and love. As the people would see His restoration in the future, their joy would return. In fact, the Lord promised that when the future Jerusalem is restored, the city would bring joy to Him (33:9).

Even though Jeremiah is remembered as a prophet of doom, he still experienced joy in his personal life. God's Word was a source of joy to him (15:16). He knew that the Lord turns people's sorrow into joy (31:13).

What about you? Are you mourning and in sorrow? Follow the example of Jeremiah and remember that you can have joy even in the midst of your pain.

**How can the Lord's promise of future joy help you experience joy from Him today?**

## Day 246
### DAVID'S RIGHTEOUS DESCENDANT

**Jeremiah 33:15.** *"In those days and at that time I will make a righteous Branch sprout from David's line; he will do what is just and right in the land...."*

Jeremiah had a growing awareness that his people needed a Savior. He knew that only a righteous Messiah could save the Judeans. He no doubt found immense satisfaction in preaching the positive message of the righteous Branch who would come.

The Messiah would be righteous Himself, but His righteousness would include much more than His own. One of His names would be "Our Righteousness" (23: 6). The Messiah would communicate His own righteousness to His people, so that they too could become righteous.

The people in Jeremiah's day saw no evidence of how this could happen. They were living during the tenth year of King Zedekiah. The powerful Babylonians were attacking Jerusalem (32:1-2).

After the Babylonians destroyed Jerusalem, the prospects for David's line worsened. King Nebuchadnezzar killed all of Zedekiah's sons (39:6). There was no one to carry on the line of David.

Zedekiah's predecessor had been living in exile in Babylon. Jeremiah had prophesied that this king would never return from Babylon (22:26). This king would have no descendants who would sit on David's throne (22:30).

Then for hundreds of years, there was no descendant of King David ruling Israel. There were centuries of national grief over their lack of a king. How could this promise of a righteous Branch on David's throne ever be fulfilled?

I had a much smaller feeling of grief when one of my favorite trees died. I tried soaking the ground around it with water, but that small tree remained brown and dead. Finally I accepted the fact that the tree would never revive and I cut it down. Only a short stump was left.

A few months later, I saw a green sprout growing from the side of the stump. A new tree was growing from the roots! I thought about how my new young tree illustrated the righteous Branch sprouting from the dead stump of David's line!

**How can you keep believing God's promises during times when your circumstances are bleak?**

## Day 247
### DAVID'S THRONE

**Jeremiah 33:17.** *"For this is what the LORD says: 'David will never fail to have a man to sit on the throne of the house of Israel....'"*

When King Jehoiachin was exiled to Babylon, people wondered about God's promise regarding David's throne. Would there ever again be a descendant sitting on a throne in Jerusalem again? Did God change His plan?

When David ruled Israel, God promised that his throne would be established forever (2 Samuel 7:16). As long as the heavens existed, David's throne would endure (Psalm 89:29). David's throne would last as long as the sun and the moon (Psalm 89:36-37).

Those promises have been fulfilled in Jesus Christ. Jesus was a descendant of David. The angel Gabriel promised Mary that God the Father would give Jesus David's throne. Jesus would reign over Israel forever (Luke 1:32-33).

In some of the last words in the Bible, Jesus claimed to be the Root and Offspring of David (Revelation 22:16). The Lamb will sit on the throne in the new Jerusalem (Revelation 22:3). Jesus is God and now sits on a throne that will last forever and ever (Hebrews 1:8).

Zechariah prophesied that the throne would be in the Lord's temple. The Messiah would sit as a priest on the throne (Zechariah 6:13). You can have confidence that Jesus is on the throne now, even as you anticipate actually seeing His throne in the new Jerusalem. He now sits on the throne of grace. You can go to Him at any time with your needs (Hebrews 4:16).

David was a prophet as well as a king. He knew that God would place one of David's descendants on David's throne (Acts 2:30). The throne of David would be established in love and faithfulness (Isaiah 16:5). The Prince of Peace would reign on David's throne forever (Isaiah 9:6-7).

Jeremiah was undoubtedly greatly encouraged by God's promises about David's throne. Jeremiah had seen some evil men sit on that throne. Yet Jeremiah had confidence that even if day and night disappeared, David would still have a descendant reigning on his throne forever (33:21).

**Why is the fact that Jesus Christ sits on David's throne important in your relationship with the Lord?**

Day 248

## The Unfailing God

**Jeremiah 33:23-24.** *The word of the LORD came to Jeremiah: "Have you not noticed that these people are saying, 'The LORD has rejected the two kingdoms he chose'? So they despise my people and no longer regard them as a nation...."*

Many cynics were saying that God had let His people down. The two nations where His people lived were failed states. The Assyrians had conquered Israel, and the Babylonians were on the verge of decimating Judah.

The cynics assumed that defeat was tantamount to rejection. They thought that the Lord had renounced His own people. The cynics then felt the freedom to scorn the Jews just like they thought the Lord had.

Cynics often do not know what they are talking about. They observe and draw conclusions, but they lack a relationship with God to give them the correct perspective. In the case of God's two kingdoms, they were absolutely wrong.

Without a king and without a priesthood, a people group could hardly be called a nation. However, Israel and Judah would again have everything that other nations have. God promised that they would have both king and priests in the future. A descendant of David would again sit on the throne, and priests would again bring offerings to the Lord (33:17-18).

God never fails His people. This simple promise is found throughout the Bible. God promised Jacob in a dream, "I am with you and I will not leave you" (Genesis 28:15).

Centuries later, when the Israelites were finally ready to go into the promised land, Moses told them twice, "The Lord will not fail you or forsake you" (Deuteronomy 31:6,8). After Moses died, God told Joshua, "Just as I have been with Moses, I will be with you; I will not fail you or forsake you" (Joshua 1:5).

After God had established the nation, King David gave the same promise to his son Solomon. He told him, "The Lord God, my God, is with you. He will not fail you nor forsake you" (1 Chronicles 28:20). Do you believe that He will never fail you? If you are one of His children, God will never leave you nor forsake you.

**How strong is your confidence that the Lord will never fail you?**

## Day 249
### GOOD PROMISE TO A BAD MAN

**Jeremiah 34:4-5.** *"'Yet hear the promise of the LORD, O Zedekiah king of Judah. This is what the LORD says concerning you: You will not die by the sword; you will die peacefully. As people made a funeral fire in honor of your fathers, the former kings who preceded you, so they will make a fire in your honor and lament, "Alas, O master!" I myself make this promise, declares the LORD.'"*

Using Jeremiah as His spokesperson, the Lord gave a personal promise to the king. King Zedekiah needed this encouragement because he had seen what happened to his predecessors. Of the four kings who immediately preceded him, one died in battle. Two went into exile, one to Egypt and the other to Babylon. And one was dragged out the city gates and given the burial of a donkey.

Of these three fates, Zedekiah probably preferred exile. He was not the kind of man who wanted to die by the sword or have a dishonorable funeral. Jeremiah had told him that he would go into exile (34:3). Looking forward to being honored with a royal funeral fire, even in exile, would have appealed to Zedekiah. In contrast to the fires that would destroy Jerusalem (34:2), Zedekiah's fire would show reverence to him.

This funeral fire would not be a cremation. The Judeans did not cremate their kings. They laid the king's body on a bed of perfumes and spices and then they built a giant bonfire to show their respect (2 Chronicles 16:14).

Zedekiah was not the kind of man whom you would expect to be honored. He feared the Jews rather than the Lord (38:19). He was profane and wicked (Ezekiel 21:25). He did not deserve any of the Lord's goodness. Yet the Lord promised that the people would honor Zedekiah at his funeral.

For reasons unknown to us, the Lord often honors people on earth who do not deserve it. How much more honor will be given to those who love the Lord! Zedekiah could have received more esteem if only he had obeyed the Lord before he was exiled. The Lord promised that He would honor those who honored Him (1 Samuel 2:30).

God's goodness to you through Jesus Christ includes giving you honor. With that honor comes the understanding that the greatest honor belongs to Him. Honor Him today.

**What are some specific ways in which you honor God in your daily relationship with Him?**

Day 250
FREEING THE SLAVES

**Jeremiah 34:8.** *The word came to Jeremiah from the LORD after King Zedekiah had made a covenant with all the people in Jerusalem to proclaim freedom for the slaves.*

The Babylonian siege of Jerusalem was intensifying (34:1), and something needed to be done. King Zedekiah decided to make an agreement with the people. Since he was a weak king, it was an agreement and not a command!

The people agreed with Zedekiah to free all of their slaves. Both male and female slaves would be released. Everyone agreed that one Hebrew should not keep another Hebrew in slavery (34:9).

There were certain conditions that the Lord had given to Moses regarding the release of slaves. All those who had become slaves because of debt were to be released after six years (Deuteronomy 15:12). Slaves who were bought had a choice. They could choose to be released or choose to serve their masters permanently (Exodus 21:2-6).

The Lord confirmed His words about slavery to Jeremiah. The Lord had originally brought the people out of slavery in Egypt. He expected them to free their own slaves after each or seven-year cycle. Sadly, the Israelites had not obeyed this command about slavery throughout much of their history (34:13-14).

If only Zedekiah and his people had obedience to the Lord's law as their motive for releasing their slaves! Sadly, they had selfish motives, for they soon reversed their agreement. They took back their slaves (34:16).

When the Babylonians surrounded the city, they cut off the food supply. Releasing the slaves would have helped to solve the food shortage problem within Jerusalem, because the slave masters would no longer be responsible to feed their slaves. Also, the freed slaves could join the soldiers who were defending the city.

Zedekiah and his people reversed their decision and took back their slaves when they saw that their circumstances had changed. The Babylonians had temporarily lifted their siege of Jerusalem and went after the Egyptians when they heard that Pharaoh's army was in the vicinity (37:5). In contrast to Zedekiah's ungodly attitude toward slavery, Jesus Christ proclaimed the permanent release of all captives (Luke 4:18).

**Why should true believers today be opposed to the institution of slavery?**

## Day 251
### "FREEDOM" FOR DEVIOUS SLAVE OWNERS

*Jeremiah 34:17. "Therefore, this is what the LORD says: You have not obeyed me; you have not proclaimed freedom for your fellow countrymen. So I now proclaim 'freedom' for you, declares the LORD—'freedom' to fall by the sword, plague and famine. I will make you abhorrent to all the kingdoms of the earth...."*

King Zedekiah had agreed with all the other slave owners in Jerusalem to release their slaves (34:8-9). The agreement had, in fact, been a covenant. However, they later changed their minds and took back their slaves (34:16). The Lord gave Jeremiah some penetrating words to say to them about their fickleness.

What if the Lord had been as fickle as they were about His own release of slaves? He had made a covenant with their ancestors. He brought them out of slavery in Egypt (34:13). He kept His covenant with them. For centuries, He had kept them from returning to slavery in Egypt.

In contrast, Zedekiah and his fellow slave owners had taken away the freedom of their recently freed slaves. The Lord's response to their disobedience was forceful. He would give "freedom" to the slave owners. The Babylonian swords would give them freedom! They would be free to fall. They would be free to be victims of warfare, plague or famine!

Zedekiah and his people had made their slave-releasing covenant by cutting a calf in half and passing between the two parts (34:18). This was the solemn way that the Lord expected covenants to be ratified. When God made His covenant with Abraham, He told him to cut the heifer, goat and ram in half (Genesis 15:9-10). In the Hebrew language, the Lord "cut" the covenant with Abram (Genesis 15:18).

Did Zedekiah and his people "cut" a covenant and then break it? Yes, they did! For their punishment, the Lord would cut them!

Their sin deserved severe divine punishment, because they had profaned the Lord's name (34:16). The king, government officials, religious leaders and many others had all cut the covenant (34:19). Then they all broke it. Because of His holy name, the Lord would bring judgment on them.

**In your opinion, why is the Lord so severe when He judges people who are unjust toward others?**

### Day 252
### Conspicuous People

**Jeremiah 35:2.** *"Go to the Rechabite family and invite them to come to one of the side rooms of the house of the LORD and give them wine to drink."*

One of my daughters lives in Lancaster County, Pennsylvania. Every time that we visit her and her family, we notice some of the Amish and Mennonites who live without the conveniences of technology. Their horse-drawn buggies share the road with speeding cars and trucks. Their farmhouses have no electricity. They plow their fields with horses instead of tractors. Because of their different lifestyle, they are noticed.

Like some Amish and Mennonites today, the Recabites in Jeremiah's day were noticed. They were nomads who had recently moved into the city. The Lord planned an unforgettable object lesson with the Recabites to illustrate Jeremiah's sermons. Jeremiah would invite them to a wine party in one of the rooms of the temple.

The Lord commanded Jeremiah to go to the community of the Recabites, in the same way that He had told the prophet to go to the potter (18:1). Jeremiah's powerful sermon illustrations came directly from the Lord, but he had to obey the Lord in order to receive them. When the Lord first called Jeremiah, He told him that he must go wherever the Lord would send him (1:7). Jeremiah went to the Recabites.

Evidently, Jeremiah had access to the temple rooms. The sovereign Lord had arranged for a room, and He worked in the hearts of the Recabites so that they would accept the invitation to the room. The Lord got everyone's attention when the Recabites joined Jeremiah in the temple area.

Many of Jeremiah's events took place in the temple area. The people had grown accustomed to the presence of the temple. The temple was supposed to remind them of the reality of the true God. They liked the temple, but they ignored God. Jeremiah had told them that the Lord would destroy their temple (7:14). As the people curiously followed the Recabites to the temple court, Jeremiah gave the people another reminder that God would bring judgment both on them and on the temple. Jeremiah's role-play with the Recabites in the temple illustrated the reason why God's judgment was coming.

People took notice of the different way of life of the Recabites. They also, more than they wished, were aware of Jeremiah. Both the prophet and the Recabites were noticed because of their obedience. Are you living in obedience to the Lord? Obey the Lord, and do not be troubled whether or not people notice you.

**In what ways can you be conspicuous for the Lord?**

Day 253

PREPARATIONS

**Jeremiah 35:4.** *I brought them into the house of the LORD, into the room of the sons of Hanan son of Igdaliah the man of God. It was next to the room of the officials, which was over that of Maaseiah son of Shallum the doorkeeper.*

The Lord told Jeremiah to invite the Recabites to drink wine (35:2), in order to illustrate true obedience. Now Jeremiah had to organize the event. He knew some men in the temple who could help.

Jeremiah made arrangements to use Hanan's room in the temple, where Hanan's sons normally met. These sons may have been his disciples. Hanan was a "man of God", which meant that he was one of the few temple workers who still followed the Lord. Hanan was willing to help Jeremiah with the task that God gave him.

Another man who viewed Jeremiah favorably was Maaseiah. He was the father of Zephaniah, an influential priest who sided with Jeremiah against a false prophet (29:24-32). Maaseiah was one of the doorkeepers, so he probably provided temple access to Jeremiah and the Recabites.

Jeremiah now had a room, but what about the wine? Who would pay for all that wine? Jeremiah had already paid out of his own pocket for another object lesson that the Lord told him to perform. He had bought a pot, which he broke. Later he would make a yoke (which a false prophet broke), he would buy a belt (which became ruined) and he would purchase some land (that would be lost to the Babylonians). Would he also need to finance the jugs of wine?

The Lord apparently provided the wine from the temple stockpile. The people routinely brought wine to the temple when they came to worship (1 Samuel 1:24). A supply of wine was kept in the temple (1 Chronicles 9:29). As it turned out, none of the Recabites drank any wine!

The Lord provided what Jeremiah needed so that he could make preparations for what the Lord wanted him to do. The Lord will do the same for you. God is able to provide more resources than you can imagine so that you can obey Him.

**How does knowing that God is your Provider help you to grow in your obedience to Him?**

## Day 254
### Awkward Social Event

**Jeremiah 35:5.** *Then I set bowls full of wine and some cups before the men of the Recabite family and said to them, "Drink some wine."*

Jeremiah already knew that the Recabites never drank wine. He knew that they would refuse the wine that he served them. He also knew that their abstinence from wine was not merely a protest against the problems of alcoholism.

The Recabites' refusal to drink wine was part of their rejection of both urban and agrarian life. They lived in tents instead of building houses. They did not stay in one place long enough to sow seeds or plant vineyards (35:7).

These were the rules that their ancestor Jonadab had given them. Jonadab wanted his descendants to move around with their livestock instead of staying in one place and depending on agriculture. Acquiring a taste for wine would have tempted them to plant vineyards and settle down.

The Recabites had survived for more than two centuries as nomadic shepherds. They lived in flawless faithfulness to their ancestor's commands. Now they faced a challenge from a prophet who was equally faithful to God.

"Drink wine!" invited Jeremiah. What would they do? Because of Jeremiah's godly reputation, perhaps they might think that his words could replace their ancestor's commands. Also, this wine-drinking occasion was in the Lord's temple, possibly adding spiritual authority to Jeremiah's appeal to imbibe.

"Drink wine!" Even though they would be perceived as gauche, they refused. They explained that their ancestor had forbidden them to drink wine (35:6). It was as simple as that.

Obedience is amazingly simple. Jeremiah used the Recabites' obedience to illustrate compliance to the Lord, which Jeremiah's people had failed to do (35:14). For the Recabites themselves, it was a test.

The Lord did not *tempt* the Recabites to disregard their own convictions about wine. He *tested* them. They passed the test.

What can you learn from the Recabites? The Lord will also test your faith. Passing divine tests, like the Recabites did, will make your faith stronger.

**How has the Lord tested you recently and how have you responded?**

## Day 255
### TENT DWELLERS

**Jeremiah 35:10.** *"We have lived in tents and have fully obeyed everything our forefather Jonadab commanded us...."*

Many generations of Recabites had lived in tents. Their tents testified of their obedience. They had obeyed all the rules of their ancestor Jonadab for nearly 250 years.

Jonadab lived during an exceptionally ungodly time in Israel's history. Idolatry had mushroomed under a series of evil kings. A man named Jehu became king, and he began to destroy both the idols and those who worshipped them.

On his way to demolish a Baal temple, Jehu met Jonadab. Jonadab was known then as Jehonadab the son of Rechab. After discerning that Jonadab's heart was against idols, Jehu helped him up into his chariot. He invited Jonadab to travel with him to see his zeal for the Lord (2 Kings 10:15).

Jehu had the reputation of being a dangerous chariot driver (2 Kings 9:20). Jonadab was risking his life by riding with him! If Jehu were living today, he would be one of the reckless drivers about whom my dad warned me each time I left on a trip. My dad always told me, "Watch out for wild drivers!"

Jonadab rode with Jehu to the temple of Baal (2 Kings 10:23). He saw how completely Jehu broke up the Baal system. Jehu wiped out Baal from Israel (2 Kings 10:28).

Then Jonadab vanished from the pages of Scripture. We can only guess the reasons why he laid out such strict rules for his descendants. Perhaps he later questioned Jehu's violent approach against idolatry, which did nothing about the idols in human hearts. Maybe he idealized the early years when the people followed Moses in the wilderness and lived in tents. Possibly he thought that comfortable city living caused people to turn to idols.

As the Recabites obeyed Jonadab's rule about always living in tents, they were also following the example of Abraham. Abraham was a tent dweller. He lived in a tent by faith, because he was looking forward to a heavenly city (Hebrews 11:8-9).

**How can your faith in God help you be content with your present earthly shelter?**

Day 256

ESCAPE

**Jeremiah 35:11.** *"But when Nebuchadnezzar king of Babylon invaded this land, we said, 'Come, we must go to Jerusalem to escape the Babylonian and Aramean armies.' So we have remained in Jerusalem."*

The Recabites avoided living in cities for centuries. They faithfully obeyed their ancestor Jonadab by living in tents (35:10). Now they found themselves living within the walls of Jerusalem.

The Recabites wanted to explain their apparent inconsistency. They had entered the city for protection. They probably planned to leave as soon as the threat ended.

If they had not moved into Jerusalem, they would not have survived. No one was safe out in the countryside. Armies from two nations were invading Judah.

Nebuchadnezzar and his Babylonian legions were on the move. They forced the Aramean army to join them. (The Arameans lived in the land that is the nation of Syria today.) They were conquering every people group that they could find.

The Recabites wanted to become neither captives nor casualties. During times of war, idealists frequently compromise. The Recabites entered the city during the reign of Jehoiakim (35:1).

The Babylonians invaded Judah several times during Jehoiakim's eleven-year reign. Their first pillage was during his fourth year, when Nebuchadnezzar won a decisive battle against Egypt (46:2). This was Nebuchadnezzar's first year as king of Babylon (25:1). Nebuchadnezzar then invaded all of Palestine, which caused the Recabites to seek safety in Jerusalem. Nebuchadnezzar took some captives from Jerusalem that included Daniel and his three friends (Daniel 1:1-7).

Nebuchadnezzar also brought Jehoiakim to Babylon, bound with bronze chains (2 Chronicles 36:5-6). Jehoiakim agreed to be Nebuchadnezzar's servant (2 Kings 24:1). Jehoiakim was then permitted to return to Jerusalem.

Before Jehoiakim returned, it was likely that Jeremiah already had his wine time with the Recabites in the temple. Jehoiakim certainly would have interfered with such an event. Later that year, Jeremiah said that he was restricted from going to the temple (36:5).

**In what way is the Recabites' escape from the Babylonians an encouragement to you as you seek to live for God?**

Day 257
OPPOSITES

**Jeremiah 35:14.** *"'Jonadab son of Recab ordered his sons not to drink wine and this command has been kept. To this day they do not drink wine, because they obey their forefather's command. But I have spoken to you again and again, yet you have not obeyed me....'"*

There were glaring differences between Recab's people and the people of Judah. The Recabites refused to drink the wine that Jeremiah offered. Conversely, the Judeans refused the living water that the Lord offered.

The Recabites obeyed a dead ancestor. In contrast, the Judeans disobeyed the living Lord. The Recabites obeyed a set of superfluous rules. Oppositely, the Judeans disobeyed the Lord's life-saving commands.

The Recabites were wanderers who tried to avoid city life. Contrarily, the Judeans believed in and loved their city. They thought Jerusalem and the temple would endure forever. Even though they had access to the temple, they disobeyed the temple's Lord.

Again and again, the Lord had spoken through His prophets. The Judeans did not listen. The Recabites' ancestor Jonadab had died 250 years earlier. Even though Jonadab had not spoken for centuries, the Recabites still obeyed his ancient commands.

The Lord would punish the Judeans for their disobedience. He would bring the disaster that He had already promised (35:17). If the choice is between reward and disaster, why did people choose disaster? They selected disaster, because they did not want to obey.

In contrast, the Lord would reward the Recabites for their obedience. Their obedience, not their ascetic rules, brought the Lord's approval. God promised that they would never lack a descendant to serve Him (35:19). An example of the Lord's reward appeared about 150 years later. A Recabite served the Lord by helping rebuild the walls of Jerusalem (Nehemiah 3:14), the same walls that the Judean disaster had leveled!

Remember the Recabites! Their example of obedience is a way to measure your own obedience to the Lord. Jesus asked the people of His day why they called Him, "Lord, Lord", but did not do what He said (Luke 6:46). Are you faithful to the Lord who calls you to obey?

**Describe a specific area of your life where you need to obey the Lord more consistently.**

## Day 258
### AGAIN AND AGAIN

**Jeremiah 35:15.** *Again and again I sent all my servants the prophets to you. They said, "Each of you must turn from your wicked ways and reform your actions; do not follow other gods to serve them. Then you will live in the land I have given to you and your fathers." But you have not paid attention or listened to me.*

Throughout the nation's history, God persistently sent prophets to warn the people about their wickedness. The prophets specifically told them not to go after other gods. In response, the people did not listen and did not obey.

These prophets were God's servants. Jeremiah was one of them. Jeremiah used the example of the Recabites to illustrate the fact that God's commands could really be obeyed. The Recabites obeyed for centuries the orders of one ancestor.

Jeremiah was the last prophet that the Lord sent to the Judeans before the Babylonians destroyed the nation. The Lord had been sending prophets to Judah for centuries. God gave the people many opportunities to repent.

Jeremiah preached again and again that the Lord had sent His prophets again and again! During King Jehoiakim's fourth year, Jeremiah preached his "again and again" message (25:4-5). On another occasion, Jeremiah told the people that God had sent His servants the prophets again and again ever since their ancestors left Egypt (7:25-26).

Jesus gave an even broader scope. He said that God has sent prophets since the beginning of the world. The people rejected His prophets by killing them, from Abel to Zechariah (Luke 11:47-51).

The Lord did everything that was divinely possible to delay the disaster of judgment. Finally, His long season of sending prophets to Judah ended. The people of Jeremiah's generation did not listen and did not obey. The Lord gave notice that their generation would be the last to reject Him. Their nation would soon end.

There is coming a day when this whole earth will end. Fire will destroy the present heavens and earth. The day of judgment is coming (2 Peter 3:7).

However, the Lord is patient. The Lord was patient with Jeremiah's generation, and He is patient with your generation as well. The Lord does not wish judgment on you or anyone else. He is waiting for more people to repent (2 Peter 3:9).

**What is your response toward the Lord's patience with you?**

Day 259
## REWARDS FOR OBEDIENCE

**Jeremiah 35:19.** *"Therefore, this is what the Lord Almighty, the God of Israel, says: 'Jonadab son of Recab will never fail to have a man to serve me.'"*

Jeremiah's wine party with the Recabites was one of his most memorable symbolic-action sermons. The Recabites were descendants of Jonadab son of Rechab. Centuries earlier, Jonadab had helped Jehu fight against idol worship (2 Kings 10:15-27).

Jonadab left commands for his descendants to help them avoid situations that were conducive to idol worship. His rules included abstaining from wine and living in tents. The Recabites had consistently obeyed Jonadab's commands.

Jeremiah used their example as an object lesson in his sermon to the Judeans. The Recabites obeyed a dead ancestor, but the Judeans disobeyed the living Lord. Because of their disobedience, the Judeans would be punished.

In contrast, the Lord promised to reward the Recabites for their obedience. Even this promise of a reward was a reward itself, because God honored them before the entire Jerusalem population. The honor continued through the centuries as believers read about their example in the Scriptures.

God promised that the massive destruction of the Babylonians would not affect the Recabites. The Recabites and their descendants would survive. Every succeeding generation of Recabites would have people who would serve the Lord.

More than one hundred years after Jeremiah's wine party, a Recabite named Malchijah served the Lord under Nehemiah. Malchijah was one of the leaders who helped rebuild the Jerusalem walls (Nehemiah 3:14). Because God keeps His promises, we know that descendants of Rechab are serving Him even today.

Jesus Christ once told a parable to teach His disciples that God does not pay wages. In the parable, the landowner paid the laborers who had worked all day the same amount that he gave those who worked only one hour. Those who had worked all day grumbled, not understanding the graciousness of the landowner (Matthew 20:1-16).

God gives rewards, not a salary. Do not work for God in order to earn something. Freely and joyfully serve the Lord, and leave the reward-giving responsibility to Him.

**How do God's rewards affect your relationship with Him?**

Day 260

JEREMIAH AND JOSIAH

**Jeremiah 36:2.** *"Take a scroll and write on it all the words I have spoken to you concerning Israel, Judah and all the other nations from the time I began speaking to you in the reign of Josiah till now...."*

After more than two decades of ministry, it was time for Jeremiah to record his messages on a scroll. Since Jeremiah could not now preach in the temple (36:5), his written words would reach more people. Also, scrolls of Jeremiah's sermons would help future generations know the Lord.

The purpose of Jeremiah's writings was to persuade the people to turn from their evil ways. It was not too late to avert the threatened disaster. If they would turn to Him, the Lord would forgive their sins (36:3).

Jeremiah began his ministry during Josiah's thirteenth year as king (1:2). Josiah reigned another eighteen years. One of his sons became king for a brief time, and then Jehoiakim came to the throne. It was now Jehoiakim's fourth year (36:1), so Jeremiah had been preaching for twenty-three years.

For most of Jeremiah's twenty-three years of ministry, Josiah had been king. The two men shared the same spiritual values. Five years before Jeremiah became a prophet, Josiah began to seek the Lord. Four years later, Josiah began tearing down the idols throughout the land. Then the Lord called Jeremiah to preach against the idols.

In Jeremiah's fifth year of ministry, Josiah began renovating the temple. During the repairs, a priest found a copy of the Scriptures. A trusted advisor read the Scriptures to Josiah and the king realized how far he and his people had strayed from the Lord. In response to God's Word, he tore his clothes. Then he went out and tore down more idols!

Josiah made a covenant to obey the Lord, and he read God's Word to all the people. He led them in a Passover celebration that was more impressive than any that had been observed for centuries. God's evaluation of Josiah was also impressive. The Lord said that Josiah had a tender heart (2 Kings 22:19). Jeremiah preached many messages about the heart. The two men must have enjoyed close fellowship with each other.

**In what ways can a close friendship with another believer help you have a tender heart toward God?**

## Day 261
### God's Words

*Jeremiah 36:4. So Jeremiah called Baruch son of Neriah, and while Jeremiah dictated all the words the Lord had spoken to him, Baruch wrote them on the scroll.*

In a secluded place in Jerusalem, two men worked. Jeremiah spoke and Baruch wrote. They were preparing to communicate the Lord's words to an entire city.

Baruch was from a wealthy and prominent family. His grandfather was Mahseiah (32:12), an important royal official under King Josiah (2 Chronicles 34:8). Baruch's brother later became a leading official under King Zedekiah (51:59).

Baruch was trained as a scribe. Most of the people in those times could neither read nor write, so educated people like Baruch were in high demand. Baruch knew the risks he took by associating with Jeremiah. He knew about the unpopularity of Jeremiah's messages. He had seen how Jeremiah was almost put to death a few years earlier (26:8). Nonetheless, Baruch became Jeremiah's scribe, his personal secretary and close friend.

Jeremiah dictated to Baruch all the words that the Lord had given him to preach during his career. He had preached for twenty-three years (25:3), so he had an abundance of material for Baruch to write on the scroll. Undoubtedly, the Lord enabled Jeremiah to remember it all as he spoke to Baruch.

It was the right time historically for Jeremiah's spoken words to become written. The fourth year of Jehoiakim was a pivotal year for international politics. The Babylonians defeated the Egyptians and became the world power. Conditions would worsen for the Judeans. It was only a matter of time before the Babylonians would conquer Jerusalem. Jeremiah's words needed to be preserved on a scroll.

During the fourth year of Jehoiakim's reign, the Lord communicated His words through Jeremiah's dictation to Baruch. Throughout the centuries, God spoke in various ways through the prophets before Jesus Christ came (Hebrews 1:1). The Lord did not "dictate" His words to all the prophets like Jeremiah did to Baruch. God used the personality, knowledge and temperament of each prophet as He "moved" (2 Peter 1:21) each prophet to speak the exact words that the Lord wanted.

Throughout human history, God has always spoken. The Scriptures are His words. Are you listening to Him through His Word?

**What particularly keeps you from listening to God's words?**

## Day 262
### RESTRICTED

**Jeremiah 36:5.** *Then Jeremiah told Baruch, "I am restricted; I cannot go to the LORD's temple...."*

The evil King Jehoiakim tried to restrict Jeremiah's public ministry during most of his reign. When Jehoiakim first became king, Jeremiah stood at the temple's entrance. Jeremiah predicted that the Lord would destroy the temple because of the evil ways of the people who worshipped there (26:1-6).

As a result, Jeremiah was arrested and demands were made for his death. A godly government official saved Jeremiah's life (26:24). Perhaps the king agreed to let Jeremiah live as long as Jeremiah stayed away from the temple.

However, Jeremiah returned to the temple during King Jehoiakim's reign. He performed a symbolic act with the Recabite people in the temple in order to expose the Judeans' disobedience. He explained that the Recabites had obeyed their ancestors, but the Judeans had disobeyed the Lord (35:14-16).

The Recabites had moved into Jerusalem in order to escape from the Babylonians (35:11). The Babylonians first came to Jerusalem during Jehoiakim's third or fourth year and took Daniel and the other captives to Babylon (Daniel 1:1). The king had prohibited Jeremiah from visiting the temple by the fourth year of his reign. Perhaps the temple spectacle with the Recabites had angered the king, so the king decided that Jeremiah would not perform in the temple again.

Even though Jeremiah's access to the temple was restricted, his ministry was not. The Lord planned to put His words to Jeremiah into writing. Jeremiah's sermons would become permanent as Baruch wrote them on a scroll. Baruch, who did have access to the temple, would speak the same words to the people that Jeremiah would have.

What about you? Do you feel restricted like Jeremiah did? Do you have certain limitations that keep you from serving the Lord as much as you would like? Do not let it bother you. The Lord is not restricted in how He can use you.

**Describe some ways that the Lord could increase your ministry in spite of your limitations.**

## Day 263
### PUBLIC READING

*Jeremiah 36:8. Baruch son of Neriah did everything Jeremiah the prophet told him to do; at the LORD's temple he read the words of the LORD from the scroll.*

Jeremiah had told Baruch that he was no longer allowed to go into the Lord's temple (36:5). Since Jeremiah could not go, Baruch needed to go to the temple the next time all the people of Judah come into Jerusalem to fast. Jeremiah told Baruch to read in a loud voice so that everyone could hear him. Jeremiah wanted Baruch to read the Lord's words that Jeremiah had told him. Baruch had written all the words in the scroll (36:6).

Jeremiah reminded Baruch that the Lord had threatened to bring His great anger against these people. Jeremiah hoped that the people would ask the Lord for mercy and would stop doing their evil deeds (36:7). If the people would repent, the Lord would forgive.

So Baruch read the Lord's words in a chamber overlooking the temple courtyard (36:10). The entire population heard Baruch read the scroll. All the people in Jerusalem were there as well as those who had come from many towns in Judah (36:9).

On that day, all of Jeremiah's words from the Lord were read aloud in their entirety three times. Baruch read the scroll once to all the people (36:10), and then he read the scroll again to some of the officials (36:11-15). Later that day one of the officials read the scroll to the king (36:21). Tragically, the king rejected God's Word and burned each section as the scroll was read (36:23).

The meaning of Baruch's name is "blessed". "Baruch" became a popular name for future parents to name their sons. Three different men in Nehemiah's time were named Baruch (Nehemiah 2:20; 10:6; 11:5).

The Lord certainly blessed Baruch that day as Baruch read God's Word publicly. It must have been an exhilarating experience for Baruch. On that day, Baruch joined the list of godly people who read God's Word publicly. Moses (Exodus 24: 7), Joshua (Joshua 8:35), Josiah (2 Kings 23:2) and Ezra (Nehemiah 8:2-3) all read God's Word to huge crowds. Paul wrote to Timothy to devote himself to the public reading of Scripture (1 Timothy 4:13).

**Why specifically is it important for you to listen to the public reading of God's Word?**

Day 264

## A TIME TO FAST

**Jeremiah 36:9.** *In the ninth month of the fifth year of Jehoiakim son of Josiah king of Judah, a time of fasting before the LORD was proclaimed for all the people in Jerusalem and those who had come from the towns of Judah.*

During national crises, government officials often called for public fasts. They summoned people to come to the city and to humble themselves before the Lord. Everyone refrained from eating.

The people of Judah were highly motivated to fast during King Jehoiakim's fifth year. The previous year had been a difficult one for the nation. The Babylonians were now the dominant world power after defeating the Egyptians (46:2). Egypt had been Judah's ally, but now Egypt could not stop King Nebuchadnezzar from coming to Jerusalem and taking some plunder.

The plunder included valuable cups and bowls from the temple. Nebuchadnezzar also brought human captives from Jerusalem back to Babylon. The Babylonians took the smartest and the handsomest young men (Daniel 1:1-7).

The Judeans feared that the Babylonians would come back for more. They assembled in the temple court (36:6). This was the same temple that had been pillaged by the Babylonians the year before.

Throughout the ancient world, fasting was an acceptable way to show reverence to God or gods when people felt helpless. For example, the pagan people of Nineveh put on sackcloth and fasted after Jonah preached to them that God would destroy their city. The Lord responded by holding back His judgment (Jonah 3:4-10).

However, fasting does not manipulate God to get Him to do what you want! Jeremiah clearly preached against this misunderstanding of fasting. Jeremiah earlier told the people that the Lord would not listen to them while they fasted (14:12). The reason was that they had not listened to Him and they had rejected His law (6:19).

At various times in my life, I have tried fasting. Due to my body type and high metabolism, I have learned that I can not go without food for long periods without getting sick! In order to stay healthy, I give up things other than food as I humble myself before the Lord.

**Would times of fasting improve your relationship with the Lord? If so, how?**

## Day 265
### A Time to Read

**Jeremiah 36:10.** *From the room of Gemariah son of Shaphan the secretary, which was in the upper courtyard at the entrance of the New Gate of the temple, Baruch read to all the people at the LORD's temple the words of Jeremiah from the scroll.*

After dictating the Lord's words to Baruch to write on a scroll, Jeremiah told Baruch to read the scroll out loud in the temple (36:6). The public reading of God's Word has been a essential ministry throughout history. (I once took a seminary course entitled "Oral Interpretation of the Bible"). If the people pondered the words that Baruch read to them, they could change their hearts toward God.

Baruch stood on the balcony of Gemariah's room and read God's Word to the crowds. Because Gemariah's father was Shaphan, the godly scribe who served under King Josiah, Gemariah was able have his living quarters within the temple courtyard. Gemariah decided to allow Baruch to read the scroll from his chamber. Like his brothers Ahikam (26:24) and Elasah (29:1), Gemariah supported Jeremiah's ministry.

The Lord's words on the scroll contained both bad news and good news. The bad news was that God planned to bring destruction on the nation of Judah. The good news was that their learning about His judgment might cause them to repent. The Lord would then forgive them (36:3).

The bad news was that God's anger against the Judeans was strong and relentless (36:6). Because of their evil deeds, God's wrath against them was like a fire that could not be quenched (4:4). He would send them to a foreign land to be slaves of their enemies (17:4). The good news was that God would not forsake Israel or Judah (51:5). The Lord would forgive the sins of both Israel and Judah (50:20). God would punish the Babylonians for their cruelty against the Judeans (51:24).

The people needed to hear the truth about their sin and God's judgment. They also needed to know how they could respond to the Lord in order to gain His forgiveness and His love. People today desperately need to know and understand these same facts. This critical information can be found only in God's Word.

Have you read the entire Bible in recent years? Do you have a regular daily or weekly time to yourself? Perhaps the Lord is providing you some breaks in your schedule for a time to read.

**When is the best time during the day or night for you to read the Bible, and what is your plan to read through the whole Bible?**

Day 266

A TIME TO TELL OTHERS

*Jeremiah 36:11-12. When Micaiah son of Gemariah, the son of Shaphan, heard all the words of the LORD from the scroll, he went down to the secretary's room in the royal palace, where all the officials were sitting: Elishama the secretary, Delaiah son of Shemaiah, Elnathan son of Acbor, Gemariah son of Shaphan, Zedekiah son of Hananiah, and all the other officials.*

Micaiah had a godly family heritage. His grandfather was Shaphan, the respected scribe who several decades earlier had read the newly discovered copy of God's Word to King Josiah (2 Kings 22:10). Micaiah's Uncle Ahikam had spoken in favor of Jeremiah's ministry four or five years earlier. Ahikam had saved the prophet's life (Jeremiah 26:24).

The influence of godly relatives had perhaps contributed to Micaiah's spiritual sensitivity. He listened to every word that Baruch read from the scroll of God's Word. He understood the urgency of the Lord's warnings.

When Baruch finished reading, Micaiah knew that it was time for him to tell others. He could not keep this critical message from the Lord to himself. Even though a large crowd heard Baruch read God's Word, many important men were noticeably absent. King Jehoiakim was not there, nor were his royal officials.

Micaiah knew that he could find his father Gemariah working at the king's palace. Micaiah needed to tell his father all the words from the Lord that Baruch had read. Baruch had read the scroll from his father's living quarters (36:10).

Gemariah was in the scribe's office in the palace, along with all the other royal officials. Micaiah felt that he had to tell the whole group. He probably knew that some would react in godly humility to the words from the Lord. Others would not.

Micaiah told them everything that he had heard Baruch read. Regardless of their personal views about God's Word, all of them recognized the seriousness of the message. They ordered that Baruch be brought to them so that they could hear the Lord's words directly from the scroll (36:13-14).

Because of Micaiah, the king eventually heard the words himself (36:20-21). Micaiah had known that it was time to tell others. It is time for you as well.

**List the people with whom you can share what the Lord is teaching you during the next few weeks. What fears do you have about how they might respond?**

## Day 267

### A Time to Hide

*Jeremiah 36:19. Then the officials said to Baruch, "You and Jeremiah, go and hide. Don't let anyone know where you are."*

The government officials heard about what Baruch had read to the people. They summoned Baruch to come to them with his scroll. He came. The officials told Baruch to read the scroll to them. He did (36:13-15).

When the government officials heard all the Lord's words in the scroll, they expressed their fear to each other. Then they told Baruch that they must certainly give the king a report about what Baruch had read. They asked Baruch if he wrote all these words. They asked him if the words actually came from Jeremiah's mouth (36:16-17).

Baruch answered that the words did definitely come from the prophet. He told them that Jeremiah had dictated the words to him and he wrote the words in ink on the scroll. Then the officials told Baruch to go hide with Jeremiah and to not let anyone know where they were (36:18-19).

The officials knew how evil King Jehoiakim was. They knew that he had earlier murdered another prophet named Uriah and had almost put Jeremiah to death (26:23-24). The king had a violent reputation (22:17). The government officials wanted Baruch and Jeremiah to save their own lives and hide.

There are times when true prophets must take cover. During the days of evil King Ahab and despicable Queen Jezebel, an administrator hid one hundred prophets of the Lord (1 Kings 18:4). Otherwise Jezebel would have slaughtered every one of these godly men.

How long did Jeremiah and Baruch stay in hiding? They undoubtedly stayed concealed until the angry king calmed down. Perhaps they remained underground until the end of Jehoiakim's reign. If so, Jeremiah and Baruch disappeared from public life for the next six years.

Perhaps the Lord has sent you underground, giving you a ministry that is not in the public arena. Instead of being well known, you are obscure. The Lord kept His renowned prophet out of sight for years, and He has excellent reasons for doing the same with you.

**What are some advantages of not being a famous believer?**

## Day 268
### BURNING GOD'S WORD

**Jeremiah 36:23.** *Whenever Jehudi had read three or four columns of the scroll, the king cut them off with a scribe's knife and threw them into the firepot, until the entire scroll was burned in the fire.*

The government officials had put the scroll containing God's words in the room of the royal secretary for safekeeping. Then they went to the court and reported everything to the king. The king sent Jehudi to get the scroll, and Jehudi read it to the king. All the officials who were standing around the king also listened. The king was sitting in his winter quarters with a warm firepot in front of him (36:20-22).

As soon as Jehudi had read three or four columns of the scroll, the king cut them off with a penknife and threw that portion of the scroll into the fire. He kept doing this procedure until the whole scroll was burned up in the fire.

The king cut pieces of the scroll with a scribe's knife before he burned them. Why did he have a scribe's knife? King Jehoiakim was not a scribe! Scribes used their knives to keep the points sharp on their writing quills. The king destroyed what another scribe had written, and with the knife he became an "anti-scribe"!

Foolish King Jehoiakim! What was he thinking? Did he think that burning a scroll would discredit Jeremiah? Did he think that he would show himself more powerful than alleged words from the Lord?

I have burned personal papers in my fireplace to prevent thieves from stealing my identity. In contrast, the king lost his royal identity when he burned God's Word. As part of God's judgment on him, he had no royal burial when he died. His body was thrown out of the city like a donkey's (22:18-19). People viewed him as an "anti-king"!

Jeremiah did not know that the burning was going on, but he knew that God's Word was a fire in his heart (20:9). And he knew that scrolls could always be replaced. In fact, later Jeremiah would give another scroll to Baruch. They would record again all the words of the scroll that Jehoiakim burned (36:32). Fire cannot permanently consume the ever-burning Word of the Lord.

How high is your confidence level in God's Word? Are you certain that no government can successfully suppress God's Word? Are you convinced that God's Word will endure forever? Is God's Word relevant to you today?

**Write down several ways that God's Word is relevant to you today.**

## Day 269
### FOOLISH FOR NOT LISTENING

*Jeremiah 36:25. Even though Elnathan, Delaiah and Gemariah urged the king not to burn the scroll, he would not listen to them.*

The scroll that the king burned was God's Word. Jeremiah had directed Baruch to write all of the words that the Lord had spoken to him (36:4). The author of the letter to the Hebrews in the New Testament considered Jeremiah's words to be from the Holy Spirit (Hebrews 10:15-16).

To burn God's Word is the ultimate in idiocy. The reason that a king has advisors is to help keep him from rash stupidity. When a king does not listen to the prudence of wise advisors, he is the greatest fool.

Elnathan, Delaiah and Gemariah were three of the king's advisors. Sadly, Elnathan had demonstrated that he was not always on the side of the godly. He was the one who had brought the prophet Uriah back from Egypt so that the king could put him to death (26:22-23). He may have been the same Elnathan who was the king's father-in-law (2 Kings 24:6,8).

However, Elnathan had heard the entire reading of God's Word. His response was fear (36:12-16). He must have finally believed the truth about God's impending judgment.

Delaiah's and Gemariah's responses to hearing God's Word were the same. They believed the truth that they heard. Gemariah's son had heard Baruch's first reading of God's word and had reported it to the other officials (36:11-12) Gemariah's father was Shaphan (36:10). Shaphan had served as scribe to the good King Josiah and had raised other godly sons.

When Josiah had heard God's Word, he tore his clothes (2 Chronicles 34:19). However, when the present king heard God's Word, he tore the Word (Jeremiah 36: 23)! (Which way would you react?) King Jehoiakim did not listen to his advisors' warning.

Hopefully, the Lord has placed wise friends and family members in your life. Listen to their words! Their counsel will be especially crucial during those times when you may tend to disregard God's Word. Their advice can help you grow closer to the Lord.

**How can the advice from wise friends help you grow closer to the Lord?**

Day 270
ANOTHER SCROLL

**Jeremiah 36:32.** *So Jeremiah took another scroll and gave it to the scribe Baruch son of Neriah, and as Jeremiah dictated, Baruch wrote on it all the words of the scroll that Jehoiakim king of Judah had burned in the fire. And many similar words were added to them.*

The king had burned the original scroll, so Jeremiah and Baruch worked on another one. This second scroll contained additional messages from the Lord that were especially relevant to the king. This was the great irony of King Jehoiakim's unspiritual legacy. His burning of God's Word resulted in an expanded second edition of God's Word. The new scroll contained specific judgments on Jehoiakim!

Jeremiah and Baruch had no reason to think that all their work on the first scroll was wasted. The Lord had mightily used the first scroll, both in the public reading of it and in the private reading before the king. Now it was time for a second scroll. The two men had important work to do as they produced another document.

The second scroll contained everything that was written on the original scroll that the king had burned (36:29). The supplementary messages included a prophecy that none of Jehoiakim's descendants would occupy the throne of David (36:30). In fact, Jehoiakim's dead body would be thrown out to be exposed to the elements of heat and frost (36:30).

The second scroll stated specifically that the Lord would punish Jehoiakim and his descendants for the wicked things they have done. He would also judge the officials who served Jehoiakim. The Lord would punish them all because they paid no heed to His words (36:31).

King Jehoiakim had it coming to him! He deserved every misfortune that the second scroll recorded against him. He truly was a man who did evil in the sight of the Lord.

Does persecution discourage you? Or do you heed God's words as revealed in the Scriptures in spite of your circumstances? Are you sensitive to the Lord's words about judgment? The Lord is intolerant toward those who despise His word. Regard His words and grow in your dearness to Him.

**What are some reasons why a person would despise God's Word? How can your knowing these reasons help you grow closer to the Lord?**

## Day 271
### POINTLESS PLEAS FOR PRAYER

*Jeremiah 37:3. King Zedekiah, however, sent Jehucal son of Shelemiah with the priest Zephaniah son of Maaseiah to Jeremiah the prophet with this message: "Please pray to the LORD our God for us."*

If a rebel becomes desperate enough, he will consider asking for prayer. If that rebel sees no hope for his situation, he will seek help from the One against whom he is rebelling. King Zedekiah was such a rebel. He knew what the Lord required. He knew, but he did not do it. He ignored the words of Jeremiah (37:2).

Zedekiah followed his earlier pattern in seeking Jeremiah's help by sending two messengers. One was antagonistic toward Jeremiah and the other friendly. Jehucal was hostile, later calling for Jeremiah's death (38:1-4). Zephaniah had earlier refused to interfere with Jeremiah's ministry (29:24-32).

Zedekiah could not contain his anxiety. He knew that King Nebuchadnezzar had the power to conquer Zedekiah's nation. Feeling bleak, Zedekiah decided that Jeremiah's prayers certainly could not make matters worse. He thought that Jeremiah's prayers might actually help the situation.

When I became a pastor, I quickly learned that many people in the church thought that my prayers were better than their prayers! They viewed me as their priest. They thought that I was the mediator between them and God.

I prayed for the people in my church. In contrast, Jeremiah did not pray. Zedekiah probably did not realize that the Lord had already told Jeremiah not to pray for his people (7:16). God had already judged them. For Zedekiah, it was too late.

Zedekiah was a pathetic potentate pleading for prayer! Do not be like him. Do not ask the Lord for help with your desires if you do not intend to comply with His desires.

In contrast to Zedekiah, all of God's legitimate children will receive answers to their prayers that exceed their grandest dreams. Through Jesus Christ, who is the only man qualified to be your mediator and high priest, God is able to do vastly more than that for which you plead. He is able to do much more than you envision. Pray to Him now.

**What is your most urgent prayer request for today?**

## Day 272
### SELF DECEPTION

**Jeremiah 37:9.** *"This is what the Lord says: Do not deceive yourselves, thinking, 'The Babylonians will surely leave us.' They will not!..."*

The situation was grim. The most powerful army in the world surrounded Jerusalem, intending to capture everyone and destroy the city. Jeremiah had preached tirelessly that this would happen, explaining the Lord would use the Babylonians to bring judgment on the city.

The people living in Jerusalem did not want to believe the truth about the Babylonians. They preferred to believe that the Egyptians would save them. They thought that the Babylonians would withdraw from Jerusalem and that Pharaoh's army would send the Babylonian soldiers back to Babylon.

Jeremiah told the people clearly that this would not happen. Pharaoh's army would go back to Egypt. The Babylonians would return to Jerusalem and attack it. They would capture everyone and then burn the city (37:7-8).

Against all reality, the people kept thinking that the Babylonians would leave and not come back. How could they deceive themselves about the Babylonians? How could they be so duped?

In one of his sermons to the nations, Jeremiah revealed the cause of self deception. He preached that the pride of one's heart deceives the person (49:16). Unbridled arrogance pushes a person toward self-deception. Unrestrained pride leads to arrogance toward the Lord. Jeremiah said that the Lord would bring down the pride of Jerusalem and the pride of Judah (13:9).

From my experience, I can recognize pride more easily in others than in myself! If I think that others are arrogant but I am not, I deceive myself. As I have talked to people who believe in other religions, I have learned that the emphasis on the problem of pride is unique to the Bible.

Do not keep clinging to a false belief, even if you believe it with all your heart. You are deceiving yourself if you think your sincerity will make a false belief into a true one. Ask the Lord to purge your pride. Allow the Lord to open your eyes to your own self deception.

**In what specific ways can the Lord keep you from deceiving yourself?**

## Day 273
### FALSE CHARGES

**Jeremiah 37:13.** *But when he reached the Benjamin Gate, the captain of the guard, whose name was Irijah son of Shelemiah, the son of Hananiah, arrested him and said, "You are deserting to the Babylonians!"*

Among the many people whom Jeremiah encountered during his life was a soldier captain named Irijah. As captain of the king's guard, Irijah knew that he could never relax. A new problem could surface suddenly. One day Irijah saw a problem walking toward him. It was Jeremiah.

Jeremiah wanted to leave the city through the gate that Irijah guarded. Leaving the city was now safe because the Babylonian army had temporarily withdrawn from surrounding Jerusalem. The Babylonians had received news that the Egyptians were coming (37:11). The Babylonians thought they could always come back to Jerusalem, but now they needed to go meet this new threat.

Jeremiah was headed toward the territory of Benjamin, which was why he chose to exit through the Benjamin Gate. He wanted to return to his hometown to get his share of property that was being divided up among his family (37:12). Later when Jeremiah was still in the courtyard of the guard, his cousin came to sell him a different piece of land (32:9).

Because Jeremiah had prophesied Babylon's future success, people thought that he was a Babylonian sympathizer. They thought that Jeremiah was anti-Judah. Irijah believed that Jeremiah was deserting his own people. Irijah thought that Jeremiah was a traitor.

Irijah had misread Jeremiah. Yes, Jeremiah had urged Judah to surrender to the Babylonians (21:9). Yes, others had already deserted to the Babylonians (38:19). And yes, Jeremiah had preached that Babylon would conquer Jerusalem (37:8). But Jeremiah was no traitor. He loved his own people.

Not only was Irijah's charge against Jeremiah false, it was also silly. The Babylonians had left (37:11). How could Jeremiah be deserting to them?

Have others falsely accused you? If so, your experience is the same as that of Jeremiah and... Jesus. Forget about the false charges! Come nearer to the Lord.

**How can the Lord help you ignore the false claims against you?**

Day 274

BEATEN

**Jeremiah 37:15. *They were angry with Jeremiah and had him beaten and imprisoned in the house of Jonathan the secretary, which they had made into a prison.***

After the Babylonians temporarily withdrew from the city, Jeremiah tried to leave. He was detained at the gate and charged with attempting to desert to the Babylonians. Jeremiah denied the accusation (37:11-14).

All the leaders refused to believe Jeremiah's story. They were angry. They unleashed their pent-up rage against Jeremiah and his sermons. They mercilessly thrashed him.

Jeremiah had already experienced the pain of being beaten. Earlier when he preached God's words, one of the leading priests had Jeremiah beaten. Then the priest locked Jeremiah in stocks (20:1-2).

This time, Jeremiah was locked up in a place worse than stocks. The officials put him in prison in Jonathan's house. This house was known as the house with the pit. The pit had a vaulted cell that was dark and airless. They left Jeremiah in this horrible place for many days (37:16).

He was locked up underground in solitary confinement. His wounds were still raw from the beatings. His prison was so foul that he could have died there if he had not been released (37:20).

You are looking at the "passion of Jeremiah." His sufferings foreshadowed the passion of Jesus Christ. Jeremiah endured unjust pain only because he was trying to warn his people about God's judgment. Jesus' sufferings were also unjust, and His pain was solely for the benefit of others. His enemies said that He saved others but could not save Himself (Matthew 27:41-42).

Before Jesus was crucified, He was mocked, spat upon and beaten (Matthew 27: 29-30). His enemies relentlessly beat His head with a staff (Mark 15:19). The soldiers beat Him and blasphemed (Luke 22:63-65). Pilate flogged Him (John 19:1).

Jesus suffered and died so that you may live. If you are suffering today, remember that Jesus understands your pain. Before long, your wounds will end.

**How can God and His love help you overcome physical abuse that you may have suffered?**

Day 275

IN PRISON

**Jeremiah 37:16. *Jeremiah was put into a vaulted cell in a dungeon, where he remained for a long time.***

Jeremiah became a member of the numberless crowds who have spent time in prison. Many of the pastors whom I have taught in Vietnam were in prison in the late 1970's and 1980's. Their government locked up these good men because of the pastors' faith.

The world is not worthy of believers who live by faith. Many believers through the ages have been cruelly mocked, beaten and imprisoned (Hebrews 11:36-38). Jeremiah joined their fellowship.

Jeremiah became a prisoner when he tried to leave Jerusalem. He was falsely accused of treason, of deserting to the Babylonians. It was obviously a false charge, because the Babylonians were no longer there (37:11-13)!

Did Jeremiah have any visitors while in prison? Perhaps Baruch and other friends were barred from seeing him. Jeremiah's next recorded conversation was with King Zedekiah. The king did not visit him, but ordered him released and brought to the palace (37:37).

How long was Jeremiah in prison? Anyone who has been imprisoned can identify with Jeremiah's feeling that it was a long time. Any length of time is long especially if the imprisoned person knows he is innocent. Jeremiah may have been in prison for at least several months, while the Babylonians were in battle with the Egyptians. The return of the Babylonians may have prompted Zedekiah to call for Jeremiah.

What did he do while he was in prison? No doubt he prayed. As a mature servant of the Lord, his prayers probably were not complaints. As a younger man, he had questioned the Lord about His justice (12:1). He had compared God to a deceptive brook (5:18), and he had cursed the day he was born (20:14).

Now he was old. He had a lifetime of fulfilled promises from the Lord behind him. I believe that his prison prayers were mostly praises. He praised the Lord as he waited expectantly for Him to deliver him again.

**If someday you were to unexpectedly go to prison, how would your relationship with the Lord be affected?**

## Day 276
### SAME WORD

*Jeremiah 37:17. Then King Zedekiah sent for him and had him brought to the palace, where he asked him privately, "Is there any word from the LORD?" "Yes," Jeremiah replied, "you will be handed over to the king of Babylon."*

Jeremiah had been locked in a hideous prison for many days (37:16). The Babylonians had withdrawn from their siege of the city (37:11). The Babylonians had apparently returned, which was why Zedekiah would seek another word from Jeremiah.

Zedekiah did not visit Jeremiah in prison. He had the prophet brought to his palace. Zedekiah probably knew how atrocious Jeremiah's cell was, and he did not want to go there.

Zedekiah met alone with Jeremiah. He did not want any of his officials to know that he was speaking to the prophet. The pitiful king was afraid of his own bureaucrats!

The fearful king was also afraid of the Babylonians. He wanted a fresh word from the Lord, and he knew that Jeremiah claimed to be God's spokesperson. Also, all the other prophets, those who had preached that the Babylonians were not a threat, were unavailable or unwanted (37:19)!

Poor King Zedekiah! Jeremiah's word from the Lord was again not the word he wanted to hear. He probably cringed when he heard Jeremiah speak. Zedekiah had heard this word before.

Jeremiah had earlier prophesied that the Lord would give Zedekiah over to the king of Babylon (21:7). He told Zedekiah that he would see the king of Babylon face to face. Zedekiah would then be taken to Babylon (34:3).

Jeremiah had also already told Zedekiah what to do about his impending doom. He had urged Zedekiah to submit to the Babylonian king (27:12). Zedekiah had not been listening to the Lord, but he could start. He chose to not listen.

Do not be like Zedekiah and try to seek a different and unbiblical word from God. The Bible may not be exhaustive, but it is perfectly adequate for you. God will use His same words to continue to transform you.

**Explain how the same familiar verses in the Bible continue to be sufficient for you.**

## Day 277
### UNEXPECTED MERCY

*Jeremiah 37:21. King Zedekiah then gave orders for Jeremiah to be placed in the courtyard of the guard and given bread be given from the street of the bakers until all the bread in the city was gone. So Jeremiah remained in the courtyard of the guard.*

Zedekiah had met secretly with Jeremiah after releasing him from the dreadful prison under Jonathan's house. Zedekiah wanted a word from the Lord. Jeremiah gave him a brief word, one that he had preached many times (37:17).

Then Jeremiah changed the subject. He asked Zedekiah in what way he had sinned against the king. Jeremiah wanted the king to tell him what sins he had committed against the king's servants or against the people of the land. Jeremiah wanted to know what he had done to deserve imprisonment (37:18).

Without waiting for Zedekiah to answer, Jeremiah asked him about all the other prophets. The rest of the prophets had foretold that the king of Babylon would not come against Zedekiah or the land. Where were these prophets now (37:19)?

Where were they!? Again, Jeremiah gave Zedekiah no time for a response. Zedekiah knew what had happened to some of them.

Hananiah, the theatrical prophet who broke Jeremiah's yoke and preached that the Babylonian captivity would last only two years, was dead (28:1-17). So were Ahab son of Kolaiah and Zedekiah son of Maaseiah. They had already been exiled to Babylon and were killed by King Nebuchadnezzar (29:21). Perhaps Zedekiah never heard about the specific fate of the false prophet Shemaiah. Shemaiah had also already been exiled to Babylon. Doom for both him and his descendants was certain (29:32).

Without dwelling on the whereabouts of the other prophets, Jeremiah asked Zedekiah for a favor. He did not ask to be released. He merely asked not to be sent back to Jonathan's prison, because he would certainly die there (37:20).

Zedekiah had an evil heart, so why would he make an effort to keep Jeremiah alive? Maybe the king had become disillusioned with the false prophets. Perhaps Jeremiah's questions about his own actions had tugged at Zedekiah's heart. Whatever the reasons, Zedekiah sent Jeremiah to another prison and made certain that the prophet would receive bread everyday.

**Describe a memorable incident in your life in which God showed mercy through an unlikely person.**

## Day 278
### FOUR BUREAUCRATS

*Jeremiah 38:1-2. Shephatiah son of Mattan, Gedaliah son of Pashhur, Jehucal son of Shelemiah, and Pashhur son of Malkijah heard what Jeremiah was telling all the people when he said, "This is what the LORD says: 'Whoever stays in this city will die by the sword, famine or plague, but whoever goes over to the Babylonians will live. He will escape with his life; he will live.'..."*

Four government officials listened to Jeremiah preach to the people. They heard him say that everyone who stayed in Jerusalem would die in battle, starvation or disease. Jeremiah's message was that only those who leave the city and surrender to the Babylonians would live. Admitting defeat was the only way to escape with their lives. (To be saved, people must first admit that they are lost.)

They also heard him say that the Lord's plan was for the city to be handed over to the Babylonian army. Jeremiah preached confidently that the Babylonians would capture Jerusalem (38:3). They did not like hearing a defeatist sermon.

The four men went to the king and demanded Jeremiah's death. They said that Jeremiah was demoralizing those soldiers who were still left in the city. They also claimed that the entire population of the city was disheartened by Jeremiah's words. They emphasized that Jeremiah was not seeking to help the people but to harm them (38:4).

The four "public servants" could not tolerate Jeremiah's words. Their hearts were hardened against God's Word. Who were these four angry men? The first man on the list is Shephatiah. To his discredit, he is last on the list of what Bible scholars know about these men! Neither Shephatiah nor his father is mentioned anywhere else in the entire Bible.

The second man is Gedaliah. He was not the same Gedaliah who was the son of the godly Shaphan. This Gedaliah was the son of Pashhur, who perhaps was the same Pashhur who had put Jeremiah in the stocks (20:2). The third man is Jehucal. The king had earlier sent Jehucal to Jeremiah asking for prayer (37:7). The fourth man is Pashhur. The king had sent this Pashhur to Jeremiah on another occasion to ask for a word from the Lord.

Even though these bureaucrats outnumbered Jeremiah, they could not defeat him. Are you, like Jeremiah, feeling like you are outnumbered four to one? Look to the Lord, whose people always have the strength of a majority when they are with Him.

**How does God's presence with you make you a majority?**

## Day 279
### SEEKING THE PEOPLE'S WELFARE

**Jeremiah 38:4.** *Then the officials said to the king, "This man should be put to death. He is discouraging the soldiers who are left in this city, as well as all the people, by the things he is saying to them. This man is not seeking the good of these people but their ruin."*

Even though Jeremiah was confined to the courtyard of the guard (37:21), he still talked to others who passed through the courtyard. He apparently talked to everyone he could, whether they wanted to listen or not. Four of the king's bureaucrats happened to be in the courtyard one day and heard what Jeremiah was saying (38:1). They did not like what they heard.

Jeremiah claimed to be telling everyone the word of the Lord. He said that staying in the city would lead to certain death. Anyone who fled from the city and went over to the Babylonians would live. Jerusalem would be handed over to the Babylonians. They would capture the city.

The four bureaucrats were furious! They went to King Zedekiah and demanded the death sentence for Jeremiah. They claimed that his death would be beneficial for the welfare of the people. During wartimes, most other politicians would have dealt with Jeremiah in a similar way. A man guilty of treason could not be allowed to continue to speak publicly. Putting national traitors to death was common.

The king's officials made a revealing comment about the soldiers. They claimed that Jeremiah was demoralizing the soldiers, but they referred to them as the soldiers who were left in the city. Many of the soldiers were deported to Babylon ten years earlier. Others had since died from battle, disease or famine. There were relatively few fighters still living in Jerusalem.

Since soldiers were in short supply, how would the city be defended? Trying to fight the Babylonians was suicidal. Thoughtful people might see Jeremiah's views as compelling. Surrendering to the enemy seemed to be the only option for saving lives.

However, public opinion in Jerusalem was opposed to both reason and God's will. The officials thought they knew what was best for the people's welfare. They overlooked the truth that the Lord has plans for the good of His people, not for their harm (29:11).

**What should you do when public opinion is contrary to God's truth?**

## Day 280
### ZEDEKIAH'S LEGACY

**Jeremiah 38:5.** *"He is in your hands," King Zedekiah answered. "The king can do nothing to oppose you."*

During an overseas trip, I asked my translator about the conditions in her country. She replied that nothing had changed since my last visit. She said that the fact that living conditions kept getting worse had not changed!

These words also describe the eleven years that Zedekiah was king. During those eleven years, nothing changed about the reality of the circumstances in his city. The circumstances were constantly becoming worse.

The city suffered from drought and food was becoming scarce. Diseases were spreading. Many people were fleeing the city and surrendering to the Babylonians.

Zedekiah personally contributed to his city's dismal situation. He did evil in the Lord's sight and did not humble himself before Jeremiah and his messages. He was stubborn and hard-hearted against the Lord. Under Zedekiah's rule, all the people and their religious leaders became even more unfaithful to God. Among other horrible sins, they defiled the Lord's temple (2 Chronicles 36:12-14).

Zedekiah was also foolish in his political decisions. The Babylonian king had put Zedekiah on the throne in Jerusalem after taking Jehoiachin captive to Babylon. However, Zedekiah listened to certain advisors and gradually rebelled against Babylon. His rebellion showed his weakness as well as his stupidity!

Zedekiah broke his treaty with Babylon, and he did not keep the covenant with the Lord (Ezekiel 17:16-19). He was a profane and wicked prince whose day of final punishment would soon come (Ezekiel 21:25).

Zedekiah was a weak and indecisive king. When his officials told him that Jeremiah should be put to death, he told them that they could do whatever they wanted with him. Zedekiah admitted that he could not do anything to stop them.

In contrast to Zedekiah, you can leave a legacy of strength and resolve. Be strong in the Lord and in the strength of His power. Do not be like Zedekiah. Be a pillar of strength like Jeremiah.

**What specific steps can you take to become a pillar of strength?**

Day 281

IN THE PIT

**Jeremiah 38:6.** *So they took Jeremiah and put him into the cistern of Malkijah, the king's son, which was in the courtyard of the guard. They lowered Jeremiah by ropes into the cistern; it had no water in it, only mud, and Jeremiah sank down into the mud.*

King Zedekiah had told his officials that he could do nothing to stop them from putting Jeremiah to death. They interpreted the king's feeble words as permission to kill the prophet. They hauled him away to the courtyard of the guard.

In the courtyard was a cistern that belonged to one of the king's sons. The purpose of cisterns was to collect and keep water. This cistern had no water in it, so the men decided it would be a useful holding tank for Jeremiah.

That waterless cistern was symbolic of what Jeremiah had preached for years. He claimed that the people had dug their own religious cisterns, which were cracked and could not hold water. They had abandoned the life-giving water of the Lord (2:13).

During times of severe drought, the cisterns had no water (14:1-3). The Lord is the One who withholds rain (Amos 4:7). Now because of drought, there was no water in Malkijah's cistern.

The officials were apparently reluctant to kill Jeremiah directly. Perhaps they did not want innocent blood on their hands. Or maybe they wanted Jeremiah to suffer an agonizingly slow death.

They used ropes to let Jeremiah down into the cistern. Jeremiah sank into the thick mire at the bottom of the cistern. They left him to die.

Jeremiah felt like what one of the psalmists described as sinking into the deep mire where there is no solid ground on which to stand (Psalm 69:2). Jeremiah could identify with Job who felt like the Lord had thrown him into the mud (Job 30:19).

Regardless of how Jeremiah felt down in that muddy cistern, the Lord had promised to be with him (1:8). The Lord was with Jeremiah in the sludge. The Lord is also with you, even if you are feeling like you are in a muddy pit. Draw close to His presence.

**What should you do when your circumstances make you doubt God's faithfulness?**

Day 282

EBED-MELECH

**Jeremiah 38:7. But Ebed-Melech, a Cushite, an official in the royal palace, heard that they had put Jeremiah into the cistern.**

Ebed-Melech was one of the four main people in the story of Jeremiah in the cistern. The other three were Jeremiah, King Zedekiah and the Lord. The Lord had told Jeremiah to preach an unpopular message. Consequently, he was arrested. Zedekiah told the officials who arrested the prophet that they could do to Jeremiah whatever they wished.

Ebed-Melech worked in the palace, so he heard about Jeremiah's plight in the cistern. He knew that Zedekiah was sitting at one of the city gates that day. Ebed-Melech left the palace immediately to find the king.

Ebed-Melech was a foreigner from the region in Africa that currently forms the nations of Sudan and Ethiopia. He was tall and black, one of the people from Cush described as smooth-skinned (Isaiah 18:2).

Ebed-Melech was Jeremiah's faithful and bold friend. As he approached the king, he knew it was not right to leave Jeremiah in the cistern to die. He did not allow the fact that he was a foreigner, with no legal rights, keep him from trying to rescue Jeremiah.

Ebed-Melech boldly told the king that his own officials had behaved wickedly. He told Zedekiah that they should not have put Jeremiah in the cistern and left him there. He warned that Jeremiah would starve (38:9).

It was an especially difficult time to be in a cistern. The Babylonians had surrounded the city, and its residents were experiencing famine and disease (38:2). Food was scarce. No one would likely toss extra scraps into the cistern for Jeremiah to eat.

Ebed-Melech wanted to help the most disliked man in the city. Why? He trusted in the Lord (39:18), and he was Jeremiah's friend. Jeremiah later gave Ebed-Melech a promise from the Lord. The Lord would deliver Ebed-Melech both from the men he feared (the Judean government officials whom Ebed-Melech had accused of wicked behavior) and from the Babylonians (39:17-18). Ebed-Melech was a courageous believer who was determined to rescue Jeremiah regardless of what might happen to him. His example is one you must consider following.

**How can God help you show kindness to an unpopular person in need?**

## Day 283
### THIRTY-ONE RESCUERS

**Jeremiah 38:10.** *Then the king commanded Ebed-Melech the Cushite, "Take thirty men from here with you and lift Jeremiah the prophet out of the cistern before he dies."*

People never knew with certainty what King Zedekiah would do from one day to the next. The king was generally unable to make up his mind. He seemed spineless when he spoke to those who wanted to kill Jeremiah. The king told them they could do what they wanted with Jeremiah. The king said that he could do nothing to stop them (38:5).

Because of the king's reputation for indecision, perhaps Ebed-Melech was surprised to hear him give both permission and a plan. To his credit, Ebed-Melech argued his case boldly before the king. He accused the officials of acting wickedly when they put Jeremiah in the cistern. Famine loomed in the city and Jeremiah was already starving in the cistern (38:9).

In spite of his evil heart, the king may have realized the inhumanity of leaving Jeremiah in the cistern. Or he may have superstitiously believed that Jeremiah's rescue would cause the Lord to send the Babylonians away. Or else, the king weakly acquiesced to the most recent person who talked to him!

When the Lord first called Jeremiah, He promised to be with him and rescue him (1:19). God planned to keep this promise and deliver Jeremiah from the cistern. No one, including King Zedekiah, could stop the Lord from keeping His promise.

The Lord works through human rulers to accomplish His purposes. God turns and directs the heart of every king (Proverbs 21:1). Nebuchadnezzar, a king much more powerful than Zedekiah, would later learn that God is the ruler over all and He gives power to whomever He wishes (Daniel 4:32).

Zedekiah decided that Ebed-Melech must act quickly before Jeremiah died in the pit. The king seemed to know that several men were needed to pull Jeremiah out of the mud. Zedekiah also apparently knew that the four angry bureaucrats (38:1-4) would try to stop the rescue operation. So the king told the Cushite to take thirty men with him.

Ebed-Melech and the thirty men were evidently armed and ready to defend Jeremiah's rescue. They would protect the liberation of the most unpopular man in the city. Would you have been one of those thirty-one rescuers?

**What unpopular cause do you believe the Lord would have you support?**

## Day 284
### PADS

**Jeremiah 38:12-13. *Ebed-Melech the Cushite said to Jeremiah, "Put these old rags and worn-out clothes under your arms to pad the ropes." Jeremiah did so, and they pulled him up with the ropes and lifted him out of the cistern. And Jeremiah remained in the courtyard of the guard.***

Ebed-Melech knew that Jeremiah would be weak from his time in the cistern. After receiving permission from the king to rescue Jeremiah, Ebed-Melech went to a storehouse to obtain old clothes and rags. He tied them to the ropes and let them down into the cistern (38:11).

Jeremiah put the rags under his arms. The rags padded his arms so that the ropes would not hurt him. Several men pulled on the ropes to gently remove Jeremiah from the deep mud. Soon the prophet was up and on dry ground.

The king had evidently given orders to transfer Jeremiah from the cistern to the courtyard of the guard. The courtyard was next to the palace (32:2). Jeremiah would be treated more humanely there, and he would be protected from his enemies.

Ebed-Melech proved himself to be the "good Samaritan" of Jeremiah's day. Ebed-Melech saw a man in need and he had a position in the palace that enabled him to help. The Lord later revealed to Jeremiah that He would reward Ebed-Melech by rescuing him from the Babylonians (39:18).

The description of Jeremiah being *drawn* up out of the cistern would remind readers of the Hebrew Bible of another verse. God had used the same Hebrew verb for *draw* in His wonderful declaration about His love. The Lord had told Jeremiah, "I have loved you with an everlasting love; I have *drawn* you with loving-kindness" (31:3). God's servants had *drawn* Jeremiah out of the cistern.

Jeremiah was down in the slimy pit, but the loving Lord used Ebed-Melech to lift him up. God delivered Jeremiah from the mire. The Lord had done the same with David (Psalm 69:14).

Jeremiah was not alone in his ups and downs. Life on earth has its ups and downs for you also. Sometimes the downs are deep, as deep as a cistern. When you are down, do not forget that the Lord loves you. At just the time when you need them, God provides pads.

**What are some "pads" that the Lord has recently provided for you?**

## Day 285
### "Lose-Lose" Situation

**Jeremiah 38:15.** *Jeremiah said to Zedekiah, "If I give you an answer, will you not kill me? Even if I did give you counsel, you would not listen to me."*

After Jeremiah was rescued from the cistern, he was brought to the king for a private meeting. The king had sent a servant to tell Jeremiah to meet him at the third entrance in the temple (38:14). Scholars today do not know where this third door was. I think I would have gotten lost trying to find it! Jeremiah certainly knew where this entry was. He had been preaching in the temple for decades. Here at the third entrance he would have his last conversation with the king before the city burned.

On previous occasions, Jeremiah had given the king the word from the Lord that he sought. Each time, the king had not responded to God's words. Jeremiah knew that Zedekiah again would not listen.

Yet, Jeremiah recognized that he had to comply with the king's request for another word from the Lord. If Jeremiah refused, the king could put him to death. If Jeremiah spoke God's words to the king, the king could still put him to death. Jeremiah was in a "lose-lose" condition. Jeremiah could lose his life no matter what he did.

Zedekiah gave Jeremiah an oath that he would not kill him. The king also promised that he would not give the prophet over to others who wanted to kill him (38:16). However, Jeremiah's past experiences indicated that Zedekiah's oath (given secretly!) meant nothing.

Jeremiah noticed that Zedekiah did not respond to his second objection. Jeremiah had told him that even if he gave the king advice, the king would not listen. The king gave no assurances that he would listen this time. Jeremiah would find himself again preaching to the spiritually deaf King Zedekiah.

Being in "lose-lose" circumstances did not paralyze Jeremiah. He knew that the Lord was in control of everything – Zedekiah, the Jerusalem bureaucrats, the Babylonians, Jeremiah's destiny. No one could do anything to Jeremiah unless the Lord allowed it.

Jeremiah then proceeded to preach God's Word to Zedekiah one more time (38:17-23). The prophet had no idea what the outcome of his preaching would be. The result did not matter. Jeremiah remembered his calling. He recalled that God would make him strong before the kings of Judah (1:18).

**Why does the Lord sometimes place you in "lose-lose" situations?**

## Day 286
### ZEDEKIAH'S CHOICE

**Jeremiah 38:17.** *Then Jeremiah said to Zedekiah, "This is what the LORD God Almighty, the God of Israel, says: 'If you surrender to the officers of the king of Babylon, your life will be spared and this city will not be burned down; you and your family will live....'"*

King Zedekiah faced a seemingly impossible choice. Jeremiah helped him understand what his two options were. The first option was for the king to surrender to Babylon. If Zedekiah chose this first option, he and all his family would live. Also, the entire city would be spared from Babylonian destruction.

If Zedekiah had paid attention to Jeremiah's words through the years, he would have known that this first option was drenched with God's grace. Twenty years earlier. Jeremiah had preached that the city would become a cursed and uninhabited area (26:6-9). Now, the Lord in His grace was extending yet another chance to the people of Judah.

Jeremiah then stated Zedekiah's second option. Zedekiah could refuse to surrender. If Zedekiah selected this option, his city would be no more. The Babylonians would burn Jerusalem and Zedekiah would not escape from them (38:18). Zedekiah used the wrong criteria as he reviewed his options. He feared the Judeans who had already deserted to the Babylonians (38:19). Fear of other people should never be a reason for a believer's decision.

God is sovereign, but He has chosen to give men and women important choices. The choices were significant because they had real consequences. The Lord gave Adam and Eve a critical command, but they chose to disobey. The world is still suffering from the results of their choice. But King Zedekiah could not blame Adam and Eve for his wretched options! Zedekiah, like everyone else, was responsible for his own choices. The king's history of ungodly decisions had resulted in his tragic two final options.

At least once during your life, you may face an extremely difficult set of options like Zedekiah did. All your outcomes may look bleak. You must avoid choosing foolishly like Zedekiah did. Even if all of your options are stressful, you can choose wisely by obeying God and trusting His promises.

When I was twenty-years-old, an evangelist explained to me the most important choice I would ever make. I am exceedingly grateful that he helped me choose wisely. I decided to believe in Jesus Christ as my Savior and Lord and to follow Him.

**What important decision do you face, and what principles will you use to make your choice?**

Day 287
FEAR

*Jeremiah 38:19. King Zedekiah said to Jeremiah, "I am afraid of the Jews who have gone over to the Babylonians, for the Babylonians may hand me over to them and they will mistreat me."*

As Jeremiah faced Zedekiah for the last time, he knew that he could not trust him. The king had allowed Jeremiah to be beaten and locked up in a dungeon (37:15). Later, King Zedekiah made no attempt to stop his officials from killing Jeremiah. They left the prophet in a cistern to die.

Jeremiah knew that the king was driven by fear. Zedekiah was probably the most fearful king whom Jeremiah knew. Fear seemed to drive him as he made desperate decisions. Dread was in his heart when he requested a private meeting with Jeremiah.

Jeremiah told the king that he was reluctant to tell him anything else. From his past experience, Jeremiah knew that the king would try to kill him and would not listen to him (38:15). Jeremiah's word from the Lord was the same message that Zedekiah had previously rejected.

The king, perhaps thinking that Jeremiah was as fearful as he was, gave the prophet his oath that nothing would happen to him. The king promised that he would not put him to death. Nor would he give Jeremiah over to any of his enemies (38:16).

Jeremiah did not contend that the king's reckless oath given to him secretly was worthless! Instead, he reminded Zedekiah that the Lord was the God of Israel. (This title meant that the Lord had an infinitely stronger motivation to save Jerusalem than the king did.) Jeremiah promised that if the king gave himself up to the Babylonians, he would live. His entire household would also survive, and the Babylonians would not burn the city (38:17).

However, if Zedekiah did not give himself up, the city would indeed burn. The Babylonians would capture Jerusalem. The king would not escape from them (38:18).

If the king gave himself up, Jeremiah assured him that the Babylonians would not give him over to the Jews who had already surrendered. He pleaded with the king to listen to and obey the Lord. If only fearful Zedekiah would obey, he would be safe (38:20).

**Are you a fearful person? Explain how your growth in obedience to the Lord would reduce your fears.**

Day 288

Feet in Mud

*Jeremiah 38:22. All the women left in the palace of the king of Judah will be brought out to the officials of the king of Babylon. Those women will say to you: "'They misled you and overcame you—those trusted friends of yours. Your feet are sunk in the mud; your friends have deserted you.'..."*

Jeremiah gave a personal prophecy to King Zedekiah. Not only would the Babylonians torment him, but also his own women would deride him. The women in Zedekiah's harem would blame him for their sufferings after their city fell to the Babylonians.

All of a king's wives and concubines were extremely vulnerable if he lost a battle. The victorious king would often force the losing king's women to have sex with him. For example, Absalom took his father's concubines into a tent in public view in order to demonstrate that he had taken the throne away from King David (2 Samuel 16:21-22).

Consistent with his weak character, Zedekiah was not even at the palace to defend his women when the Babylonians conquered the city. He tried to escape at night with his soldiers. The Babylonians captured him (39:4-5).

Zedekiah's women would blame the king for allowing himself to be misled by his own advisors. He mistakenly thought that they were his friends. The truth was that he often seemed to fear his advisors.

Among his advisors had been the false prophets. Jeremiah asked King Zedekiah where these prophets were now (37:19). They had deserted him.

Zedekiah faced imminent distress, symbolized by his feet sinking in mud. King David had also faced distresses that he described as like sinking in the mud. Unlike Zedekiah, David prayed to the Lord about his problems. He asked God to deliver him from the mud (Psalm 69:14).

Because of Zedekiah's stubborn refusal to obey the Lord, Zedekiah sank deeper in the mud than Jeremiah did! Jeremiah was in the mud in the cistern for a brief time. Zedekiah was still stuck in the metaphorical mud, and he was sinking. His city would soon end in tragedy. He would never escape.

**Describe how the Lord can deliver you from the mud in your own life.**

## Day 289
### DISCREET WORDS

*Jeremiah 38:27. All the officials did come to Jeremiah and question him, and he told them everything the king had ordered him to say. So they said no more to him, for no one had heard his conversation with the king.*

King Zedekiah had a secret talk with Jeremiah, but the king again rejected the truth that the prophet spoke. Yet the king gave assurance that Jeremiah would not die if the prophet would not reveal what they had talked about. Zedekiah knew that his officials would question Jeremiah about their conversation (38:24-25).

The king apparently did not trust his own officials. He knew that some of them had already tried to put Jeremiah to death. Zedekiah also feared that they might try to harm their own king as well!

The king told Jeremiah exactly what to tell anyone who asked about their discussion. The only statement coming from Jeremiah's lips should be his plea about his prison conditions. The king wanted Jeremiah to tell them that he was only asking not to be sent back to the prison in Jonathan's house (38:26).

Jonathan's prison must have been a horrible place. Jeremiah had earlier requested not to be sent there (37:20). The men who questioned Jeremiah were satisfied with his brief answer.

Jeremiah could easily obey the king's order about what to say. The prophet knew that the king's men cared nothing about God's Word. Jeremiah knew that he was under no obligation to give them any information.

He also knew what Solomon knew. Solomon wrote a proverb about speaking discreetly. In that proverb Solomon taught that a wise person conceals his knowledge from others (Proverbs 12:23).

Concealing knowledge means knowing when to keep your big mouth shut!

Are you reserved in your speech? Do you choose your words carefully before speaking? Do not be like the fool who blurts out indiscretions. Follow the example of Jeremiah.

**In what ways can your dependence on the Lord help you speak more discreetly?**

## Day 290
### SAFE PRISON

**Jeremiah 38:28. *And Jeremiah remained in the courtyard of the guard until the day Jerusalem was captured.***

This is a pivotal verse in Jeremiah's book. This sentence about Jeremiah's imprisonment connects two major sections. Chapters 37 and 38 explain why Jeremiah was in prison. Chapter 39 describes the capture of Jerusalem and the release of Jeremiah by the Babylonians.

The Babylonians found Jeremiah still confined in the courtyard of the guard. The Babylonian king had ordered his soldiers to do no harm to Jeremiah. They took him out of the prison and entrusted him to his friend Gedaliah (39:11-14).

The courtyard of the guard was the safest place for Jeremiah to be during the fall of Jerusalem. When he predicted the city's demise, he often repeated the three dangers of sword, famine and disease. Prison kept Jeremiah safe from all three.

When the Babylonians stormed the city, Jeremiah was safe from the initial chaotic and random killing with swords. He was safe from famine, because King Zedekiah had ordered that Jeremiah be given bread everyday (37:21). And he was safe from disease, because his imprisonment kept him isolated from the spreading pestilence.

The Lord arranged the circumstances so that Jeremiah was in the safest place. God had promised to be with Jeremiah and to rescue him (1:8:19). The Lord kept His promise by using the prison to rescue Jeremiah from the sword, famine and disease.

Like Jeremiah, the Apostle Paul also experienced imprisonment. He knew that the Lord had His reasons for keeping him locked up. And he knew how to be content no matter what his circumstances (Philippians 4:10).

After many years of exciting ministry in a major city in Europe, my family and I had to move back to a small town in Texas. I began to question why the Lord put me in an obscure place. I finally learned that God sends His people to the most unlikely places, and sooner or later we will understand why.

What about you? What do you think about your current situation? Like He did with Jeremiah, the Lord has arranged for you to be in the place that is best for you? Your circumstances are under His loving control.

**How is the Lord helping you to be content with where you are right now?**

Day 291

BROKEN WALLS

*Jeremiah 39:1-2. This is how Jerusalem was taken: In the ninth year of Zedekiah king of Judah, in the tenth month, Nebuchadnezzar king of Babylon marched against Jerusalem with his whole army and laid siege to it. And on the ninth day of the fourth month of Zedekiah's eleventh year, the city wall was broken through.*

It finally happened. The Babylonian army had been attacking Jerusalem since the tenth month of the ninth year that Zedekiah ruled over Judah. It was inevitable that the day would come when the Babylonians would break through the city walls.

All the Babylonian officers came and set up quarters in one of the city gates (39:3). Forty years earlier, the Lord had told Jeremiah that this would happen (1:15). The city now belonged to Babylon.

When Zedekiah and all his soldiers saw that the Babylonians had taken the city, they tried to escape. They left the city during the night. They took a path through the king's garden and secretly went through the gate between the two walls. They headed toward the Jordan Valley (39:4).

However, the Babylonian army chased after them. They caught up with Zedekiah in the plains of Jericho and captured him. They took him to King Nebuchadnezzar who then passed sentence on Zedekiah. The king of Babylon had Zedekiah's sons put to death while Zedekiah watched. Nebuchadnezzar also had all the nobles of Judah put to death. Then he had Zedekiah's eyes put out and bound him in chains to be led off to Babylon. (39:5-7).

The Babylonians burned down the royal palace, the peoples' homes and even the temple. They tore down the walls of Jerusalem. Then Nebuzaradan, the captain of the royal guard, captured the rest of the people who were left in the city. He took them to Babylon, along with the people who had deserted to him. He left behind some of the poorest people who owned nothing. He gave fields and vineyards to them (39:8-10).

Sooner or later, every human wall will fail. Even the walls of Jerusalem failed against the Babylonians. They broke through the walls and destroyed them. The only walls that will endure are the strong people who follow the Lord. The Lord promised that He would make Jeremiah as strong as a bronze wall (1:18). Be like Jeremiah and be strong in the Lord.

**What are some ways in which you can become strong in the Lord?**

## Day 292
### LIGHT AND DARKNESS

**Jeremiah 39:7.** *Then he put out Zedekiah's eyes and bound him with bronze shackles to take him to Babylon.*

The Babylonians had conquered King Zedekiah's city. King Nebuchadnezzar's officials now sat at the entrance to Jerusalem. Zedekiah saw the hopelessness of his plight and tried to flee. The Babylonians overtook him and brought him before King Nebuchadnezzar (39:3-5).

There was no one left to help Zedekiah. As Jeremiah had said, Zedekiah's friends would mislead him and Zedekiah's feet would sink in the sludge (38:22). Zedekiah's army had accompanied him as he fled from the city, but the army scattered (52:8).

Jeremiah had foretold that Zedekiah would be handed over to the king of Babylon (37:17). Zedekiah now saw the king of Babylon with his own eyes, as Jeremiah had predicted (32:4). Once the Judean king was a prisoner, the Babylonian king killed Zedekiah's sons and his aristocrats before his eyes (39:6).

The deaths of his sons and nobles were the last images that Zedekiah saw. Nebuchadnezzar then blinded Zedekiah's eyes. Nebuchadnezzar's cruel act was a symbolic judgment on a man who had closed his eyes to the light of God's Word.

Another prophet had preached that Zedekiah would not see the land of Babylon (Ezekiel 12:13). Jeremiah had prophesied that Zedekiah would be taken to Babylon as a prisoner (32:5). At first, these seemed to be contradicting prophecies. The blinding of Zedekiah clarified how both would be fulfilled.

Zedekiah the king lived in Jerusalem for eleven years. During those eleven years, Jeremiah the prophet lived in the same city. The king had more than a decade to hear God's Word from the prophet. The king chose not to respond to the spiritual light that Jeremiah preached.

Zedekiah preferred to live in spiritual darkness. He would now spend his remaining years in physical darkness. His blindness was a unique metaphor of the darkness of spiritual denial and unbelief. Many blind people today cope with their handicap in exceptional ways and look forward to the ultimate fulfillment of Jesus' mission to proclaim recovery of sight to the blind (Luke 4:18).

**In what specific ways can you follow the Light today?**

## Day 293
### DELIVERANCE

*Jeremiah 39:11-12. Now Nebuchadnezzar king of Babylon had given these orders about Jeremiah through Nebuzaradan commander of the imperial guard: "Take him and look after him; don't harm him but do for him whatever he asks."*

Jeremiah was still in prison when the Babylonians conquered the city. He heard them breaking down the city walls. He saw the smoke from the king's palace, which the enemy soldiers set on fire. He knew they were burning every building in Jerusalem.

The Babylonians captured everyone in the city. They carried all but the poorest back to Babylon. Jeremiah, however, did not become a captive. Even if he had been taken into custody, he probably would have remembered God's promise that He would always rescue him. Unbeknownst to Jeremiah, the Babylonian king had given specific orders about Jeremiah's deliverance.

The king told his chief officer, the captain of the guard, to take responsibility for Jeremiah's welfare. Absolutely no harm should come to the prophet. The king told the captain to give to Jeremiah whatever he asked. The captain had to first find Jeremiah. He commanded all the other officers to search for him. They finally found him in the courtyard of the guard (39:13-14).

The Babylonian officers were probably pleased to obey the king's orders, since they assumed Jeremiah was in prison for siding with Babylon. They did not realize that the God in whom they did not believe was using them. God rewarded His faithful prophet through the kindness of enemy pagan soldiers.

Centuries earlier, Solomon wrote a proverb about a faithful man's enemies. Solomon taught that God rewards a person who pleases Him. These rewards from heaven include peace with one's enemies (Proverbs 16:7).

Solomon also wrote that a king's heart is like a stream of water in the Lord's hand. God turns the king's heart in whatever direction He wishes (Proverbs 21:1). The Lord moved King Nebuchadnezzar's heart so that he was good to Jeremiah.

Before the end of that day, Jeremiah was moved from a Jerusalem prison to Babylonian freedom and honor. Through his many years of suffering, Jeremiah knew that God was always good. He knew that the Lord laid up goodness for those who trusted Him (Psalm 31:19). On the day of his deliverance, Jeremiah dramatically experienced some of the goodness that God had stored for him.

**How can you grow close to the Lord even during those times when you do not feel that He is delivering you His goodness?**

Day 294

EBED-MELECH'S FUTURE

**Jeremiah 39:16-17.** *"Go and tell Ebed-Melech the Cushite, 'This is what the LORD Almighty, the God of Israel, says: I am about to fulfill my words against this city through disaster, not prosperity. At that time they will be fulfilled before your eyes. But I will rescue you on that day, declares the LORD; you will not be handed over to those you fear....'"*

Where was Ebed-Melech when the Babylonians destroyed Jerusalem? He could easily have died amidst the confusion and chaos of battle. Or he could have been chained with the rest of the Judean prisoners and taken to Babylon.

Ebed-Melech met neither of these fates. Jeremiah had given him a personal promise from the Lord. God promised to rescue him from the fall of Jerusalem.

The Lord fulfilled this personal prophecy of deliverance as completely as the fulfillment of His national prophecy of disaster. Jerusalem's demise was obvious. Ebed-Melech's rescue would be just as certain.

Ebed-Melech had helped a true prophet of the Lord. His good deed was an expression of his faith in the Lord (39:18). Ebed-Melech had rescued Jeremiah from the cistern (38:7-13). Now God would reward Ebed-Melech by delivering him from an even greater danger.

As a Cushite from Africa, Ebed-Melech was tall (Isaiah 18:2). I met many of the descendants of Ebed-Melech's people during my teaching ministry in Sudan. I am a tall man, but many of them were taller. King Zedekiah probably felt a tinge of fear as Ebed-Melech towered over him and criticized his officials for putting Jeremiah in the cistern (38:9)!

At the beginning of Jeremiah's career, the Lord had promised to deliver him. Throughout Jeremiah's life, the Lord rescued him by using various people. Now as Jerusalem's fall was eminent, God expanded His promise of deliverance to include Ebed-Melech.

Sometime in the future you might face a situation in your life that seems to be as horrible as the destruction of Jerusalem. You might feel like your problems are too big for you. In situations like these, remember men like Jeremiah and Ebed-Melech. Just like God was faithful to them, God will be faithful to you.

**How have you trusted God's faithfulness in recent weeks?**

## Day 295
### EBED-MELECH'S FAITH

**Jeremiah 39:18.** *"'I will save you; you will not fall by the sword but will escape with your life, because you trust in me,' declares the LORD."*

Ebed-Melech's legacy was his trust in the Lord. He had expressed his godly trust by boldly rescuing Jeremiah from the cistern (38:8-13). Now the Lord declared that He would reward Ebed-Melech by protecting him from violent death from the sword.

The meaning of Ebed-Melech's name was "king's servant". Not only did he serve King Zedekiah, but he was also the Lord's servant. God was his heavenly king. Ebed-Melech served the Lord by rescuing His prophet.

Even as they shared the same faith in the same God, Ebed-Melech was different from Jeremiah in many ways. Ebed-Melech was a foreigner with a different skin color from Jeremiah. Ebed-Melech worked for the government and he faced daily decisions in his work that Jeremiah did not have to think about.

Ebed-Melech had leadership abilities that were recognized by other government officials. King Zedekiah did not hesitate to put thirty men under his authority (38: 10). Ebed-Melech successfully led the operation to rescue Jeremiah from the cistern.

Ebed-Melech was perhaps a eunuch (38:7). The Hebrew word can mean either "eunuch" or "an official". If he was a eunuch, Ebed-Melech was excluded from worshipping in the assembly of the Lord (Deuteronomy 23:1).

However, the Lord was already changing the eunuchs' situation as the time of the fulfillment of the New Covenant approached. The Lord promised to reward eunuchs who obeyed Him (Isaiah 56:3-5). Later, another eunuch who was also from Africa placed his faith in Jesus Christ (Acts 8:27-39).

Even though they were considered to be less than true men, eunuchs could still have faith. People who lack an important body part or function can still have faith. They will be made whole in the future Kingdom.

Ebed-Melech's faith saved him. Do you have confidence that your faith has saved you? Do not trust in your good deeds. You can only be saved by grace through faith (Ephesians 2:8).

**Describe in one sentence how your faith in Jesus Christ has saved you.**

Day 296

BOUND

*Jeremiah 40:1. The word came to Jeremiah from the LORD after Nebuzaradan commander of the imperial guard had released him at Ramah. He had found Jeremiah bound in chains among all the captives from Jerusalem and Judah who were being carried into exile to Babylon.*

Nebuchadnezzar himself had ordered that Jeremiah be set free when the Babylonians conquered Jerusalem. His trusted commander named Nebuzaradan had released Jeremiah from the courtyard of the guard. He and the other Babylonian leaders treated Jeremiah with respect. The Babylonians told Jeremiah that he was free to stay in Judah with his friend Gedaliah. (39:11-14).

For forty years, Jeremiah had not received this kind of esteem from his own people! Now the Babylonians treated him like a celebrity. He finally received the honor that he as God's prophet deserved.

It must have been a bitter-sweet time for Jeremiah. He saw his prophecies about Jerusalem fulfilled, but it was the city that he knew and loved. The same soldiers who conquered his city were now holding him in high regard.

However, during the confusion and chaos of battle, the Babylonian soldiers had bound Jeremiah along with the rest of the Judean prisoners. They then began their long journey to Babylon. What a series of emotional up-and-downs for Jeremiah!

What was Jeremiah thinking when he was forced to begin a long walk in chains to Babylon? He may have thought that he would not survive the long march. Did he remember God's promise that God would always deliver him (1:19)? Did he think about his calling, that he was a prophet to the nations and Babylon was one of those nations?

The Babylonian commander finally discovered the mistake when they reached Ramah. Nebuzaradan had released Jeremiah in Jerusalem (39:14). Now Nebuzaradan released him again.

Do you feel bound like Jeremiah was on that march to Babylon? Do circumstances restrict you from having the life you would like? Use the time to grow closer to the Lord. God will set His captives free at His appointed time.

**During times when you feel restrained, what specific words should you pray to the Lord?**

## Day 297
### A Pagan Preaching to the Prophet

**Jeremiah 40:2.** *When the commander of the guard found Jeremiah, he said to him, "The Lord your God decreed this disaster for this place...."*

The Babylonian commander of the guard had not necessarily become a true believer. He was merely following orders. King Nebuchadnezzar had told him what to say (39:11). The king was acquainted with Jeremiah's prophecies. He had learned about Jeremiah's sermons either from Daniel and the other exiles who were already in Babylon for a while, or from the recent captives from Jerusalem.

The commander summarized Jeremiah's message and preached it back to him. Years earlier, Jeremiah had bought a jar from a potter to use as an illustration. Before he broke the jar, had preached that the Lord would make the city a disaster and that everyone who passed by the ruins of Jerusalem would be amazed (19:8). After Jeremiah broke the jar, he had preached that the Lord would bring disaster on the city because the people had ignored His words (19:15).

The commander went on to say that the Lord has now done exactly what He warned He would do. The commander said that the Jerusalem disaster happened because Jeremiah's people sinned against the Lord (40:3).

The commander, like most others in that day, believed in the supernatural. The Babylonians believed that each city had its own god. The commander said, "The Lord *your* God." The Babylonians did not realize that the Lord God of Jerusalem is the Lord of every nation on earth.

Also, the Babylonians did not comprehend the fact that the Lord does not tolerate sin in any city. If a nation persists in its sin long enough, God will bring that nation down. And that is exactly what would happen to Babylon about fifty years later.

Not only did the Babylonians misunderstand about the Lord, they also misread Jeremiah. They thought that he was "pro-Babylon" in his politics. They were wrong. Jeremiah knew that God was going to use the Babylonians to punish the Judeans, but Jeremiah still loved his own people. The commander would soon learn from Jeremiah's decision how much the prophet loved his fellow Judeans.

A pagan soldier said that Judah's sins caused the nation's disaster! The Lord may surprise you with a word from Him through an unlikely vessel. Listen to the Lord.

**What are some reasons why God might cause disasters?**

Day 298
DECISION

**Jeremiah 40:4.** *"But today I am freeing you from the chains on your wrists. Come with me to Babylon, if you like, and I will look after you; but if you do not want to, then don't come. Look, the whole country lies before you; go wherever you please."*

Jeremiah now faced a major decision. The Babylonians had liberated him. Jeremiah could go wherever he wanted. He could go to Babylon as a free man, and the Babylonians would take care of him. He would have no financial worries.

If I were Jeremiah, I would have seriously considered the Babylon offer! I would have looked at this offer as a reward from the Lord for all the difficult years resulting from faithfully following Him. Babylon was a city of great wealth, and Jeremiah could finally live comfortably.

There was a spiritual dimension to the possibility of going to Babylon. Godly men were already there. Influential Judeans like Daniel, Shadrach, Meshach, Abednego and Ezekiel lived in Babylon. What a great time of fellowship Jeremiah could have with these people, if only he would choose to go to Babylon! Jeremiah was now in his sixties. Maybe it was time for him to retire. He could have a comfortable retirement home in Babylon. What a temptation!

The other major option was for Jeremiah to stay in war-torn Judah. If he stayed behind, he would demonstrate that he was not a Babylonian sympathizer. (Daniel, his three friends and Ezekiel were earlier forced by the Babylonians to go to Babylon.) If Jeremiah stayed behind, he would prove that he really did love the people of Judah.

If Jeremiah decided to stay in Judah, the Babylonian commander advised that he stay with the newly appointed Governor Gedaliah. The governor of Judah, backed by Babylon, could offer both the safety and the support that Jeremiah would need.

Jeremiah decided to stay.

It must have been an arduous decision. Growing older does not mean that decisions get easier. God continues to shape your character as long as you live, and He often does it through your decisions. Are you facing a difficult decision? Allow Jeremiah's God to make you stronger through the process of dealing with that decision.

**How can having a close relationship with the Lord help you make difficult decisions?**

## Day 299
### BASIC NEEDS

*Jeremiah 40:5. However, before Jeremiah turned to go, Nebuzaradan added, "Go back to Gedaliah son of Ahikam, the son of Shaphan, whom the king of Babylon has appointed over the towns of Judah, and live with him among the people, or go anywhere else you please." Then the commander gave him provisions and a present and let him go.*

The Babylonian commander gave Jeremiah a gift. The gift was not like the small wooden frog that I once brought back from Asia as a gift to my wife! When the Babylonians gave a gift, it was expensive and lavish. Its market value could meet a person's basic needs for months, perhaps years.

They also gave Jeremiah an ample supply of food. The Lord met Jeremiah's needs through the generosity of pagans, not through His own people! After years of suffering from the hands of the Judeans, Jeremiah finally received honor and material goods. The Babylonians gave him the respect that was long overdue. They provided for his emotional and physical needs.

They also provided for his need for future safety. Amidst the chaos of the destroyed city, the Babylonian commander wanted Jeremiah to choose a safe place to live. The two safest places would be Babylon and Gedaliah's house. When Nebuzaradan sensed that Jeremiah wanted to stay, the commander suggested staying with Gedaliah.

Before the city's destruction, there had been famine inside the walls. Jeremiah still received food until it was completely gone (37:21). The Lord not only faithfully delivered the prophet from starvation. He also saved him from the sword and from the deadly plague. The Lord used various means to supply Jeremiah with what he needed all his life. Otherwise, Jeremiah would not have lived as long as he did.

The Lord promises to meet the needs of all of His people when they live for Him and generously give of their resources (Philippians 4:19-20). Jesus told His disciples not to worry about what they would eat, drink or wear (Matthew 6:25). If they lived for God's kingdom and His righteousness, they would have everything they would need (Matthew 6:33).

Are you worried about how you will make ends meet? Are you living primarily for the physical instead of the spiritual? If so, you must adjust your attitude. Grow closer to the Lord. He will give you what you need.

**How can the Lord help you overcome anxiety about your basic needs?**

Day 300
LIFE AFTER JERUSALEM

*Jeremiah 40:6. So Jeremiah went to Gedaliah son of Ahikam at Mizpah and stayed with him among the people who were left behind in the land.*

Jerusalem's destruction was not the end of Jeremiah's story. Providentially, the Babylonians did not capture or kill every resident of Judah. They left behind the poorest of the poor. And the Babylonian king chose a good man named Gedaliah to govern the remnant in Judah.

Gedaliah was the son of Ahikam. Ahikam was Jeremiah's friend in the Jerusalem government who saved him from being put to death (26:24). Gedaliah had grown up in a godly family. The king of Babylon chose him to be Jeremiah's next political leader.

Jerusalem was gone, so Gedaliah's people would live in Mizpah. At least Mizpah was not destroyed. It was located on a hill, so its residents had a great view of the surrounding countryside. The town of Mizpah had had a rich religious heritage for centuries. In Mizpah there would be some feeling of links with the past.

People who had fled to neighboring countries heard about Mizpah. They returned to live in Judah under Gedaliah's leadership. Gedaliah was now responsible for all the refugees and the poor in the land. How could he provide for all these people? Providentially, the Babylonians had given farmland and vineyards to the poor people whom they did not capture or kill. The fields produced an abundance of food that year (40:12).

For Jeremiah, even though it would be temporary, living in Mizpah would be one of the special inns along life's difficult journey. Jeremiah needed a season of rest and peace. And he got even more. He finally received, at least for a short time, the respect he deserved.

Providence rules! Even after the destruction of Jerusalem, providence continued to reign. Providence is another way of expressing the reality that the sovereign Lord controls everything that happens. The Lord manages even the bad things, in order to bring about a greater good. This is a challenging lesson to learn.

What about you? Are you wondering if there is life after Jerusalem for you? Perhaps you have suffered loss, and you have seen the destruction of your own personal Jerusalem. Remember that nothing is beyond the Lord's hand of provision.

**How is your understanding of God's providence affecting your life today?**

## Day 301
### UNSAFE WORLD

*Jeremiah 40:13-14. Johanan son of Kareah and all the army officers still in the open country came to Gedaliah at Mizpah and said to him, "Don't you know that Baalis king of the Ammonites has sent Ishmael son of Nethaniah to take your life?" But Gedaliah son of Ahikam did not believe them.*

The king of Babylon had chosen Gedaliah to govern the war ravaged nation of Judah. Jeremiah was staying with him (40:5-6). What should have been a quiet and peaceful season was disrupted by news of an assassination plot.

Gedaliah heard that a certain man named Ishmael was conspiring to kill him. Why did Ishmael want to do this? Perhaps King Baalis of the Ammonites had offered a generous sum of money to Ishmael to slay Gedaliah. The nation of Ammon had earlier formed an alliance to oppose the Babylonians (27:3), and King Baalis probably saw Gedaliah as a Babylonian minion. According to the historian Josephus, Baalis had thoughts of ruling Judah himself.

Ishmael was a member of the royal family through Elishama (41:1), who was a son of King David (2 Samuel 5:16). Maybe Ishmael wanted to retaliate against the Babylonians for their capturing and murdering some of the royal family. Or possibly, Ishmael thought that he should have been governor instead of Gedaliah, since Gedaliah did not belong to the royal family.

Whatever Ishmael's motive, Johanan believed that Ishmael was a menace to Gedaliah. Johanan was not the only one who knew about the murder plot. All of the army officers also knew about it, and they warned Gedaliah.

Why didn't Gedaliah believe them? He probably did not trust Johanan. Johanan turned out to be a man of shady character who may have had his own political ambitions. He offered to kill Ishmael, but Gedaliah refused to permit it (40:15-16).

Johanan proved himself later to be arrogant and ungodly. He refused to obey the Lord's words. He called Jeremiah a liar, and he accused the prophet of scheming with Baruch to give Johanan and the others over to the Babylonians (43:1-4). With men like Johanan and Ishmael, the post-Jerusalem world was just as dangerous as before the Babylonians conquered Judah. You live in a dangerous world today. Living close to the Lord is your hope.

**In what areas of life do you feel most unsafe, and how can the Lord help you feel safe in Him?**

## Day 302
### WHOM CAN YOU TRUST?

*Jeremiah 40:16. But Gedaliah the son of Ahikam said to Johanan the son of Kareah, "Don't do such a thing! What you are saying about Ishmael is not true."*

Gedaliah had the challenging task of leading a war-shocked people. He had seen the Babylonians brutalize his tiny country. The king of Babylon handpicked Gedaliah to govern the remnant. Gedaliah was a good man, capable of doing the job.

As shown by his choice of Daniel to serve him in Babylon, the Babylonian king was skilled in discerning reliable people. Unfortunately, Gedaliah did not have this ability to judge character. Gedaliah's lack of discernment would cost him his life.

Gedaliah trusted Ishmael. He dismissed Johanan's offer to kill Ishmael. Gedaliah, who did not have the ability to discern like the king of Babylon did, thought the warning about Ishmael was groundless. Ishmael had been one of the first to come to Gedaliah after the king of Babylon had appointed Gedaliah to be governor. So Gedaliah trusted him.

It was tragic that the governor did not believe Johanan. Johanan had reliable information that Baalis, who was the king of Ammon, was sending Ishmael to assassinate Gedaliah. Johanan saw Gedaliah as the only hope for the safety of the Judean remnant. Johanan also feared Babylonian vengeance if their chosen governor was killed.

Gedaliah should have considered Johanan's counsel. He was wise to dismiss Johanan's offer to kill Ishmael, but he should have discerned Ishmael as a dangerous threat to his own life. Gedaliah should have assigned bodyguards to protect him from a possible assassination attempt. He needed to listen to wise advisers.

An entire nation can fall for lack of guidance, but many advisers will assure national victory (Proverbs 11:14). Plans will fail for lack of consultation, but the plans will succeed with many advisers (Proverbs 15:22). King Solomon had many elders who advised him (1 Kings 12:6).

God did not intend for you to privatize your relationship with Him to the extent that you ignore human advice. Draw closer to Him, and listen to the others who are also drawing nearer.

**List some ways in which you can find other believers who will give you wise counsel.**

## Day 303
### LIFE AFTER GEDALIAH

**Jeremiah 41:2.** *Ishmael son of Nethaniah and the ten men who were with him got up and struck down Gedaliah son of Ahikam, the son of Shaphan, with the sword, killing the one whom the king of Babylon had appointed as governor over the land.*

People want to have stability in their lives. After the downfall of Jerusalem, Jeremiah thought that Gedaliah would give the refugees a stable government. His expectations did not last long. Ishmael murdered Gedaliah.

Ishmael came with ten of his men to have dinner with Gedaliah (41:1). Gedaliah extended his complete hospitality to Ishmael, which was the cultural expectation. It was also expected that guests would be equally gracious to their host. But Ishmael completely violated both cultural and divine standards.

While they were eating their meal together, Ishmael and his ten men stood up. They pulled out their swords and killed Gedaliah. They also killed the Judeans who were with Gedaliah at Mizpah. They even slaughtered the Babylonian soldiers who happened to be there (41:3).

No words can adequately describe what Ishmael and his men did. It was a hideous crime. Ishmael's actions were subhuman. His treachery could even be considered "sub-animal"! Gedaliah and the others were totally unsuspecting of their violent fate.

Would Nebuchadnezzar look at these murders as rebellion against Babylonian authority? It was inevitable that he would. He later sent the Babylonians to carry more Judeans into exile (52:30).

Gedaliah's death ended any hope of a normal life for the remnant in Judah. They fell into despair about the future. If some of them remembered that the Lord had promised to give them hope and a future (29:11), they would know that the fulfillment of the promise would be in the distant future. Their immediate future looked bleak.

How does your immediate future look? Are you wondering if you have a secure life ahead of you? Believers do not need to worry about the future. They know that they have the Lord with them in the immediate future, and they will have a wonderful life in eternity.

**What can you anticipate in your future because of God's promises?**

## Day 304
### JONATHAN THE RESCUER

**Jeremiah 41:11-12.** *When Johanan son of Kareah and all the army officers who were with him heard about all the crimes Ishmael son of Nethaniah had committed, they took all their men and went to fight Ishmael son of Nethaniah. They caught up with him near the great pool in Gibeon.*

On the day after Ishmael had murdered the governor, eighty men arrived from the north. They had shaved off their beards, torn their clothes, and cut themselves to demonstrate their grief over the destruction of Jerusalem. They were carrying offerings and incense to present at the temple in Jerusalem. Ishmael went out to meet them and pretended to weep with them. He invited them to meet with the governor. But as soon as they were inside the city, Ishmael and his men slaughtered them. Ishmael threw their bodies into a cistern (41:4-7).

There were ten men among them who pleaded for their lives. They told Ishmael they would give him their supplies of wheat, barley, olive oil, and honey that they had hidden in a field. So Ishmael let them live. Then Ishmael took captive all the people who were still left alive in the city of Mizpah. Ishmael's prisoners included the royal princesses from Jerusalem and all the rest of the people in Mizpah that the Babylonians had put under the authority of Governor Gedaliah. Then Ishmael started traveling with all his captives toward the country of the Ammonites (41: 8-10).

Having all the wheat, barley, olive oil and honey probably influenced Ishmael to take prisoners instead of continuing his murder spree. He could sell his captives as slaves in the country of Ammon and he would become a wealthy man.

Ishmael's prisoners included women and children as well as soldiers and court officials (41:16). Jeremiah and Baruch were likely his prisoners also, because Jeremiah was with them after their rescue (42:2-6).

What a memorable rescue it was! Johanan and his men caught up with Ishmael, and all the prisoners turned and went over to Johanan. When Ishmael saw that he no longer had any prisoners, he managed to flee to Ammon with eight of his men. (41:14-15).

Are your circumstances looking bleak? Are you praying for a rescuer? The Lord raised up Jonathan to rescue many, and He can raise up a rescuer for you too!

**List some ways in which God rescues His people.**

## Day 305
### ARE YOU ON YOUR WAY TO EGYPT?

*Jeremiah 41:17-18. And they went on, stopping at Geruth Kimham near Bethlehem on their way to Egypt to escape the Babylonians. They were afraid of them because Ishmael son of Nethaniah had killed Gedaliah son of Ahikam, whom the king of Babylon had appointed as governor over the land.*

Johanan was a hero. He had rescued all those whom Ishmael had taken captive. Sadly, Johanan's courage soon dissipated into fear. He was brave against Ishmael, but he was afraid of facing the anger of Babylon. The rest of the people also feared Babylon's revenge.

The murderer of Gedaliah had escaped to Ammon. The Babylonians would have difficulty trying to find him among the Ammonites. However, The Babylonians could easily find Johanan and his followers.

Johanan was an impressive rescuer, but he proved to be an unwise leader. He remembered neither the counsel of Gedaliah (40:9) nor the sermons of Jeremiah. Gedaliah and Jeremiah had both warned the people to stay in the land. Johanan ruined his legacy as a rescuer by ignoring their words. Their words were the Word of the Lord.

The people stopped near Bethlehem, as if uncertain about what to do next. They knew where they wanted to go, but they wanted some confirmation of their plan. They asked Jeremiah what the Lord wanted them to do (42:1-3).

Jeremiah prayed for ten days, and then told them the Lord's answer. Then Lord would protect them from the Babylonians. They must not go to Egypt (42:7-17). Sadly, in their hearts they had already decided that their destination was Egypt.

Are you on your way to the metaphorical Egypt? Do not let fear propel you to trust in the ungodly world system. The world cannot remedy your fearfulness. Stop immediately on that road to Egypt. Turn around and come back to the Lord.

Friendship with the world is hate toward God (James 4:4). You are either the Lord's friend or His enemy. A friend of the world embraces the world's ungodly values. Stop traveling that road to Egypt!

**Which of the world's values are tempting you and keeping you from a more intimate relationship with the Lord?**

## Day 306
### DRAWING NEAR TO JEREMIAH

*Jeremiah 42:1-2. Then all the army officers, including Johanan son of Kareah and Jezaniah son of Hoshaiah, and all the people from the least to the greatest approached Jeremiah the prophet and said to him, "Please hear our petition and pray to the LORD your God for this entire remnant. For as you now see, though we were once many, now only a few are left...."*

In times of crisis and confusion, people seek out spiritual leaders. So it was with the remnant that approached Jeremiah. The people had confidence that Jeremiah was close to the Lord. They wanted him to pray for them.

This is the first mention of Jeremiah since he went to live with Gedaliah (40: 6). Much had happened since that calm period of time immediately following the destruction of Jerusalem. Now we know that was with the remnant that was going toward Egypt.

This latest chain of unfortunate events started with the assassination of Gedaliah. The king of Ammon sent a man named Ishmael to kill the newly appointed governor of Judah. Ishmael struck him down with a sword (40:13-41:2).

Jeremiah had shed so many tears over the city of Jerusalem, but I suppose that he still had a few spare tears for his friend Gedaliah. If only that ruthless Ishmael had stopped after he murdered Gedaliah! Ishmael and his men went on to kill everyone who was with Gedaliah. On the next day, they murdered eighty men who had come from Samaria to worship at the ruins of the temple (41:3-7).

Then Ishmael made captives of everyone else in the town, including Jeremiah. Once again Jeremiah was a prisoner! Ishmael's plan was to take all of them across the border to Ammon. But Johanan and his men rescued them while they were still in Judah. Ishmael and most of his men escaped (41:10-16).

Johanan the rest of the Judean remnant thought they had a serious problem. Now they feared retaliation from the Babylonians for the assassination of Gedaliah. They were thinking that they should flee to Egypt (41:17-18).

Apparently, Jeremiah was the only prophet among them. Every other prophet was either dead or exiled. The people had no one else to whom to turn, so they drew near to Jeremiah. Jeremiah did not waver from telling them the truth.

**How does your relationship with the Lord strengthen your resolve to tell people the truth?**

## Day 307
### WHERE TO GO AND WHAT TO DO

**Jeremiah 42:3.** *"Pray that the LORD your God will tell us where we should go and what we should do."*

The Judean refugees asked Jeremiah to pray to his God. They referred to the Lord as Jeremiah's God because they recognized that he had an especially close relationship with the Lord. They wanted Jeremiah, after he prayed, to tell them the Lord's will for their lives.

They wanted to know where they should go and what they should do. They wanted divine guidance, just like you and countless other believers want today. Have you prayed lately for God's will for your life?

Jeremiah agreed to ask the Lord for them what His plans were for them. He reminded them that He was their God also (42:4). They could have prayed to the Lord directly without going through the prophet.

Also, they could have contemplated their recent history and known what they should do. Before he was assassinated, Gedaliah had told them to stay in the land and serve the king of Babylon. He told them to harvest grapes, figs and olives from the land (40:9-10). The king of Babylon had appointed Gedaliah to be governor over the conquered nation of Judah (40:5), so Gedaliah spoke with authority.

Before the Babylonians destroyed Jerusalem, Jeremiah preached for many years that the Judeans should submit to the king of Babylon (27:11). When the Babylonians surrounded Jerusalem, Jeremiah told the people inside the city that they would live if they surrendered (38:2). He told King Zedekiah to give himself up to the Babylonian officers (38:17).

The Judeans should have known that yielding to Babylon was God's will for their lives. They were not to blame for the assassination of Gedaliah, so his death would not have changed God's plan for them. If they had only reflected on their past, they would have known that their future did not include going to Egypt.

How has the Lord led you in the past? One of my favorite hymns, "Be Still, My Soul", affirms that God will guide the future as He has the past. Trust His guidance!

**Where does God want you to go (or stay) and what does He want you to do during the next few years? How do you know?**

Day 308
ALL GOD'S WORD

**Jeremiah 42:4.** *"I have heard you," replied Jeremiah the prophet. "I will certainly pray to the LORD your God as you have requested; I will tell you everything the LORD says and will keep nothing back from you."*

The people asked Jeremiah to pray for them, and he agreed to do it. Many years earlier, the Lord had told Jeremiah not to pray for the people of Judah (11:14). They were judged when Jerusalem burned, so now Jeremiah felt that he could make a fresh start with this small remnant. He could pray for them.

He promised them that he would tell them the whole word that the Lord would reveal to him. He said that he would hide nothing from them. Perhaps he already suspected that they would not like his answer!

The entire group had approached Jeremiah (42:1). Their leaders were Johanan and Jezaniah son of Hoshaiah. Jezaniah was also called Azariah in the next chapter.

Johanan and Jezaniah were leading the people from Judah to Egypt. All of them wanted to go to Egypt to escape from the Babylonians. They feared that the Babylonians would retaliate against them because of the assassination of Gedaliah (41:17).

The people sought Jeremiah's advice even though they had already decided what they wanted to do! They thought that fleeing to Egypt was their only option. They wanted to make Egypt their permanent home (42:14).

Perhaps they wanted Jeremiah (and the Lord) to approve their plan to go to Egypt. Maybe they wanted him to tell them which route to travel. It was apparent that they did not really want to hear all of God's Word.

The Apostle Paul proclaimed to the Ephesians the whole purpose of God (Acts 20:27). Jeremiah would do the same to the renegades of Judah. Both Jeremiah and Paul knew that many do not want to hear all of God's will. Many people just want to know the part that makes them feel snug.

Isaiah had to deal with people who had the same attitude. Many in his day did not want to hear prophecies. They did not even want to hear about the Holy One of Israel (Isaiah 30:10-11)! Reject this attitude! You can do better!

**Which sections of God's Word have you neglected in recent years? What plan can you make to read or study those sections?**

## Day 309
### CONDITIONAL OBEDIENCE

**Jeremiah 42:5-6.** *Then they said to Jeremiah, "May the LORD be a true and faithful witness against us if we do not act in accordance with everything the LORD your God sends you to tell us. Whether it is favorable or unfavorable, we will obey the LORD our God, to whom we are sending you, so that it will go well with us, for we will obey the LORD our God."*

Even though the people seemed willing to go anywhere the Lord might send them, their willingness was conditional. They apparently assumed that the Lord wanted them to go to Egypt. Instead of wanting to obey, they desired for the Lord to approve their plan!

They were already on their way to Egypt when they asked Jeremiah for the Lord's guidance (42:3). They said that they would obey even if they perceived that the command was unfavorable to them. Sadly, they had a different standard in their hearts.

The people made a big mistake when they told Jeremiah that they would do what God said (42:20). They had asked the prophet to pray for them for guidance. They pledged to do whatever the Lord told them, but Jeremiah knew that they were lying.

Jeremiah learned about the dangers of conditional obedience early in his life. When the Lord first called him to serve Him, Jeremiah tried to set some conditions. He told the Lord that he was too young (1:6). Jeremiah wanted to obey the Lord's call when he was older. As an older and more mature man, Jeremiah would know more. With years of maturity, he thought he would be a more experienced speaker. Jeremiah was using his age for his conditional obedience excuse!

My wife and I taught our children that delayed obedience is the same as disobedience. Also, conditional obedience is the same as disobedience. In God's eyes, the Judeans who were on their way to Egypt were disobedient.

Is your obedience to the Lord conditional? Are you willing to obey only if you like the command? Grow closer to Him so that you can trust His commands unconditionally.

**Which New Testament commands do you have the most difficulty desiring to obey? Ask the Lord for His grace to change your attitude.**

## Day 310
## Ten Days

**Jeremiah 42:7-8.** *Ten days later the word of the LORD came to Jeremiah. So he called together Johanan son of Kareah and all the army officers who were with him and all the people from the least to the greatest.*

The people had to wait ten days before they heard Jeremiah speak again. Undoubtedly, they became fidgety. Ten days was a long time to wait for a message that might radically change the remaining years of their lives.

The people had told Jeremiah that they would respond positively to the whole word that the Lord would give to Jeremiah. They assured him that they would listen to God's words, even if the words were unpleasant. They even said that obeying the Lord would cause their lives to turn out well (42:5-6).

They had ten days to think about what they had said to Jeremiah. They had uttered the right religious words, but they had not fooled the prophet. Jeremiah had encountered this duplicitous attitude during his entire ministry in Jerusalem. He especially saw this attitude in King Zedekiah.

Shortly before Jerusalem fell, Zedekiah had come to Jeremiah requesting a word from the Lord. Based on his past experiences with the king, Jeremiah replied that Zedekiah would not listen to him (38:15). The prophet lived eleven years under Zedekiah's reign, and he knew well the king's persistent rejection of God's Word.

Jeremiah prayed for ten days before receiving the Lord's answer for him to give to the people. The prophet was willing to wait for as long as it took for him to clearly receive God's will. He wanted God's pure words, unmingled with his own personal desires.

Jeremiah knew that he could not give God a closing date! It was the Lord's message, and it would come according to the Lord's timing. Jeremiah may have thought that the ten-day wait would prepare the people to follow the Lord. If he thought this, he would be disappointed.

If only the people had used those ten days for spiritual growth! They then would have realized that the Lord took care of them during that time. They had enough food. The Babylonians did not suddenly attack them. God was with them. They had nothing to fear.

**How has God cared for you during the past ten days?**

## Day 311
### THE GRIEVING GOD

*Jeremiah 42:10. "'If you stay in this land, I will build you up and not tear you down; I will plant you and not uproot you, for I am grieved over the disaster I have inflicted on you....'"*

The Lord gave the Judean refugees some wonderful promises. Using the same metaphors of builder and farmer that He employed when He first called Jeremiah (1:10), the Lord gave them hope. He would plant them and build them up, just like He was doing to the exiled Judeans in Babylon (24:5-6).

However, the promises were conditional on their obedience. The condition was that they were required to stay in their native land of Judah. They must not go to Egypt, or anywhere else.

The Lord went on to make the remarkable statement that He was grieved over the disaster of Jerusalem. Even though the Babylonians had destroyed the city, the Lord took responsibility for it. Through His perfect personality, the Lord grieved over the pain that His people suffered from the Babylonians. During times when you mourn, you can take comfort in knowing that the Lord also grieves.

The Hebrew word for "grieve" can also be translated as "repent", "relent" or "change one's mind". The Lord used this same word when He told Jeremiah that if a nation turns from evil, He would "repent" from bringing catastrophe on it (18:8). However, the Lord would not "repent" from bringing judgment on those people whom He knew would not change (4:28).

Since the Hebrew word has more than one meaning, this verse does not necessarily teach that God has now "repented" over the Jerusalem disaster. Since His thoughts and purposes are unchanging, this verse should not be interpreted that God has now "changed His mind" about whether He should have inflicted destruction on the Judean city. The potential contradictions about God's dependability are solved when we see in this verse that the Lord was "grieved."

The Lord used this word early in the history of humankind. When He saw the intensity of wickedness on the earth, He was grieved. He was sorry that He had made men and women. He felt sorrow over the sinful choices that His creation had made (Genesis 6:6).

**How does knowing that God grieves help you to grow closer to Him?**

## Day 312
### REASONS FOR FEARLESSNESS

**Jeremiah 42:11-12. *Do not be afraid of the king of Babylon, whom you now fear. Do not be afraid of him, declares the LORD, for I am with you and will save you and deliver you from his hands. I will show you compassion so that he will have compassion on you and restore you to your land.***

After the Babylonians conquered Judah, they appointed a governor who was soon assassinated. A group of Judeans wanted to immigrate to Egypt because they feared revenge from the Babylonians for the governor's murder. Jeremiah told these Judeans that the Lord wanted them to stay in Judah. He told them that they had nothing to fear.

The Lord's message to them was that they should not be afraid of the king of Babylon. If they stayed in Judah, the Babylonians would not harm them. Jeremiah gave them four foundations for fearlessness.

The first foundation was the Lord's promise to be with them. God gave this same promise to Jeremiah forty years earlier (1:8). The Lord had been in close relationship with Jeremiah for four decades, so Jeremiah could personally confirm that the Lord keeps this promise.

The second foundation was God's promise to save them. He would keep them safe from physical harm. The third foundation was God's deliverance. God promised that He would deliver them from the Babylonians. God used the same word when He promised to rescue Jeremiah from all of his enemies (1:8). God extended the same promise of deliverance to the remnant.

The fourth foundation was God's compassion. God's compassion would motivate the king of Babylon to show them mercy. God's compassion would allow them to return to their homes in Judah.

If only they listened to Jeremiah! They would have experienced the truth that Solomon wrote centuries earlier. One of his proverbs taught that fear of other people will result in being trapped, but trusting in the Lord will bring safety (Proverbs 29:25).

Do you have true security? Do you trust in the Lord and not in human beings? If so, you have nothing to fear.

**Have you been strongly secure in the Lord in recent months? Why or why not?**

## Day 313
### ENTERING EGYPT

**Jeremiah 43:7.** *So they entered Egypt in disobedience to the LORD and went as far as Tahpanhes.*

After Jeremiah told all the people that the Lord did not want them to go to Egypt, several arrogant men called Jeremiah a liar. They claimed that the Lord had not sent Jeremiah to tell them to stay out of Egypt. They accused Baruch of stirring Jeremiah up against them. They thought that Baruch wanted to hand them over to the Babylonians so that they would kill them or carry them off into exile in Babylon (43:1-3).

Jeremiah did not respond to their false accusations. Even though they were wrong, Jeremiah sensed that their hardened attitudes did not warrant any further words from him. He had already told them that they would all die if they went to Egypt (42:22).

The people did not obey the Lord's command to stay in the land. Johanan and his military leaders took the entire Judean remnant to Egypt. The group included everyone who had returned to Judah after being dispersed throughout the nations. Also in the group were all the men, women, children, and royal princesses whom the Babylonians had left with Gedaliah. With the exceptions of Jeremiah and Baruch, who were forced to go with them, they went to Egypt because they refused to obey the Lord (43:4-7).

Why did they force Jeremiah and Baruch to go with them? Possibly they thought that Jeremiah would be a useful hostage in case the Babylonians pursued them. Or perhaps they wanted to keep Jeremiah accessible to consult in the event of a new crisis. The ungodly King Zedekiah had kept Jeremiah alive for the same purpose.

In the opening sermon of his career, Jeremiah had fondly remembered his ancestors' devotion to God in the wilderness soon after they had left Egypt (2:1). Jeremiah then rebuked the people of his day for relying on Egypt for help (2:18). Now at the end of his career, Jeremiah was being taken to the very country where his ancestors had been enslaved.

Tahpanhes was an Egyptian border town. The travel-weary crowd from Judah stopped there to get permission to enter Egypt. The Egyptians allowed them to come in.

Egypt is a symbol of everything that is opposed to God's good plan for your life. Do not go to where God has forbidden. Do not even consider visiting the border!

**What is specifically tempting to you about disobedience? How can you grow stronger in your obedience to God?**

## Day 314
### HIDDEN STONES

**Jeremiah 43:9.** *"While the Jews are watching, take some large stones with you and bury them in clay in the brick pavement at the entrance to Pharaoh's palace in Tahpanhes...."*

In the Egyptian town of Tahpanhes, the Lord spoke to Jeremiah. God wanted Jeremiah to perform one more symbolic act. The Lord told him to take some large stones and bury them under the pavement that led to Pharaoh's palace. (The Pharaoh had several palaces throughout Egypt, and probably he did not reside in Tahpanhes at this time.)

If only the people had remembered Jeremiah's earlier symbolic performances! The meanings behind the prophet's ruined belt, smashed pot and yoke on his shoulders had all come to pass. The Babylonians had conquered Judah.

The people from Judah were Jeremiah's audience. They watched the old prophet move and bury the huge stones. Presumably they did not offer to help!

Then Jeremiah told them the Lord's words – Egypt was not safe from the Babylonians. God would bring King Nebuchadnezzar and the Babylonians to Egypt. The Lord would set Nebuchadnezzar's throne and royal tent over the stones that Jeremiah had buried (43:10).

The large stones symbolized pedestals that were worthy of supporting a king's throne. Jeremiah buried the stones so that the Egyptians would not remove them. The permanency of the buried stones demonstrated that Jeremiah's prophecy would certainly happen.

The Babylonians would attack Egypt. Many people would die, and many others would be carried off into exile. The Babylonians would set fire to the temples of the gods of Egypt. They would burn some of the Egyptian idols and carry others off as captives (43:11-13).

The large concealed stones symbolized God's words about Babylon's future conquest of Egypt. All of God's words are like unseen stones. The world's people act as if the stones are not there. They do not realize that the Lord will fulfill every one of His hidden stones.

**What large hidden stone from God's Word will you claim for your life today?**

## Day 315
### UNLEARNED LESSONS

**Jeremiah 44:1.** *This word came to Jeremiah concerning all the Jews living in Lower Egypt—in Migdol, Tahpanhes and Memphis—and in Upper Egypt....*

Several years had passed since Jeremiah and Baruch arrived in Egypt. The Jews lived in their own communities throughout Egypt. Many Jews had moved to Egypt before Johanan's remnant arrived.

Unfortunately, none of them had learned the lessons from recent history. They had changed their country of residence, but they had not changed their hearts. Jeremiah began preaching to his people once again.

Jeremiah reminded them that they saw the destruction that the Lord had brought on Jerusalem. The Lord also demolished all the other cities in Judah. The cities were still abandoned and in ruins (44:2).

Jeremiah also recapped why the devastation happened. They lost their cities and their nation because of their wickedness. Specifically, they served and worshipped other gods (44:3).

The Lord sent prophets again and again to warn the people that their idol worship was an outrage to Him. But the people did not listen. They continued to sacrifice to other gods. Consequently, the Lord finally poured out His anger on the cities of Judah (44:4-6).

Then Jeremiah spoke about their present situation in Egypt. They were again provoking the Lord to anger, because they were now worshipping other gods in Egypt. They were setting themselves up to be without a remnant and to become a curse among all the nations of the earth (44:7-8).

They had not learned basic spiritual lessons. They thought that moving to Egypt would give them a safe and blissful life. They were wrong.

Changing your geographical location will not solve your basic problems. Every place you choose to live will have its own idolatrous snares. You need to grow closer to the Lord right where you are.

**Write a prayer in which you express your contentment with the place in which the Lord has placed you.**

Day 316
FLAWED THINKING

**Jeremiah 44:18.** *"But ever since we stopped burning incense to the Queen of Heaven and pouring out drink offerings to her, we have had nothing and have been perishing by sword and famine."*

The people were flawed in their thinking about the reason for their unfortunate circumstances. When their parents lived in Judah and worshipped the idol called the queen of heaven, they remembered that everything was going well for them. They had plenty of food and carefree lives. Then Josiah became king. He made them give up their idols. In fact, he destroyed the idols.

After being deprived of their gods and goddesses, their circumstances worsened. King Josiah was killed in a battle with the Egyptians. Eventually the Babylonians destroyed their nation of Judah. The Judeans feared that the Babylonians would pursue them as long as they remained in Judah.

The Judeans blamed their misfortunes on their neglect of the queen of heaven. Josiah's death, drought, disease, famine, Jerusalem's destruction, and now Gedaliah's assassination – they thought all these bad things happened because they stopped burning sacrifices to their favorite goddess. They were determined to reverse their fortunes.

A minority of Judeans had managed to escape to Egypt. They were determined to restore the queen idol to her rightful place on their idol pedestals. They were free in Egypt to worship the queen of heaven as much as they desired.

The direct cause of their flawed thinking was their rejection of God's truth. Decades earlier, Jeremiah had preached specifically about the queen of heaven. He described how entire families were involved in her worship. He warned about how their devotion to her was showing spitefulness to the Lord (7:18-19).

Commitment to idols was a foolish challenge to the sovereign Lord God! How could any idol do more for them than the all-powerful living God? How could any idol do anything for anybody!?

Combat your own blurry thinking. Focus your thoughts on God as you grow in your awareness of His presence in your life. No other god or goddess has power like His.

**Write a prayer in which you ask God to keep you from erroneous thinking about your circumstances.**

Day 317

In Harm's Way

*Jeremiah 44:26. But hear the word of the LORD, all Jews living in Egypt: 'I swear by my great name,' says the LORD, 'that no one from Judah living anywhere in Egypt will ever again invoke my name or swear, "As surely as the Sovereign LORD lives."*

The Judeans living in Egypt were in harm's way. Their lives were in imminent danger because of their disobedience. They had defied the Lord's command to stay in Judah. Now that they were in Egypt, they were worshipping other gods (44:15-16).

Jeremiah had some words for them! He spoke to a large group of Judeans, both men and women. He told them to go ahead and keep their vows to their idols (44:24-25)!

Jeremiah was preaching with sarcasm. He knew that they would remain devoted to other gods no matter what he said. He was distressed that they were not keeping their vows to the Lord. The Judeans living in Egypt were a complete contrast to the Recabites. The Recabites, who were foreigners in Jerusalem, still kept their vows to their ancestor (35:1-11). The Judeans, who were foreigners in Egypt, snubbed the vows they had made to their ancestors' God.

The Lord had asked the refugees in Egypt why they were bringing such great harm to themselves (44:7). Because of their disobedience and idolatry, they were running toward ruin. They would experience famine and sword (44:12). They would have no descendants.

In the past, the Lord watched over them for good. Now He would watch over them for harm (44:27). The Lord is the God who watches. He watches over His Word to carry it out (1:12). In the future, He will watch over His people as they are built and planted (31:28).

Jeremiah gave them a glimmer of hope. A few would escape from Egypt and return to Judah (44:14). He repeated this promise. Some would escape the sword and go back to live in Judah (44:28).

As the Lord watches over all people, you can have hope. The Lord builds and plants His people. Jesus Christ hung on the cross, in harm's way, so that He might plant you and build you for His kingdom.

**Are you confident that you are not in harm's way like those renegade Judeans? Why or why not?**

Day 318

JEREMIAH'S UNKNOWN DEATH

**Jeremiah 44:28. *Those who escape the sword and return to the land of Judah from Egypt will be very few. Then the whole remnant of Judah who came to live in Egypt will know whose word will stand—mine or theirs.***

Jeremiah's messages often contained hope for a few. His last recorded sermon in Egypt predicted that a small group would return to Judah. Total judgment would fall on all those who stayed in Egypt and worshiped the Queen of Heaven. The return of the few, who presumably would carry these words from Jeremiah with them, would demonstrate that the Lord's words were true.

It is possible that Jeremiah returned with them. Or as an old man, he may have died in Egypt. The Bible is silent about Jeremiah's death.

Ancient tradition asserts that Jeremiah's own people stoned him in Egypt. Even though Jesus taught that Jerusalem's people had stoned their prophets through the centuries (Luke 13:34), Jesus mentioned nothing about Jeremiah being stoned.

If Jeremiah suffered a violent death at the hands of his own people, it would have been a startling breach of one of God's promises to him. The Lord had promised to be with Jeremiah and to rescue him from hostile people (1:8). Even though they would fight against him, the Lord would deliver him (1:19).

Jeremiah's biography in the Bible records a lifetime of rescues. Why would the Lord revoke His promise at the end of Jeremiah's life and permit him to be stoned? The promise-keeping faithful Lord would not!

The Lord was with all of His other prophets, but He did not promise each one that He would rescue them when their lives were in danger. Nor does the Lord promise you that He will deliver you from every life-threatening difficulty. However, a true believer in Jesus Christ can confidently expect deliverance through death. Death for the believer means entrance into His kingdom.

Unless Jesus Christ returns during your lifetime, you will die. If you are a true believer, the Lord will be with you like He was with Jeremiah. Live closely with Him and face death fearlessly. Remember that victory is on the other side of death (1 Corinthians 15:55-57)!

**Describe how you can anticipate your deliverance through death.**

## Day 319
### PHARAOH'S FATE

*Jeremiah 44:30. "This is what the LORD says: 'I am going to hand Pharaoh Hophra king of Egypt over to his enemies who seek his life, just as I handed Zedekiah king of Judah over to Nebuchadnezzar king of Babylon, the enemy who was seeking his life.'"*

The refugees from Judah were trusting in the Egyptian government for their protection. They considered Pharaoh Hophra to be one of the most powerful kings in the world. Jeremiah gave them a prophetic dose of truth about Hophra. The reality was that Pharaoh Hophra would meet a disastrous fate similar to King Zedekiah's doom.

Hophra had agreed to help Zedekiah defend Jerusalem against the Babylonians. Hophra's help did nothing to save Judah from being conquered. Hophra's army temporarily distracted the Babylonians (37:5), but the Babylonians returned to Jerusalem and destroyed the city. Hophra had led his weakened army back to Egypt.

King Nebuchadnezzar captured Zedekiah, killed his sons, and took him to Babylon as a blinded prisoner. Jeremiah prophesied that Hophra would meet a similar fate. The prophet had earlier performed a symbolic act that Nebuchadnezzar and the Babylonians would invade Egypt, but Jeremiah did not say that this would happen during Hophra's lifetime (43:8-13). Historians now know that Hophra was killed before the Babylonians came.

Even secular historians who have no regard for the Bible acknowledge the historicity of Pharaoh Hophra. Hophra became Pharaoh three years before Nebuchadnezzar destroyed Jerusalem, and he ruled Egypt for less than twenty years. Toward the end of his reign, some of his army rebelled. The military leader who ended the rebellion was made a co-ruler, and Hophra was put to death several years later.

Hophra was a mere mortal. The refugees from Judah should not have put their trust in Pharaoh Hophra. They should have learned from history that most national leaders prove to be weak and disappointing.

God is in control of the rise and fall of every king and political leader. The Lord is not giving prophetic words today about those national rulers about whom you may be concerned. It does not matter that you do not know their future. What does matter is to know that God is the Cosmic Ruler. Leave the fate of the pharaohs to Him.

**Are there any national leaders that you are prone to trust as much as you trust the Lord? How can you keep your trust exclusively in the Lord?**

Day 320

BARUCH'S FUTURE

*Jeremiah 45:1. This is what Jeremiah the prophet told Baruch son of Neriah in the fourth year of Jehoiakim son of Josiah king of Judah, after Baruch had written on a scroll the words Jeremiah was then dictating....*

Jeremiah and Baruch were in Egypt (43:1-44:13), and history is silent about what happened to them next. Chapter 45 is a flashback to King Jehoiakim's reign. More than fifteen years before the Babylonians destroyed Jerusalem, Baruch had a personal crisis.

Baruch was Jeremiah's scribe when the Lord told the prophet to write down His words (36:1-2). Jeremiah dictated as Baruch wrote. When he finished the writing project, Baruch broke down.

From all the Lord's words that he had written, Baruch clearly understood that judgment was coming. His reaction was, "Woe is me!" (45:3) He was emotionally exhausted. He knew that the catastrophic Babylonian invasion would finish his nation, his family and his career. He along with everyone else in the fourth year of King Jehoiakim saw the Babylonians as a real threat.

The fourth year of Jehoiakim was the first year that Nebuchadnezzar was king of Babylon (25:1). The Babylonians defeated the Egyptians in an important battle that year (46:2). Egypt was now no longer the world power. It seemed like no one could stop Nebuchadnezzar from conquering the world.

The Lord had built Jerusalem, but He would use the Babylonians to tear it down. He had planted the nation of Judah, but He would use Nebuchadnezzar to uproot the whole land (45:4). Baruch felt pain as a result of understanding the Lord's words, but God had a special promise to encourage Baruch.

The Lord promised Baruch that He would preserve his life (45:5). The Lord kept His promise. Baruch survived the Babylonian annihilation of Jerusalem, and he was still living with the rebellious Judeans who went to Egypt. He probably lived many years after that and probably never forgot the gift of life that the Lord had given him.

You also have the gift of life. The Lord has extended your life on earth to at least today. You do not know how many days or years you have left on earth. Use the remainder of your days to seek the Lord.

**What are your specific plans for seeking the Lord for the rest of your life?**

## Day 321
### REFUSING GOALS OF GREATNESS

**Jeremiah 45:5.** *"'Should you then seek great things for yourself? Seek them not. For I will bring disaster on all people, declares the LORD, but wherever you go I will let you escape with your life."*

Baruch needed encouragement, and Jeremiah had a word for him. The Lord knew Baruch's heart. God knew that Baruch was emotionally exhausted and feeling sorry for himself. Baruch believed what Jeremiah had dictated to him about the city falling to the Babylonians. However, his own career goals conflicted with God's plans for judgment. Baruch was grieving.

Baruch's sorrow was trivial compared with the Lord's. The Lord had personally built and planted the city (45:4). He loved that city more than Baruch could understand. But it would soon be time for God to overthrow and uproot those rebellious people.

A person should not try to achieve selfish goals in the midst of a national disaster! The Lord told Baruch to stop pursuing personal greatness. Baruch should not keep seeking a successful career.

Baruch's brother Seraiah had a successful career under King Zedekiah (51:59). Perhaps Baruch had wanted to be on a similar career path. If so, Baruch should have stopped looking at his brother's life as a model for his own. The Lord has unique plans for each individual.

There would be no political or economic structures left in Judah to confer greatness on any man or woman. Career plans would be meaningless in those days. The Lord was warning Baruch about the eminent death of all significant jobs.

Baruch would survive the Babylonian disaster. The Lord promised that Baruch would escape with his life wherever he went. He went to Egypt and lived to tell about it. Legends claim that he then went to Babylon.

Baruch lived many years and continued to trust in the Lord. Everyday he would experience the simple gift of life. He did not attain his professional aspirations, but he discovered something much better. He had a long life that was fulfilling and complete. Baruch responded well to the Lord's words. Then God made him great!

What about you? Are you dreaming of becoming great? Forget it! Live for the great God whose greatness shrinks all human greatness into oblivion.

**How might your career plans be in conflict with God's purposes?**

## Day 322
### JEREMIAH'S WORLD

**Jeremiah 46:1. *This is the word of the LORD that came to Jeremiah the prophet concerning the nations....***

Jeremiah lived six hundred years before the time of Jesus Christ. He lived in a world filled with international tension. His nation and other small nations were trying to form alliances against the rising (Babylon) and falling (Egypt) super powers.

The Lord had called Jeremiah to be a prophet to the nations (1:5). The Lord gave him messages to warn individual nations of their destruction and also encourage the nations about future rebuilding (1:10). Jeremiah preached these international messages throughout his career.

Jeremiah messages to the nations appear in the latter section of his book (46:1-51:64). Up until this section, Jeremiah recorded his messages to his own nation of Judah. The Lord gave him messages to nine other nations.

The messages to the two most powerful nations, Egypt (46:1-28) and Babylon (50:1-51:64), form large bookends between which the messages to the seven other nations are found. The messages are mostly in chronological order. The message to Egypt begins with the fourth year of King Jehoiakim (46:2). The last recorded message to Babylon was in the fourth year of King Zedekiah (51:59).

Apparently, Jeremiah did not travel to all these nations to deliver his international sermons. The Lord intended for the people of Judah to hear these messages to the nations. Likewise, God planned for you to read Jeremiah's messages to these nations.

Many similarities exist between your world and Jeremiah's world. God knows what every nation is doing in your world today. The Lord is in the process of bringing some nations down and raising others up.

Jesus Christ praised God the Father as Lord of heaven and earth (Luke 10:21). Whether they acknowledge it or not, all nations are accountable to the Lord. God will judge the nations by His own standards. All nations have evidence that God exists (Romans 1:19-20). It is their fateful choice if they suppress the evidence and fall under judgment.

**Explain your confidence that Lord rules over nations today just like He did in Jeremiah's world.**

Day 323

EGYPT

*Jeremiah 46:2. Concerning Egypt: This is the message against the army of Pharaoh Neco king of Egypt, which was defeated at Carchemish on the Euphrates River by Nebuchadnezzar king of Babylon in the fourth year of Jehoiakim son of Josiah king of Judah....*

Jeremiah preached his first international message to the nation of Egypt. He directed his sermon toward Pharaoh Neco's army. This was the same Pharaoh who had killed the good King Josiah five years earlier (2 Kings 23:29).

King Jehoiakim was one of Josiah's evil sons. In King Jehoiakim's fourth year, the Pharaoh lost a major battle. The Babylonians defeated the Egyptians at Carchemish. This was one of the most decisive military battles during Jeremiah's lifetime. Egypt's dominance as a world power ended. Under King Nebuchadnezzar, Babylon became the prevailing force in the world.

Egyptian pride seemed to blind the nation to the reality of defeat. In a sarcastic manner, Jeremiah preached to the Egyptian army. He commanded the soldiers to line up their shields and harness their horses. Jeremiah played the role of an imaginary military commander as he told the soldiers to put on their helmets and polish their spears (46:3-4).

In spite of the commands, Egypt lost the battle. The Babylonians terrified the Egyptians. Jeremiah preached that terror was on every side (46:5).

All the Egyptian soldiers tried to escape. Amidst the great confusion of their retreat, many stumbled and fell. This caused even the strong soldiers to be able to flee from the Babylonians (46:6). The Babylonians destroyed the Egyptian army.

Egypt had tried to be like the Nile River during its periods of flooding. Egypt had tried to cover the earth with its military conquests. The Pharaoh had hired mercenary soldiers from Ethiopia and other nations in order to fulfill his dream of his invasion of the world (46:7-9).

The Lord used the Babylonians to shatter Pharaoh's dream. The victory at the Battle of Carchemish belonged to the Lord. The Lord took vengeance on the Egyptian army (46:10). The Egyptians trusted their own strength, which proved insufficient. You can do much better than they by looking beyond yourself.

**How are you specifically depending on the Lord to fight for you in your battles with the world?**

Day 324

INCURABLE

**Jeremiah 46:11.** *"Go up to Gilead and get balm, O Virgin Daughter of Egypt. But you multiply remedies in vain; there is no healing for you...."*

There was no hope for Egypt. Egypt's military defeat was a day of vengeance for the Lord (46:10). The Lord was bringing Egypt's world power to an end.

Jeremiah preached mockingly for Egypt to go up to Gilead in order to get some balm for the nation's wounds. The land of Gilead was famous for its medicinal herbs. When he preached about the wounds of his own nation of Judah, Jeremiah asked if there were no balm in Gilead to restore his people to health (8:22).

It was unusual for Jeremiah to refer to Egypt as a "virgin daughter". Jeremiah had preached that Israel was the Lord's virgin (18:13). In the future, the Lord will rebuild Israel as His virgin (31:4).

Egypt was like a virgin because of Egypt's strategic geographical position. Like a virgin daughter living in the safety of her father's house, the Egyptians thought they lived in a secure part of the world. They were wrong.

Like Judah (14:19), Egypt was beyond healing. There is no healing for those nations that have an incurable wound (30:12-13). Even balm from Gilead would not help.

Balm is a salve or ointment that the people could apply directly on their sores. Jeremiah ironically told Egypt to get their needed medicine from Gilead. It was irony, because Egypt prided herself on having skilled physicians and amply medicine. However, Egypt's medicine was not working. Jeremiah told the Egyptians to go to Gilead and try the medicinal creams from there.

Other nations would hear about Egypt's shame. Word would spread about Egypt's incurable wound. Egypt's proud army would prove to be inept as they stumbled and fell all over each other in trying to escape from the Babylonians (46:12).

Without medical attention, a serious wound will keep getting worse. Like the nations of Egypt and Judah, everyone in the world has an incurable wound. Without Jesus Christ, there is no healing of that incurable wound of sin.

**How do you know that the incurable wound of sin is not obstructing your relationship with the Lord?**

## Day 325
### OPPORTUNITY

**Jeremiah 46:17. *There they will exclaim, 'Pharaoh king of Egypt is only a loud noise; he has missed his opportunity.'***

Jeremiah wrote that the king of Egypt missed his moment. Pharaoh had an opportunity to change the course of history, but he squandered it. If Pharaoh had defeated the Babylonians during the battle at Carchemish in the fourth year of King Jehoiakim, many subsequent events would have been different.

Or if Pharaoh had pursued the Babylonians after the battle, he might have still been victorious. Nebuchadnezzar had to return to Babylon when he learned about his father's death. While the Babylonians retreated, Pharaoh did not take advantage of this opportunity.

Nebuchadnezzar did not invade Egypt until much later (43:8-13). Apparently, Pharaoh did nothing effective against the Babylonians until this invasion. The Egyptian king missed his opportunity.

Pharaoh's army could not fight successfully against the Babylonians, because the Lord had pushed them down. The Egyptian army stumbled all over each other. All they could shout to each other was retreat (46:15-16).

One of the problems was that the Egyptian military was not composed entirely of Egyptians. Pharaoh had hired mercenaries from other countries to fight for Egypt. They could not stand their ground against the Babylonians (46:21).

All of Pharaoh's foreign soldiers eventually realized that he was nothing more than a big blare! He was merely a loud noise. He talked about how he would accomplish mighty triumphs for Egypt, but he was only blowing smoke. He was an incessant talker, but an underachiever. He could not deliver on his promises. His major "accomplishment" was to give his nation's position of super power over to Babylon!

In contrast to Pharaoh, you can choose to seize the opportunities that God provides for you. Jesus said His followers should do His work now, because night would soon come when no one could work (John 9:4). Paul wrote that believers should redeem their time (Ephesians 5:16).

**What opportunities has the Lord given you that you need to seize now?**

Day 326

## PHILISTIA

**Jeremiah 47:1. *This is the word of the LORD that came to Jeremiah the prophet concerning the Philistines before Pharaoh attacked Gaza....***

Five city-states were in the land of the Philistines. One of these was Gaza. The Lord singled out this city in particular to fall under judgment. The Lord would use the Egyptians who later attacked the city.

The Lord would also use the Babylonians to judge Gaza. The Lord described the Babylonians as the rising waters in the north (47:2). The Babylonian army would overflow the land of the Philistines.

The Philistines would be caught in the middle of the power struggle between Babylon and Egypt. As a result, they would be destroyed. They would not be able to help their two allies, Tyre and Sidon (47:4).

Tyre and Sidon had sent representatives to Jerusalem to try to form an alliance against Babylon (27:3). It was a futile attempt. God's judgment fell upon the kings of Tyre and Sidon (26:22).

Jeremiah warned that the Philistines, especially the cities of Gaza and Ashkelon, that they should shave their heads and cut themselves as signs that they were in mourning. They will come to ruin (47:5).

God described the process of His judgment as the sword of the Lord. Jeremiah described the longing of the Philistines for that sword to withdraw into its sheath. But the sword could not rest, because the Lord had given it His orders (47:6-7).

Jeremiah gave no reason why God chose to bring devastation upon the Philistines. King David had subdued the Philistines during his reign, and they were no longer a military threat. Jeremiah mentioned no idols that they were continuing to worship. So why did God judge them?

Ezekiel gave a clue for the reason in his prophecy against the Philistines. Even though they were weak, the Philistines continued to carry out vengeance against Judah. Their goal was to destroy Judah (Ezekiel 25:15-17).

**How can you grow closer to the Lord even when you don't understand the reasons for His destruction of your world?**

## Day 327
### MOAB

*Jeremiah 48:1. Concerning Moab: This is what the LORD Almighty, the God of Israel, says: "Woe to Nebo, for it will be ruined. Kiriathaim will be disgraced and captured; the stronghold will be disgraced and shattered.*

The land of Moab is the central part of the nation of Jordan today. Jeremiah preached that the Lord would tear down the cities of Moab. The Lord would use a destroyer (48:8) to judge Moab. The world would learn that the destroyer was King Nebuchadnezzar, who conquered every nation that he could.

The Moabite town of Nebo was near the mountain where Moses stood to view the promised land (Deuteronomy 32:49). The Moabite town of Kiriathaim was an ancient settlement that existed during the time of Abraham (Genesis 14:5). Both cities had a long history.

However, cities do not prosper forever. The Lord would bring shame on the towns of Moab. Jeremiah preached that the nation of Moab was known for its pride (48:29). Moab's haughtiness would halt its success and bring national shame.

This disgrace would spread to Moab's national god. The nation itself would be ashamed of its idol named Chemosh (48:13). Chemosh had led God's people astray. Sadly, King Solomon had popularized the worship of Chemosh in Jerusalem (1 Kings 11:7).

The fact that the king of Moab had sacrificed his oldest son as a burnt offering (2 Kings 3:26-27) demonstrates how morally detestable Chemosh should have been to God's people. The practice of child sacrifice was prevalent in Jeremiah's day (7:31). Moab would be ashamed!

God would uproot and destroy Moab because the Lord has the highest standards of justice and holiness. Amazingly, the Lord will restore the fortunes of Moab in the future (48:47). Why?

The Lord also has the highest standards of grace and love. God's measure of grace and love is more extensive than you can imagine! His gracious kindness to you is beyond your understanding!

**Describe a specific incident that confirmed to you that the Lord is giving you His love and grace.**

## Day 328
### SWORDS

**Jeremiah 48:10. "*A curse on him who is lax in doing the LORD's work! A curse on him who keeps his sword from bloodshed!...*"**

The Lord had chosen the Babylonian soldiers to use their swords on the Moabites. The Lord did not want those soldiers to hold back their swords from bloodshed. The Lord was bringing judgment on the Moabites, and the Babylonians would fall under a curse if they did not carry out the Lord's vengeance on them. The Lord had revealed to Jeremiah that the king of Babylon was His servant (27:6).

What had Moab done to deserve divine wrath? The Lord was displeased with the way that the Moabites trusted both in their wealth and in their idols (48:7). Idols always bring judgment.

The Lord also judged other nations because of their idols. He said through Jeremiah that the chief idol of Ammon would go into exile (49:3). The Lord was going to punish both Egypt and the Egyptian gods (46:25). And the Lord would punish the idols of Babylon (51:47). Babylon was a land of idols (50:38), and the Lord would fill the idols with shame and terror (50:2). In the same way, the Lord judged Israel and Judah because they left Him to serve idols. The Lord has the same standards of righteousness by which He judges each nation.

Moab also had other problems that made the nation ripe for God's judgment. Moab was famous for its pride (48:29). Moab had become arrogant toward the Lord (48:42).

Jeremiah 48:10 was the favorite verse of Pope Gregory the Seventh, who lived about one thousand years ago. Critics today call it the "bloodthirsty verse" of the Bible. However, these critics need to understand that this verse refers only to the Babylonian sword against the Moabites. These critics need to read the rest of the Bible!

When Jesus Christ came to earth, many things changed. Jesus said that those who take up the sword will die by the sword (Matthew 26:52). He taught his disciples to love their enemies and to pray for those who persecuted them (Matthew 5:44).

Believers today have a sword. Their sword is God's Word (Ephesians 6:17). God's Word is living, active and sharper than any double-edged sword (Hebrews 4:12).

**Explain how God's Word is a sword to you.**

Day 329

AMMON

*Jeremiah 49:1. Concerning the Ammonites: This is what the LORD says: "Has Israel no sons? Has she no heirs? Why then has Molech taken possession of Gad? Why do his people live in its towns?..."*

The Ammonites were enduring enemies of Jeremiah's people. The prophet's first rebuke of them was because of their settlement of the northern city of Gad. The Ammonites stole the city after the Israelites had gone into exile. Depending on how the Hebrew is translated, either the Ammonite king, or Malcam, or Milcom or Molech took possession of Gad.

Malcam, Milcom and Molech were names of the leading idol of Ammon. If one of these names is the correct rendering of the original Hebrew document, a pagan god was given credit for the Ammonites' occupation of Gad. Their idolatry would be their downfall.

The Ammonites squandered their nation in other foolish ways. Ignoring Jeremiah's message to them, they tried to form an alliance against the Babylonians (27:3). The Ammonite king was behind the assassination of Jeremiah's friend Gedaliah (40:14), whom the Babylonians had appointed to govern Judah. Ammon was a military aggressor, trusting in its geographical defenses and wealth (49:4).

Jeremiah served notice that the Lord would judge the nation of Ammon. Rabbah, the capital city, would become a desolate heap. A future war would bring much loss to Ammon (49:2).

The ancient city of Rabbah was in the area that is today the modern city of Amman. I have stood among the Rabbah ruins, which are on the highest point of Amman. As I looked around from that height, I could understand why the Ammonites believed they were safe from any military attack.

As I explored the ruins, I found the remains of a Byzantine Church. The church was obviously built at a later time, after Jesus Christ had come. Christians had worshipped on the ruins of Rabbah! Countless other believers will worship there in the future, because the Lord promised to restore the fortunes of Ammon (49:6).

**How can you have confidence that the Lord will totally restore you in the future?**

## Day 330
### EDOM

**Jeremiah 49:7. Concerning Edom: This is what the LORD Almighty says: "Is there no longer wisdom in Teman? Has counsel perished from the prudent? Has their wisdom decayed?..."**

Jeremiah issued a prophecy against the nation of Edom (49:7-22). Edom had a long history of warring against Israel and Judah. The Edomites must have inherited their hostility toward God's people from their ancestor Esau! Even though Esau was Isaac's older son, the younger son Jacob received the father's blessing (Genesis 27:1-29). Isaac predicted that Esau would live by the sword. Esau responded with a desire to kill Jacob (Genesis 27:40-41).

Esau was red and hairy (Genesis 25:25), and his descendants ironically settled in a red-colored land. "Edom" means "red". When I visited the region of Edom that is now southern Jordan, I was impressed by the rich redness of the sand and cliffs.

Teman was one of the major cities in Edom. The name Teman was also used to refer to the whole nation of Edom (50:20). One of Job's self-appointed counselors, Eliphaz, was from Teman (Job 2:11). Eliphaz the Temanite attempted to give wise advice to Job. Perhaps in part due to Eliphaz's legacy, the land of Teman became famous for its wisdom. There were many wise men in Edom (Obadiah 8). Now that wisdom had rotted!

Their corroded wisdom manifested itself when envoys from Edom met in Jerusalem to try to form an alliance against Babylon. Jeremiah preached clearly that Babylon would prevail (27:1-7). In Jeremiah's days, rebelling against Babylon was the same as resisting God's will. Going against Babylon was not wise.

Having worldly wisdom often results in conceit. Edom had grown into an arrogant land. Because of the nation's pride, God would judge Edom (49:16).

The answer to Jeremiah's rhetorical question was, "Yes, there is still wisdom in Teman. However, that wisdom will soon vanish. For now, that wisdom has a rancid smell!"

Whatever wisdom you may have, you must guard it against decay. Keep asking the Lord for wisdom (James 1:5). Grow closer to Jesus Christ who is our wisdom (1 Corinthians 1:30).

**In what particular areas do you need the Lord to give you wisdom?**

## Day 331

### DAMASCUS

**Jeremiah 49:25.** *Why has the city of renown not been abandoned, the town in which I delight?*

In the midst of his prophecy against Damascus, Jeremiah praised the city. He called Damascus the city of in which someone delighted. The question is, who delighted in the city of Damascus? Was Damascus the city of the Lord's joy, or Jeremiah's joy, or the joy of the king of Damascus?

Jeremiah left no record that he ever visited Damascus. The prophet would have no reason to single out this city as his delight. Jeremiah's joy was in God's Word (15:16).

Babylon was also called a city of praise, but it was clearly praised by men (51:41). In the future, Jerusalem will be a city of praise to the Lord (33:9). In the context of the description of Damascus, the Lord Himself would set fire to the city wall (49:27). It is therefore the Lord Himself who rejoices in Damascus.

When I visited Syria, I walked the streets of Damascus. I walked down the Street called Straight, the same street where Paul stayed in a house immediately after his conversion (Acts 9:11). As I walked, I pondered this question of how Damascus could be the city of God's joy.

Damascus has a rich spiritual history. Abraham's faithful servant was from Damascus (Genesis 15:2). During the time of Elisha, a servant girl in Damascus advised a Damascus military general to go to the man of God for healing. He did (2 Kings 5:1-27). During the time of Paul, Damascus had many synagogues (Acts 9:2).

Jeremiah had preached that the city of God's joy in the future would be Jerusalem (33:9). God will rejoice in the Jerusalem that is yet to come because His people will be there. In the meantime, the Babylonians would destroy the Jerusalem that Jeremiah knew. While Jerusalem was under God's judgment, where on earth would He then dispense His joy? On which other people would He bestow His favor? Which city would be a temporary substitute for Jerusalem? Damascus!

The Lord rejoiced in those people who found their joy in Him. One of the Apostles rejoiced when he heard that God's people were living according to the truth (3 John 4). What causes you to rejoice?

**How can you more closely align the sources of your joy to what gives joy to God?**

## Day 332
## KEDAR AND HAZOR

*Jeremiah 49:28. Concerning Kedar and the kingdoms of Hazor, which Nebuchadnezzar king of Babylon attacked: This is what the LORD says: "Arise, and attack Kedar and destroy the people of the East...."*

Not even the wandering tribes in the desert east of Palestine could escape Jeremiah's prophecies! One of those tribes was Kedar, which Jeremiah had mentioned in one of his early sermons (2:10). Kedar was a wealthy ethnic group (Isaiah 21:16-17), known for their extensive flocks of sheep and goats (Ezekiel 27:21).

Kedar and Hazor were among the many peoples and nations that Nebuchadnezzar conquered. Compared to other nations about whom Jeremiah preached, these people of the East were rather unimportant. By human standards, they were insignificant desert nomads. However, even they could not flee from God's judgment.

Jeremiah prophesied that the Babylonians would be the Lord's means of carrying out His judgment. They would take away the tents and all the possessions of the people of Kedar. They also had a plan to conquer the people of Hazor (49:29-30).

God's evaluation of Kedar and Hazor was that they were carefree. Kedar and Hazor had no walled cities and gates to protect them, but they still felt protected. They lived in isolation in the desert, so they thought they were secure from enemies (49:31).

However, they would not be safe from the Babylonians. The Babylonians would find them in the desert and would plunder their cattle and camels. They would scatter the people of Kedar and Hazor like chaff in the winds (49:32).

Hazor would become a haunt of jackals (49:33). The stomping ground for jackals was a metaphor that Jeremiah liked to use to describe places where no humans lived any more. Whenever people were removed from cities, the jackals would move in.

Jeremiah had preached that the Lord would also make Jerusalem a meeting place for jackals (9:11). He added that all the cities of Judah would become haunts for jackals (10:22). Jeremiah saw the ruins of Jerusalem after the Babylonians destroyed it. He observed that jackals had taken up residence in the city ruins and were nursing their young (Lamentations 4:3). He also predicted that eventually even Babylon would become a haunt of jackals (51:37).

**What metaphors would you use to describe the desolation and emptiness that result from God's judgment on those who reject Him?**

## Day 333
### ELAM

**Jeremiah 49:34.** *This is the word of the LORD that came to Jeremiah the prophet concerning Elam, early in the reign of Zedekiah king of Judah ....*

Elam was a distant country from Judah, two hundred miles further east than Babylon was. Elam was located in the land that is now southwestern Iran. Jeremiah may have considered Elam to be in the uttermost part of the earth!

During King Jehoiakim's fourth year, Jeremiah had preached that Elam was one of the nations that God would judge (25:25). Now, early in King Zedekiah's reign (about six years later), Jeremiah gave more details about Elam's fate. Breaking the bow of Elam (49:35) was a vivid description of Elam's defeat, because the Elamites were famous for their skill as archers (Isaiah 22:6).

Elam's downfall was her pride in her strength with the bow. Instead of submitting to God, Elam depended solely on her own resources. Any nation that has this political attitude will become a failed state.

God would send enemy soldiers into Elam, and they would disperse the Elamites in all directions. Elam's exiles would end up in every nation. Elam would be shattered (49:36-37).

The Lord would set His throne in Elam (49:38). This was a metaphorical way to assert the Lord's absolute power as He decisively brought judgment. When the Lord first called Jeremiah, He told the prophet that kings from the north would set their thrones at the gates of Jerusalem (1:15). When Jeremiah was in Egypt at the end of his career, he prophesied that the king of Babylon would set his throne in front of Pharaoh's palace (43:9-10).

Jeremiah gave a hopeful conclusion in his sermon against Elam. He preached that the Lord would restore the fortunes of Elam in the last days (49:39). The Lord had given comparable words of hope to the nations of Egypt (46:28), Moab (48:47) and Ammon (49:6).

In Jeremiah's day, the Lord was sovereign over absolutely every nation on earth. God's universal power over the nations continues today. He holds every nation accountable to Him.

**Since the God whom you know is sovereign over every nation, for which nations do you wish to pray to Him now?**

## Day 334
### BABYLON

**Jeremiah 50:1-2a.** *This is the word the LORD spoke through Jeremiah the prophet concerning Babylon and the land of the Babylonians: "Announce and proclaim among the nations, lift up a banner and proclaim it; keep nothing back, but say, 'Babylon will be captured...'"*

Jeremiah lived much of his life under the looming shadow of Babylon. During his day, Babylon became the most powerful city in the world. The city was situated on the Euphrates River in an area that is now southern Iraq.

Nebuchadnezzar became one of the most famous kings in the ancient world. Along with the nation of Babylonia, the city of Babylon is mentioned more than two hundred times in the Bible. The Old Testament refers to Nebuchadnezzar almost one hundred times.

Like every other nation that has ever existed, the time would come for Babylon's demise. The Lord chose Jeremiah to announce it clearly and eloquently. The central theme of his long sermon (50:1-51:64) was Babylon's defeat and the Jew's restoration to their land.

The Babylonians ravaged the Jewish homeland more violently and completely than any other nation had done. So it was fitting that Babylon would receive the longest message about her judgment. Jeremiah began his sermon with the clear message that Babylon would be captured. After hearing his sermon, no reasonable person could accuse Jeremiah of belonging to the "pro-Babylon" political party!

Jeremiah preached against Babylon during Zedekiah's reign (51:59), before the Babylonians destroyed Jerusalem. The Lord wanted this message to be public information. He told Jeremiah to proclaim it among the nations.

Even earlier, during Jehoiakim's reign (25:1), Jeremiah also predicted the end of Babylon. Jeremiah said that God would judge Babylon and every other nation according to their deeds. He prophesied that Babylon would become completely deserted (25:12-14).

Babylon became symbolic of the earthly forces that oppose God and His people. God will ultimately defeat His enemies. Knowing the final outcome can help you live securely today.

**How can the Lord help you live wisely under your "Babylon" today?**

## Day 335
### IDOLS OF BABYLON

**Jeremiah 50:2b.** *"... 'Babylon will be captured; Bel will be put to shame, Marduk filled with terror. Her images will be put to shame and her idols filled with terror.' ... "*

Jeremiah prophesied that both the nation of Babylon and the idols of Babylon would be defeated. Specifically, the images of Bel and Marduk would meet their doom. Jeremiah spoke about these idols as if they actually could feel shame and terror!

However, Jeremiah used Hebrew words to show that both he and the Lord did not believe that the Babylonian gods had any real human emotions. The words translated as "images" and "idols" literally mean "wooden blocks" and "dung pellets"! The Lord had a low opinion of idols!

Those who worshipped the gods believed that their national welfare depended on the condition of their carved images. If the idols fell, the nation fell. Jeremiah preached later that God would punish Bel, and the walls of Babylon would collapse (51:44). God would punish the Babylonian idols, and many people would die in the land (51:47).

Jeremiah referred to this same superstitious belief when he preached about other nations. When he prophesied against Egypt, he said that the Lord would punish Pharaoh along with the Egyptian gods (46:25). When he preached against Moab, he predicted that the nation would be conquered and its god Chemosh would be deported (48:7). When he spoke against Ammon, he foretold that the nation's god Molech would go into exile along with the priests and princes (49:3).

In the same vein, Jeremiah put Babylon on notice that its idols were in harm's way. What were these Babylonian gods? The Canaanite god Baal had become the Babylonian idol named Bel. Both "Baal" and "Bel" mean "lord". So Bel was the leader of all the gods.

Marduk was the national god of Babylon. In the minds of idolaters, there was no competition for leadership between Marduk and Bel. The two became one god, who was sometimes called Bel Marduk!

Bel Marduk had no future, except God's judgment. Even though there are no known followers of Bel or Marduk today, other idols have replaced them. The warnings to believers today are unambiguous. Keep yourselves from idols (1 John 5:21).

**How can a close relationship with the Lord help keep you from being tempted by idols?**

## Day 336
### JUDGMENT OF BABYLON

**Jeremiah 50:3. *A nation from the north will attack her and lay waste to her land. No one will live in it; both men and animals will flee away.***

Jeremiah's assertion of Babylon's total defeat was unmistakable. Just like Jeremiah announced an army from the north would attack his own nation of Judah (1:14-15), a nation from the north would assail Babylon. The attacks would be so complete that the Babylonian countryside would lie desolate.

After Babylon's defeat, no one would live in the devastated land. Even the animals would run away. It would be a complete reversal of Nebuchadnezzar's empire in which the wild animals submitted to him (27:6).

However, Babylon was not razed to ruins when the great city was conquered. Daniel was in the city on the last night of the Babylonian Empire when the Medes took control (Daniel 5:30-31). Daniel stayed in Babylon and served the new king (Daniel 6:1-2). There was no battle that laid waste to the land.

It is possible that the many prophecies about Babylon's complete destruction (50:9) and God's people fleeing for their lives from Babylon (51:6) refer to a future Babylon. Maybe a literal Babylon will be rebuilt in the future. That Babylon will fall into complete catastrophe (Revelation 17-18).

It is also possible that when King Nebuchadnezzar finally humbled himself before the Lord (Daniel 4:34-37), God released His mercy. Nebuchadnezzar, the most powerful man in the ancient world, praised the Lord as the King of heaven. Perhaps the Lord then softened His intended judgment on Babylon.

Why? Didn't the sovereign Lord already plan for Babylon's demise? Yes, but God's intentions to bring judgment always take into account human responses. Jeremiah preached that God withholds His planned judgment on a nation if that nation repents of its evil (18:7-8).

Jonah experienced this truth when he reluctantly went to Nineveh to prophesy God's judgment on that pagan city. He preached that Nineveh would be destroyed in forty days. However, God did not destroy Nineveh after forty days, because the entire population repented (Jonah 3:4-10).

**How does the fact that God often extends His mercy to nations that deserve His judgment affect your relationship with Him?**

## Day 337
### WEEPING AND SEEKING

*Jeremiah 50:4. "In those days, at that time," declares the LORD, "the people of Israel and the people of Judah together will go in tears to seek the LORD their God...."*

Jeremiah was preaching about the future judgment of Babylon. Babylon's fall would mean freedom for people of both Israel and Judah. Jeremiah urged them to use their freedom to seek the Lord.

God had sent the people into captivity under the terms of the old covenant that He made with Moses. The Lord would bring His people home under the terms of the everlasting covenant (50:5). They had neglected the old covenant, but they would never forget the New.

Their many years in Babylon prepared them to seek the Lord. When released, they would weep as they kept seeking the Lord. They would weep while the Lord led them by streams of water (31:9).

When a few of the people finally returned to the land, some did shed tears. Nehemiah wept before he led some of the people back (Nehemiah 1:4). Ezra was already in the land and wept before the Lord (Ezra 10:1).

However, this was merely a "mini-fulfillment" of Jeremiah's prophecy. Under Ezra and Nehemiah, there was partial repentance. Jeremiah spoke of a yet future age which he described as "in those days, at that time."

At that time, there will be total national repentance. The Deliverer (Jesus Christ) will remove all ungodliness from the nation. All of Israel will receive salvation (Romans 11:26-27).

There will also be complete unity. Jeremiah said that both the Israelites and the Judeans together would seek God. The Lord made the New Covenant with both Israel and Judah (31:31).

Unity and repentance are essential values today. As you grow in your relationship with the Lord, you will have days when you will weep. Also, growing closer to the Lord will cause you to desire unity with others who are on the same spiritual journey.

**How has the Lord led you in recent weeks in the areas of repentance and/or unity?**

## Day 338
### EVERLASTING COVENANT

**Jeremiah 50:5.** *They will ask the way to Zion and turn their faces toward it. They will come and bind themselves to the Lord in an everlasting covenant that will not be forgotten.*

Interspersed in Jeremiah's sermon about Babylon's judgment were brilliant glimmers of hope for God's people. The brightest gleam was his mention of the everlasting covenant. Jeremiah's record of this covenant was his greatest contribution to the Bible.

"Everlasting" was a memorable and appropriate word to describe this covenant. All the main points of the covenant were everlasting. God revealed to Jeremiah that His law on human hearts and His forgiveness would last forever (31:31-34).

Centuries later, the author of the letter to the Hebrews quoted from Jeremiah the terms of the New Covenant. The author called it a "better covenant" and Jesus became the mediator of it. The New Covenant made the old covenant given to Moses obsolete (Hebrews 8:6-13).

In contrast to the old covenant, the everlasting covenant will never become out of date. Every sin that anyone committed under the old covenant can be forgiven under the New. This forgiveness is possible because Jesus died to redeem everyone who sinned under the old covenant (Hebrews 9:15).

Jeremiah knew all about the sins of his people under the old covenant. Early in his career, Jeremiah traveled throughout his nation looking for anyone who kept God's law. He could find no one (5:1-5).

I used to wonder and worry about people who died before the time of Jesus. They did not know about Jesus Christ's death, so how could they be forgiven? Gradually I realized that they could be saved through faith, just like faith brings forgiveness to believers today. Old Testament believers placed their faith in a future sacrifice for sins, and the Lord started giving revelation about this sacrifice at the beginning of human history (Genesis 3:15).

The people in Jeremiah's day could join themselves in the Lord through the promises of the everlasting covenant. Through faith they could ask the way to the heavenly Zion (Hebrews 12:22) and turn their faces toward it. You can do the same.

**In your own words, describe everlasting forgiveness.**

## Day 339
### SCATTERED SHEEP

**Jeremiah 50:17.** *"Israel is a scattered flock that lions have chased away. The first to devour him was the king of Assyria; the last to crush his bones was Nebuchadnezzar king of Babylon."*

The Lord had chosen Babylon to punish His sinful people, but the Babylonians went too far. They enjoyed devastating God's people too much! As they slaughtered the people of Israel, they acted like a joyful calf threshing the grain (50:11).

Under King Nebuchadnezzar, the Babylonians crushed the bones of God's people. Nebuchadnezzar was like a lion gnawing on mutton bones. He chewed on what was left after the Assyrians had slaughtered many.

God's people had been as helpless as sheep being chased by lions. Both Babylon (4:7) and Assyria (Isaiah 15:9) were like lions. They were ferocious and dangerous. They attacked and killed the weak and helpless.

Earlier in his prophecy against Babylon, Jeremiah said that God's people had become like lost sheep. Their shepherds, who were the political leaders of Judah, had led them astray. Instead of remaining in safe pastures, the sheep had wandered among the mountains and hills (50:6). Altars to idols were on these mountains!

As the sheep drifted on the hills and mountains, the Babylonians devoured them. The Babylonians admitted no guilt as they devoured every sheep they could find. However, they sinned against the Lord as they cruelly assaulted the sheep (50:7).

Because of Babylon's brutality, all their captives would be released. Jeremiah called on them to wander away from Babylon. Like goats pushing the sheep aside as they run though the gate, God's people would be the first to leave Babylon (50:8).

Throughout ancient history, lions of nations have savagely attacked God's people. However, the situation began to change when the Lion of Judah came. God's people today can live fearlessly among the nations.

The coming of Jesus Christ severely weakened national lions. He saw the people of Israel as sheep without a shepherd (Matthew 9:36). Jesus is the good shepherd who came to earth to lay down His life for the sheep (John 10:11).

**What are some specific "lions" that are threatening you, and how can you trust the Good Shepherd to protect you from them?**

Day 340

FUTURE GRAZING

*Jeremiah 50:19. But I will bring Israel back to his own pasture and he will graze on Carmel and Bashan; his appetite will be satisfied on the hills of Ephraim and Gilead.*

Jeremiah had described the Babylonians captives as lost sheep (50:6). They were brutalized by the Babylonian lions (50:7). Someday they would wander away from Babylon; indeed they would run out of the gates like male goats (50:8).

However, they would not continue to wander without a shepherd. The Lord Himself would bring them home. He would take them to His pasture.

Another prophet, who was Jeremiah's contemporary, wrote that God would search for His sheep and would rescue them. The Lord would bring them back to their land and would feed them on the mountains and by the streams. They would rest and eat in the lush pastures (Ezekiel 34:11-16).

Carmel, Bashan, Ephraim and Gilead would evoke much emotion as the Babylonian captives heard these names. The exiled people remembered these places. These four regions were green and fertile.

Prophets compared the splendid beauty of Mount Carmel with the majesty of the Lord (Isaiah 35:2). Healthy herds fed on the pastures of Bashan (Deuteronomy 32:14). The Ephraim hill country was a scenic and desirable location for fields (Obadiah 19). Gilead contained many fruitful meadows where flocks could find food (Micah 7:14).

Even though King Nebuchadnezzar gnawed on the bones of the Judeans (50:17), the Lord would reverse their fortunes. The Judeans would no longer be food for the Babylonians. They would return to a land that would feed them plentifully.

The Lord was reversing His judgment on the nation of Judah. Jeremiah had earlier preached that the whole land would become barren (4:27). Because of God's grace, the Judge became the Shepherd.

If the Lord is your shepherd, He has promised to lead you to green pastures (Psalm 23:1-2). As the good shepherd, Jesus promised His people that they would through Him find pasture (John 10:9). In God's presence are eternal pleasures (Psalm 16:11).

**How has the Lord been your shepherd in recent weeks, and what "green pastures" is He leading you toward?**

## Day 341
### SEARCHING FOR SINS THAT ARE NOT THERE

**Jeremiah 50:20.** *"In those days, at that time," declares the LORD, "search will be made for Israel's guilt, but there will be none, and for the sins of Judah, but none will be found, for I will forgive the remnant I spare...."*

"In those days" refers to a future time when Israel and Judah will totally accept the New Covenant. The Lord promised in this covenant to forgive wickedness and forget sins (31:34). The covenant became effective through Jesus Christ's blood (Luke 22:20).

For a nation under judgment, the New Covenant offered a radical change to the existing situation. Instead of their sins being a permanent stain (2:22), the Lord would forgive. Instead of their sins being great and numerous (30:15), the Lord would forget.

Absolute forgiveness will be the climax of Israel's history. The nation has gone through cycles of intense suffering throughout the centuries. Jeremiah knew about the pain that the Assyrians inflicted (50:17), and he experienced some of the sufferings brought by the Babylonians.

After they suffered, the people were always vindicated by God. God always brought judgment on Israel's enemies. Just as the Lord punished the Assyrians, He would also condemn the Babylonians (50:18).

After judging their enemies, the Lord would then lead His people like a Shepherd back to green pastures. He would meet their needs (50:19). The cycles of history repeatedly reveal God's goodness to His people after they suffered. That goodness will culminate in His complete forgiveness.

Those who receive His forgiveness are called "the remnant". Jeremiah did not believe in universal salvation. Like Isaiah (Isaiah 10:20), Jeremiah believed that a remnant of people would trust in the Lord. Only a remnant would be forgiven.

When I became a believer, I had difficulty believing that God forgave me. The man who led me to Jesus showed me an important verse. I learned that by confessing my sins, God would forgive my sins and cleanse me from all unrighteousness (1 John 1:9).

Are you searching for sins that are not there? If you are looking for sins in other believers, stop the search! Jesus said to take the log out of your own eye first (Matthew 7:5)! If you are searching for sins in your own heart, stop! Give the hunt over to the Lord, and embrace His forgiveness through Christ.

**What is keeping you from fully accepting the forgiveness of your sins through Jesus Christ?**

## Day 342
### PRICE OF DEFIANCE

**Jeremiah 50:29. "Summon archers against Babylon, all those who draw the bow. Encamp all around her; let no one escape. Repay her for her deeds; do to her as she has done. For she has defied the LORD, the Holy One of Israel...."**

Jeremiah described how the Lord would bring judgment on Babylon. Taking on the role of a military commander, God would call for a mighty army to surround the city. He would beckon expert archers to defeat the Babylonians.

God's vengeance on Babylon was totally justified. In His perfect judgment, He would repay Babylon for all the sins that she had committed. What had she done?

First of all, the Babylonians had defied the Lord by being arrogant against Him. Also, they had opposed the Lord by being in open conflict with Him (50:24). In addition, they had destroyed His temple in Jerusalem, for which God would take vengeance on them (50:28).

What Babylon had meted to Judah, the Lord would give back to Babylon. He reminded the Babylonians that He is the Holy One of Israel. They had trampled on those people whom He had called His own.

Even though the Lord had chosen Babylon to be His instrument of judgment against Judah, Babylon had remained haughty against Him. Also, the Babylonians had gone too far in pillaging His people (50:11). They had sinned against the Lord (50:14).

The Babylonians would pay the penalty for their insolence toward God. Babylon would become an object of horror among the nations. The Lord would set a snare for Babylon. God would use many people to conquer Babylon (50:23-25).

The Lord would bring armies from the furthest borders of the Babylonian empire. They would slaughter all the people of Babylon and they would destroy the nation. They would turn the empire of Babylon into heaps of rubble (50:26-27).

There are many people living today who have this same Babylonian attitude of arrogance. All who are defiant against the Lord will pay a price. If only they understood what the complete cost will be!

**How can your growing closer to the Lord help you discard any lingering attitudes of arrogance that you may have?**

## Day 343
### THE STRONG REDEEMER

**Jeremiah 50:34.** *Yet their Redeemer is strong; the LORD Almighty is his name. He will vigorously defend their cause so that he may bring rest to their land, but unrest to those who live in Babylon.*

The Babylonians thought that they were strong enough to keep God's people in exile indefinitely. The captives from Judah wondered how and if they would ever return to their own land. They did not understand the power of the Strong Redeemer.

God's people could not set themselves free from the Babylonians. They learned that they needed a Redeemer stronger than they. Just like the Lord delivered their ancestors from Egypt, He would release them from Babylon.

As He redeemed His people, He would bring unrest to Babylon just like He did to Egypt. The unrest was His judgment on the Babylonians for their sins against His people. The Lord was the prosecuting attorney.

Earlier, he had been the prosecutor of the Judeans as he brought serious charges against them (2:9). Now that the Judeans had served their term of punishment, He would put the Babylonians on trial. The Lord was also the Babylonians' judge as well as the prosecutor. He would find them guilty as charged.

Now that the Judeans had served their sentence, the Lord could serve as their defense attorney. He was their Strong Redeemer who would release them from Babylon. The Babylonians refused to recognize that the prison term had ended for God's people.

In his sermon about the New Covenant, Jeremiah preached that the Lord would redeem His people from the grip of a stronger nation (31:11). Redeeming them meant that God would set them free and restore them. They would finally have the best life possible.

Since the days of Jeremiah, the Strong Redeemer has revealed Himself to be even stronger. Jesus Christ's death gave us redemption from sins (Ephesians 1: 7). I still remember clearly that night many years ago when I was redeemed. Also, believers can look forward to the redemption of their bodies (Romans 8:23), on that future glorious day of redemption (Ephesians 4:30).

**How has your Strong Redeemer helped you face challenges in the past, and how confident are you that He will offer the same help to you in the future?**

## Day 344
### Swords against Babylon

**Jeremiah 50:35-36.** *"A sword against the Babylonians!" declares the Lord – "against those who live in Babylon and against her officials and wise men! A sword against her false prophets! They will become fools. A sword against her warriors! They will be filled with terror...."*

When I was a young boy, a friend of my parents gave me a real sword. He had picked it up from a dead officer during World War II. For many years that sword was one of my favorite possessions.

Throughout my life, swords have fascinated me. During a recent trip to Thailand, I watched a man perform a traditional sword dance. He used more than a dozen knives and swords, but he never cut himself. During Jeremiah's time, Ezekiel wrote the words to a sword song that possibly accompanied an ancient sword dance (Ezekiel 21:9-10).

Like Ezekiel, Jeremiah also recorded poetry about the sword. He used the word "sword" five times in this section of his sermon about Babylon (50:35-37). Jeremiah often used repetition in his preaching and he used it effectively.

Before Jerusalem fell, Jeremiah continually warned the people about the coming of sword, famine and disease. He used this trio of words at least fifteen times in his writings. Along with famine and disease, the sword of the Babylonians caused Judah's defeat.

Now Jeremiah announced that the Babylonians would be on the receiving end of the sword. The sword would especially target soldiers, political leaders and false prophets. No inhabitant of Babylon would be safe.

The Lord as the strong Redeemer would send the sword to the Babylonians (50: 34). Jesus Christ died on the cross as our Redeemer. One of His followers saw a vision of Him with a symbolic sword coming out of His mouth (Revelation 1:16). When Jesus Christ comes again to earth, He will use a sword (Revelation 19:15).

Throughout history, violent people have used swords to threaten decent people like you and me. Fortunately, a sword in a good man's hand can protect all of us from evil. The day is coming when the righteous sword of Jesus Christ will bring an end to all wickedness.

**Explain how the sword of Jesus Christ can be a comfort to you.**

## Day 345
### NOT FORSAKEN

*Jeremiah 51:5. For Israel and Judah have not been forsaken by their God, the LORD Almighty, though their land is full of guilt before the Holy One of Israel.*

My mother has lived as a widow for many years since my father died. As with most widows, it was a difficult adjustment for her. Her husband of many years left her to go to the next world.

During Jeremiah's time, many people from Israel and Judah were feeling that the Lord had left them. The Hebrew word for "forsaken" is literally "widowed". While he preached about God's judgment against Babylon, Jeremiah assured his own people that God had not "widowed" them.

The Lord still had a problem with the people of Israel and Judah. Their land was full of guilt. As the Holy One of Israel, in order to honor His own holiness, the Lord could have abandoned them forever.

Babylon was also guilty (50:29). However, the Babylonians denied their guilt and claimed that they had not sinned against the Lord (50:7). Jeremiah did not preach about Babylon here in 51:5. He said that the land was guilty before the Holy one of Israel. He emphasized Israel. God had chosen Israel to know His holiness, but the nation had become guilty of ungodliness.

For a moment in history, the Lord apparently did forsake His people when they went to Babylon as exiles. Jeremiah was now describing the end of that time in exile. After the exile, the Lord would have everlasting compassion on His people (Isaiah 54:7-8).

God spared Israel and Judah from the permanent destruction that He would bring upon Babylon. Babylon's destruction would be so complete that Jeremiah urged everyone to flee from Babylon when they could (51:6). Babylon would suddenly fall and break (51:8), like the egg named Humpty in the children's nursery rhymes.

Jeremiah's life was a vivid illustration of not being forsaken by the Lord. Jeremiah experienced much hardship, but the Lord was always with him like He had promised (1:8, 19). At the end of his life Jeremiah could certainly testify that God had not forsaken him.

**Describe your confidence that the Lord will never forsake you.**

## Day 346
### GOLDEN CUP

**Jeremiah 51:7. *Babylon was a gold cup in the Lord's hand; she made the whole earth drunk. The nations drank her wine; therefore they have now gone mad.***

Like many people, I am fascinated by gold. In the past when I had occasional reveries that I was wealthy, I would imagine having sets of gold cups on my lavish dinner table. I do not think about that anymore. I remember that Babylon was a gold cup and the cup turned deadly!

Babylonia was the wealthiest nation on earth. Gold as a symbol for Babylon was certainly appropriate. The king of Babylon was the head of gold on the statue that Daniel dreamed about (Daniel 2:38).

This excessively wealthy nation, however, was not beyond God's rule. Jeremiah preached that Babylon was a golden cup in the Lord's hand. God used this superpower to intoxicate many nations with the measureless Babylonian riches.

Getting drunk from the wine in the cup was a metaphor for receiving God's judgment. Jeremiah preached that the Lord would fill all the people in Judah with drunkenness (13:12-13). Isaiah had prophesied that Jerusalem would drink from the cup of God's anger (Isaiah 51:17).

Inevitably, Babylonia herself would move to the receiving end of the wrathful cup. Jeremiah preached in another sermon that God would cause all the nations, including the land of the Babylonians, to drink from the cup of His anger (25:15-26). The Lord's pure and perfect holiness prompts His righteous anger against what is not holy.

Another prophet of the Lord preached that Babylon in particular would become drunk from the cup in the Lord's hand. Getting drunk results in shame (Habakkuk 2:16). God's judgment is the ultimate disgrace.

Shortly before His death, Jesus Christ said that He would drink the cup that the Father gave Him (John 18:11). Christ drank from the cup of God's wrath, even though He is the innocent sinless Savior. He took God's judgment upon Himself so that you and I might be spared. By believing in Jesus, you will never have to drink from the judgment cup.

**How does freedom from the cup of God's wrath affect your relationship with Him?**

## Day 347
### HELPING BABYLON

**Jeremiah 51:9.** *"'We would have healed Babylon, but she cannot be healed; let us leave her and each go to his own land, for her judgment reaches to the skies, it rises as high as the clouds.'..."*

The Lord put some words into the mouths of a people group. These people would say that they tried to heal Babylon, but Babylon was not healed. In fact, Babylon could not be healed. It was too late for Babylon.

Who were these people speaking these words? They were the ones whom the Lord told to flee from the midst of Babylon (51:6). They would give an account of the Lord's work when they were back in Zion (51:10). They were the people of Judah and Israel.

Why would the Jews have tried to heal Babylon? Through Jeremiah's letter to the exiles, the Lord had instructed them to pray for Babylon. They were supposed to work toward the best interests of the Babylonian empire (29:7).

Through the years, Babylon required an increasing amount of help to sustain herself. The Lord would finally call upon a medical team to bring balm for Babylon's pain, but Babylon would be too broken. Babylon's condition would be terminal and untreatable. The Lord would summon professional mourners to wail for her (51:8).

The Babylonians apparently did not show any appreciation toward the Judeans for their contribution to the empire. They taunted and tormented them instead (Psalm 137:1-9). The time would come when Babylon's judgment reached to the skies. In other words, the reasons for God's judgment of Babylon would attain maximum proportions.

Finally the time would come, after seventy years, when the Judeans could leave Babylon (29:10). Indeed, they would need to flee lest they be trapped in Babylon's destruction (51:6). They would serve Babylon no more.

What about you? Are you praying for the nation in which you live? Are you working toward your nation's welfare? The time will come when even your nation will fall under the Lord's judgment. Until that time, you can serve the Lord in many ways through serving your nation.

**In what specific ways is the Lord calling you to serve the nation in which you live?**

Day 348

## VINDICATION

**Jeremiah 51:10.** *"'The LORD has vindicated us; come, let us tell in Zion what the LORD our God has done.'..."*

In his sermon about God's judgment of Babylon, Jeremiah explained about God's vindication of His people. Jeremiah anticipated the day when freed prisoners would spontaneously start singing, "The Lord has vindicated us!" Babylon's fall would free the singing people to travel to Zion.

One of the reasons why the Lord would bring Babylon down was because of what the Babylonians did to His temple (50:28). By judging Babylon, God would save His own people. Returning to Zion would publicize their salvation.

The Babylonians might try to argue with the God of Zion. They had been attentive to Jeremiah's words that the Lord was bringing disaster against Jerusalem. The Babylonian captain told Jeremiah that Jeremiah's people had sinned against their Lord (40:2-3). They deserved to lose their nation.

Jeremiah's sermon against Babylon anticipated this argument. He had preached that Judah's enemies claimed that they were not guilty. The Babylonians charged the Judeans were the ones who were guilty because they had sinned against the Lord (50:7).

The idolatrous Babylonians did not understand the higher ways of the true Lord. They did not realize that their treatment of God's people had caused the Judeans to receive full punishment for their sins (Isaiah 40:2). Vindication, not further punishment, was now the Lord's plan for His people.

In a court of law, a vindication is the same as an acquittal. The guilty party has gone through the legal process, and now is no longer accused of breaking the law. The acquittal gives that person freedom to get on with his or her life.

God's people could sing about the Lord's vindication even though they had previously sinned against Him. The Lord was now executing justice for them. He was bringing them out so that they could see His righteousness (Micah 7:9).

Can you join that happy throng as they sing about the Lord's vindication? Today, are you confidant that God has vindicated you? Only through Jesus Christ will you have forgiveness (Ephesians 1:7).

**Explain your level of confidence that the Lord has completely vindicated you.**

## Day 349
### CREATION BY WISDOM

**Jeremiah 51:15.** *"He made the earth by his power; he founded the world by his wisdom and stretched out the heavens by his understanding...."*

As Jeremiah prophesied about Babylon's demise, he inserted some powerful truths about God in his sermon (51:15-19). He wanted his people to think about the Creator God bringing about the "un-creation" of Babylon. Jeremiah taught that the Lord who created is also the Judge who will destroy.

Jeremiah had preached these exact words in an earlier sermon about the uselessness of idols (10:12-16). In contrast to God's power and wisdom, idols are totally impotent and foolish. Idols have never created anything.

Since Babylon trusted heavily on her idols, it was just a matter of time before Babylon would collapse. Babylon had made herself great through her own power. Before long, that power would be no more.

Unlike Babylon's fleeting power, God's dominance persists eternally. He created the earth by His power. He continues to sustain the universe by that same power (Hebrews 1:3).

Babylon rose and fell by human wisdom. The Babylonians lacked wisdom from God. They did not understand that God's wisdom is immeasurably better than the wisdom of Babylon. His wisdom was sufficient to create our whole world.

Amazingly, God has made His wisdom available to you and me. Through Jesus Christ you can freely ask God for wisdom (James 1:5). Do you have a goal to grow in wisdom as you grow closer to the Lord?

Our three children were teenagers when our family lived in Europe. When one of them would start to leave our apartment to go out with friends, my wife or I would give that child a reminder. We always told each child, "Be wise!" He or she would then answer in German, "Wie immer," which means, "as always"! (My children were trying to be humorous!)

Do not be "wise guys" like the Babylonians. Seek true wisdom from the Lord. Be wise.

**How can you consistently grow in wisdom?**

Day 350
## THE GOD WHO THUNDERS

*Jeremiah 51:16. When he thunders, the waters in the heavens roar; he makes clouds rise from the ends of the earth. He sends lightning with the rain and brings out the wind from his storehouses.*

In his long sermon about God's judgment of Babylon, Jeremiah inserted some of his earlier sermon material (10:12-13) about God as creator. Not only did the Lord create the heavens and earth, He also actively maintains His creation. Even today God sustains His creation. Life on earth continues to need rain, and God is the One who supplies it.

The Lord sends rain in spectacular ways to remind people about His power. He could just as easily replenish the water supply by using a quiet unnoticed method. No, the Lord usually sends rain with the unforgettable accompaniments of thunder, lightning and wind.

In the immediate context, Jeremiah preached about the stupidity and shamefulness of idols (51:17). Since Babylon was a nation of idols (50:38), the Babylonians worshipped storm gods instead of bowing to the God who Thunders. God would judge both the nation and its idols (50:2).

Before falling to the Babylonians, Judah experienced severe drought. All the farmland was dried up and cracked (14:1-4). I have seen severely cracked earth like this during droughts in Texas.

The Lord was withholding rain showers from the Judeans (3:3). All the vegetation was withering (12:4). The Lord was allowing the land to dry up because the people had forsaken Him to do evil (23:10).

Drought conditions evidently continued through the end of Zedekiah's reign. When Jeremiah was lowered into a cistern, there was no water in it (38:6). The Judeans should have returned to the God who Thunders and pleaded with Him for rain.

Jeremiah earlier preached that those who trust in the Lord will not be anxious during times of drought (17:8). When wise believers pray to God about the weather, they do not always ask that He change it. Often they pray that His will be done and that they might have His grace to accept whatever weather He sends their way.

**How does your relationship with the God who Thunders help you accept the weather that He sends to you?**

## Day 351
### JACOB'S PORTION

*Jeremiah 51:19. He who is the Portion of Jacob is not like these, for he is the Maker of all things, including the tribe of his inheritance—the LORD Almighty is his name.*

Of all the Biblical writers, only Jeremiah gave to God the title "Portion of Jacob." He used the same title for God in another sermon (10:16). Because the Judeans were suffering in exile, Jeremiah encouraged them with the thought that God was Jacob's Portion.

The psalmists referred to God as "my portion" (Psalm 119:57). David wrote that the Lord was his portion in the land of the living (Psalm 142:5). Asaph wrote that the Lord was his portion forever (Psalm 73:26).

What does it mean for the Lord to be someone's portion? In Biblical times, the word "portion" had a special connotation. A portion was an inheritance. The Lord told Aaron that he would have no inheritance or portion in the land, but the Lord Himself would be His portion and inheritance (Numbers 18:20).

As the people followed Moses out of Egypt, they knew that they needed land in order to survive. In order to meet their needs, the Lord gave land as an inheritance to all the tribes of Jacob except one. The people of Levi would own no land. The Levites were priests who served the Lord on behalf of all the other people.

How could the priests survive if they had no land for farming or ranching? Where would they get their food? The Lord provided for them by setting up a system of tithes and offerings (Numbers 18:25-31).

However, the tithe was not their portion! The Lord made it clear that He would be their portion. He would provide for them even during the dark days when the people had no land and the Levites had no tithes. Jacob was another name for Israel. The Lord was Jacob's Portion.

After the Babylonians conquered Judah, Jeremiah walked through the ruins of Jerusalem. He wept for his people and his city (Lamentations 3:48). Babylon now owned all the inheritance that had belonged to Jeremiah's people. However, Jeremiah had hope in the fact that the Lord was his portion (Lamentations 3:24). He knew that the Lord was his Maker, and He would care for His people.

**Write a praise to the Lord for being your portion.**

## Day 352
### ENDING THE PAIN

**Jeremiah 51:59. *This is the message Jeremiah gave to the staff officer Seraiah son of Neriah, the son of Mahseiah, when he went to Babylon with Zedekiah king of Judah in the fourth year of his reign.***

Jeremiah had written a description of all the tragedies that would come upon Babylon. Jeremiah told Seraiah to read this entire scroll aloud when he arrived in Babylon. Jeremiah told him to emphasize the total destruction of Babylon (51:60-62).

When Seraiah finished reading the scroll in Babylon, he was to tie a stone to it. Then he was to throw the scroll into the Euphrates River. Seraiah's concluding words to the people would be that Babylon would sink and rise no more. The Lord would bring great catastrophes upon Babylon (51:63-64).

Seraiah was Baruch's brother. Baruch was Jeremiah's faithful scribe and friend. Throughout many of his years of ministry, Jeremiah relied on Baruch's help. Now Jeremiah depended on Baruch's brother to help him with this symbolic act.

Later, Jeremiah himself performed a symbolic act in Egypt. While some Jews watched, Jeremiah hid some large stones under the brick pavement in front of one of the Egyptian palaces. Then Jeremiah explained the meaning of his symbolic act. The Babylonians would invade Egypt and put their king's throne over the stones that Jeremiah had buried (43:8-13). Neither Egypt nor Babylon was safe from God's judgment.

Seraiah went to Babylon during the fourth year of King Zedekiah. The Judeans did not have a good life under Zedekiah. The Babylonians had put Zedekiah on the throne and they continued to control him. In a sense, the Judeans were already experiencing Babylonian captivity under the weak Zedekiah.

The meaning behind Seraiah's symbolic act would encourage God's people. Babylon, and all that the nation represented, would collapse. Babylon would bring pain, but the Lord would end the pain by destroying Babylon.

In the same way, the Lord will eventually bring to an end everything that causes you pain. All the evil that Babylon represents will come to an end (Revelation 18:21). The Lord will wipe away all of your tears (Revelation 21:4).

**How can the Lord's destruction of Babylon give you hope in the midst of your pain and problems?**

## Day 353
### SIMILARITIES AND CONTRASTS

*Jeremiah 52:1-2. Zedekiah was twenty-one years old when he became king, and he reigned in Jerusalem eleven years. His mother's name was Gametal daughter of Jeremiah; she was from Libya. He did evil in the eyes of the LORD, just as Jehoiakim had done.*

The words of Jeremiah ended in the previous verse (51:64). Another author, perhaps Baruch, penned this last chapter in Jeremiah. Chapter 52 forms a fitting epilogue to Jeremiah's book. The historical account in chapter 52 is remarkably similar to 2 Kings 24:18 – 25:30. The authors of each narrative used the same resources. Neither author copied from the other, because each had his distinctive perspectives.

Chapter 52 concludes Jeremiah's book in similarities and contrasts to the introduction in chapter one. Jeremiah's call (1:1-19) and this historical appendix (52:1-34) form thoughtfully paired bookends for Jeremiah's life and words.

Jeremiah wrote most of his prophecies between Josiah's thirteenth year and Zedekiah's eleventh year (1:1-2). Chapter 52 begins with the last years of Zedekiah's reign. The Babylonians began their last siege of Jerusalem during King Zedekiah's ninth year (52:4).

Jeremiah's introduction noted that the exile occurred in the fifth month of Zedekiah's eleventh year (1:3). The exile included all the people who were left in the city as well as deserters (52:15). During Nebuchadnezzar's reign, there were several exiles of the Judeans (52:28-30).

The Lord used the Babylonians to attack Jerusalem because He was angry (52:3). The Judeans had angered the Lord because of their sin against Him. The Lord had explained to Jeremiah that the people had left Him and worshipped other gods (1:16).

The Lord promised to deliver Jeremiah from every enemy (1:19). Throughout Jeremiah's long book, the Lord kept His promise. In the end, the Lord delivered Jehoiachin (52:31).

The Lord promised Jeremiah that he would be strong (1:18). Jeremiah was like a fortified city. But the Babylonians broke into the city of Jerusalem (52:6). Jeremiah was like an iron pillar. But the Babylonians broke into pieces the pillars of the temple (52:17). Jeremiah was like a bronze wall. But the Babylonians broke down the city walls (52:14).

**What are some similarities and contrasts between Jeremiah's life and circumstances and yours?**

## Day 354
### Spiritual Sight and Spiritual Blindness

**Jeremiah 52:11.** *Then he put out Zedekiah's yes, bound him with bronze shackles and took him to Babylon, where he put him in prison till the day of his death.*

Poor King Zedekiah! He had a pathetic end to his reign over Judah. His kingdom and his eyesight ended at the same time. The last scene he saw before his eyes were blinded was the killing of all his sons and officials (52:10). He was left with no heirs to sit on the throne.

Because he did not submit to God's light, King Zedekiah kept his nation in spiritual darkness for eleven years. Even though he occasionally sought Jeremiah's counsel when he did not know what else to do, he always chose to reject Jeremiah's words.

Jeremiah was the only light in Jerusalem during Zedekiah's dark reign. At the beginning the king's reign, Jeremiah warned him against listening to the false prophets (27:12-15). The king chose darkness.

During Zedekiah's fourth year, the Lord revealed a long message about Babylon to Jeremiah (51:59-60). In that sermon Jeremiah preached spiritual light about God. He said that the Lord made an everlasting covenant with His people (50:5), that the Lord is our strong Redeemer (50:34), and that He is the Holy One of Israel (51:5). But Zedekiah chose darkness.

During Zedekiah's tenth year (32:1), Jeremiah praised the Lord for being the Creator. He exclaimed that nothing was too difficult for the Lord (32:17). Instead of allowing God to handle his difficulties, Zedekiah chose darkness.

The brightest light in Jeremiah's ministry was his Book of Comfort (chapters 30-33). The most dazzling section in the Book of Comfort is the report about the New Covenant (31:31-34). The Lord revealed all this to Jeremiah was Zedekiah was king.

Zedekiah was oblivious to these wonderful truths. He went to Babylon as a blind man. He left behind his shameful legacy of being a spiritually blind king.

Take Zedekiah's pitiful life as a warning to you. Are you looking at your own life through the spiritual eyes that Jesus Christ gives? Choose His light!

**How does your relationship with the Lord provide you with spiritual light for everyday living?**

Day 355

## TEMPLE'S BURNING!

**Jeremiah 52:13.** *He set fire to the temple of the LORD, the royal palace and all the houses of Jerusalem. Every important building he burned down.*

Nebuzaradan's destruction of the city was total. He burned everything that he could. He even burned the Lord's temple.

Why did God want His own temple to burn? The answer is that He no longer lived there. The temple had ceased to be His primary residence on earth, because the entire temple system had become corrupt.

That burning temple was the fire of God's judgment. Jeremiah had preached that fire would come. He had said that the Lord would give Jerusalem over to the Babylonians who would burn it with fire (21:10). They would burn every building where the people had worshipped other gods (32:29).

In the temple, people had worshipped the sun instead of the Lord (Ezekiel 8:16). They had defiled the temple (2 Chronicles 36:14). The temple that King Solomon built had become like any other pagan shrine.

Consequently, the Lord's presence left the temple. First He moved to one of the temple gates (Ezekiel 10:19). Then He moved to the mountain to the east of the city (Ezekiel 11:23). The temple was now spiritually empty, and it was time for the temple to end.

If the temple had been spared, its continued operation would have been the epitome of hypocrisy. The priests would have pretended to offer sacrifices to the One who was no longer there. They would have sunk deeper into sin.

The temple had to go, and the Babylonians knew how to eradicate it. The Babylonians were skilled destroyers. They later burned all the idolatrous temples in Egypt (43:12).

The Lord's residence is in a different temple today. If you are a believer, your body is the Lord's temple (1 Corinthians 6:19-20). The Spirit lives in you. Honor Him with your body.

**In what specific ways can you honor God with the temple of your body?**

## Day 356
### WALLS

**Jeremiah 52:14.** *The whole Babylonian army under the commander of the imperial guard broke down all the walls around Jerusalem.*

When the Lord first called Jeremiah to the ministry, He promised the young man that he would be like a bronze wall against all of his enemies (1:18). The Lord later repeated this promise to Jeremiah, assuring him that he would be like a fortified wall of bronze (15:20). The Lord gave this promise to Jeremiah, not to the city of Jerusalem! Jerusalem's walls of stones fell to the enemy.

Jeremiah was there in Jerusalem when the city walls came down. But Jeremiah was the bronze wall, and the Lord protected him from the Babylonian slaughter. Jeremiah knew that eventually even the walls of Babylon would fall (51:44).

My wife and I have lived in relative safety so far. We have not needed the protection of city walls. The only wall that we have is a short one made of stones by the street in front of our house. The purpose of the wall is to keep our front yard from eroding away. However, I know that my wall will be gone sooner or later.

There will be walls in the future that no one will be able to destroy. The walls of the New Jerusalem coming down from heaven will be great and high. The walls will have twelve gates, and an angel will be at each gate (Revelation 21:12-21).

The gates of the New Jerusalem will never be closed. God's glory will continually illuminate the city. Nothing unclean will ever enter the city (Revelation 21:23-27).

The Lord promised that He would be a wall of fire around Jerusalem in the future (Zechariah 2:5). God is like a wall of fire around His people today. He protects believers from the unseen spiritual enemies.

The Lord is your wall. He will always protect you. Even if political and national walls collapse around you, the Lord will be your protector and your helper.

You can believe with confidence that God will always help you. When you have God as your wall, you need no other wall. People may mock you like they did Jeremiah. But you can have courage against spiritual enemies as you trust in God as your wall.

**In what ways do you need the Lord to be your wall today?**

## Day 357
### BLESSED ARE THE POOR

**Jeremiah 52:16.** *But Nebuzaradan left behind the rest of the poorest people of the land to work the vineyards and fields.*

Nebuzaradan was the Babylonian military commander under King Nebuchadnezzar. He carried out the king's orders to spare some of the poorest Judeans from captivity and exile. He left them to take care of the farmland and vineyards.

Not every poor person was spared. Some of the poorest were taken into exile, along with the rest of the artisans who were in the city (52:15). No social class escaped the Babylonian captivity.

It was economically wise for the Babylonians to leave people behind in Judah to work the land. The produce from the vineyards and fields would contribute to the prosperity of the Babylonian Empire. Perhaps the Babylonians left the poorest people because these people were uneducated and would pose no political threat.

It is clear that compassion was *not* the reason that the Babylonians spared the poor. King Nebuchadnezzar did not have a heart for poor people. Daniel boldly told King Nebuchadnezzar that he should turn away from his sins and show mercy to the poor (Daniel 4:27).

A king should treat poor people fairly (Proverbs 29:14). It is only by justice that a king can give stability to his land (Proverbs 29:4). Many of the kings of Israel did not help the poor and needy (Ezekiel 16:49).

In contrast, the Lord lifts up the poor and the needy (Psalm 113:7). He scatters His gifts freely to the poor (Psalm 112:9). He upholds justice for the poor (Psalm 140:12). The church leaders told Paul to remember the poor, and he was very eager to do so (Galatians 2:10). James wrote to visit widows and orphans in their distress (James 1:27).

Do you consider yourself poor? You are in perfect company, because Jesus Christ was poor. Do you consider yourself rich? If so, you should be rich in good deeds (1 Timothy 6:17-18). Help the poor.

**How is the Lord directing you to think wisely about the poor and about your own economic situation?**

Day 358
PILLARS

*Jeremiah 52:20. The bronze from the two pillars, the Sea and the twelve bronze bulls under it, and the movable stands, which King Solomon had made for the temple of the LORD, was more than could be weighed.*

During the Christmas season every year while I was growing up, my family and I enjoyed looking at the decorated houses close to our neighborhood. I especially liked looking at the houses that had pillars. Pillars seemed to give the houses a sense of strength and permanence.

When King Solomon's workmen built the temple, they made two large pillars for the front entrance. Solomon gave each of the pillars a name. The right pillar he named Jachin and the left one he named Boaz (2 Chronicles 3:17). Jachin means, "He establishes," and Boaz means, "Strength is in Him."

Jeremiah preached an unpopular sermon about the temple 350 years after Solomon built it. Jeremiah predicted that the temple would become like Shiloh, meaning that the temple would be destroyed. The reason for the destruction was the disobedience of the people (26:4-6).

The people continued to disobey God. The Babylonians came and destroyed both the temple and the entire city. Even the Babylonian military commander said that the reason for the devastation was that the Judeans sinned against the Lord (40:2-3).

The Babylonians broke the bronze temple pillars into pieces. They also broke the bronze basin and the stands. They carried the pillar parts back to Babylon (52:17). Back in Babylon, perhaps King Nebuchadnezzar displayed the pillar pieces in a museum. When he had invaded Jerusalem during the year that he became king, he had taken some of the temple vessels and placed them in one of his pagan temples (Daniel 1:2).

Even though Solomon's temple was destroyed, God's heavenly temple lives on. The Lord's heavenly temple has pillars, and you could be one of them! Jesus Christ will make into pillars those who, living faithfully for Him, persevere through trials (Revelation 3:12).

**What trial are you currently enduring as you look toward being a pillar in God's temple?**

Day 359

POMEGRANATES

*Jeremiah 52:22-23. The bronze capital on top of the one pillar was five cubits high and was decorated with a network and pomegranates of bronze all around. The other pillar, with its pomegranates, was similar. There were ninety-six pomegranates on the sides; the total number of pomegranates above the surrounding network was a hundred.*

My wife and I planted a small pomegranate tree several years ago. We are pleased that luscious fruit now grows on our tree every year. I think that the pomegranate is one of the most beautiful and interesting-shaped fruit that I have seen.

The pomegranate appears on many pages of Scripture. The land that the Lord promised to Moses and his people was flowing with abundance, including pomegranates (Deuteronomy 8:8). When Moses sent out spies to investigate the land, they brought back grapes, figs and pomegranates (Numbers 13:23).

The Lord instructed Moses that the high priest's robe should have pomegranates sewn on its hem. The pomegranates were made of blue, purple and scarlet material. Bells of gold were between them (Exodus 28:33-34). Since the high priest offered gifts and sacrifices to God for sins (Hebrews 5:1), the high priest's robe symbolized the life that he provided for the people when he met with God.

A husband comparing his wife to an orchard of pomegranates was an extraordinary compliment (Song of Solomon 4:13). The pomegranates blooming in the spring provided a wonderful moment (Song of Solomon 7:12). The juice from the pomegranate offered special refreshment (Song of Solomon 8:2).

When King Solomon built the temple, his workmen carved pomegranates into the bronze capitals that were on top of the pillars (1 Kings 7:18-20). The total number of carved pomegranates was four hundred (1 Kings 7:42). When the Babylonians destroyed the temple, they carried the bronze pieces back to Babylon. Their plunder included the bronze pieces with the carved pomegranates (2 Kings 25:13-17).

Even though the Babylonians destroyed the temple, the carved pomegranates survived. The pomegranates would remind the Judean exiles in Babylon that God's plan for them also survived. Through Jesus Christ, God offers the quality of life represented by the pomegranate. May you enjoy a pomegranate-like life today!

**Describe in your own words how the symbolism of the pomegranate encourages you today.**

## Day 360
### LOOKING BEYOND THE CIRCUMSTANCES

**Jeremiah 52:28-30.** *This is the number of the people Nebuchadnezzar carried into exile: in the seventh year, 3,023 Jews; in Nebuchadnezzar's eighteenth year, 832 people from Jerusalem; in his twenty-third year, 745 Jews taken into exile by Nebuzaradan the commander of the imperial guard. There were 4,600 people in all.*

The Babylonians carried the people of Jerusalem into exile in several stages. The author of the epilogue of Jeremiah listed three of the deportations. There were others. It was a total banishment. The first deportation occurred during the first year that Nebuchadnezzar became king. The Babylonians took some of the young men from the nobility and the royal family in Jerusalem and brought them back to Babylon. Among this group were Daniel, Shadrach, Meshach and Abednego (Daniel 1:1-7).

The second deportation happened during King Nebuchadnezzar's seventh year. The Babylonians carried away 3,023 Jews. No other Scripture refers to this particular exile.

The third deportation, which occurred during Nebuchadnezzar's eighth year, was the largest. Ten thousand captives from Jerusalem were exiled to Babylon, along with King Jehoiachin (2 Kings 24:10-16). Among these exiles were the queen mother, princes, court officials, craftsmen and smiths (Jeremiah 29:1-2).

The fourth deportation was during King Nebuchadnezzar's eighteenth year. The Babylonians carried away 832 people from Jerusalem. This happened the year before the Babylonians' devastating attack on Jerusalem, when the city was already under siege.

The fifth deportation occurred during Nebuchadnezzar's nineteenth year. The Babylonians burned the temple and the whole city of Jerusalem. They exiled everyone except for some of the poorest (2 Kings 25:8-12). Four years after Jerusalem's destruction, the sixth and final deportation happened during King Nebuchadnezzar's twenty-third year. The Babylonians carried off 745 Jews, probably in retaliation for the murder of Gedaliah. The Babylonians had appointed Gedaliah as governor of the devastated nation, and his assassination was seen as rebellion against Babylon (41:17-18).

With six deportations, the exile was crushingly complete. No visible evidence remained that Judah and Israel would ever become a nation again. Yet the Jews obeyed Jeremiah's letter and multiplied in number (29:6). The Lord kept His promises and later restored them to their land.

**Do you see any circumstances that tempt you to doubt God's promises? How can you look beyond the circumstances and trust the Lord?**

## Day 361
### PRISON TERM ENDS

*Jeremiah 52:31. In the thirty-seventh year of the exile of Jehoiachin king of Judah, in the year Evil-Merodach became king of Babylon, he released Jehoiachin king of Judah and freed him from prison on the twenty-fifth day of the twelfth month.*

King Jehoiachin had been a prisoner in Babylon for thirty-seven years. He had reigned in Judah for only three months before the Babylonians deported him. Even though he was an evil king (2 Kings 24:8-9), Jehoiachin was among the good figs to whom the Lord promised blessing (Jeremiah 24:1-6).

Sooner or later, every powerful political ruler will die. Nebuchadnezzar was no exception. During his long reign, Nebuchadnezzar apparently never considered releasing Jehoiachin. When Nebuchadnezzar finally died, Evil-Merodach became king and showed the kindness to Jehoiachin that Nebuchadnezzar never did.

Evil-Merodach was one of Nebuchadnezzar's sons. According to Josephus, Evil-Merodach was an ineffective Babylonian king who ruled recklessly and lawlessly. He was assassinated after a short reign. Yet Evil-Merodach was responsible for the one incident that would encourage future generations of God's people – Jehoiachin's release from prison. Evil-Merodach probably gave the orders for Jehoiachin's release on the twenty-fifth day, but Jehoiachin did not appear before the king until the twenty-seventh (2 Kings 25:27).

The release of King Jehoiachin symbolized the freeing of all Judeans who were captives and exiles in Babylon. Jeremiah had prophesied that God would gather the scattered nation (31:10). The Judean descendants would return to their own land (31:17).

When the people finally returned to Judah, Jehoiachin's grandson Zerubbabel became governor (Haggai 1:1). But Zerubbabel was never considered a king. Jeremiah had earlier prophesied that Jehoiachin would be cast out of Judea (22:28). Jeremiah had also preached that Jehoiachin might as well have been childless, because none of Jehoiachin's descendants would sit on David's throne (22:30).

Jesus' mother Mary was not a descendant of Jehoiachin. Her ancestry was through David's son Nathan (Luke 3:31). She was Jesus' physical parent. Joseph's ancestry was through David's son Solomon (Matthew 1:6-7), and Joseph was one of Jehoiachin's descendants (Matthew 1:12). Through Jesus, the curse against Jehoiachin's descendants was removed!

**Explain how Jesus Christ has taken the curse of the law away from you and set you free.**

Day 362

THRONES

**Jeremiah 52:32.** *He spoke kindly to him and gave him a seat of honor higher than those of the other kings who were with him in Babylon.*

Jehoiachin had lived as a prisoner in exile in Babylon for thirty-seven years (52: 31). He was eighteen years old when he was first taken to Babylon (2 Kings 24:8). He lived in prison in Babylon a little more than twice the number of years that he had lived in freedom in Jerusalem.

Jehoiachin had been king in Jerusalem for only three months. During that short reign, he had done evil in the sight of the Lord (2 Kings 24:8-9). Three months as an evil king had sentenced him to thirty-seven years as a prisoner!

King Nebuchadnezzar had kept Jehoiachin in prison until Nebuchadnezzar died. Nebuchadnezzar had also been cruel to other Judean kings. He had bound Jehoiachin's father in chains and taken him to Babylon for a brief time (2 Chronicles 36:6). Nebuchadnezzar probably instigated the violent death and dishonorable burial of Jehoiachin's father that Jeremiah had prophesied (22:19).

Also, Nebuchadnezzar unleashed his vengeance on Jehoiachin's successor to the Judean throne, Zedekiah. Nebuchadnezzar blinded Zedekiah after killing his sons and royal officials before his eyes (52:10-11). Zedekiah spent the remainder of his years as a blind exile in Babylon.

For unknown reasons, Nebuchadnezzar's son decided to show kindness to Jehoiachin. He gave Jehoiachin a throne that was more honorable than any of the other captive kings. Jehoiachin had no power as he sat on that throne, but he had honor. He had more honor than he deserved. Thirty-seven years earlier he had sat on the throne of David. He squandered the throne because of his wickedness.

Jesus Christ received the throne of David (Luke 1:32), and He is the only man who deserves it. The throne on which Jesus now sits is the throne of grace (Hebrews 4:16). Because of His grace, you also might sit on a throne! Faithful Christians will sit on thrones (Revelation 3:21), and Jesus promised His disciples that they would sit on thrones (Matthew 19:28). Followers of Jesus Christ who endure for Him will someday reign with Him (2 Timothy 2:12).

**How does God's promise that believers will reign with Jesus alter the way you will live today?**

## Day 363
### CLOTHING CHANGE

*Jeremiah 52:33. So Jehoiachin put aside his prison clothes and for the rest of his life ate regularly at the king's table.*

The new Babylonian king freed Jehoiachin from prison. Jehoiachin was finally a free man. It was time to change out of his prison clothes.

Jehoiachin was no longer locked up as a prisoner. He was now free. He could eat freely from the table of the most powerful king in the world. The change of clothes symbolized the transformation of Jehoiachin's life.

Many decades earlier, Jeremiah performed a symbolic act with a piece of clothing. He buried the piece of clothing by the Euphrates River, symbolizing the exile in Babylon. When Jeremiah later dug it up, it was ruined and useless (13:1-11). In the same way, Jehoiachin had been wasting away in his prison clothes.

When the exiles finally returned from Babylon to rebuild Jerusalem, the prophet Zechariah had a vision. He saw the high priest standing before the angel of the Lord, and Satan was accusing him. The high priest's clothes were filthy, representing sin. The Lord ordered that the dirty garments be removed from the high priest, and that he be clothed with lavish robes and a clean hat. This was symbolic of what the Branch (Jesus Christ) would do (Zechariah 3:1-10).

The believers who persevere through trials will wear white clothing (Revelation 3:4-5). The Lord sent a letter to the believers in the church at Laodicea that they should let Him clothe them with white garments (Revelation 3:18). Each martyr for Jesus Christ was given a white robe in heaven (Revelation 6:11).

When my son was young, he wanted me to talk to him every night about heaven. One of his interests was what he would wear in heaven. He did not especially want to wear a white robe. He told me that he wanted to wear white pants. I told him that whatever clothing God gave him to wear in heaven, he would be very happy with his heavenly wardrobe!

Think about your future heavenly clothing. Believers have clothed themselves with Jesus Christ now (Galatians 3:27). Live for Him today.

**Describe your awareness of how Jesus Christ has clothed you with His righteousness.**

## Day 364
### A HOPEFUL ENDING

Jeremiah 52:34. *Day by day the king of Babylon gave Jehoiachin a regular allowance as long as he lived, till the day of his death.*

The king of Babylon who succeeded Nebuchadnezzar pardoned Jehoiachin and released him from prison. He spoke kindly to Jehoiachin and gave him a more exalted position than the other captive kings. Jehoiachin took off his prison clothes. He ate daily with the king of Babylon for the rest of his life. The king gave daily provisions to Jehoiachin until the day that Jehoiachin died (52:31-34).

The new king of Babylon was named Evil-Merodach (2 Kings 25:27). He was named after the pagan idol Marduk. He ruled Babylon for only two years, so he did not have time to achieve the political greatness that Nebuchadnezzar did. However, Evil-Merodach facilitated the one event that was the worthy ending for Jeremiah's book. He released Jehoiachin.

In contrast to Zedekiah who stayed in prison until he died (52:11), Jehoiachin was free. Zedekiah's eyes were put out, but Jehoiachin received favor. Zedekiah's sons were killed, but Jehoiachin had sons who survived (1 Chronicles 3:17-18).

If Jeremiah were still alive during the time of Jehoiachin's release, he would be about ninety years of age. Even if he died before hearing the news about Jehoiachin, Jeremiah would have known the encouraging news about the king's future. Jeremiah had preached that descendants of David would sit on the throne of Israel (33:17). Jehoiachin's release was the beginning of the fulfillment of that promise.

After nonstop descriptions of gigantic judgment and destruction, Jeremiah's book ends on a note of hope. The Babylonian captivity did not obliterate God's people. Judah's king was now free. The nation also would one day be free. After uprooting and destroying the people, the Lord would rebuild and replant them in the future.

The Lord restored Jehoiachin, who was also known as Jeconiah. One of Jeconiah's descendants was Joseph, the legal father of Jesus Christ (Matthew 1:12-16). Jesus Christ would provide the ultimate hope for God's people.

As you face this day, and indeed as you face the rest of your life, you must never forget that Jesus Christ is your hope (1 Timothy 1:1). He is your only hope. Your life will have a hopeful ending as you trust in Him.

**As you grow closer to the Lord today, describe your hope.**

## Day 365
### JESUS AND JEREMIAH

*Matthew 16:13-14. When Jesus came to the region of Caesarea Philippi, he asked his disciples, "Who do people say the Son of Man is?" They replied, "Some say John the Baptist; others say Elijah; and still others, Jeremiah or one of the prophets."*

Jesus Christ had qualities that reminded people about the holy prophets, especially Jeremiah. Jesus was the Man of Sorrows, and Jeremiah was the prophet with the broken heart. Both men wept over the city of Jerusalem.

Jeremiah's preaching against sin brought him rejection and suffering. Jeremiah compared himself to a gentle lamb that was being led to slaughter (11:19). And Jesus was the Lamb of God whom His own people rejected.

Both Jesus and Jeremiah made the temple a central location for their teaching. When Jesus made a whip out of cords and chased the moneychangers from the temple, He quoted Jeremiah 7:11: "Has this house, which bears My name, become a den of robbers to you?" Both Jeremiah and Jesus sharply criticized the godless religious leaders of their day. Jesus told the priests, "The tax collectors and the prostitutes are entering the kingdom of God ahead of you" (Matthew 21:31). Jeremiah said in his day, "Prophets and priests alike, all practice deceit" (Jeremiah 6:13).

Both Jesus and Jeremiah had close relationships with God the Father. Their whole lives were devoted to doing God's will. They had their critics, as does anyone who tries to live in holiness before God. Both of them were accused of political treason. They were persecuted, put on trial and imprisoned. But they followed God consistently to the end.

The greatest honor for anyone on this earth is for people to think that he or she is Jesus Christ. Jeremiah was such a person.

In contrast to Jeremiah, Jesus had a unique birth, death and resurrection. He was born to die for the sins of the world, which He could do because He was God. One of the implications of Jesus' resurrection is that all who believe can have hope. Because Jesus rose from the dead, He is alive, and He will come again.

In the midst of all his messages about judgment, Jeremiah was a man of hope. Jeremiah saw how completely God brought judgment to Jerusalem, but as Jeremiah walked through the ruins of that city, he had hope. Why? Because he knew that this was not the end of Jerusalem. He knew that one day God would raise Jerusalem from those ruins and restore the city.

**What Christ-like trait that Jeremiah had do you most want in your life?**

## ANALYSIS OF JEREMIAH'S BOOK

With 52 chapters that contain 1364 verses, Jeremiah has more words than any other book in the Bible. Jeremiah's secretary Baruch is the most likely compiler of the book. Baruch wrote much of the material as Jeremiah dictated it to him (36:32). We can trust Jeremiah's book not only as historically accurate, but also as theologically trustworthy. Jeremiah's book is Scripture that God inspired (2 Timothy 3:16). Jeremiah was a prophet who spoke the word of the Lord.

The book of Jeremiah is not arranged in chronological order. However, neither is it pieced together as a disorganized collection. Here is an outline of Jeremiah:

   I.    Introduction: God's Call of Jeremiah (Jeremiah 1)
   II.   God's Words in Jeremiah's Mouth (Jeremiah 2-25)
   III.  God's Rescue of Jeremiah and Others (Jeremiah 26-36)
   IV.   God's Judgment on Judah (Jeremiah 37-45)
   V.    God's Judgment on the Nations (Jeremiah 46-51)
   VI.   Epilogue: God's Uprooting and Replanting (Jeremiah 52)

God's call of Jeremiah in chapter 1 actually summarizes the entire book. Much of Jeremiah's record refers back to chapter 1. Chapters 2-25 include many of Jeremiah's sermons, which fulfill Jeremiah 1:9. "Then the Lord reached out His hand and touched my mouth and said to me, 'Now, I have put My words in your mouth.'"

Chapters 26-36 describe God's deliverance, how the Lord faithfully protected Jeremiah and others. Within this section are the messages in chapters 30-33 that include the New Covenant, showing God's faithfulness to all His people in the future. Chapter 34 describes God's plan to faithfully protect slaves, and chapter 35 shows how the Lord faithfully protected the Recabites, a people known for their obedience. Jeremiah faced many enemies during his long career, but the Lord always kept His promise to Jeremiah that He gave in Jeremiah 1:8. "'Do not be afraid of them, for I am with you to rescue you,' declares the Lord."

Chapters 37-45 narrate how the Lord brought judgment on Judah. God used the Babylonians to carry out His punishment on the nation, which fulfilled Jeremiah 1:14. "The Lord said to me, 'From the north disaster will be poured out on all who live in the land.'"

The Lord clearly explained why He brought judgment on His own people in Jeremiah 1:10. "I will pronounce My judgments on My people because of their wickedness in forsaking Me, in burning incense to other gods and in worshipping what their hands have made." Even in the midst of the devastation, the Lord continued to faithfully protect Jeremiah and those few individuals who were faithful to Him. The Lord took care of Baruch (45:1-5) and Ebed-Melech (39:15-18).

Lastly, Chapters 46-51 contain Jeremiah's messages of judgment on nine other nations. The Lord had appointed Jeremiah to be a prophet to the nations (1:5). These international prophecies fulfilled the Lord's words to Jeremiah in 1:10. "See, today I appoint you over nations and kingdoms to uproot and tear down, to destroy and overthrow, to build and to plant."

Chapter 52 is a retelling of the Babylonians' annihilation of Jerusalem. The Babylonians destroyed the city's walls (52:18) and the temple's pillars (52:17). In contrast, the Lord had promised to make Jeremiah as strong as a fortified city, an iron pillar and walls of bronze (1:18).

The Babylonians had earlier carried many people from Jerusalem to Babylon. King Jehoiachin was among those exiled people. Jeremiah's book ends with Jehoiachin being released from prison. So Jeremiah ends on a hopeful note. Even though the Lord had uprooted an entire nation, He was in the process of replanting His people. God judged His people, and then He restored their descendants. God is faithful!

## INDEX TO TITLES

## INDEX OF SCRIPTURE REFERENCES
## OUTSIDE THE BOOK OF JEREMIAH

## ACKNOWLEDGMENTS

My personal meditations on Jeremiah began early in my ministry. The writing of this book took decades. I am grateful to the following people, books, and mission organizations that greatly influenced the writing of *Jeremiah's God*.

*To* the prophet himself, whose long-term faithfulness to God continues to inspire me.

*To* Francis Schaeffer (*Death in the City,* 1969), James Sire (*Jeremiah, Meet the 20th Century,* 1975) and Eugene Peterson (*Run with the Horses,* 1983), whose books helped me understand the urgent relevance of Jeremiah and enabled me to introduce Jeremiah to the 21st century.

*To* the congregation in the 1970's of Alief Community Church (Houston, Texas) who helped shape me as a young pastor for a lifetime of running with the horses.

*To* InterVarsity Christian Fellowship, Search Ministries and Biblical Education by Extension. It was a privilege for me to serve the Lord through these missions while the truths of Jeremiah matured in my heart. Many colleagues in these three organizations contributed to my life.

*To* Michael Kerns, my long-time good friend in Memphis. His suggestions for *Jeremiah's God* were invaluable.

*To* Vern Meyer and Vaughn Akins. Our many Saturday mornings together, drinking coffee and discussing truth, gave my writing more depth and extra realism.

*To* my brother Chris Coldwell. Without his editing skills and publishing knowledge from his work with Naphtali Press, *Jeremiah's God* might have remained as only a few copies from Kinko's.

*And finally to* Barbara, the wife of my youth, my best friend and companion through many adventures together, whose loving patience and understanding made it possible for me to spend much time with "Jerry" and his God.

CPSIA information can be obtained at www.ICGtesting.com

234830LV00001B/132/P